VISUAL QUICKSTART GUIDE

FOR THE WORLD WIDE WEB
Second Edition

Larry Ullman

Peachpit Press

Visual QuickStart Guide

PHP for the World Wide Web, Second Edition

Larry Ullman

Peachpit Press
1249 Eighth Street
Berkeley, CA 94710
510/524-2178
510/524-2221 (fax)

Find us on the Web at www.peachpit.com.
To report errors, please send a note to errata@peachpit.com.
Peachpit Press is a division of Pearson Education.

Editor: Rebecca Gulick
Production Editor: Lupe Edgar
Copy Editor: Tiffany Taylor
Compositor: Owen Wolfson
Indexer: Karin Arrigoni
Technical Reviewer: Henrik Hansen
Cover Design: Peachpit Press
Cover Production: George Mattingly / GMD

ISBN 0-321-24565-2

9 8 7

Printed and bound in the United States of America

For Jessica, Gina, and Rich,
with gratitude for all of their love and support.

Special thanks

Many, many thanks to everyone at Peachpit Press for their assistance and hard work, especially:

The best darn editor in the world, Rebecca Gulick. Thanks for, well, just about everything. As always, it's my pleasure to be able to work with you.

Tiffany Taylor, for her attention to detail and her willingness to replace every errant "that" with the appropriate "which," or vice versa.

Lupe Edgar and Owen Wolfson, who take a bunch of disparate stuff and turn it into a book. Karin Arrigoni for her excellent indexing.

Nancy Aldrich-Ruenzel, Nancy Davis, Marjorie Baer, Suzie Lowey, Rebecca Ross, Kim Lombardi, Gary-Paul Prince, Alexa Smith, Lisi Baldwin, Jim Bruce, and a probably a few other people, whose value is immense (even if I may not fully understand what they do).

Henrik Hansen, for his spot-on technical review and many suggestions (on yet another book).

My sincerest thanks to the readers of the first edition of this book and my other books. Thanks for your feedback and support and for keeping me in business.

Finally, thanks to: Rasmus Lerdorf (who got the PHP ball rolling); the people at PHP.net, Zend.com, Spoono.com; those who frequent the various newsgroups and mailing lists; and the greater PHP and open source communities for developing, improving upon, and supporting such wonderfully useful technology.

TABLE OF CONTENTS

INTRODUCTION

When I began the first edition of this book, back in the year 2000, PHP was a little-known *open source* project. It was adored by technical people in the know but not yet recognized as the popular choice for Web development that it is today. When I taught myself PHP, very little documentation was available on the language—and that was my motivation for writing this book in the first place.

Today things are different. The Internet has gone through a boom and a bust and seems to be righting itself. Furthermore, PHP is now the reigning king of dynamic Web design tools and has begun to expand beyond the realm of Web development. But despite PHP's popularity and the increase in available documentation, sample code, and examples, a good book discussing the language is still relevant. Particularly as PHP makes its fifth major release, a book such as this—which teaches the language in simple but practical terms—can be your best guide in learning the information you need to know.

This book is intended to help you learn PHP, giving you both a solid understanding of the fundamentals and a sense of where to look for more advanced information. Although it isn't a comprehensive programming reference, through demonstrations and real-world examples, this book provides the knowledge you need to begin building dynamic Web sites and Web applications using PHP.

What Is PHP?

PHP originally stood for *Personal Home Page.* It was created in 1994 by Rasmus Lerdorf to track the visitors to his online résumé. As its usefulness and capabilities grew (and as it began to be utilized in more professional situations), PHP came to mean *PHP: Hypertext Preprocessor.* (The definition basically means that PHP handles data before it becomes HTML—which stands for HyperText Markup Language.)

According to the official PHP Web site, found at www.php.net (**Figure i.1**), PHP is an HTML embedded scripting language. I'll explain this definition in more detail.

To say that PHP is *HTML embedded* means that it can be written within your HTML code—HTML being the code with which all Web pages are built. Therefore, programming with PHP can be only slightly more complicated than hand-coding HTML.

Also, PHP is a *scripting language*, as opposed to a *programming language*. This means that PHP is designed to do something *only after an event occurs*—for example, when a user submits a form or goes to a URL (Uniform Resource Locator—the technical term for a Web address). Conversely, programming languages such as Java, C, and Perl, can be used to write stand-alone applications, which may or may not involve the Web. The most popular example of a scripting language is JavaScript, which commonly handles events that occur within the Web browser. Another way to refer to the different types of languages is to use the term *interpreted* for languages such as PHP and JavaScript, which can't act on their own, and *compiled* for those like C and Java, which can.

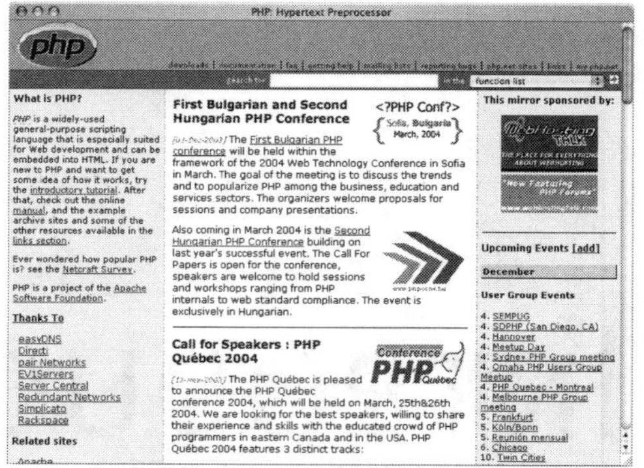

Figure i.1 At the time of this writing, this is the appearance of the official PHP Web site, located at www.php.net. Naturally, this should be the first place you look to address most of your PHP questions and curiosities. This site contains the latest edition of the PHP manual with other user's comments added, as well as links to more resources.

Figure i.2 This is the home page of Zend, creators of the programming at the heart of PHP. The site contains much useful software as well as a code gallery and well-written tutorials.

You should also understand that PHP is a *server-side* technology. This refers to the fact that everything PHP does occurs on the server (as opposed to on the *client*, which is the computer being used by the person viewing the Web site). A *server* is a special computer that houses the pages you see when you go to a Web address with your browser (for example, Netscape Navigator, Microsoft Internet Explorer, Safari, or Mozilla). I'll discuss this process in more detail later (see "How PHP Works").

Finally, PHP is *cross-platform*, meaning that it can be used on machines running Unix, Windows, Macintosh, and other operating systems. Again, we're talking about the *server's* operating system, not the client's. Not only can PHP run on almost any operating system, but, unlike most other programming languages, you can switch your work from one platform to another with few or no modifications.

At the time this book was written, PHP was in version 4.3.4, with version 5 in development. This book was tested using both versions of the language, and allowances were made for those of you who are using an earlier version. More information about PHP 5.0 can be found at PHP.net and `www.zend.com`, the minds behind the core of PHP (**Figure i.2**).

What PHP Is Not

The thing about PHP that confuses most new learners is what PHP can't do. Although you can use the language for an amazing array of tasks, its main limitation is that PHP can't be used for client-side features found in some Web sites.

Using a client-side technology like JavaScript, you can create a new browser window, add mouseovers, make pop-up alerts, resize the browser window, find out the screen size on the user's machine, and dynamically generate and alter forms. None of these tasks can be accomplished using PHP (because PHP is server-side, whereas those are client-side issues). But, you can use PHP to create JavaScript, just as you can use PHP to create HTML.

When it comes time to develop your own PHP projects, remember that you can only use PHP to send information (HTML and such) to the Web browser. You can't do anything else within the Web browser until another request from the server has been made (a form has been submitted or a link has been clicked).

Why Use PHP?

Put simply, PHP is better, faster, and easier to learn than the alternatives. When you're designing Web sites, your primary alternatives to PHP are simple HTML, CGI scripts (Common Gateway Interface, commonly, but not necessarily written in Perl), ASP (Active Server Pages) and the newer ASP.NET, Macromedia ColdFusion, and JSP (JavaServer Pages). JavaScript isn't truly an alternative to PHP (or vice versa) because JavaScript is a client-side technology and can't be used to create HTML pages the same way PHP or CGI can.

PHP's advantage over basic HTML is that the latter is a limited system allowing for no flexibility or responsiveness. Visitors accessing HTML pages see simple pages with no level of customization or dynamic behavior. With PHP, you can create exciting and original pages based on whatever factors you want to consider (for example, the time of day or the user's operating system). PHP can also interact with databases and files, handle email, and do many other things that HTML can't.

Webmasters learned a long time ago that HTML alone won't produce enticing and lasting Web sites. Toward this end, server-side technologies such as CGI scripts have gained widespread popularity. These systems allow Web-page designers to create Web applications that are dynamically generated, taking into account whichever elements the programmer desires. Often database-driven, these advanced sites can be updated and maintained more readily than static HTML pages.

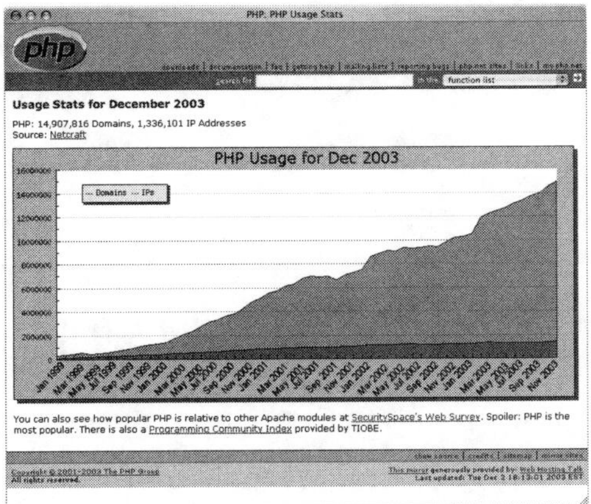

Figure i.3 Netcraft's (www.netcraft.com) graphic shows PHP's phenomenal growth over the past five years.

So the question is, why should a Web designer use PHP instead of CGI, ASP.NET, or JSP to make a dynamic Web site?

- **PHP is much easier to learn and use.** People—perhaps like you—without any formal programming training can write PHP scripts with ease after reading this one book. In comparison, ASP.NET requires an understanding of VBScript, C#, or another language; and CGI requires Perl (or C). These are more complete languages and, therefore, are more difficult to learn.
- **PHP was written specifically for dynamic Web page creation.** Perl (and VBScript and Java) were not, inferring that, by its very intent, PHP can do certain tasks faster and more easily than the alternatives. I'd like to make it clear, however, that although I'm suggesting PHP is better for certain things (specifically those it was created to do), PHP isn't a better programming language than Java or Perl—they can do things PHP can't.
- **PHP is both free and cross-platform.** So, you can learn and use it on nearly any computer and incur no cost. Furthermore, its open source nature means that PHP's users are driving its development, not some corporate entity.
- **PHP is currently the most popular tool available for developing dynamic Web sites.** At the time of this writing, PHP is in use on nearly 15 million domain names (**Figure i.3**). By mastering this technology, you'll provide yourself with either a usable hobby or a lucrative skill.

How PHP Works

PHP is a server-side language, which means the code you write in PHP resides on a host computer that serves Web pages to Web browsers.

When you go to a Web site (`www.DMCinsights.com`, for example), your Internet Service Provider (ISP) directs your request to the server that holds the `www.DMCinsights.com` information. The server reads the PHP code and processes it according to its scripted directions. In this example, the PHP code tells the server to send the appropriate Web page data to your browser in the form of HTML (**Figure i.4**). In short, PHP creates an HTML page on the fly based on parameters of my choosing.

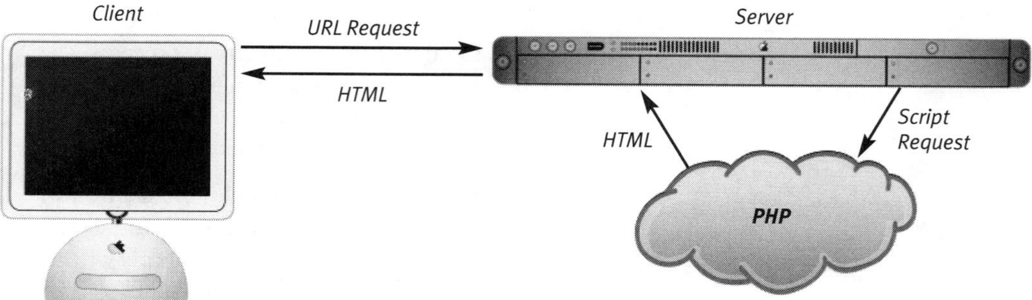

Figure i.4 This graphic demonstrates (albeit in very simplistic terms) how the process works between a client, the server, and a PHP module (an application added to the server to increase its functionality) to send HTML back to the browser. All server-side technologies use a third-party module on the server to process the data that's sent back to the client.

This differs from an HTML-generated site in that when a request is made, the server merely sends the HTML data to the Web browser—no server-side interpretation occurs (**Figure i.5**). Hence, to the end user's browser, there may or may not be an obvious difference between what `home.html` and `home.php` look like, but how you arrive at that point is critically altered. The major difference is that by using PHP, you can have the server *dynamically* generate the HTML code. For example, different information could be presented if it's Monday as opposed to Tuesday or if the user has visited the page before. Dynamic Web page creation sets apart the less appealing, static sites from the more interesting and, therefore, more visited, interactive ones.

The central difference between using PHP and using straight HTML is that PHP does everything on the server and then sends the appropriate information to the browser. This book covers how to use PHP to send the right data to the browser.

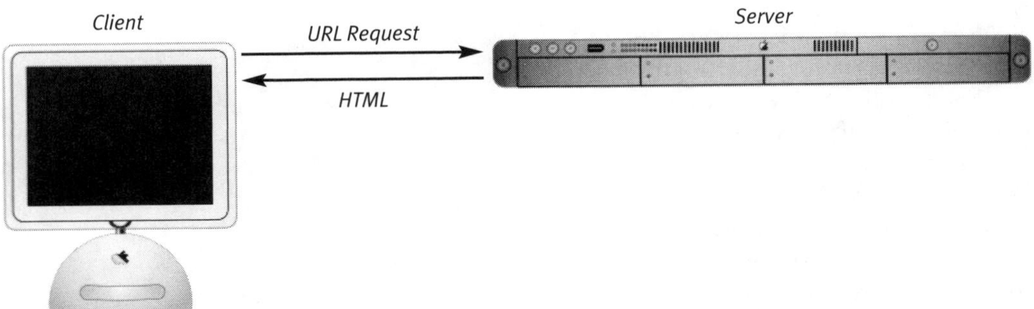

Figure i.5 Compare this direct relationship of how a server works with basic HTML to that of Figure i.4. This is also why HTML pages can be viewed in your browser from your own computer—they don't need to be "served," but dynamically generated pages need to be accessed through a server that handles the processing.

What You'll Need

The most important requirement for working with PHP—because it's a server-side scripting language—is access to a PHP-enabled server. Considering PHP's popularity, your ISP or Web host most likely has this option available to you on their servers. You'll need to contact them to see what technology they support.

Your other option is to install PHP and a Web server application (like Apache or Personal Web Sharing) on your own computer. Users of Windows, Mac OS X, or Linux can easily install and use PHP for no cost. Directions for installing PHP are available in Appendix A, "Installation and Configuration." If you're up to the task of using your own PHP-installed server, you can take some consolation in knowing that PHP is available for free from the PHP Web site (`www.php.net`) and comes in easy-to-install packages.

The second requirement is almost a given: You must have a text editor on your computer. Crimson Editor, WordPad, TextEdit, and similar freeware applications are all sufficient for your purposes; and BBEdit, EditPad, Homesite, and other commercial applications offer more features that you may appreciate. If you're accustomed to using graphical interface (also referred to as WYSIWYG—What You See Is What You Get) editors like Macromedia Dreamweaver or Adobe GoLive, you can consult your manual to see how to program within that application. For a list of PHP-capable text editors, see Keith's PHP Editors at `http://phpeditors.linuxbackup.co.uk` (**Figure i.6**).

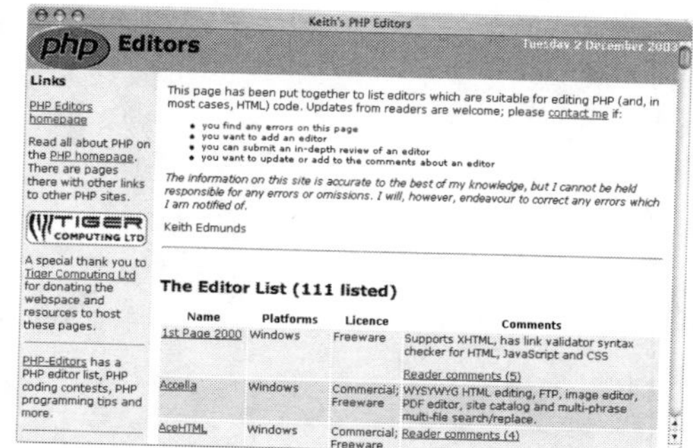

Figure i.6 Dozens of text editors that support PHP are available for every platform. Many are free, whereas some cost a modest amount (presumably these come with more features).

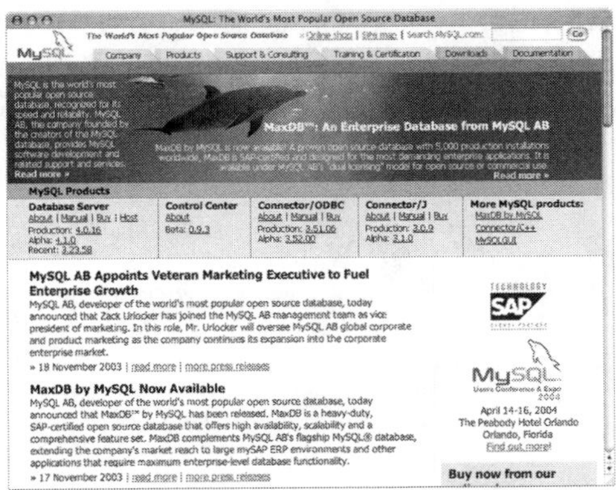

Figure i.7 MySQL is a popular database application that you can download and run on your computer for free.

Third, you need a method of getting the scripts you write in your text editor to the server. If you're working directly on your own server, you can save the scripts to the appropriate directory. However, if you're using a remote server with your ISP or Web host, you'll need an FTP (File Transfer Protocol) program to send the script to the server.

Fourth, if you want to follow the examples in Chapter 12, "Introduction to Databases," you need access to MySQL (`www.mysql.com`, **Figure i.7**) or another database application.

This book assumes only a basic knowledge of HTML, although the more comfortable you are handling raw HTML code *without* the aid of a Web-creation application such as Dreamweaver, GoLive, or Microsoft FrontPage, the easier the transition to using PHP will be. Every programmer will eventually turn to an HTML reference at some time or other, regardless of how much you know, so I encourage you to keep a good HTML book by your side. One such introduction to HTML coding is Elizabeth Castro's *HTML for the World Wide Web with XHTML and CSS: Visual QuickStart Guide* (Peachpit Press, 2002).

Previous programming experience is certainly not required. However, it may expedite your learning, because you'll quickly see numerous similarities between, for example, Perl and PHP or JavaScript and PHP.

About This Book

This book attempts to convey the fundamentals of programming with PHP while hinting at some of the more advanced features you may want to consider in the future, without going into overwhelming detail. It uses the following conventions to do so.

The step-by-step instructions indicate what coding you're to add to your scripts and where. The specific text you should type is printed in a unique type style to separate it from the main body text. For example:

```
<?php print "Hello, World!"; ?>
```

The PHP code is also written as its own complete script and is numbered by line for reference (**Script i.1**). You shouldn't insert these numbers yourself, because doing so will render your work inoperable. I recommend using a text editor that automatically displays the line numbers for you—the numbers will help when you're debugging your work. In these blocks, I also highlight in red the particular parts being discussed in the step-by-step instruction section to draw attention to new or relevant material.

Because of the nature of how PHP works, you need to understand that there are essentially three views of every script: the PHP code, the code that's sent to the browser (mostly HTML), and what the browser displays to the end user.

Script i.1 Better text editors automatically put in line numbers for you as you work. You should never put them in yourself!

Script

```
<!DOCTYPE html PUBLIC "-//W3C//DTD XHTML 1.0 Transitional//EN"
        "http://www.w3.org/TR/xhtml1/DTD/xhtml1-transitional.dtd">
<html xmlns="http://www.w3.org/1999/xhtml">
<head>
    <meta http-equiv="content-type" content="text/html; charset=iso-8859-1" />
    <title>Hello, World!</title>
</head>
<body>
<?php
print "Hello, World!";
?>
</body>
</html>
```

Which Book Is Right For You?

This is the second edition of my first book on PHP. Like the original, it's written with the beginner or nonprogrammer in mind. If you have little or no programming experience, prefer a gentler pace, or like to learn things in bite-sized pieces, this is the book for you. Make no mistake: This book covers what you need to know to begin develop dynamic Web sites (while using practical examples), but it does so without any in-depth theory or advanced applications.

Conversely, if you pick up new technologies really quickly or already have some experience developing Web sites, you may find this to be too basic. In that case, you should consider my *PHP and MySQL for Dynamic Web Sites: Visual QuickPro Guide* instead (Peachpit Press, 2003). It discusses SQL and MySQL in much greater detail and goes through several more complex examples, but it does so at a quick jog.

Figure i.8 This is the view you'll see of the browser window. For the purposes of this book, it won't make any difference whether you use Netscape Navigator or Internet Explorer (or something else) on Macintosh, Windows, Linux, or any other operating system.

Figure i.9 By viewing the source code received by the Web browser, you can see the HTML created by PHP and sent by the server.

Where appropriate, sections of or all of the browser window are revealed, showing the end result of the exercise (**Figure i.8**). Occasionally, you'll also see an image displaying the HTML source that the browser received (**Figure i.9**). You can normally access this view by choosing View Source or View Page Source from the appropriate Web browser menu. To summarize, Figure i.9 displays the HTML the browser receives, and Figure i.8 demonstrates how the browser interprets that HTML. Using PHP, you'll create the HTML that's sent to the browser.

Because the column in this book is narrower than the common text editor screen, sometimes lines of PHP code printed in the steps have to be broken where they would not otherwise break in your editor. A small gray arrow indicates when this kind of break occurs. For example:

```
print "This is going to be a longer line
→ of code.";
```

You should continue to use one line in your scripts, or else you'll encounter errors when executing. (The gray arrow isn't used in scripts that are numbered.)

While demonstrating new features and techniques, I'll do my best to explain the why's and how's of them as I go. Between reading about and using a function, you should clearly comprehend it. Should something remain confusing, though, this book contains a number of references where you can find answers to any questions (see Appendix B, "Resources"). If you're confused by a particular function or example, your best bet will be to check the online PHP manual or the book's supporting Web site (and its user support forum).

Companion Web Site

While you're reading this book, you may also find it helpful to visit the *PHP for the World Wide Web 2nd Edition: Visual QuickStart Guide* Web site, located at www.DMCinsights.com/phpvqs2. There you'll find every script in this book available in a downloadable form. (However, I strongly encourage you to type the scripts yourself in order to become more familiar with the structure and syntax of PHP.)

The site also includes a more detailed reference section with links to numerous useful Web pages where you can continue learning PHP. In addition, the site provides an errata section listing any mistakes made in this text.

What many users find most helpful, though, is the book's supporting forum, found through the Web site or directly at www.DMCInsights.com/phorum/list.php?f=10 (**Figure i.10**). Using this site, you can:

- Find answers to problems you're having
- Receive advice on how to approach an idea you have
- Get debugging help from other readers
- See how changes in the technologies have affected the examples in the book
- Learn what other people are doing with PHP
- See a faster reply from me than if you send me a direct email

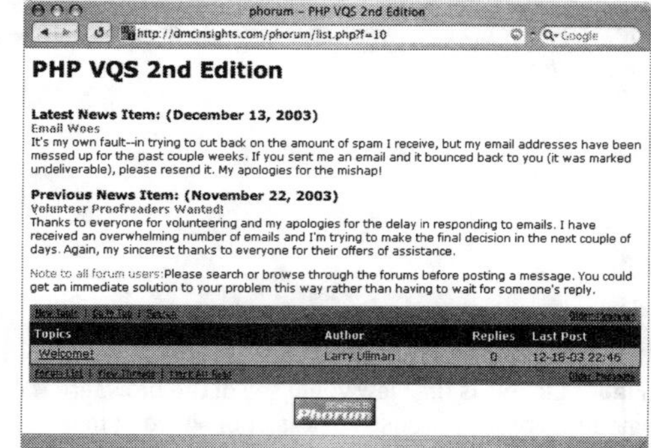

Figure i.10 If you need more assistance, use the book's supporting forum, where readers and myself post problems and solutions.

How to Ask Questions the Smart Way

Whether you're posting a message to the book's supporting forum, sending me an email, or asking a question in a newsgroup, knowing how to most effectively ask a question improves the quality of the response you'll receive as well as the speed with which you'll get your answer. To receive the best answer in the shortest amount of time, follow these steps:

1. Search the Internet, read the manuals, and browse any applicable documentation.
2. Ask your question in the most appropriate forum (newsgroup, mailing list, and so on).
3. Use a clear and concise subject.
4. Describe your problem in detail, show any relevant code, say what went wrong, indicate what version of PHP you're using, and state what operating system you're running.

For more tips and an enlightening read, see Eric Steven Raymond's "How to Ask Questions the Smart Way" at `www.catb.org/~esr/faqs/smart-questions.html`. The 10 minutes you spend on it will save you hours in the future. Those people who will answer your questions, like myself, will be most appreciative!

Questions, comments, or suggestions?

If you have a PHP-specific question, there are newsgroups, mailing lists, and question-and-answer sections available on PHP-related Web sites for you to turn to. These are discussed in more detail in Appendix B. Browsing through these references or searching the Internet with Google will almost always provide you with the fastest answer.

You can also direct your questions, comments, and suggestions to me via email at `phpvqs2@DMCinsights.com`. I try to answer every email I receive, but I can't guarantee a quick reply. Also, understand that faster and more detailed responses are given to emails directly pertaining to the content of the book.

1 Getting Started with PHP

When you're learning any new programming language you should always begin with an understanding of the basic syntax, and that's what I'll introduce in this chapter. I'll primarily discuss the fundamentals, but I'll also cover some recommended programming techniques that will improve your work in the long run.

If you've never programmed before, a deliberate reading of this chapter will start you on the right track. If you have some programming experience, you'll be able to breeze through this section, gaining a reference for the book's remaining material in the meantime. By the end of this chapter you will have successfully written and executed your first PHP scripts and be on your way to developing dynamic Web applications.

Basic XHTML Syntax

As you should know already, all Web pages are made using HTML (HyperText Markup Language). Every Web browser, be it Microsoft's Internet Explorer, Apple's Safari, or Netscape's Navigator, turns HTML code into the stylized Web page seen by the user. In this book, I'm using a slight variant of HTML called XHTML; so, I wanted to give it special mention up front.

The World Wide Web Consortium (W3C)—the group responsible for defining HTML and other protocols—created XHTML as a transition between HTML and XML (Extensible Markup Language), a potent new technology. XHTML is almost exactly like HTML, with the following differences:

- All tags are written in lowercase.
- Nested tags must be well formed.

  This rule isn't as complicated as it sounds. It means that you can't code `<b><big>text</b></big>`; instead you write `<b><big>text</big></b>`.
- All tag attributes must be quoted.

  In HTML, you might write `<table border=2>`; but in XHTML, you must use `<table border="2">`.
- All tags must be closed.

  This rule is the most confusing for most people. Many HTML tags have both an open and a close, like `<div class="classname">text</div>`. However, a few don't have implicit closing tags. These include `<hr>`, `<br>`, `<img>`, and `<input>`. To make these valid XHTML tags, you need to close them by adding a space and a slash at the end, like this:

  ```
  <hr />
  <br />
  <img src="image.jpg" width="100"
  → height="42" />
  <input type="text" name="age" size="3" />
  ```

Figure 1.1 BBEdit and most other Web development applications will create the basics of an XHTML document for you.

Script 1.1 This sample document shows the basics of XHTML code.

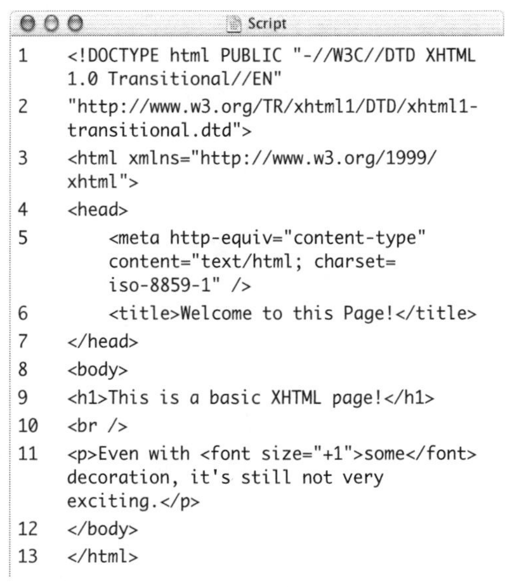

```
<!DOCTYPE html PUBLIC "-//W3C//DTD XHTML 1.0 Transitional//EN"
"http://www.w3.org/TR/xhtml1/DTD/xhtml1-transitional.dtd">
<html xmlns="http://www.w3.org/1999/xhtml">
<head>
    <meta http-equiv="content-type" content="text/html; charset=iso-8859-1" />
    <title>Welcome to this Page!</title>
</head>
<body>
<h1>This is a basic XHTML page!</h1>
<br />
<p>Even with <font size="+1">some</font> decoration, it's still not very exciting.</p>
</body>
</html>
```

As a clear-cut example of these rules, let's write a simple but valid XHTML document before getting into the syntax of PHP.

To create an XHTML page:

1. Open your HTML or text editor.

   You can use pretty much any application to create HTML, XHTML, and PHP pages. Popular choices include Macromedia's DreamWeaver, Adobe's GoLive, Microsoft's WordPad (Windows only), and Bare Bones' BBEdit (Macintosh only).

2. Choose File > New to create a new, blank document.

   Some text editors allow you to start by creating a new document of a certain type—for example, a new XHTML file (**Figure 1.1**). If your application has this option, feel free to use it.

3. Start with the XHTML header lines (**Script 1.1**):

   ```
   <!DOCTYPE html PUBLIC "-//W3C//DTD
   → XHTML 1.0 Transitional//EN"
   "http://www.w3.org/TR/xhtml1/DTD/
   → xhtml1-transitional.dtd">
   <html xmlns="http://www.w3.org/1999/
   → xhtml">
   ```

   A valid XHTML document begins with these lines. They tell the Web browser what type of document to expect.

continues on next page

4. Create the head section of the page:

```
<head>
   <meta http-equiv="content-type"
   → content="text/html; charset=
   → iso-8859-1" />
   <title>Welcome to this Page!</title>
</head>
```

The head section includes the content-type meta tag (required for valid XHTML) and the title tags. JavaScript could also be placed here.

5. Create the body section:

```
<body>
<h1>This is a basic XHTML page!</h1>
<br />
<p>Even with <font size="+1">
→ some</font> decoration, it's still
→ not very exciting.</p>
</body>
```

Per XHTML rules, the break tag (`<br />`) includes a space before the slash that closes it. All the other tags are similar to their standard HTML counterparts except that they're in lowercase.

6. Type `</html>` to complete the HTML page.

7. Choose File > Save As. In the dialog box that appears, choose Text Only (or ASCII) for the format, if you're given the option.

8. Navigate to the location where you wish to save the script.

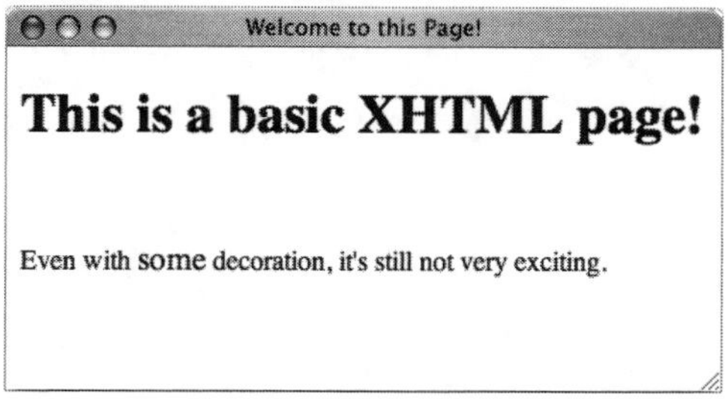

Figure 1.2 The XHTML document as it's interpreted by the Web browser.

9. Save the file as `welcome.html`.

   Even though you're coding with XHTML, the page will still use the standard `.html` or `.htm` extension.

10. Test the page by viewing it in your Web browser (**Figure 1.2**).

    Unlike PHP scripts (as you'll soon discover), you can test your XHTML and HTML pages by opening them directly in your Web browser.

✔ Tips

- I'll be using XHTML throughout the book, but that doesn't mean you have to. If you're more comfortable with HTML, stick with what you know. It won't affect the operability of your PHP scripts.
- For more information on XHTML, XML, and HTML, check out the W3C's Web page at www.w3c.org or Elizabeth Castro's excellent book, *HTML for the World Wide Web: Visual QuickStart Guide.*
- For many reasons, including sheer convenience, I'll use the terms *HTML* and *XHTML* interchangeably throughout the book. In fact, you'll probably see just *HTML* the majority of the time, but understand that I mean XHTML as well.
- For a thorough listing of PHP editors, see http://phpeditors.linuxbackup.co.uk. The page also lists the operating system each application runs on and its cost.

Basic PHP Syntax

Now that you've seen how I approach the HTML side of things, it's time to begin PHP scripting. To create your first PHP page, you'll start exactly as you would if you were creating an HTML document from scratch.

There are three main differences between a standard HTML document and a PHP document. First, PHP scripts should be saved with the `.php` file extension (for example, `index.php`). Second, you wrap your PHP code with the `<?php` and `?>` tags to indicate which code is PHP as opposed to HTML. Finally, PHP scripts must be run on a PHP-enabled Web server (whereas HTML pages can be viewed on any computer).

To make this first PHP script do something without too much programming fuss, you'll use the `phpinfo()` function. This function, when called, sends a table of information to the Web browser that itemizes the specifics of the PHP installation on that particular server. It's a great way to test your PHP installation, and it has a high "bang for your buck" quality.

To create a new PHP script on your computer:

1. Create a new HTML document in your HTML or text editor (**Script 1.2**):

```
<!DOCTYPE html PUBLIC "-//W3C//
→ DTD XHTML 1.0 Transitional//EN"
"http://www.w3.org/TR/xhtml1/DTD/
→ xhtml1-transitional.dtd">
<html xmlns="http://www.w3.org/1999/
→ xhtml">
<head>
   <meta http-equiv="content-type"
   → content="text/html; charset=
   → iso-8859-1" />
   <title>First PHP Script</title>
```

Script 1.2 Taking a minimal HTML page, I've inserted PHP tags into the body section and made use of a PHP function.

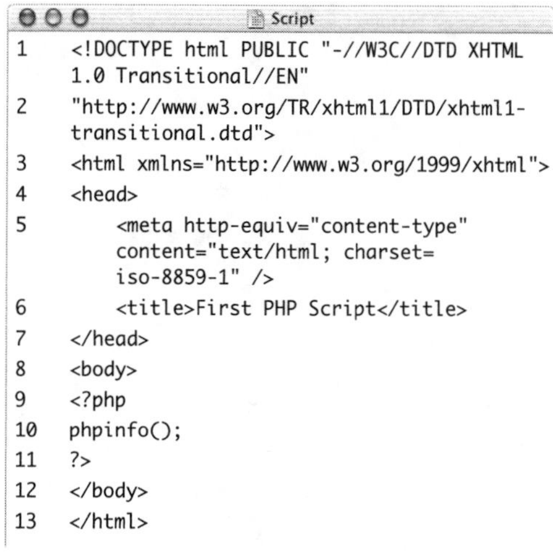

```
<!DOCTYPE html PUBLIC "-//W3C//DTD XHTML
1.0 Transitional//EN"
"http://www.w3.org/TR/xhtml1/DTD/xhtml1-
transitional.dtd">
<html xmlns="http://www.w3.org/1999/xhtml">
<head>
    <meta http-equiv="content-type"
    content="text/html; charset=
    iso-8859-1" />
    <title>First PHP Script</title>
</head>
<body>
<?php
phpinfo();
?>
</body>
</html>
```

```
</head>
<body>
</body>
</html>
```

This particular code is largely irrelevant to the overall point of creating a PHP page; but, for consistency sake, you're using the same format as the basic XHTML example (Script 1.1).

2. Create some blank lines between the opening and closing body tags by pressing Return.

3. Type `<?php` on its own line, just after the opening body tag.

   This initial PHP tag tells the server that the following code is PHP and should be handled as such.

4. Add the following line:

   ```
   phpinfo();
   ```

   I'll explain the syntax in detail later. For the time being, add this code exactly as it appears here.

5. Type `?>` on its own line, just before the closing body tag.

   The closing PHP tag tells the server that the PHP section of the script is over. Any text outside of the PHP tags is immediately sent to the Web browser as HTML and isn't treated as PHP code.

6. Save the script as `test.php`.

   Not to overstate the point, but remember that PHP scripts must use a valid file extension. Most likely you'll have no problems if you save your files as *filename*.php.

continues on next page

✔ Tips

- Just as a file's extension on your computer tells the operating system what application to open the file in, a Web page's extension tells the server how to process the file: `file.php` goes through the PHP module, `file.aspx` is processed as ASP.NET, and `file.html` is a static HTML document (normally). This is determined by the Web server application's settings.
- Check with your ISP to learn which file extensions you can use for PHP documents. In this book you'll see `.php`, the most common extension. Servers still running PHP version 3 commonly use `.php3` as the default extension, and you might come across `.phtml` as well.
- You can also check with your ISP to see if short tags (using `<?` and `?>` instead of `<?php` and `?>`) or ASP-style tags (`<%` and `%>`) are acceptable. You'll occasionally see these in other people's scripts, although it's best to stick with the formal tags as I do in this book.
- `Phpinfo()` is an example of a built-in function that comes standard with PHP. In Chapter 10, "Creating Functions," you'll learn more about functions and how to create your own.
- You'll find it handy to have a copy of the `test.php` file around. You can use it to check the PHP capabilities of a new server or see what features are supported, such as databases, image creation, and so on. You can also use this file to experiment with different file extensions and learn which ones the server will process correctly and which it won't.

Figure 1.3 Fetch is a popular FTP application for the Macintosh.

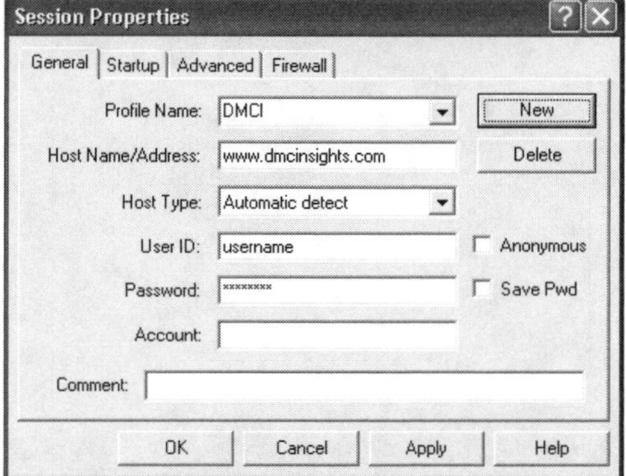

Figure 1.4 WS_FTP is a common FTP application for Windows users.

Testing Your Script

Unlike HTML, which can be tested on your own computer using a Web browser, your PHP script needs to be run from a PHP-enabled server in order for you to see what the output will look like. Fortunately, PHP is open source software (meaning, in part, that it's free) and is easy to install. To do so, follow the directions in Appendix A, "Installation and Configuration."

If you have PHP and a Web server application (such as Internet Information Server, Personal Web Server, or Apache) installed on your personal computer, then you can test your PHP scripts by saving them in, or moving them to, the Web document root. This is normally

- `C:\Inetpub\www` for Windows users running IIS or PWS
- `~/Sites` for Mac OS X users (where ~ stands for your home directory)

If you're using a server to host your PHP scripts, you need to transfer them to their destination using FTP (File Transfer Protocol). Your ISP or Web host will provide you with FTP access; you'll also need an FTP application such as Fetch (for the Macintosh) or WS_FTP (for Windows).

To FTP your script to the server:

1. Open your FTP application.
2. Connect to the server using the information provided by your ISP or Web host (**Figures 1.3** and **1.4**).

   Enter the username and password the ISP or Web host provided to you. If you know the directory where the files are to be stored, you can enter that here as well.

continues on next page

3. Navigate to the proper directory for your Web pages (for example, `www/` or `htdocs/`).

   The FTP application won't necessarily drop you off in the appropriate directory. You may need to do some navigation to get to the Web document root. This directory is the location on the server to which a URL points (for example, www.dmcinsights.com).

4. Save your script (`test.php`) on the server.

   As a rule, most FTP applications save transferred pages to the server with the same filename you're using for those files on your computer. If your particular FTP program gives you the option to specify the filename, use `test.php`.

To test your script in the browser:

1. Open your favorite Web browser.

   For the most part, PHP doesn't behave differently on different browsers (because PHP runs on the server). Conversely, HTML garners inconsistent results on various browsers and operating systems.

2. Enter the URL of the site where your script has been saved.

   In my case, this is www.DMCinsights.com/phpvqs2, but your URL will certainly be different. If you're running PHP on your own computer, the URL is http://localhost (Windows); or http://localhost/~*username* (Mac OS X), where you should replace *username* with your actual username.

3. Add `/test.php` to the URL.

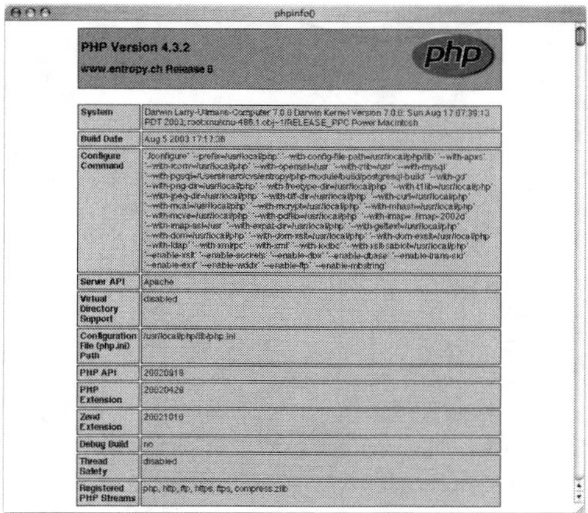

Figure 1.5 If your script has been executed correctly, your browser should look like this (woohoo!).

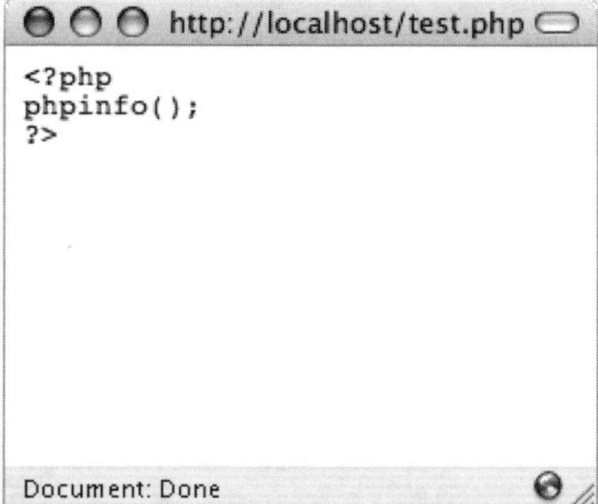

Figure 1.6 If you see the raw PHP or HTML code, then either PHP isn't installed correctly or the extension you used (`.php`) isn't treated as a PHP file by the server.

4. Press Return.

   The page should load in your browser window (**Figure 1.5**). If you see the PHP code (**Figure 1.6**) or a blank page, it most likely means that PHP has not been enabled on the server or you're using an unrecognized file extension.

✔ Tips

- Some text editors, such as BBEdit, have built-in FTP capability, allowing you to save your scripts directly to the server.
- It's very important to remember that you can't open a PHP file directly in your Web browser as you would open HTML pages or files in other applications. PHP scripts must be processed by the Web server, which means you must access them via a URL (an address that starts with `http://`).
- Even if you aren't a seasoned computer professional, you should consider installing PHP on your computer. Doing so isn't too difficult, and PHP is free. Again, see Appendix A for directions.
- Technically speaking, you don't need to add any HTML to a `phpinfo()` script. It will generate its own proper tags.

Sending Text to the Browser

PHP wouldn't be very useful if all you could do was see what PHP features were installed. You'll use it most frequently to send information to the browser in the form of plain text and HTML tags. For this, you'll use the `print()` function:

```
print ("Hello, world!");
```

Functions in PHP are followed by parentheses in which *arguments* are passed to the function. Here the argument is the text you want printed. Because this argument is a string of text, you pass it to the function by surrounding it with quotation marks (which aren't sent to the browser).

Also notice that the line is terminated with a semicolon (`;`). Every statement in PHP code must end with a semicolon, and forgetting this requirement is a common cause of errors. A *statement* in PHP is an executable line of code, like

```
print();
```

or

```
phpinfo();
```

Conversely, comment lines, PHP tags, control structures (conditionals, loops, and so on), and certain other constructs I'll discuss in this book don't merit a semicolon.

PHP Functions in the Manual

The PHP manual—accessible online at www.php.net/manual—lists every function available in the language, but using it takes a bit of know-how. The manual starts with general notions (installation, syntax, variables) and finishes with the functions by topic (MySQL, string functions, and so on). A reference for a particular function begins like so:

```
print
(PHP 3, PHP 4 )
print -- Output a string
Description
int print (string arg)
```

It first lists the function itself and then the version of PHP in which it's available. (As the language grows, new functions are added that aren't usable in older versions.) Then there's a textual description of the function, followed by its basic usage—the most important and confusing part.

In this example, the first value, `int`, says that the `print()` function returns an integer value (specifically, `print()` returns `1` if it worked and `0` if it didn't). Within the parentheses, `string arg` shows that the function takes one argument, which should be in the form of a string.

In comparison, the listing for the `echo()` function (which also sends text to the browser) looks like this:

```
void echo (string arg1 [, string argn...])
```

The `void` states that `echo()` returns no values whatsoever. The square brackets indicate optional arguments, which, as you'll discover in Chapter 10, must be listed last. Therefore, the `echo()` function must take one string as an argument but can take multiple strings as arguments if they're separated by commas.

If you're ever confused by a function or how it's properly used, check the PHP manual's reference page for it.

To print a simple message:

1. Begin a new HTML document in your text editor (**Script 1.3**):

```
<!DOCTYPE html PUBLIC "-//W3C//DTD XHTML 1.0 Transitional//EN"
"http://www.w3.org/TR/xhtml1/DTD/xhtml1-transitional.dtd">
<html xmlns="http://www.w3.org/1999/xhtml">
<head>
   <meta http-equiv="content-type" content="text/html; charset=iso-8859-1" />
   <title>Hello, world!</title>
</head>
<body>
The following was created by PHP:
```

   The last line distinguishes between the hard-coded HTML and the PHP-generated HTML.

2. Type `<?php` to create the initial PHP tag.

3. Add

```
print ("Hello, world!");
```

   Printing the phrase *Hello, world!* is the first step most programming references teach. Even though it's a trivial reason to use PHP, you're not really a programmer until you've made at least one *Hello, world!* application.

4. Close the PHP section and the HTML page:

```
?>
</body>
</html>
```

5. Save your file as `hello.php`, upload the script to your server, and test it in your browser (**Figure 1.7**).

   If you're running PHP on your own computer, remember that you can save the file to the proper directory and access the script via http://localhost/.

Script 1.3 By putting the print statement between the PHP brackets, we have the server send the *Hello, world!* greeting to the browser. It's the same as if we had put *Hello, world!* within the HTML code.

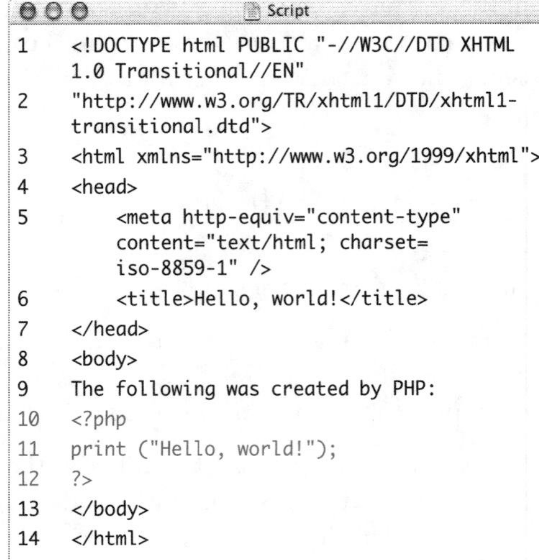

```
<!DOCTYPE html PUBLIC "-//W3C//DTD XHTML 1.0 Transitional//EN"
"http://www.w3.org/TR/xhtml1/DTD/xhtml1-transitional.dtd">
<html xmlns="http://www.w3.org/1999/xhtml">
<head>
    <meta http-equiv="content-type" content="text/html; charset=iso-8859-1" />
    <title>Hello, world!</title>
</head>
<body>
The following was created by PHP:
<?php
print ("Hello, world!");
?>
</body>
</html>
```

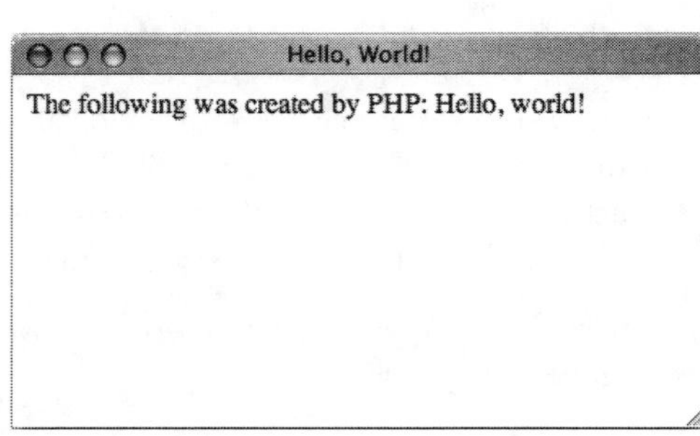

Figure 1.7 A simple *Hello, world!* example is your first foray into programming.

✔ Tips

- For better or worse, PHP is rather liberal when it comes to case sensitivity of built-in functions like `phpinfo()` and `print()`: `print()`, `Print()`, and `PRINT()` net the same results. Later in the book (for example, in Chapter 2, "Variables") you'll see examples of instances where case makes a crucial difference.
- You can use different functions to send text to the browser, including `echo()` and `printf()`. In this book, I'll primarily use `print()`.
- You can use `print()` with or without the parentheses because technically it's a language construct rather than a function (but this is irrelevant to your use of it). Most programmers don't use the parentheses, and I will omit them from here on.
- Failure to use an opening or closing quotation mark or parenthesis and neglecting to include the required trailing semicolon for every statement are common causes of errors when using the `print()` statement. If your script isn't executing properly, check these items first.
- To look up any function in the PHP manual, go to www.php.net/*functionname* in your Web browser (for example, www.php.net/print).
- You can—and commonly will—use the `print()` function over multiple lines.

Sending HTML to the Browser

As those who first learned HTML quickly discovered, viewing plain text in a Web browser leaves a lot to be desired. Indeed, HTML was created to make plain text more appealing and useful. Because HTML works by adding tags to text, you can use PHP to send HTML tags to the browser, along with other data:

```
print "<b>Hello, world!</b>";
```

There is one situation where you have to be careful, though. HTML tags that require quotation marks (for example, `<font color="#000000">`) cause problems when printed by PHP, because the `print()` function uses quotation marks as well. To avoid complications, you *escape* the quotation marks using the backslash (\). Here's an example statement:

```
print "<font color=\"#000000\">
→ Hello, world!</font>";
```

By escaping each quotation mark within your `print()` statement, you make PHP print the mark itself instead of interpreting it as either the beginning or end of the `print()` statement.

Script 1.4 With the `print()` function, you can send HTML tags along with your text to the browser, where the formatting will be applied.

```
Script
1   <!DOCTYPE html PUBLIC "-//W3C//DTD XHTML
    1.0 Transitional//EN"
2   "http://www.w3.org/TR/xhtml1/DTD/xhtml1-
    transitional.dtd">
3   <html xmlns="http://www.w3.org/1999/xhtml">
4   <head>
5       <meta http-equiv="content-type"
        content="text/html; charset=
        iso-8859-1" />
6       <title>Hello, world!</title>
7   </head>
8   <body>
9   The following was created by PHP:
10  <?php
11  print "<font color=\"red\">Hello,
    <big>world!</big></font>";
12  ?>
13  </body>
14  </html>
```

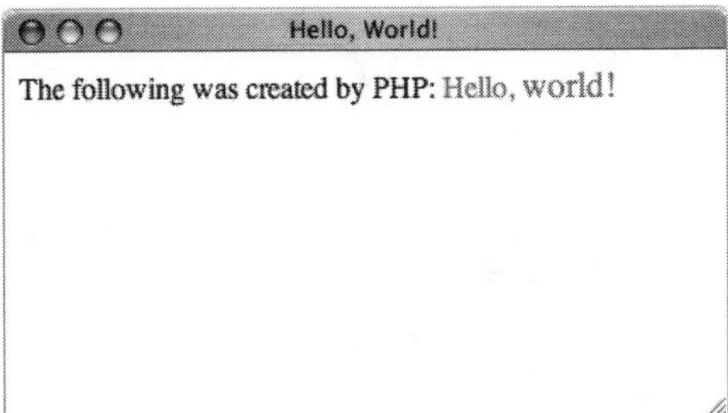

Figure 1.8 The new version of the script, with a little more decoration and appeal. Any HTML tag can be sent to the browser from PHP.

To send HTML to the browser using PHP:

1. Open the `hello.php` script (Script 1.3) in your text editor.
2. Edit the *Hello, world!* text on line 11 by adding HTML tags so that it reads as follows (**Script 1.4**):

   ```
   print "<font color=\"red\">
   → Hello, <big>world!</big></font>";
   ```

   Per the earlier discussions, you need to escape the quotation marks within the font tag so that it doesn't conflict with the `print()` statement's quotation marks. Also, you can drop the parentheses from the `print()` line while you're at it (which is allowed and the norm).
3. Save the script as `hello2.php`, upload it to your server, and reload the page in your browser (**Figure 1.8**).

✔ Tips

- Understanding the role of quotation marks and how to escape problematic characters is crucial to programming with PHP. These topics will be covered in more detail in the next two chapters.
- The HTML you send to the Web browser from PHP doesn't need to be this simple. You can create tables, CSS (Cascading Style Sheet) data, and even JavaScript.
- Remember that any HTML outside of the PHP tags will automatically go to the browser, but within the PHP tags, `print()` statements are used for this purpose.

Using White Space in PHP and HTML

As those who hand-code HTML understand, white space (blank lines, tabs, and other extra spaces) in your code can help maintain an uncluttered programming environment while not affecting what the viewer sees in the browser. By inserting blank lines between sections of code, placing nested elements one tab-stop in from their predecessor, and spacing out code, you can make a script look more organized; it will also be easier to program initially and debug later. Thus, judicious use of white space in your work is highly encouraged and can be utilized in both your PHP and the resulting HTML.

This book addresses three areas of Web development: the PHP scripts themselves, the data (HTML) that the PHP scripts send to the Web browser, and how the Web browser interprets or displays that data. I'll briefly address the issue of white space for each of these areas.

When you're programming in PHP, you should understand that white space is generally (but not universally) ignored. Any blank line (just one or several in a row) is irrelevant to the end result. Likewise, tabs and spaces are normally inconsequential to PHP.

The spacing of HTML code shows up in the HTML source of a Web page but has only a minimal effect on what's viewed in the Web browser. To adjust that spacing, you need to use special HTML tags. Let's rewrite the previous script to demonstrate.

Script 1.5 The script now has three different kinds of white space: blank lines in the PHP, a newline in the HTML source (created by \n), and space in the browser result (thanks to the <p>).

```
1   <!DOCTYPE html PUBLIC "-//W3C//DTD XHTML
    1.0 Transitional//EN"
2   "http://www.w3.org/TR/xhtml1/DTD/xhtml1-
    transitional.dtd">
3   <html xmlns="http://www.w3.org/1999/xhtml">
4   <head>
5       <meta http-equiv="content-type"
        content="text/html; charset=
        iso-8859-1" />
6       <title>Hello, World!</title>
7   </head>
8   <body>
9   The following was created by PHP:
10  <?php
11
12  print "<p><font color=\"red\">Hello,
13  <big>world!</big></font></p>\n";
14
15  ?>
16  </body>
17  </html>
```

To change the spacing of your PHP and the data sent to the browser:

1. Open `hello2.php` (Script 1.4) in your text editor.
2. Insert a new line before and after the PHP `print()` function by pressing Return at the appropriate places (**Script 1.5**).

   The new lines within the PHP serve only to add focus and clarity to the script.
3. Make the `print()` statement extend over two lines by pressing Return with your cursor between *Hello,* and *<big>world!*.

   As I stated earlier, you can print text over multiple lines because the end of the function is marked by the closing quotation mark and the semicolon.
4. At the beginning and end of the `print()` statement, add `<p>` tags.

   The `<p>` tag is an HTML element designed to create space (it defines paragraphs) within the resulting browser window.
5. At the end of the `print()` command (now on line 13), add `\n` within the quotation marks.

   The `\n` character combination sends a command to the Web browser to start a new line in the HTML source. Think of it as the equivalent of pressing the Return key.

   The line should now read

   ```
   print "<p><font color=\"red\">Hello,
   <big>world!</big></font></p>\n";
   ```

continues on next page

6. Save the script as `hello3.php`, upload it to your server, and view it with your browser (**Figure 1.9**).

   Although blank lines and printing the newline character (`\n`) can make your PHP and HTML more readable, they don't affect the appearance of your page in the Web browser (compare with Figure 1.8). To do that you must use HTML tags (the code to create a space in your browser is ` `, and the HTML equivalent of pressing Return is `<br />`).

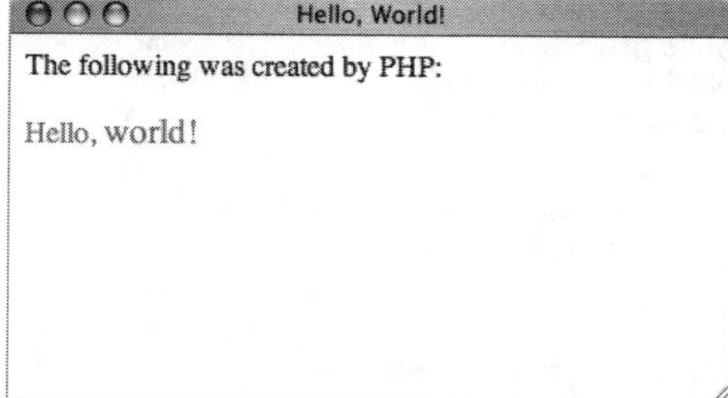

Figure 1.9 The blank lines have not affected the resulting Web page, but the <p> tag added some spacing.

✔ Tips

- One exception to the rule of immaterial white space in PHP is extra spaces within a `print()` statement that result in extra spaces being printed to the browser. However, HTML largely ignores these white spaces (technically, one space is recognized but multiple spaces aren't).

- Conversely, you can space out your functions in other ways. These two lines will both work and are equivalent:

```
print   (   "message "   );
print("message");
```

- To see the code that was sent to the browser, use the View Source or View Page Source feature built into all browsers. You'll quickly be able to tell the difference between using a newline and not using a newline (compare **Figures 1.10** and **1.11**). It may be hard to appreciate the benefits of white space on a twelve-line script, but it will become more significant as your scripts grow larger and more complicated.

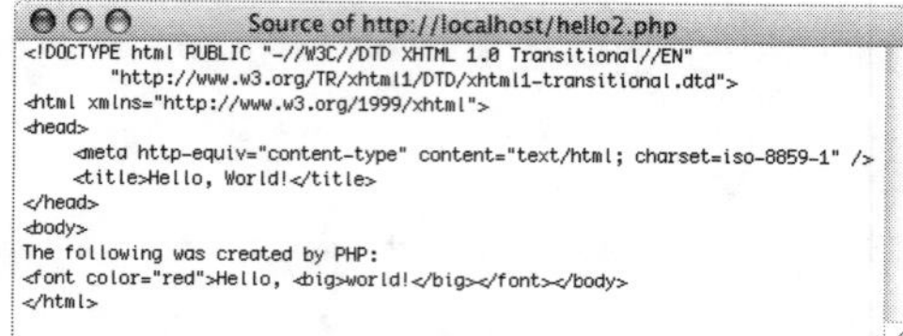

Figure 1.10 Viewing the source of a Web page is a good way to determine where a formatting problem may exist. This is the source code from the script before you added the \n, <p>, and blank lines.

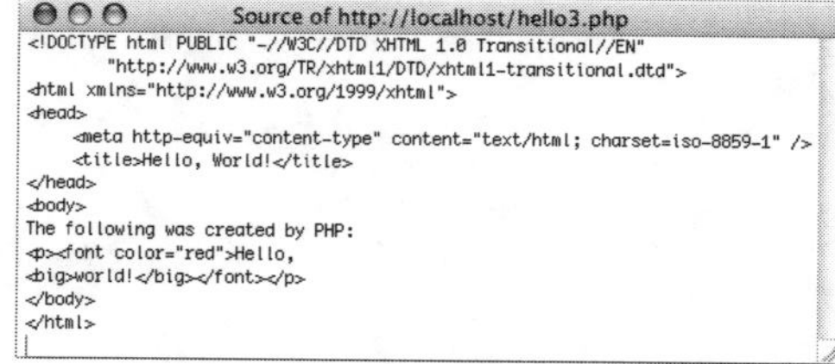

Figure 1.11 The \n in the print statement separates the *Hello, world!* line from the other HTML tags. When you send more complicated HTML code to your browser, using newlines helps to simplify the look of the source code.

Script 1.6 By putting either // or # in front of a single line of code, that line will no longer be processed by the server.

```
<!DOCTYPE html PUBLIC "-//W3C//DTD XHTML 1.0 Transitional//EN"
"http://www.w3.org/TR/xhtml1/DTD/xhtml1-transitional.dtd">
<html xmlns="http://www.w3.org/1999/xhtml">
<head>
    <meta http-equiv="content-type" content="text/html; charset=iso-8859-1" />
    <title>Hello, World!</title>
</head>
<body>
The following was created by PHP:
<?php
/*
Filename: hello4.php
Book reference: Script 1.6
Created by: Larry Ullman
*/

// print "<p><font color=\"red\">Hello, <big>world!</big></font></p>\n";

?>
<!-- This is an HTML comment. -->
</body>
</html>
```

Adding Comments to Your Scripts

The final fundamental concept I'll cover is that of comments. Comments are integral to programming not because they do anything but because they help you remember why *you* did something. The computer ignores these comments when it processes the script. Furthermore, PHP comments are never sent to the Web browser and therefore remain your secret.

PHP supports three methods of adding comments. You can comment out one line of code by putting either // or # at the beginning of the line you want ignored. For example:

```
// This is a comment.
```

You can also use // or # to begin a comment at the end of a PHP line, like so:

```
print ("Hello."); // Just a greeting.
```

You can comment out multiple lines by using /* to begin the comment and */ to conclude it:

```
/* This is a
multi-line comment. */
```

To add comments to your script:

1. Open the `hello3.php` (Script 1.5) in your text editor.

2. After the initial PHP tag, add some comments to your script (**Script 1.6**):

   ```
   /*
   Filename: hello4.php
   Book reference: Script 1.6
   Created by: Larry Ullman
   */
   ```

   This is just a sample of the kind of comments you can write. I highly recommend that you document what the script does, what information it relies upon, who created it, when you created it, and so forth.

continues on next page

3. On line 17, before the `print()` statement, type `//`.

   By preceding the `print()` statement with two slashes, you comment out the function, meaning it will never be executed.

4. Delete the Return between lines 17 and 18 so that the `print()` function is entirely on one line.

   Line 17 should now read

   ```
   // print "<p><font color=\"red\">
   → Hello, <big>world!</big></font>
   → </p>\n";
   ```

   Because the `print()` statement flows over two lines, you either need to precede each line with `//` or place it back on one line as you've done here. If you don't do one of those two things, you'll get a parse error when you run the script (**Figure 1.12**).

5. After the closing PHP tag (line 19), add an HTML comment.

   ```
   <!-- This is an HTML comment. -->
   ```

   This line of code just helps you comprehend the different comments and where they appear.

6. Save the script as `hello4.php`, upload it to the server, and view the page in your Web browser (**Figure 1.13**).

7. View the source of the page to see the HTML comment (**Figure 1.14**).

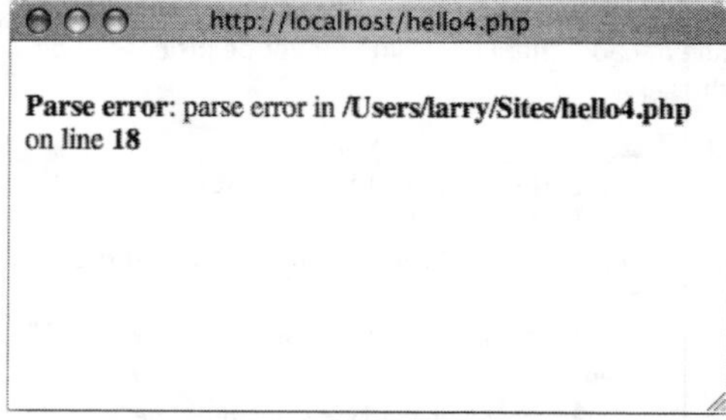

Figure 1.12 Parse errors are frequently caused by an imbalance of quotation marks or parentheses, or by omitting a semicolon.

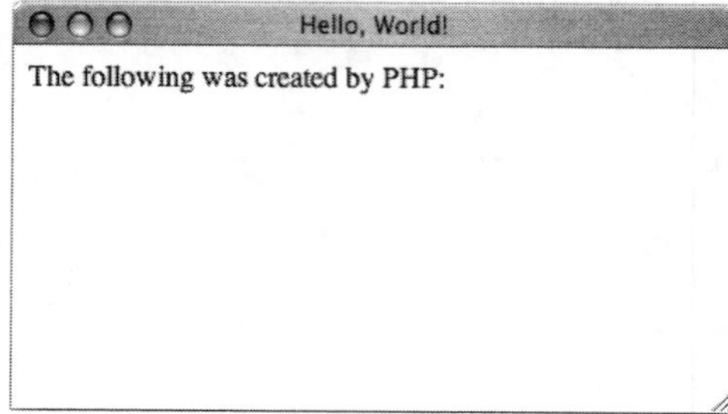

Figure 1.13 With the print statement commented out, the page looks just like it would if the `print()` function wasn't there. The server never processes this line, so the browser never receives the *Hello, world!* text.

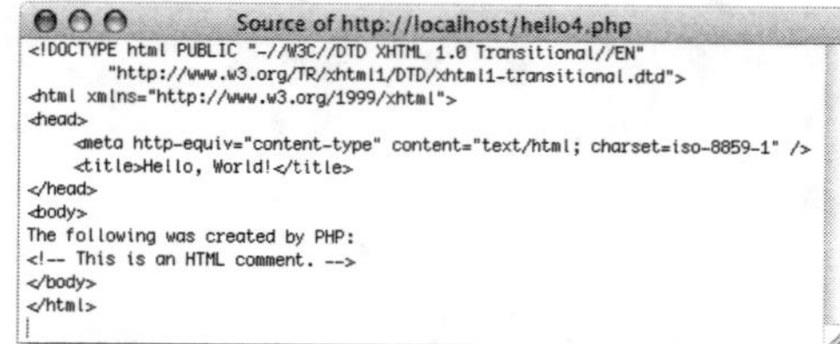

Figure 1.14 HTML comments don't appear in the Web browser but are in the HTML source. PHP comments remain in the PHP script on the server.

✔ Tips

- You can comment out just one line of code or several using the /* and */ method. With // or #, you can negate only one line at a time.
- Different programmers prefer to comment code in different ways. The important thing is to find a system that works for you and stick to it. Those who also do JavaScript programming will most likely use // and /* */ because these are the same in both languages. Perl programmers are more familiar with the # method.
- Note that you can't use HTML comment characters (<!-- and -->) within PHP to comment out code. You could have PHP print those tags to the browser, but in that case you'd create a comment that appeared in the HTML source code on the client's computer (but not in the browser window). PHP comments never make it as far as a user's computer.
- Text that's commented out in PHP isn't sent to the browser (Figure 1.13), so this is a good place to leave notes that only the programmer will ever be able to see.
- More advanced text editors such as BBEdit use colors to indicate which code is commented out. This can be very helpful when you're working on large scripts.
- Despite my strong belief that you can't over-comment your scripts, the scripts in this book aren't as documented as they should be, in order to save space. I will begin documenting the script name and number, for cross-reference purposes.

2

VARIABLES

In the last chapter, you used PHP to send simple text and HTML code to a Web browser—in other words, something for which you don't need PHP at all! Don't worry, though; this book will teach you how to use the `print()` function in conjunction with other PHP features to do useful things with your Web site.

To make the leap from creating simple, static pages to dynamic Web applications and interactive Web sites, you need to use variables. Variables are an essential concept in PHP, as well as in any other programming language. Understanding what variables are, the types that a language supports, and how to use them is critical to your work.

This chapter will discuss the fundamentals of variables used in PHP, and later chapters will cover the different types in greater detail. If you've never dealt with variables before, this chapter will be a good introduction. If you're familiar with the concept, then you should be able to work through this section with ease.

What Are Variables?

A *variable* is best thought of as a container for data. Once data has been stored in a variable (or, put differently, once a variable has been assigned a value), that data/variable can be altered, printed to the Web browser, saved to a database, emailed, and so forth.

Variables in PHP are, by their nature, flexible: You can put data into a variable, retrieve that data from it (without affecting the value of the variable), put new data in, and continue this cycle as long as necessary. But variables in PHP are also temporary: They only exist—that is, they only have a value—for the duration of a script. Once you're in a new page, those variables cease to exist, unless you take special measures to alter their longevity.

Before I get too deep into the discussion of variables, let's write a quick script to access some of PHP's predefined variables (see the sidebar). In doing so, you'll use the `$GLOBALS` variable together with the `print_r()` function, which displays information about a variable in a human-readable format.

PHP's Predefined Variables

A predefined variable is a special type of variable that the Web server application (for example, Apache), the Web server operating system (Linux, Mac OS X, or Windows XP), or the PHP module uses. The first two categories are also referred to as *environmental variables*.

Examples of a server's environmental variables are `HOSTNAME` (how the server refers to itself) and `OSTYPE` (what operating system the server is running).

Examples of Apache's environmental variables are `DOCUMENT_ROOT`, which indicates where the files are stored on the server; and `HTTP_USER_AGENT`, which details the browser and platform of the person viewing the page.

The `PHP_SELF` variable is commonly used and is equal to the name of the current script, possibly including the directory where the script is located on the server.

Script 2.1 The `print_r()` function is used to examine the contents and structure of the `$GLOBALS` variable.

Script

```
<!DOCTYPE html PUBLIC "-//W3C//DTD XHTML 1.0 Transitional//EN"
"http://www.w3.org/TR/xhtml1/DTD/xhtml1-transitional.dtd">
<html xmlns="http://www.w3.org/1999/xhtml">
<head>
    <meta http-equiv="content-type" content="text/html; charset=iso-8859-1" />
    <title>Using Print_R()</title>
</head>
<body>
<pre>
<?php // Script 2.1 - print_r.php

print_r ($GLOBALS);

?>
</pre>
</body>
</html>
```

To print PHP's predefined variables:

1. Begin a new PHP script, starting with the HTML code (**Script 2.1**).

2. Create the initial HTML tags:

```
<!DOCTYPE html PUBLIC "-//W3C//
→ DTD XHTML 1.0 Transitional//EN"
"http://www.w3.org/TR/xhtml1/DTD/
→ xhtml1-transitional.dtd">
<html xmlns="http://www.w3.org/1999/
→ xhtml">
<head>
    <meta http-equiv="content-type"
    → content="text/html; charset=
    → iso-8859-1" />
    <title>Using Print_R()</title>
</head>
<body>
<pre>
```

   This code is a repetition of the XHTML template created in the previous chapter. You use the HTML `<pre>` tags to make the generated PHP information more legible (the `print_r()` function is useful but its results can be messy).

3. Add the PHP code:

```
<?php // Script 2.1 - print_r.php
print_r ($GLOBALS);
?>
```

   This PHP code is just one function call, `print_r()`. You feed it the `$GLOBALS` variable, which is a special variable in PHP. `$GLOBALS` contains all the variables accessible to the script, including both pre- and user-defined ones. (This will make more sense once you see the script in action.)

continues on next page

4. Complete the HTML page:

```
</pre>
</body>
</html>
```

5. Save the file as `print_r.php`, upload it to your server (or save it to the appropriate directory on your computer), and test it in your Web browser (**Figure 2.1**).

6. If possible, save the file on another computer or server running PHP and run the script in your Web browser again (**Figure 2.2**).

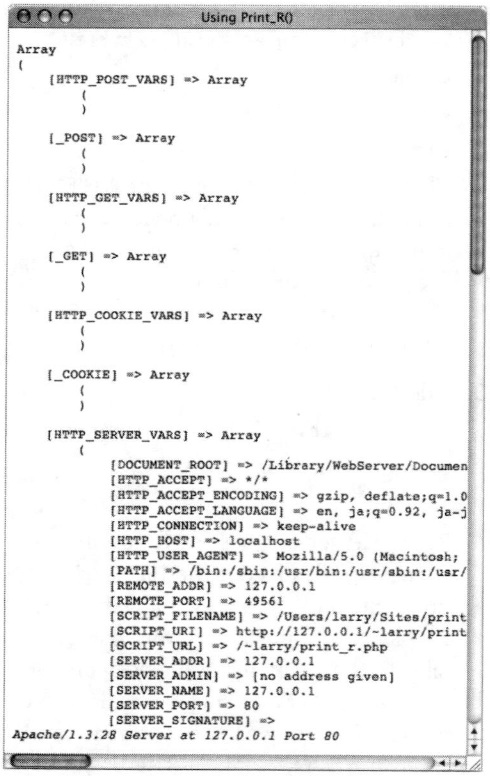

```
Using Print_R()

Array
(
    [HTTP_POST_VARS] => Array
        (
        )

    [_POST] => Array
        (
        )

    [HTTP_GET_VARS] => Array
        (
        )

    [_GET] => Array
        (
        )

    [HTTP_COOKIE_VARS] => Array
        (
        )

    [_COOKIE] => Array
        (
        )

    [HTTP_SERVER_VARS] => Array
        (
            [DOCUMENT_ROOT] => /Library/WebServer/Documen
            [HTTP_ACCEPT] => */*
            [HTTP_ACCEPT_ENCODING] => gzip, deflate;q=1.0
            [HTTP_ACCEPT_LANGUAGE] => en, ja;q=0.92, ja-j
            [HTTP_CONNECTION] => keep-alive
            [HTTP_HOST] => localhost
            [HTTP_USER_AGENT] => Mozilla/5.0 (Macintosh;
            [PATH] => /bin:/sbin:/usr/bin:/usr/sbin:/usr/
            [REMOTE_ADDR] => 127.0.0.1
            [REMOTE_PORT] => 49561
            [SCRIPT_FILENAME] => /Users/larry/Sites/print
            [SCRIPT_URI] => http://127.0.0.1/~larry/print
            [SCRIPT_URL] => /~larry/print_r.php
            [SERVER_ADDR] => 127.0.0.1
            [SERVER_ADMIN] => [no address given]
            [SERVER_NAME] => 127.0.0.1
            [SERVER_PORT] => 80
            [SERVER_SIGNATURE] =>
Apache/1.3.28 Server at 127.0.0.1 Port 80
```

Figure 2.1 The `$GLOBALS` variable, as printed out by this script, is a master list of variables available to the script and what their current values are.

```
Using Print_R()

Array
(
    [PWD] => /home/root
    [HOSTNAME] => host25.webserver1010.com
    [MACHTYPE] => i386-redhat-linux-gnu
    [LOGNAME] => root
    [SHLVL] => 2
    [SHELL] => /bin/sh
    [HOSTTYPE] => i386
    [OSTYPE] => linux-gnu
    [HOME] => /root
    [TERM] => dumb
    [PATH] => /usr/bin:/bin
    [_] => /etc/httpd/bin/httpd
    [DOCUMENT_ROOT] => /home/leullman/dmcinsights-www
    [HTTP_ACCEPT] => */*
    [HTTP_ACCEPT_ENCODING] => gzip, deflate;q=1.0, identi
    [HTTP_ACCEPT_LANGUAGE] => en, ja;q=0.92, ja-jp;q=0.96
    [HTTP_CONNECTION] => keep-alive
    [HTTP_HOST] => dmcinsights.com
    [HTTP_USER_AGENT] => Mozilla/5.0 (Macintosh; U; PPC M
    [REMOTE_ADDR] => 68.48.73.89
    [REMOTE_PORT] => 10030
    [SCRIPT_FILENAME] => /home/leullman/dmcinsights-www/p
    [SERVER_ADDR] => 65.109.106.125
    [SERVER_ADMIN] => webmaster@dmcinsights.com
    [SERVER_NAME] => dmcinsights.com
    [SERVER_PORT] => 80
    [SERVER_SIGNATURE] =>
    [SERVER_SOFTWARE] => Apache/1.3.27 (Unix) PHP/4.2.3 F
    [GATEWAY_INTERFACE] => CGI/1.1
    [SERVER_PROTOCOL] => HTTP/1.1
    [REQUEST_METHOD] => GET
    [QUERY_STRING] =>
    [REQUEST_URI] => /phpvqs2/print_r.php
    [SCRIPT_NAME] => /phpvqs2/print_r.php
    [PATH_TRANSLATED] => /home/leullman/dmcinsights-www/p
    [PHP_SELF] => /phpvqs2/print_r.php
    [argv] => Array
        (
        )

    [argc] => 0
    [HTTP_POST_VARS] => Array
        (
        )

    [_POST] => Array
```

Figure 2.2 With the `print_r.php` page, different servers generate slightly different results (compare with Figure 2.1).

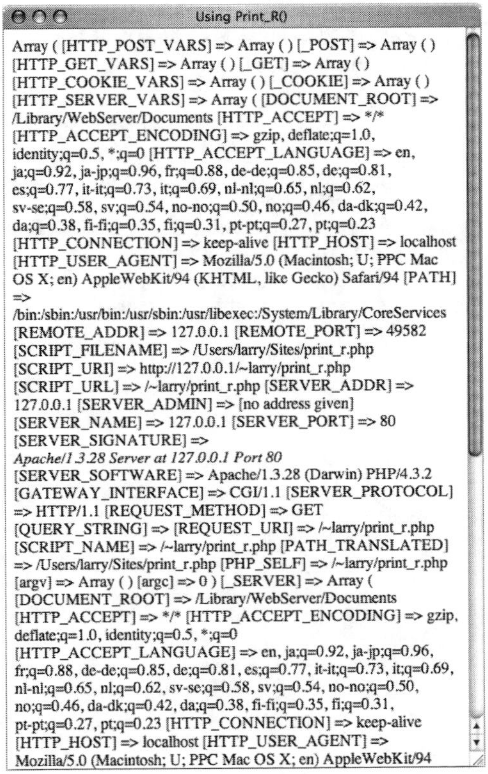

Using Print_R()

```
Array ( [HTTP_POST_VARS] => Array ( ) [_POST] => Array ( )
[HTTP_GET_VARS] => Array ( ) [_GET] => Array ( )
[HTTP_COOKIE_VARS] => Array ( ) [_COOKIE] => Array ( )
[HTTP_SERVER_VARS] => Array ( [DOCUMENT_ROOT] =>
/Library/WebServer/Documents [HTTP_ACCEPT] => */*
[HTTP_ACCEPT_ENCODING] => gzip, deflate;q=1.0,
identity;q=0.5, *;q=0 [HTTP_ACCEPT_LANGUAGE] => en,
ja;q=0.92, ja-jp;q=0.96, fr;q=0.88, de-de;q=0.85, de;q=0.81,
es;q=0.77, it-it;q=0.73, it;q=0.69, nl-nl;q=0.65, nl;q=0.62,
sv-se;q=0.58, sv;q=0.54, no-no;q=0.50, no;q=0.46, da-dk;q=0.42,
da;q=0.38, fi-fi;q=0.35, fi;q=0.31, pt-pt;q=0.27, pt;q=0.23
[HTTP_CONNECTION] => keep-alive [HTTP_HOST] => localhost
[HTTP_USER_AGENT] => Mozilla/5.0 (Macintosh; U; PPC Mac
OS X; en) AppleWebKit/94 (KHTML, like Gecko) Safari/94 [PATH]
=>
/bin:/sbin:/usr/bin:/usr/sbin:/usr/libexec:/System/Library/CoreServices
[REMOTE_ADDR] => 127.0.0.1 [REMOTE_PORT] => 49582
[SCRIPT_FILENAME] => /Users/larry/Sites/print_r.php
[SCRIPT_URI] => http://127.0.0.1/~larry/print_r.php
[SCRIPT_URL] => /~larry/print_r.php [SERVER_ADDR] =>
127.0.0.1 [SERVER_ADMIN] => [no address given]
[SERVER_NAME] => 127.0.0.1 [SERVER_PORT] => 80
[SERVER_SIGNATURE] =>
Apache/1.3.28 Server at 127.0.0.1 Port 80
[SERVER_SOFTWARE] => Apache/1.3.28 (Darwin) PHP/4.3.2
[GATEWAY_INTERFACE] => CGI/1.1 [SERVER_PROTOCOL]
=> HTTP/1.1 [REQUEST_METHOD] => GET
[QUERY_STRING] => [REQUEST_URI] => /~larry/print_r.php
[SCRIPT_NAME] => /~larry/print_r.php [PATH_TRANSLATED]
=> /Users/larry/Sites/print_r.php [PHP_SELF] => /~larry/print_r.php
[argv] => Array ( ) [argc] => 0 ) [_SERVER] => Array (
[DOCUMENT_ROOT] => /Library/WebServer/Documents
[HTTP_ACCEPT] => */* [HTTP_ACCEPT_ENCODING] => gzip,
deflate;q=1.0, identity;q=0.5, *;q=0
[HTTP_ACCEPT_LANGUAGE] => en, ja;q=0.92, ja-jp;q=0.96,
fr;q=0.88, de-de;q=0.85, de;q=0.81, es;q=0.77, it-it;q=0.73, it;q=0.69,
nl-nl;q=0.65, nl;q=0.62, sv-se;q=0.58, sv;q=0.54, no-no;q=0.50,
no;q=0.46, da-dk;q=0.42, da;q=0.38, fi-fi;q=0.35, fi;q=0.31,
pt-pt;q=0.27, pt;q=0.23 [HTTP_CONNECTION] => keep-alive
[HTTP_HOST] => localhost [HTTP_USER_AGENT] =>
Mozilla/5.0 (Macintosh; U; PPC Mac OS X; en) AppleWebKit/94
```

Figure 2.3 Use the HTML preformatting tags to avoid an ugly page like this (compare to Figures 2.1 and 2.2).

✔ Tips

- Printing out the value of the `$GLOBALS` variable as you've done here is a great debugging trick for your scripts, because it details the variables that exist and what their values are.
- If you don't use the HTML `<pre></pre>` tags, the result will be like the mess in **Figure 2.3**.

Variable Syntax

Now that you've had a quick dip in the variable pool, it's time to investigate the subject further. In the previous example, the `$GLOBALS` variable revealed PHP's predefined variables. You can also create your own variables, once you understand the proper syntax. To create appropriate variable names, you must follow these rules:

- All variable names must be preceded by a dollar sign (`$`).
- Following the dollar sign, the variable name must begin with either a letter (A–Z, a–z) or an underscore (_). It can't begin with a number.
- The rest of the variable name can contain any combination and quantity of letters, underscores, and numbers.
- You may not use spaces within the name of a variable. (Instead, the underscore is commonly used to separate words.)
- Variable names are case-sensitive. Consequently, `$variable` and `$Variable` are two different constructs, although it would be a bad idea to use two variables with such similar names.

You should quickly get into the habit of creating variable names that make sense on their own, as well as using comments to indicate the purpose of variables (**Script 2.2**), redundant as that may seem. These habits will reduce errors and make revisiting your work less taxing.

Script 2.2 This script shows how to document the purpose of variables. It's always better to include too many comments than too few.

```
<!DOCTYPE html PUBLIC "-//W3C//DTD XHTML 1.0 Transitional//EN"
"http://www.w3.org/TR/xhtml1/DTD/xhtml1-transitional.dtd">
<html xmlns="http://www.w3.org/1999/xhtml">
<head>
    <meta http-equiv="content-type" content="text/html; charset=iso-8859-1" />
    <title>Variable Comments</title>
</head>
<body>
<pre>
<?php // Script 2.2

// Define my variables.

$year = 2003; // The current year.
$june_avg = 88; // The average temperature for the month of June.
$page_title = 'Weather Reports'; // A title for the page.

// ... and so forth.

?>
</pre>
</body>
</html>
```

For example, as a variable name, `$FirstName` is better than `$FN`, and putting in a comment that details a variable's purpose makes your work abundantly clear. In fact, you may decide that `$first_name` is a better variable name than `$FirstName` (although both are valid) because there are no capital letters to remember and the words are separated for clarity.

No matter how you decide to name your variables, the most important consideration is remaining consistent with whatever convention you use. Doing so will help you avoid making trivial errors in your programming.

✔ Tips

- The case-sensitivity of PHP's variables is a common cause of problems for programmers of all levels. Using the wrong case or misspelling a variable's name can lead to results that are unpredictable—and difficult to debug.

- Unlike some other languages, PHP generally doesn't require you to declare or initialize a variable prior to use. In other words, you can refer to variables without first defining them. That being said, it's best not to do that; I try to write my scripts so that every variable is defined before use.

- There are two main variable naming conventions, determined by how you delineate words. These are the so-called *camel-hump* (named because of the way capital letters break up the word—for example, `$FirstName`) and *underscore* (`$first_name`) styles. I'll use the latter convention in my examples.

Types of Variables

In this book, I'll cover three variable types: numbers, strings, and arrays. I'll introduce them quickly here, and later chapters will discuss them in more detail (Chapter 4, "Using Numbers"; Chapter 5, "Using Strings"; and Chapter 7, "Using Arrays"). A fourth variable type, objects, is introduced here but isn't covered in this book because the subject is too advanced to be given its due.

Numbers

Technically speaking, PHP breaks numbers into two types: *integers* and *floating-point* (also known as *double-precision floating-point* or *doubles*). Due to the lax way PHP handles variables, it won't affect your programming to group the two categories of numbers into one all-inclusive membership. Still, I'll briefly discuss the differences between the two, for clarity's sake.

The first type of numbers—integers—are the same as whole numbers. They can be positive or negative but include neither fractions nor decimals. Numbers that use a decimal point (even something like 1.0) are floating-point numbers. You must also use floating-point numbers to refer to fractions, because the only way to express a fraction in PHP is to convert it to its decimal equivalent. Hence 1¼ is written as 1.25. **Table 2.1** lists some sample valid numbers and their formal type; **Table 2.2** lists invalid numbers and the rules they violate.

✔ Tips

- As you'll soon see, you can quote invalid numbers to turn them into valid strings.
- PHP doesn't have a *date* type of variable like that used in database applications and other programming languages. The dates you work with in your PHP scripts will therefore be comprised of numbers and/or strings.

Valid Numbers in PHP

Number	Type
1	Integer
1.0	Floating-point
1972	Integer
19.72	Floating-point
–1	Integer
–1.0	Floating-point

Table 2.1 All of these are valid number values in PHP.

Invalid Numbers in PHP

Number	Reason
1 1/4	Contains a space and a slash
1972a	Contains a letter
02.23.72	Contains multiple decimals

Table 2.2 All of these are invalid number values in PHP.

Strings

A variable is a string if it consists of characters (some combination of letters, numbers, symbols, and spaces) enclosed within a pair of either single (`'`) or double (`"`) quotation marks. Strings can contain any combination of characters, including variable names.

Examples of valid strings values include:

```
"Hello, world!"
"Hello, $FirstName!"
"1 1/4"
'Hello, world! How are you today?'
"02.23.72"
"1972"
```

An example of an invalid string would be:

```
"I said, "How are you?""
```

This last example can be tricky. I hinted at this problem in Chapter 1, "Getting Started with PHP," with respect to printing HTML code. When PHP hits the second quotation mark, it assumes the string ends there; the continuing text (*How...*) causes an error. As I mentioned previously, to use a quotation mark within a string you can *escape* the quotation mark by putting a backslash (\) before it. By changing this string to `"I said, \"How are you?\""`, you tell PHP to include the two quotation marks as part of the value of the string, rather than treat them as the string's opening or closing indicators.

You can similarly circumvent this problem by using different quotation mark types:

```
'I said, "How are you?"'
"I said, 'How are you?'"
```

continues on next page

✔ Tips

- Notice that the "1972" example converts an integer into a string by putting it within quotes. Essentially, the string contains the characters *1972*, whereas the number (a non-quoted value) would be equal to 1972. It's a fine distinction, and one that won't matter in your code, because you can perform mathematical calculations with the string *1972* just as you can with the number.
- In Chapter 1, I demonstrated how to create a new line by printing the `\n` character within double quotation marks. Although escaping a quotation mark prints the quotation mark, escaping an *n* prints a new line, escaping an *r* creates a carriage return, and escaping a *t* inserts a tab into your HTML source code.
- Understanding strings, variables, and the single and double quotation marks is critical to programming with PHP. For this reason, I've dedicated a section at the end of this chapter to the subject.

Indexed Array	
KEY	VALUE
0	Toby
1	Josh
2	CJ
3	Will

Table 2.3 A sample indexed array: The keys are numbers.

Associative Array	
KEY	VALUE
VT	Vermont
NH	New Hampshire
IA	Iowa
PA	Pennsylvania

Table 2.4 A sample associative array: The keys are strings (here, the state's abbreviation).

Arrays

I'll cover arrays more thoroughly in Chapter 7, but I'll introduce them briefly here. Whereas a string or a number contains a single value, an array can have more than one value assigned to it. You can think of an array as a list of values. In other words, you can put multiple strings and/or numbers into one array.

Arrays use *keys* to create and retrieve the values they store. The resulting structure—a list of key-value pairs—looks similar to a two-column spreadsheet. Interestingly, the array structure in PHP is so flexible that it can use either numbers or strings for both the keys and the values. The array doesn't even need to be consistent in this respect. (All of this will make more sense in Chapter 7, when you start working with specific examples.)

PHP has two different types of arrays, based on the format of the keys. If the array uses numbers for the keys (**Table 2.3**), it's an *indexed* array. If it uses strings for the keys (**Table 2.4**), it's an *associative* array. In either case, the values in the array can be of any variable type (string, number, and so on).

✔ Tips

- Due to a significant change in the default PHP configuration, understanding arrays is a must for today's PHP programmers.
- The array's key is also called its *index*. You'll see these two terms used interchangeably.
- An array can, and frequently will, contain other arrays, creating what is called a *multidimensional* array.

Objects

The fourth most common type of variable in PHP is the object, which is not formally approached in this book. An object is a very special type of variable: You define its structure (called a class) and then create instances of that structure (the instances are the objects). The structural definition of the object may include variables of different types as well as user-defined functions. All of this leads to object-oriented programming (OOP), a powerful concept in the world of computing that allows you to modularize your code.

Fortunately, as a beginning PHP developer you can accomplish everything you need to do without touching a single object. I decided not to cover objects in this book, as such a chapter would be either too advanced for beginning users or too superficial in its approach. But, once you are comfortable with PHP, you can start learning about objects by looking at the dozens of tutorials on this subject available online.

Viewing a Variable's Type

Script 2.1 uses the `print_r()` function to examine the contents of the `$GLOBALS` variable. If you instead used the `var_dump()` function, the single line of PHP would read

```
var_dump ($GLOBALS);
```

and the script would also report on the variables' types in detail (**Figure 2.4**). The format is

```
var_name var_type (var_length)
var_value
```

If you run this example, you'll see that `$GLOBALS` is an array (consisting of 14 items in my case). Within `$GLOBALS` are other arrays; they contain primarily strings but also the occasional number.

Using Var_Dump()

```
array(14) {
  ["HTTP_POST_VARS"]=>
  array(0) {
  }
  ["_POST"]=>
  array(0) {
  }
  ["HTTP_GET_VARS"]=>
  array(0) {
  }
  ["_GET"]=>
  array(0) {
  }
  ["HTTP_COOKIE_VARS"]=>
  array(0) {
  }
  ["_COOKIE"]=>
  array(0) {
  }
  ["HTTP_SERVER_VARS"]=>
  array(29) {
    ["DOCUMENT_ROOT"]=>
    string(28) "/Library/WebServer/Documents"
    ["HTTP_ACCEPT"]=>
    string(3) "*/*"
    ["HTTP_ACCEPT_ENCODING"]=>
    string(42) "gzip, deflate;q=1.0, identity;q=0.5, *;q=0"
    ["HTTP_ACCEPT_LANGUAGE"]=>
    string(249) "en, ja;q=0.92, ja-jp;q=0.96, fr;q=0.88, de-de;q=0
    ["HTTP_CONNECTION"]=>
    string(10) "keep-alive"
    ["HTTP_HOST"]=>
    string(9) "localhost"
    ["HTTP_USER_AGENT"]=>
    string(89) "Mozilla/5.0 (Macintosh; U; PPC Mac OS X; en) Apple
    ["PATH"]=>
    string(71) "/bin:/sbin:/usr/bin:/usr/sbin:/usr/libexec:/System
    ["REMOTE_ADDR"]=>
    string(9) "127.0.0.1"
    ["REMOTE_PORT"]=>
    string(5) "49599"
    ["SCRIPT_FILENAME"]=>
    string(30) "/Users/larry/Sites/print_r.php"
    ["SCRIPT_URI"]=>
    string(35) "http://127.0.0.1/~larry/print_r.php"
    ["SCRIPT_URL"]=>
    string(19) "/~larry/print_r.php"
```

Figure 2.4 The `var_dump()` function prints even more information about a variable than `print_r()` does.

Assigning Values to Variables

I mentioned at the beginning of this chapter that you don't need to initialize or declare your variables (as a general rule), but you still need to know how to assign a value to one. To assign a value to a variable, regardless of the variable type, you use the equal sign (=). Therefore, the equal sign is called an *assignment operator*, because it assigns the value on the right to the variable on the left. For example:

```
$number = 1;
$floating_number = 1.2;
$string = "Hello, world!";
```

To print out the value of a variable, you include the variable's name in a `print()` statement, within the double quotation marks:

```
print "Number is $number";
print "String is $string";
```

This method works for the scalar (single-valued) variable types, which is to say numbers and strings. Arrays and objects use more complex syntax for defining and accessing their values, as you'll learn.

For better or worse, because variable types aren't locked in (PHP is referred to as a *weakly typed* language, as is JavaScript), they can be changed on the fly:

```
$variable = 1;
$variable = "Greetings";
```

If you were to print the value of `$variable` now, the result would be *Greetings*. The following script better demonstrates the concept of assigning values to variables and then accessing those values.

To assign values to and access variables:

1. Begin a new PHP script, starting with the HTML code (**Script 2.3**).

2. Create the initial HTML tags.

```
<!DOCTYPE html PUBLIC "-//W3C//
→ DTD XHTML 1.0 Transitional//EN"
"http://www.w3.org/TR/xhtml1/DTD/
→ xhtml1-transitional.dtd">
<html xmlns="http://www.w3.org/1999/
→ xhtml">
<head>
   <meta http-equiv="content-type"
   → content="text/html; charset=
   → iso-8859-1" />
   <title>Variables</title>
</head>
<body>
```

3. Begin the PHP code:

```
<?php // Script 2.3 - variables.php
```

4. Define some number and string variables:

```
$street = "100 Main Street";
$city = "State College";
$state = "PA";
$zip = 16801;
```

These lines create some different variables of string and number types. The strings are defined using quotation marks, and each variable name follows the syntactical naming rules.

Because this is the first true multi-lined PHP script you've written, let me remind you to conclude each statement with a semicolon.

Script 2.3 This script defines some basic variables and then prints out their values.

```
<!DOCTYPE html PUBLIC "-//W3C//DTD XHTML 1.0 Transitional//EN"
"http://www.w3.org/TR/xhtml1/DTD/xhtml1-transitional.dtd">
<html xmlns="http://www.w3.org/1999/xhtml">
<head>
    <meta http-equiv="content-type" content="text/html; charset=iso-8859-1" />
    <title>Variables</title>
</head>
<body>
<?php // Script 2.3 - variables.php

// An address:
$street = "100 Main Street";
$city = "State College";
$state = "PA";
$zip = 16801;

// Print the address.
print "The address is:<br />$street <br />$city $state $zip";

?>
</body>
</html>
```

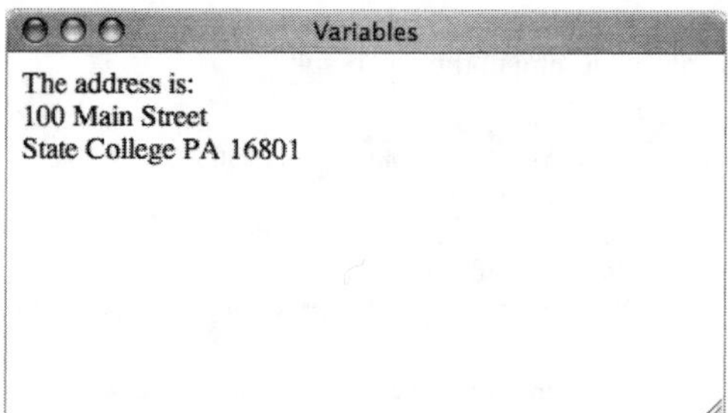

Figure 2.5 Creating and using variables in PHP can be remarkably simple.

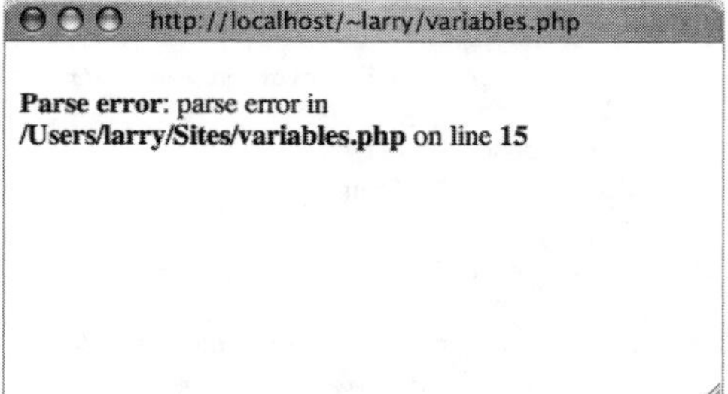

Figure 2.6 Parse errors are the most common type of PHP error, as you'll discover. They're frequently caused by missing semicolons or an imbalance of quotation marks or parentheses.

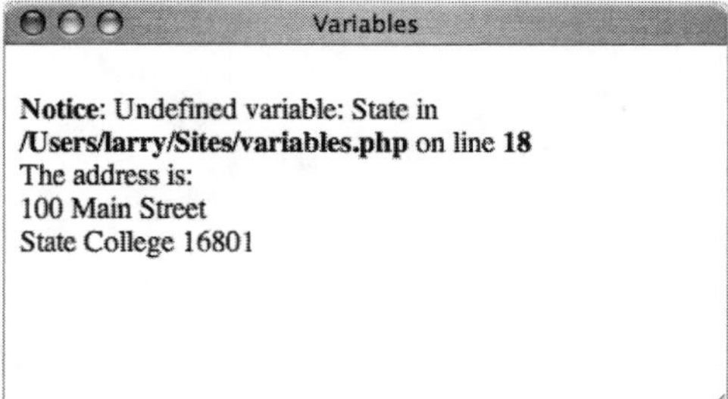

Figure 2.7 The *Undefined variable* error indicates that you used a variable with no value (it hasn't been defined). This can happen with misspellings and capitalization inconsistencies.

5. Print out the variables:

```
print "The address is:<br />$street
→ <br />$city $state $zip";
```

Here you use a single `print()` statement to access all the variables. The entire string to be printed (consisting of text, HTML tags, and variables) is enclosed within double quotation marks. The HTML `<br />` tags make the text flow over multiple lines in the browser window (remember, the extra space and slash in the break tag is there for XHTML compliance purposes).

6. Complete the PHP section and the HTML page:

```
?>
</body>
</html>
```

7. Save the file as `variables.php`, upload it to your server (or save it to the appropriate directory on your computer), and test in your Web browser (**Figure 2.5**).

✔ Tips

- If you see a parse-error (**Figure 2.6**) when you run this script, you probably either omitted a semicolon or have an imbalance in your quotation marks.
- If one of the variable's values isn't printed out or you see an *Undefined variable* error (**Figure 2.7**), you most likely failed to spell a variable name the same way twice.
- You can set the variable type by *casting* it upon first use (casting a variable is similar to declaring it, where you formally establish its type). The syntax for doing so is:

  ```
  $varname = (type) value;
  ```

  For example:

  ```
  $number = (integer) 5;
  $string = (string) "Hello, World!";
  ```

Understanding Quotation Marks

Now that you know the basics of variables and how to create them, I'll clarify the important concept of quotation marks. PHP, like most programming languages, supports both double (") and single (') quotation marks—but they give vastly different results.

The rule of thumb is this: Items within single quotation marks are treated literally; items within double quotation marks are extrapolated (that is, a variable's name is replaced with its value, as you saw in Script 2.3). This rule applies anywhere in PHP you might use quotation marks, including the creation of string variables and using the `print()` function. An example is the best way to explain.

To use quotation marks:

1. Begin a new PHP script, starting with the HTML code (**Script 2.4**).

2. Create the initial HTML tags:

```
<!DOCTYPE html PUBLIC "-//W3C//
→ DTD XHTML 1.0 Transitional//EN"
"http://www.w3.org/TR/xhtml1/DTD/
→ xhtml1-transitional.dtd">
<html xmlns="http://www.w3.org/1999/
→ xhtml">
<head>
    <meta http-equiv="content-type"
    → content="text/html; charset=
    → iso-8859-1" />
    <title>Quotes</title>
</head>
<body>
```

3. Begin the PHP code:

```
<?php // Script 2.4 - quotes.php
```

Script 2.4 The type of quotation mark you use with variables is vital to the end result.

Script

```
<!DOCTYPE html PUBLIC "-//W3C//DTD XHTML 1.0 Transitional//EN"
"http://www.w3.org/TR/xhtml1/DTD/xhtml1-transitional.dtd">
<html xmlns="http://www.w3.org/1999/xhtml">
<head>
    <meta http-equiv="content-type" content="text/html; charset=iso-8859-1" />
    <title>Quotes</title>
</head>
<body>
<?php // Script 2.4 - quotes.php

// Single or double quotation marks won't matter here:
$first_name = 'Larry';
$last_name = "Ullman";

// Single or double quotation marks DOES matter here:
$name1 = '$first_name $last_name';
$name2 = "$first_name $last_name";

// Single or double quotation marks DOES matter here:
print "<p>name1 is $name1 <br />
name2 is $name2</p>";

print '<p>name1 is $name1 <br />
name2 is $name2</p>';

?>
</body>
</html>
```

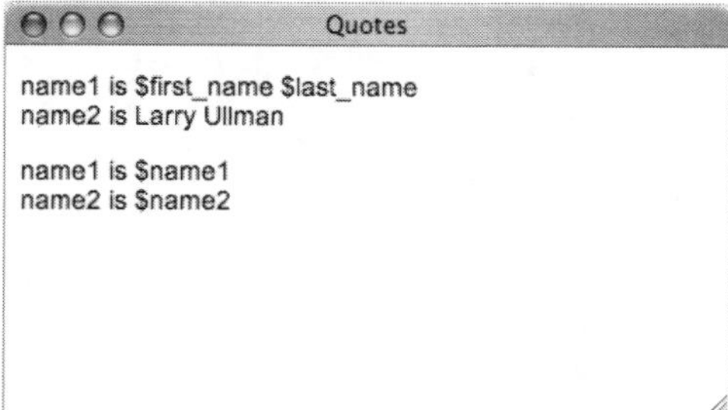

Figure 2.8 The different quotation marks (single versus double) dictate whether the variable's name or value is printed.

4. Create two string variables:

```
$first_name = 'Larry';
$last_name = "Ullman";
```

It doesn't matter whether you use single or double quotation marks, as each string should be treated literally.

5. Create two different name variables, using the first- and last-name variables:

```
$name1 = '$first_name $last_name';
$name2 = "$first_name $last_name";
```

In these lines it makes a huge difference which quotation marks you use. The `$name1` variable is literally equal to *$first_name $last_name*, because no extrapolation occurs. Conversely, `$name2` is now equal to *Larry Ullman*, presumably the result you're shooting for.

6. Print out the variables using both types of quotation marks:

```
print "<p>name1 is $name1 <br />
name2 is $name2</p>";
print '<p>name1 is $name1 <br />
name2 is $name2</p>';
```

Again, the quotation marks make all the difference. The first `print()` statement prints out the values of the `$name1` and `$name2` variables, whereas the second prints out *$name1* and *$name2*.

The HTML in the `print()` statements makes them more legible in the browser, and each statement is executed over two lines, which is perfectly acceptable.

7. Complete the PHP section and the HTML page:

```
?>
</body>
</html>
```

8. Save the file as `quotes.php`, upload it to your server (or save it to the appropriate directory on your computer), and test in your Web browser (**Figure 2.8**).

continues on next page

✔ Tips

- If you're still confused about the distinction between the two types of quotation marks, stick with double quotation marks and you'll be safe.
- Arguably, using single quotation marks when you can is preferable, as PHP won't need to search the strings looking for variables. This rule is more of a finesse issue—the performance won't be measurably affected regardless.
- The shortcuts for creating newlines (`\n`), tabs (`\t`), and double quotation marks (`\"`) must also be used within double quotation marks to have the desired effect.
- You can also print a variable's value without using quotation marks, assuming you print nothing else:

```
print $number;
```

3

HTML Forms and PHP

In the previous chapter, you had a brief introduction to variables. Although you'll often create your own variables, you'll also commonly use variables in conjunction with HTML forms. Forms, as you've certainly seen, are a fundamental unit of today's Web sites, enabling such features as registration and login systems, search capability, and online shopping. Even the most basic site will find logical reasons to incorporate HTML forms. And, with PHP, it's stunningly simple to receive and handle data generated by them.

With that in mind, this chapter will cover the basics of creating HTML forms and how the form data is transmitted to your PHP script. Simultaneously, this chapter will introduce several key concepts of real PHP programming, including how to debug and manage errors in your scripts.

Creating a Simple Form

For the HTML form example in this chapter, you'll create a feedback page that takes the user's salutation, name, email address, response, and comment. You'll need to create the necessary fields with this in mind. First, let's briefly revisit the topic of XHTML.

As stated in the first chapter (which introduced the fact that this book would use XHTML), the language has some rules that result in a significantly different syntax than HTML. For starters, the code needs to be in all lowercase letters, and every tag attribute must be enclosed in quotes. Further, every tag must be closed; those that don't have formal closing tags, like `<input>`, are closed by adding a blank space and a slash at the end. Thus, in HTML you might write

```
<INPUT TYPE=TEXT NAME=address SIZE=40>
```

but in XHTML it's

```
<input type="text" name="address"
→ size="40" />
```

This explanation will help to avoid confusion as the following page follows XHTML standards.

To start a basic HTML form:

1. Open your text editor and begin a new document (**Script 3.1**):

```
<!DOCTYPE html PUBLIC "-//W3C//
→ DTD XHTML 1.0 Transitional//EN"
"http://www.w3.org/TR/xhtml1/DTD/
→ xhtml1-transitional.dtd">
<html xmlns="http://www.w3.org/1999/
→ xhtml">
<head>
    <meta http-equiv="content-type"
    → content="text/html; charset=
    → iso-8859-1" />
    <title>Feedback Form</title>
</head>
```

Script 3.1 Every HTML form begins and ends with the `<form> </form>` tags. When you're hand-coding forms, take care not to forget either one. Also be sure to direct the form to the proper handling script using the `action` attribute.

```
<!DOCTYPE html PUBLIC "-//W3C//DTD XHTML
1.0 Transitional//EN"
"http://www.w3.org/TR/xhtml1/DTD/xhtml1-
transitional.dtd">
<html xmlns="http://www.w3.org/1999/xhtml">
<head>
    <meta http-equiv="content-type"
    content="text/html; charset=
    iso-8859-1" />
    <title>Feedback Form</title>
</head>
<body>
Please complete this form to submit your
feedback: <br />

<form action="handle_form.php">

</form>

<!-- Script 3.1 - feedback.html -->
</body>
</html>
```

```
<body>
Please complete this form to submit
→ your feedback: <br />
```

2. Add the opening and closing <form> tags:

```
<form action="handle_form.php">
</form>
```

The <form> tags dictate where a form begins and ends. Every element of the form must be entered between these two lines. The action attribute tells the server which page (or script) will receive the data from the form and is one of the most important considerations.

3. Complete the page with the closing body and HTML tags.

```
<!-- Script 3.1 - feedback.html -->
</body>
</html>
```

4. Save the page as feedback.html.

✔ Tips

- Note that you use the HTML extension (.html) here because it's a standard HTML page (not a PHP page). You could use the .php extension without a problem, even though there's no actual PHP code. (Remember that in a PHP page, anything not within the PHP brackets—<?php and ?>—is assumed to be HTML.)

- Be certain that your action attribute correctly points to an existing file on the server, or your form won't be processed properly. In this case, you indicate that the form should be submitted to handle_form.php, which is located in the same directory as the feedback.html page.

Now that you've been introduced to the fundamental form tags, let's add the various form elements (inputs for the user's name, email address, and so on) to complete the form.

To create form elements:

1. After the opening `form` line (line 11) but before the closing `form` tag, press Enter (or Return) to create a new line.

2. Add three radio buttons for the person's title (**Script 3.2**):

```
Mr. <input type="radio" name="title"
→ value="Mr." />
Mrs. <input type="radio" name="title"
→ value="Mrs." />
Ms. <input type="radio" name="title"
→ value="Ms." />
<br />
```

   This HTML code creates three radio buttons (clickable circles; see **Figure 3.1**). Because they all have the same `name` value, only one of the three can be selected at a time. Per XHTML rules, the code is in lowercase except for the values, and an extra space and slash are added to the end of each input to close the tag.

   In the interest of spacing out the form, the `<br />` tag is added at the end.

3. Add text inputs for the user's name and email address:

```
Name: <input type="text" name="name"
→ size="20" />
<br />
Email Address: <input type="text"
→ name="email" size="20" />
<br />
```

   Follow a consistent naming convention within your form by giving each field a logical and descriptive name. Use letters, numbers, and the underscore (_) when naming fields. These text inputs make the text boxes in the browser (**Figure 3.2**).

continues on page 48

Mr. Mrs. Ms.

Figure 3.1 The title radio buttons.

Name:
Email Address:

Figure 3.2 Text input types make boxes like these.

Script 3.2 You can add any combination of input types to your form—just ensure that all of them are within the <form> tags, or they won't appear.

Script

```
<!DOCTYPE html PUBLIC "-//W3C//DTD XHTML 1.0 Transitional//EN"
"http://www.w3.org/TR/xhtml1/DTD/xhtml1-transitional.dtd">
<html xmlns="http://www.w3.org/1999/xhtml">
<head>
    <meta http-equiv="content-type" content="text/html; charset=iso-8859-1" />
    <title>Feedback Form</title>
</head>
<body>
Please complete this form to submit your feedback: <br />

<form action="handle_form.php">

Mr. <input type="radio" name="title" value="Mr." />
Mrs. <input type="radio" name="title" value="Mrs." />
Ms. <input type="radio" name="title" value="Ms." />
<br />
Name: <input type="text" name="name" size="20" />
<br />
Email Address: <input type="text" name="email" size="20" />
<br />
Response: <select name="response">
<option value="excellent">This is excellent.</option>
<option value="okay">This is okay.</option>
<option value="boring">This is boring.</option>
</select>
<br />
Comments: <textarea name="comments" rows="3" cols="30"></textarea>
<br />
<input type="submit" name="submit" value="Send My Feedback" />

</form>

<!-- Script 3.2 - feedback.html -->
</body>
</html>
```

4. Add a select menu for a response:

```
Response: <select name="response">
<option value="excellent">This is
→ excellent.</option>
<option value="okay">This is okay.
→ </option>
<option value="boring">This is boring.
→ </option>
</select>
<br />
```

You add a *response* drop-down menu here mostly to use another popular form field type, the select menu (**Figure 3.3**). Each option listed between the select tags is an answer the user can choose.

5. Add a textarea to record the comments:

```
Comments: <textarea name="comments"
→ rows="3" cols="30"></textarea>
<br />
```

A textarea (**Figure 3.4**) gives the user more space to enter their comments than a text field would. However, the text input lets you limit how much information the user can enter, which you can't do with the textarea (not without using JavaScript, that is). When you're creating a form, choose input types appropriate to the information you wish to retrieve from the user.

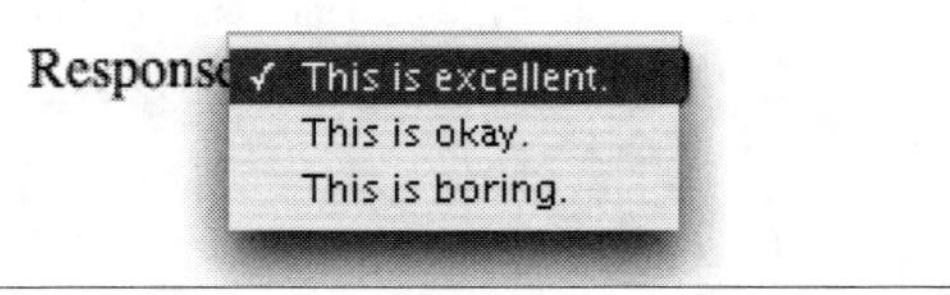

Figure 3.3 The select tag creates a drop-down menu.

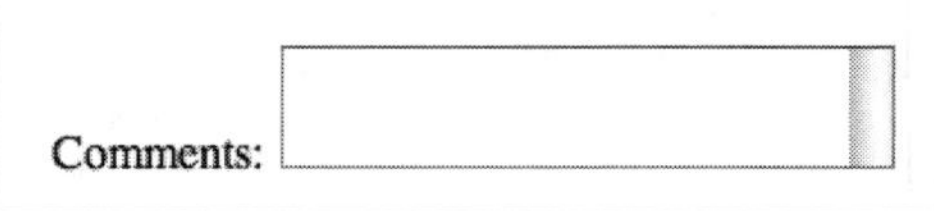

Figure 3.4 The textarea tags generate a larger text box.

Figure 3.5 Every form needs to have a submit button, which may look different from one Web browser to another.

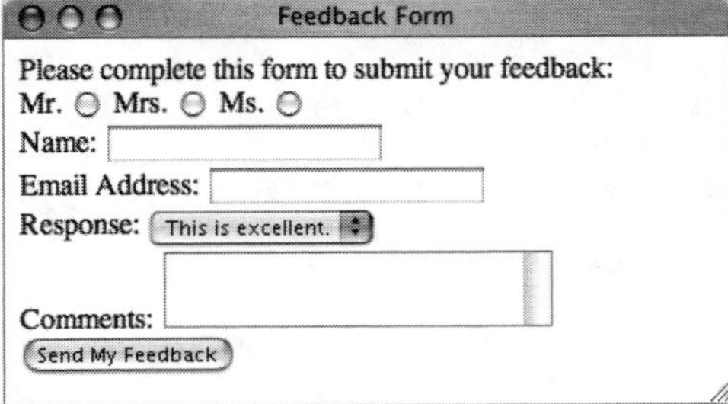

Figure 3.6 If you've typed in your form correctly, it should look like this in your Web browser.

6. Add the submit button:

```
<input type="submit" name="submit"
→ value="Send My Feedback" />
```

The `value` attribute of a submit type is what appears on the button in the Web browser (**Figure 3.5**). You could also use *Go!* or *Enter*, for example.

7. Save your script, upload it to your server (or store it in the appropriate directory on your computer in which you've installed PHP), and view it in your browser (**Figure 3.6**). (Because this is an HTML page, not a PHP script, you could view it in your Web browser directly from your computer.)

✔ Tip

- In this example you create the form by hand-coding the HTML, but you can do this in a Web page application (such as Macromedia Dreamweaver or Adobe GoLive) if you're more comfortable with that approach.

Using GET or POST

The experienced HTML developer will notice that the feedback form is missing one thing: The initial `<form>` tag has no `method` value. This attribute tells the server how to transmit the data from the form to the handling script.

You have two choices with `method`: GET and POST. Many HTML coders may not be entirely clear on the distinction and when to use which. In truth, for the most part it doesn't make much difference (especially as you first begin using them), because either will generally get you the results you need.

The difference between using GET and POST is squarely in how the information is passed from the form to the processing script. The GET method sends all the gathered information along as part of the URL. The POST method transmits the information invisibly to the user. For example, upon submitting your form, if you use the GET method, the resulting URL will be something like this:

```
http://www.DMCinsights.com/phpvqs2/handle_form.php?title=Mr.&name=Larry%20Ullman...
```

Whereas using the POST method, the end user will only see the following:

```
http://www.DMCinsights.com/phpvqs2/handle_form.php
```

When choosing which method to use, you may want to keep in mind these three factors:

- With the GET method, a limited amount of information can be passed.
- The GET method sends the input to the handling script publicly (which means, for example, that a password entered in a form can be viewed by anyone within eyesight of the Web browser, creating a larger security risk).
- A page generated by a form that used the GET method can be bookmarked, but one based on POST can't be.

Script 3.3 The `method` attribute with a value of *post* has been added to complete the form.

Script

```
<!DOCTYPE html PUBLIC "-//W3C//DTD XHTML 1.0 Transitional//EN"
"http://www.w3.org/TR/xhtml1/DTD/xhtml1-transitional.dtd">
<html xmlns="http://www.w3.org/1999/xhtml">
<head>
    <meta http-equiv="content-type" content="text/html; charset=iso-8859-1" />
    <title>Feedback Form</title>
</head>
<body>
Please complete this form to submit your feedback: <br />

<form action="handle_form.php" method="post">

Mr. <input type="radio" name="title" value="Mr." />
Mrs. <input type="radio" name="title" value="Mrs." />
Ms. <input type="radio" name="title" value="Ms." />
<br />
Name: <input type="text" name="name" size="20" />
<br />
Email Address: <input type="text" name="email" size="20" />
<br />
Response: <select name="response">
<option value="excellent">This is excellent.</option>
<option value="okay">This is okay.</option>
<option value="boring">This is boring.</option>
</select>
<br />
Comments: <textarea name="comments" rows="3" cols="30"></textarea>
<br />
<input type="submit" name="submit" value="Send My Feedback" />

</form>

<!-- Script 3.3 - feedback.html -->
</body>
</html>
```

Source of http://localhost/~larry/feedback.html

```
<!DOCTYPE html PUBLIC "-//W3C//DTD XHTML 1.0 Transitional//EN"
        "http://www.w3.org/TR/xhtml1/DTD/xhtml1-transitional.dtd">
<html xmlns="http://www.w3.org/1999/xhtml">
<head>
     <meta http-equiv="content-type" content="text/html; charset=iso-8859-1" />
     <title>Feedback Form</title>
</head>
<body>
Please complete this form to submit your feedback: <br />
<form action="handle_form.php" method="post">

Mr. <input type="radio" name="title" value="Mr." />
Mrs. <input type="radio" name="title" value="Mrs." />
Ms. <input type="radio" name="title" value="Ms." />
<br />
Name: <input type="text" name="name" size="20" />
<br />
Email Address: <input type="text" name="email" size="20" />
<br />
Response: <select name="response">
<option value="excellent">This is excellent.</option>
<option value="okay">This is okay.</option>
<option value="boring">This is boring.</option>
</select>
<br />
Comments: <textarea name="comments" rows="3" cols="30"></textarea>
<br />
<input type="submit" name="submit" value="Send My Feedback" />

</form>

<!-- Script 3.3 - feedback.html -->
</body>
</html>
```

Figure 3.7 View the source of an HTML page to validate its contents.

This book uses POST almost exclusively for handling forms, although you'll also see a useful technique where the GET method theory adds capabilities to your Web site (see "Manually Sending Data to a Page" at the end of this chapter). Either method will successfully pass along the data from the form, and the final decision about which method to use should be based on mitigating factors in your form and whether the resulting page should be bookmark-able. Experience will make the distinction clearer, but you can safely use POST most of the time.

To add a method to your script:

1. Open `feedback.html` (Script 3.2) in your text editor.
2. Within the initial `<form>` tag, add `method="post"` (**Script 3.3**, line 11).

   The form's `method` attribute tells the browser how to send the form data to the receiving script.
3. Save the script and test again in your Web browser.
4. View the source of the page to make sure all the required elements are present (**Figure 3.7**).

✔ Tip

- In the discussion of the methods, GET and POST are written in capital letters to make them stand out. However, the form uses *post* for XHTML compliance. Don't worry about this inconsistency (if you caught it at all)—the method will work regardless of case.

USING GET OR POST

Receiving Data from a Form in PHP

Now that you've created a basic HTML form, you need to write the `handle_form.php` script that will receive and process the data generated by the `feedback.html` page. For this example, the PHP script will simply repeat what the user entered into the form. In later chapters, you'll learn how to take this information and store it in a database or send it in an email.

For many readers, this example will be surprisingly simple, and the script will work flawlessly. But some may encounter a small hiccup or two, thanks to major changes in PHP's default configuration. In many PHP installations, you can access form values by taking the `name` attribute of the various inputs and adding a dollar sign to create the variable. In this example, those variables would be `$title`, `$name`, `$email`, `$response`, `$comments`, and `$submit`.

You'll write the script using this standard method, which will work for many readers. If it doesn't, then this leads nicely into the debugging techniques covered next. So, as a heads up, if you see unexpected results with this example, fear not: The next three sections of the chapter explain everything and teach some valuable lessons in the process.

To create the PHP script:

1. Open your text editor and create a new document (**Script 3.4**):

```
<!DOCTYPE html PUBLIC "-//W3C//DTD XHTML 1.0 Transitional//EN"
"http://www.w3.org/TR/xhtml1/DTD/xhtml1-transitional.dtd">
<html xmlns="http://www.w3.org/1999/xhtml">
<head>
   <meta http-equiv="content-type" content="text/html; charset=iso-8859-1" />
```

Script 3.4 By taking the value of the `name` elements in the HTML form and adding a dollar sign, you create variables that contain the values the user entered in the corresponding form fields.

Script

```
<!DOCTYPE html PUBLIC "-//W3C//DTD XHTML 1.0 Transitional//EN"
"http://www.w3.org/TR/xhtml1/DTD/xhtml1-transitional.dtd">
<html xmlns="http://www.w3.org/1999/xhtml">
<head>
    <meta http-equiv="content-type" content="text/html; charset=iso-8859-1" />
    <title>Your Feedback</title>
</head>
<body>
<?php // Script 3.4 - handle_form.php

// This page receives the data from feedback.html.
// It will receive: title, name, email, response, comments, and submit.

print "Thank you $title $name for your comments. <br />";
print "You stated that you found this example to be $response and added: $comments";
?>
</body>
</html>
```

```
    <title>Your Feedback</title>
</head>
<body>
```

2. Insert the opening PHP tag and add any comments:

```
<?php // Script 3.4 - handle_form.php
// This page receives the data from
→ feedback.html.
// It will receive: title, name, email,
→ response, comments, and submit.
```

You add comments to the script to remind yourself of its purpose. Even though the `feedback.html` page indicates where the data is sent (via the `action` attribute), a comment here indicates the reverse (from where this script is getting its data).

3. Print out the user information:

```
print "Thank you $title $name for your
→ comments. <br />";
print "You stated that you found this
→ example to be $response and added:
→ $comments";
```

Again, to access what the user typed into the Name input box, you refer to the `$name` variable. The same applies to all the other form inputs, regardless of their type.

4. Close the PHP section and complete the HTML page.

```
?>
</body>
</html>
```

5. Save the script as `handle_form.php`.

6. Upload the script to the server (or store it in the proper directory on your computer if you've installed PHP), making sure it's saved in the same directory as `feedback.html`.

continues on next page

7. Test the script in your Web browser by going to `feedback.html` and then submitting the form (**Figures 3.8** and **3.9**).

   If the values of the variables aren't printed when you run the script (**Figure 3.10**), or they're not printed and you see many error messages, these are the aforementioned hiccups. Some of you may see nothing at all (a blank page). In any of these cases, continue reading the next three sections of the book for the appropriate solutions.

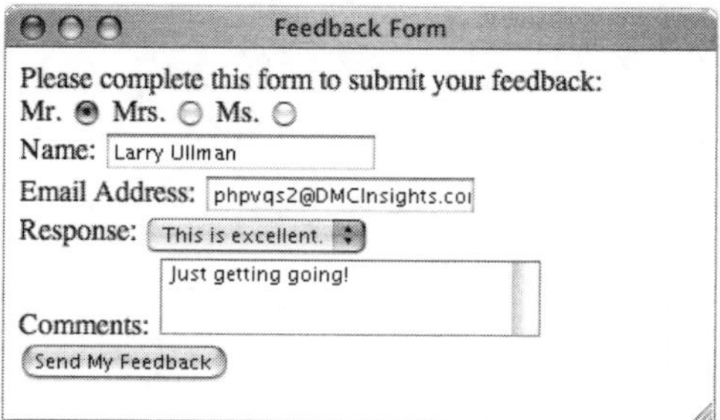

Figure 3.8 Whatever the user enters into the HTML form should be printed out to the Web browser by the `handle_form.php` script (see Figure 3.9).

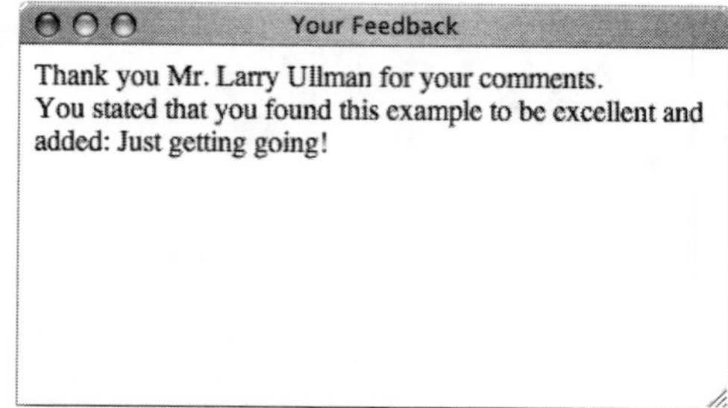

Figure 3.9 This is another application of the `print` statement discussed in Chapter 1, but it constitutes your first dynamically generated Web page.

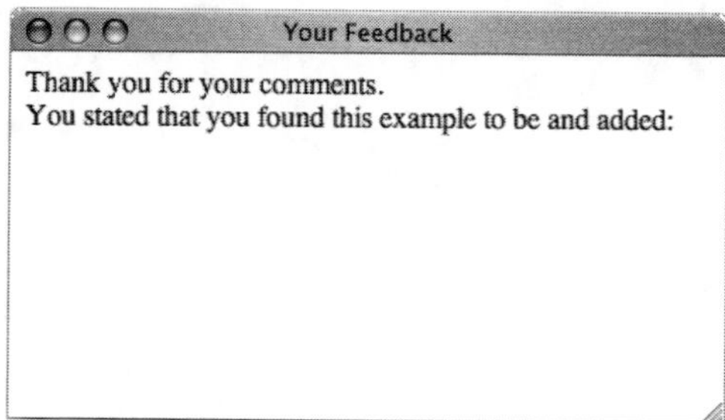

Figure 3.10 If the page doesn't display the submitted information, read the *The Register Globals Problem* section of the chapter.

✔ Tips

- If you want to pass a preset value along to your script, use the hidden type of input within your HTML form. For example, the line

  ```
  <input type="hidden" name="this_page"
  → value="feedback.html" />
  ```

  inserted between the form tags will create a variable in your handling script called `$this_page` with the value *feedback.html*.

- Notice that the value of radio button and select menu variables is based on the `value` attribute of the selected item (for example, *excellent* in the select menu). This is also true for check boxes. As you saw, for text boxes, the value of the variable is what the user typed.

- Even the submit button is sent to the receiving page as a variable.

- If the `handle_form.php` script displays extra slashes in submitted strings see the "Combating Magic Quotes" section of Chapter 5, "Using Strings."

- You should know that the method of handling form data demonstrated here (referring to `$name`, `$title`, etc.) is not the preferred method and can introduce some security risks—although it can work, obviously. Rest assured that you will learn better, more secure methods soon, but I wanted to keep things simple for the time being.

Displaying Errors

After you install PHP on a Web server, it will run under a default configuration with respect to security, how it handles data, performance, and so forth. Since this book was first written, three significant changes have been made in that default configuration, and all PHP programmers should be aware of them. The first has to do with whether error messages are displayed.

PHP can be set to give you feedback if it encounters problems. Whether it does so is based on the `display_errors` setting in PHP's configuration file (which is called `php.ini`). In current versions of PHP, this setting is disabled by default, so errors generated by a script result in a blank screen. You may have experienced this result in the previous example.

To have PHP display errors, you can

- Turn `display_errors` back on (see the "Configuring PHP" section of Appendix A, "Installation and Configuration," for more information)
- Turn `display_errors` back on for a particular script.

Although the first option is best for people learning PHP, it's only an option for those with administrative control over the server. Anyone can use the second option by including this line in your script:

```
ini_set ('display_errors', 1);
```

The `ini_set()` function allows a script to temporarily override a setting in PHP's configuration file. In this example, you'll turn the `display_errors` setting to *on*, which is represented by the number `1`.

To display errors:

1. Open `handle_form.php` in your text editor.
2. As the first line of PHP code, enter the following (**Script 3.5**):

   ```
   ini_set ('display_errors', 1);
   ```

   Again, this line tells PHP you'd like to see any errors that occur. You should call it first thing in your PHP section so the rest of the PHP code will abide by this new setting.
3. Save the file as `handle_form.php`.
4. Upload the file to your Web server and test it in your Web browser (**Figures 3.11** and **3.12**).

   If the resulting page has no errors in it, then the script will run as it did before. If you saw a blank page when you ran the form earlier, you should now see messages like those in Figure 3.12. If so, keep reading this chapter to find the solutions.

Script 3.5 Turning on the `display_errors` directive should eliminate blank pages that occur when an error is found.

```
<!DOCTYPE html PUBLIC "-//W3C//DTD XHTML 1.0 Transitional//EN"
"http://www.w3.org/TR/xhtml1/DTD/xhtml1-transitional.dtd">
<html xmlns="http://www.w3.org/1999/xhtml">
<head>
    <meta http-equiv="content-type" content="text/html; charset=iso-8859-1" />
    <title>Your Feedback</title>
</head>
<body>
<?php // Script 3.5 - handle_form.php (second version after Script 3.4)

ini_set ('display_errors', 1); // Let me learn from my mistakes.

// This page receives the data from feedback.html.
// It will receive: title, name, email, response, comments, and submit.

print "Thank you $title $name for your comments. <br />";
print "You stated that you found this example to be $response and added: $comments";

?>
</body>
</html>
```

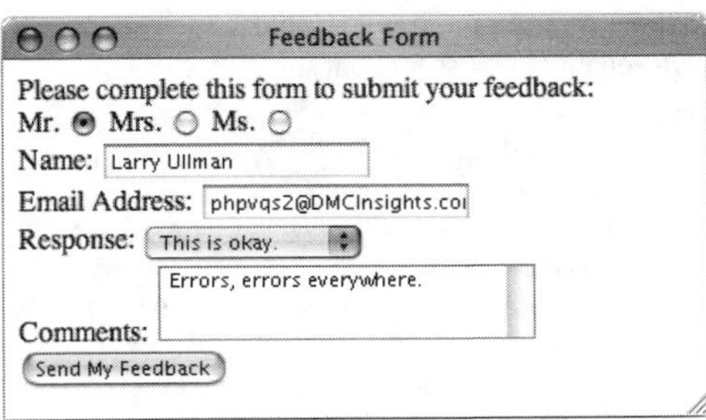

Figure 3.11 Trying the form again...

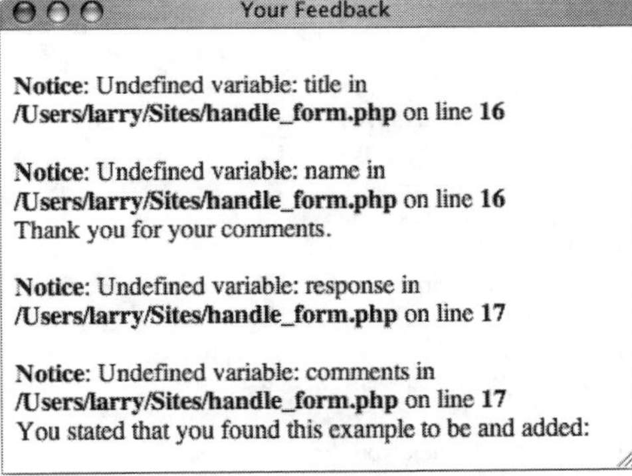

Figure 3.12 ...and now any error messages are displayed.

✔ Tips

- Make sure `display_errors` is enabled any time you're having difficulties debugging a script. If you installed PHP on your computer, I *highly* recommend enabling it in your PHP configuration while you learn (again, see Appendix A).
- If you see a blank page when running a PHP script, also check the HTML source code for errors or other problems.
- The `ini_set()` function can only be used to alter certain settings. See the PHP manual for details.
- Remember that the `display_errors` directive only controls whether error messages are sent to the Web browser. It doesn't create errors or prevent them from occurring in any way.
- It's recommended that `display_errors` be kept off for production (live) Web sites, because errors are both unseemly and a security risk. You should turn on `display_errors` while you develop a site, though.
- It's entirely possible that the makers of PHP will change other settings that will affect the usability of the scripts in this book. If so, information and updates can be found through the book's Web site at www.DMCInsights.com/phpvqs2.

Error Reporting

The second of the three PHP configuration issues you should be aware of is error reporting. There are eight types of errors in PHP plus three user-defined errors (which aren't covered here). **Table 3.1** lists the four most important error types, along with a description and example.

You can determine what errors PHP reports on using the `error_reporting()` function. The function takes either a number or a constant (a nonquoted string with a predetermined meaning) to adjust the levels. For example:

```
error_reporting (0); // Turn off entirely.
error_reporting (E_ALL); // Report everything.
error_reporting (E_ALL & ~E_NOTICE); // Don't show notices.
```

The last example states that you want to see all error messages except notices (the & ~ means *and not*). You'll apply this setting to the `handle_form.php` page to get rid of those pesky error messages (Figure 3.12).

Script 3.6 You adjust PHP's level of error reporting to give you more or less feedback.

```
<!DOCTYPE html PUBLIC "-//W3C//DTD XHTML 1.0 Transitional//EN"
"http://www.w3.org/TR/xhtml1/DTD/xhtml1-transitional.dtd">
<html xmlns="http://www.w3.org/1999/xhtml">
<head>
    <meta http-equiv="content-type" content="text/html; charset=iso-8859-1" />
    <title>Your Feedback</title>
</head>
<body>
<?php // Script 3.6 - handle_form.php (third version after Scripts 3.4 and 3.5)

ini_set ('display_errors', 1); // Let me learn from my mistakes.
error_reporting (E_ALL & ~ E_NOTICE); // Don't show notices.

// This page receives the data from feedback.html.
// It will recieve: title, name, email, response, comments, and submit.

print "Thank you $title $name for your comments. <br />";
print "You stated that you found this example to be $response and added: $comments";

?>
</body>
</html>
```

PHP Error Types

Type	Description	Example
Notice	Nonfatal error that may or may not be indicative of a problem	Referring to a variable that has no value
Warning	Nonfatal error that is most likely problematic	Passing the wrong type of parameter to a function
Parse error	Fatal error caused by a syntactical mistake	Omission of a semicolon or an imbalance of quotation marks, braces, or parentheses
Error	A general fatal error	Memory allocation problem

Table 3.1 The four most common error types in PHP.

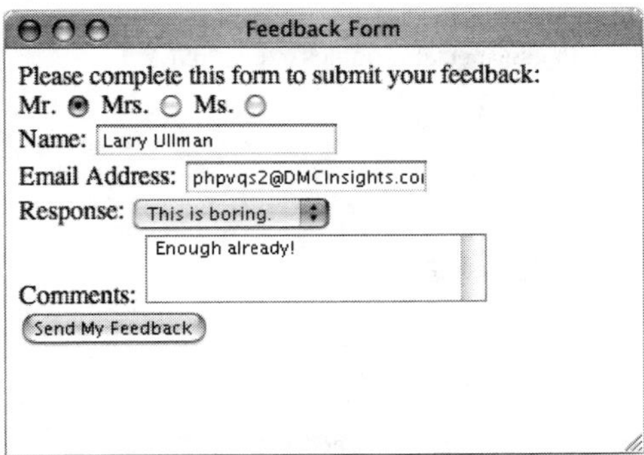

Figure 3.13 Trying the form one more time...

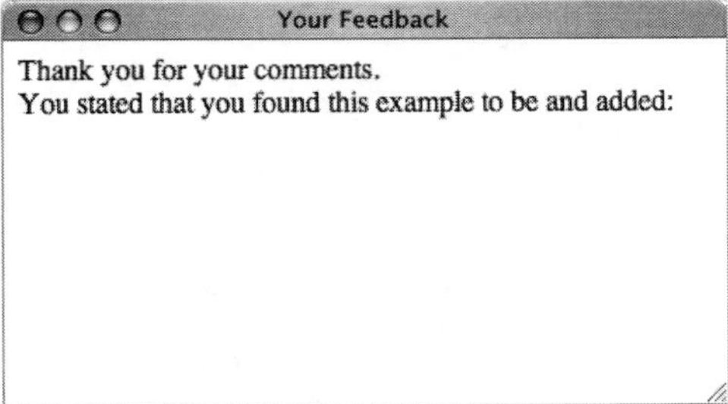

Figure 3.14 ...and now the notices are gone.

To adjust error reporting:

1. Open `handle_form.php` in your text editor (Script 3.5).
2. After the `ini_set()` line, enter the following (**Script 3.6**):
   ```
   error_reporting (E_ALL & ~ E_NOTICE);
   ```
3. Save the file as `handle_form.php`.
4. Upload the file to your Web server and test it in your Web browser (**Figures 3.13** and **3.14**).

   At this point, you should either see a successful handling of the form (Figure 3.9) or be missing the variable values but not see the error messages (Figure 3.14). The next section of this chapter will address the missing variable values.

✔ Tips

- The PHP manual lists all the error-reporting levels, but the three listed here are the most useful.
- You can also adjust the level of PHP error reporting in the `php.ini` file, although such a change affects every script. If you are running your own PHP server, you'll probably want to tweak this while developing your scripts. See the "Configuring PHP" section of Appendix A.
- In the current script, `handle_form.php`, the notices are indicative of a problem—namely, that the variables aren't being assigned their values. But this problem is also evident in the resulting Web page, so it makes sense to disable the notices.

The Register Globals Problem

The last of the three major configuration changes in PHP is the most serious (and has been a real bugaboo to readers of this book's first edition and nearly every beginning PHP programmer). As of version 4.2 of PHP, the creators decided to change one of the most important settings, called `register_globals`.

If `register_globals` is turned on (which was the case in versions of PHP prior to 4.2), form data is automatically stored in variables with simple names like `$name` and `$email`. In other words, the form data is registered as a global variable in the script. If `register_globals` is turned off (as you might have witnessed), these variables aren't automatically assigned the form values and are therefore blank.

There are two ways to combat this issue:

- Turn `register_globals` back on (see the "Configuring PHP" section of Appendix A for more information).
- Refer to the form data using a different set of variables.

While the first method will certainly work, the latter is far and away the better choice. It's more secure, more exacting, and what you're likely to see in real-world applications.

You'll try the second method by rewriting the `print()` statements, replacing each occurrence of a variable (`$var`) with `{$_POST ['var']}`. `$_POST` refers to an array of data sent to the page via the POST method (because the form uses POST), which is automatically global and therefore doesn't need to be registered. The curly braces are used to avoid parse errors in the `print()` statements. The syntax, and the reasoning behind why it works, will make much more sense after you read Chapter 7, "Using Arrays."

Script 3.7 To combat `register_globals` being off, you need to use special variables like `$_POST`.

```
<!DOCTYPE html PUBLIC "-//W3C//DTD XHTML 1.0 Transitional//EN"
"http://www.w3.org/TR/xhtml1/DTD/xhtml1-transitional.dtd">
<html xmlns="http://www.w3.org/1999/xhtml">
<head>
    <meta http-equiv="content-type" content="text/html; charset=iso-8859-1" />
    <title>Your Feedback</title>
</head>
<body>
<?php // Script 3.7 - handle_form.php (fourth version after Scripts 3.4, 3.5, and 3.6)

ini_set ('display_errors', 1); // Let me learn from my mistakes.
error_reporting (E_ALL & ~ E_NOTICE); // Don't show notices.

// This page receives the data from feedback.html.
// It will recieve: title, name, email, response, comments, and submit.

// Adjust for register_globals being off.
print "Thank you {$_POST['title']} {$_POST['name']} for your comments. <br />";
print "You stated that you found this example to be {$_POST['response']} and added: {$_POST['comments']}";

?>
</body>
</html>
```

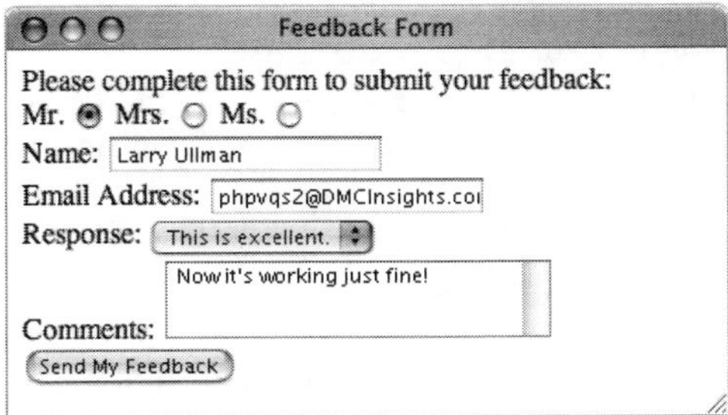

Figure 3.15 Once again, the form...

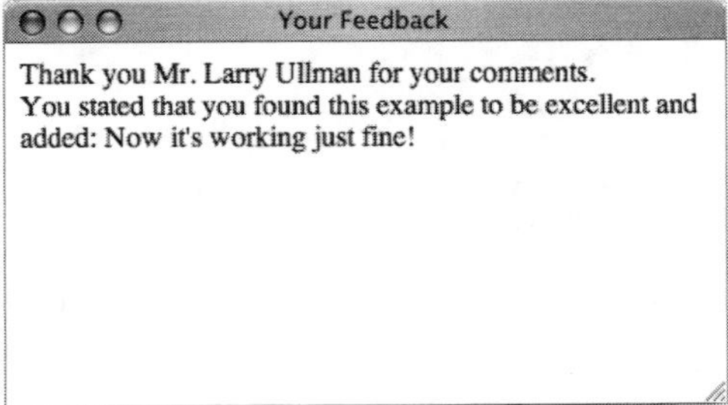

Figure 3.16 ...and it will now work without the need for `register_globals`.

To adjust for register_globals:

1. Open `handle_form.php` (Script 3.6) in your text editor.
2. Replace the two print lines with the following (**Script 3.7**):

```
print "Thank you {$_POST['title']}
→ {$_POST['name']} for your comments.
→ <br />";
print "You stated that you found this
→ example to be {$_POST['response']}
→ and added: {$_POST['comments']}";
```

   To get this particular script to work without `register_globals`, you needed to change the variable references from, for example, `$name` to `{$_POST['name']}`. The reasoning behind this change will make more sense later, if it doesn't already.

3. Save the file, upload it to your server, and test it again in your Web browser (**Figures 3.15** and **3.16**).

✔ Tips

- This revised version of the script will work for all users, regardless of whether `register_globals` is enabled.
- Remember that you used the `$_POST` variable because the form used the POST method. If you set the form's method attribute to GET, you'd need to use `$_GET` here.
- The `$_POST` and `$_GET` variables replace `$HTTP_POST_VARS` and `$HTTP_GET_VARS`. If you're using a version of PHP prior to 4.1, use these instead (for example, `{$HTTP_POST_VARS['name']}`).
- `$_POST`, `$_GET`, `$HTTP_POST_VARS`, and `$HTTP_GET_VARS` are all examples of arrays, which you'll formally learn about in Chapter 7.

Manually Sending Data to a Page

The last example for this chapter is a slight tangent to the other topics but plays off the idea of handling form data with PHP. As you learned in the section "Using GET or POST," if a form uses the GET method, the resulting URL is something like

```
http://www.DMCinsights.com/phpvqs2/
→ handle_form.php?title=Mr.&name=
→ Larry%20Ullman...
```

The receiving page (here, `handle_form.php`) is sent a series of *name=value* pairs, each of which is separated by an ampersand (&). The whole sequence is preceded by a question mark (immediately after the handling script's name). In this example, `handle_form.php` has a `$title` variable with a value of *Mr.*, a `$name` variable with a value of *Larry Ullman* (the *%20* is a URL-encoded version of a space), and so forth.

Using this knowledge, you can send data to a PHP page without the use of the form. A simple script will easily demonstrate this concept, sometimes called the "GET method trick."

To create a simple greeting script:

1. Create a new document within your text editor (**Script 3.8**):

```
<!DOCTYPE html PUBLIC "-//W3C//
→ DTD XHTML 1.0 Transitional//EN"
"http://www.w3.org/TR/xhtml1/DTD/
→ xhtml1-transitional.dtd">
<html xmlns="http://www.w3.org/1999/
→ xhtml">
<head>
   <meta http-equiv="content-type"
   → content="text/html; charset=
   → iso-8859-1" />
   <title>Greetings!</title>
</head>
<body>
```

Script 3.8 This script will receive a variable and its value in the URL.

```
<!DOCTYPE html PUBLIC "-//W3C//DTD XHTML 1.0 Transitional//EN"
"http://www.w3.org/TR/xhtml1/DTD/xhtml1-transitional.dtd">
<html xmlns="http://www.w3.org/1999/xhtml">
<head>
    <meta http-equiv="content-type" content="text/html; charset=iso-8859-1" />
    <title>Greetings!</title>
</head>
<body>
<?php // Script 3.8 - hello.php

// Adjust display_errors and error_reporting, if desired.
ini_set ('display_errors', 1);
error_reporting (E_ALL & ~ E_NOTICE);

// This page should receive a name value in the URL.

// Say "Hello".
print "<p>Hello, <b>$name</b>!</p>";

?>
</body>
</html>
```

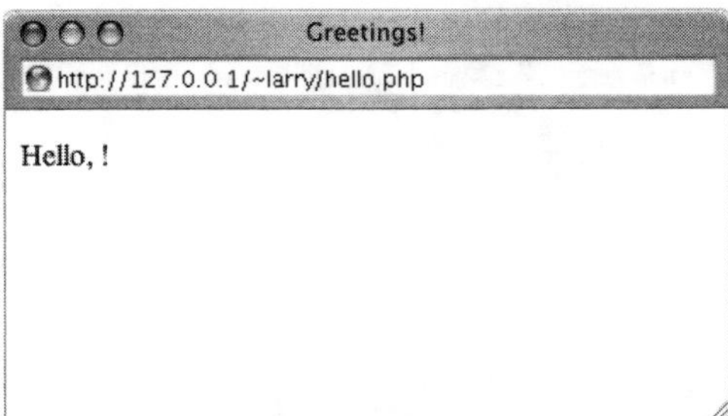

Figure 3.17 If the $name variable isn't assigned a value, the browser prints out this awkward message.

2. Begin the PHP code:

```
<?php // Script 3.8 - hello.php
```

3. Address the error management, if desired:

```
ini_set ('display_errors', 1);
error_reporting (E_ALL & ~ E_NOTICE);
```

These two lines, which configure how PHP responds to errors, may or may not be necessary but can be helpful.

4. Print a message using an assumed $name variable:

```
print "<p>Hello, <b>$name</b>!</p>";
```

The $name variable is sent to the page through the URL. To access it, you can use $name if register_globals is enabled or {$_GET['name']} if it isn't. Again, you would use $_GET (as opposed to $_POST) because the value is coming from a GET method, and the curly braces help avoid parse errors.

5. Complete the PHP code and the HTML page:

```
?>
</body>
</html>
```

6. Save the script as hello.php and upload it to your Web server.

If you were to view this script now, it would only display *Hello, !*, because the $name variable has no value (**Figure 3.17**). To pass the script a $name value, use the GET method trick.

To manually send data to a PHP script:

1. View the `hello.php` script in your Web browser by going to the appropriate URL, in this case, `http://127.0.0.1/~larry/hello.php` (Figure 3.17).
2. Append to the URL the text `?name=Michael`.

   You can (or, frankly, should) use your own name; just ensure that there are no spaces in your entry.
3. Press Enter (or Return) to reload the page in your browser with the new URL (**Figure 3.18**).

   If you don't see the name printed in the browser, then you made a mistake. Check to be sure you included the question mark, which separates the file name from the data itself. Then be sure you used *name*, because that's what `hello.php` is expecting as a variable (remember that *Name* would constitute a different variable).
4. If desired, change the `name` value in step 2 and press Enter (or Return) to reload the page again (**Figure 3.19**).

   Each new `name` value creates a new dynamically generated greeting.

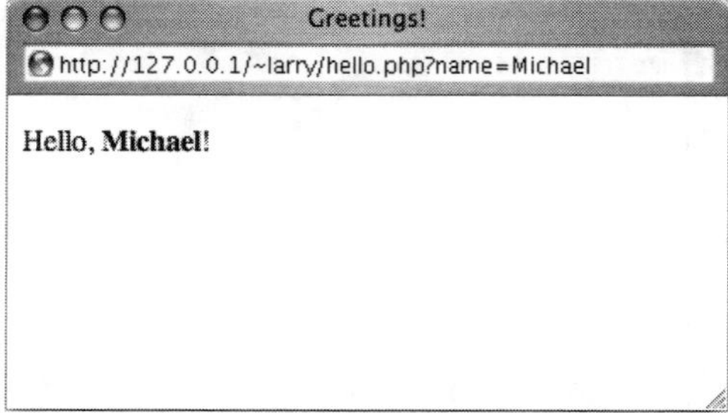

Figure 3.18 By setting the `$name` variable to *Michael* or some other name, you create a dynamic page that changes to address the specific user.

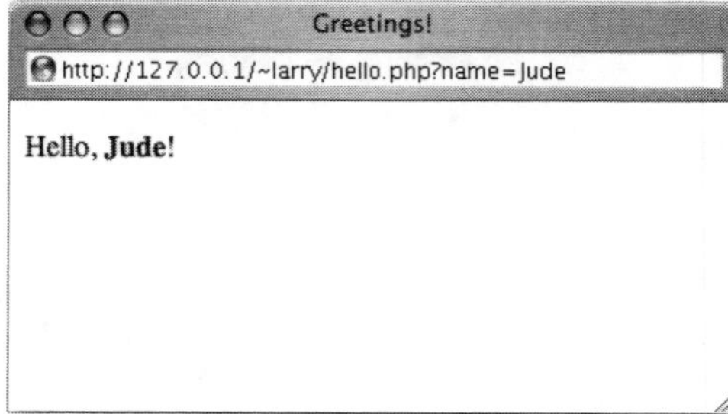

Figure 3.19 Setting the value of `$name` to *Jude* has the same effect as changing the `print()` line to read `print "<p>Hello, <b>Jude</b>!</p>";`.

✔ Tips

- If you want to use the GET method to send data to your script, you can pass multiple values by separating the `variable=value` pairs (for example, `first_name=Larry`) with the ampersand (&). So, an appended URL may be `hello.php? first_name=Larry&` → `last_name=Ullman`.

- Although the example here—setting the value of a person's name—may not be very practical, this basic technique is useful on many occasions. For example, a PHP script might constitute a template, and the resulting Web page would differ based on the values the page received in the URL.

- Because the `register_globals` issue is a big (and annoying) issue for PHP programmers, this book includes constant reminders about it. With this script, you'd use `$_GET['name']` instead of `$name`, and place that construct within curly braces to avoid parse errors.

Using Numbers

Chapter 2, "Variables," loosely discussed the different types of variables, how to assign values to them, and how they're generally used. In this chapter, you'll work specifically with number variables—both integers (whole numbers) and floating-point (decimals).

The chapter begins by showing you how to create an HTML form that will be used to generate number variables. Then you'll learn how to perform basic calculations, how to format numbers, and how to use multiple operators at once. The last two sections of this chapter cover incrementing and decrementing numbers, generating random numbers, and, finally, manipulating numbers using several pre-existing functions.

Creating the Form

The first few PHP examples in this chapter perform various calculations based on an e-commerce situation. They take quantity, price, tax rate, shipping cost, and discount values and come up with a total cost. This value is then divided by the number of payments to generate a monthly expense value.

You could use the GET method trick introduced at the end of the last chapter to submit each value to the PHP script in the URL, but that approach would be needlessly complicated. Instead you'll write one HTML page that allows the user to enter the different values.

To create the HTML form:

1. Begin a new HTML document in your text editor (**Script 4.1**):

```
<!DOCTYPE html PUBLIC "-//W3C//
→ DTD XHTML 1.0 Transitional//EN"
"http://www.w3.org/TR/xhtml1/DTD/
→ xhtml1-transitional.dtd">
<html xmlns="http://www.w3.org/1999/
→ xhtml">
<head>
    <meta http-equiv="content-type"
    → content="text/html; charset=
    → iso-8859-1" />
    <title>Product Cost Calculator
    → </title>
</head>
<body>
Fill out this form to calculate the
→ total cost: <br />
```

Script 4.1 This basic HTML form generates the numbers upon which mathematical calculations will be performed in PHP.

Script

```
<!DOCTYPE html PUBLIC "-//W3C//DTD XHTML 1.0 Transitional//EN"
"http://www.w3.org/TR/xhtml1/DTD/xhtml1-transitional.dtd">
<html xmlns="http://www.w3.org/1999/xhtml">
<head>
    <meta http-equiv="content-type" content="text/html; charset=iso-8859-1" />
    <title>Product Cost Calculator</title>
</head>
<body>
Fill out this form to calculate the total cost: <br />

<form action="handle_calc.php" method="post">

Price: <input type="text" name="price" size="5" />
<br />
Quantity: <input type="text" name="quantity" size="5" />
<br />
Discount: <input type="text" name="discount" size="5" />
<br />
Tax: <input type="text" name="tax" size="3" />
<br />
Shipping method: <select name="shipping">
<option value="5.00">Slow and steady</option>
<option value="8.95">Put a move on it.</option>
<option value="19.36">I need it yesterday!</option>
</select>
<br />
Number of payments to make: <input type="text" name="payments" size="3" />
<br />
<input type="submit" name="submit" value="Calculate!" />

</form>

<!-- Script 4.1 - calculator.html -->
</body>
</html>
```

2. Create the initial form tag:

```
<form action="handle_calc.php"
→ method="post">
```

This form tag begins the HTML form. Its `action` attribute indicates that the form data will be submitted to a page called `handle_calc.php`. Its `method` tells the page to use POST to send the data.

3. Create the inputs for the price, quantity, discount, and tax:

```
Price: <input type="text"
→ name="price" size="5" />
<br />
Quantity: <input type="text"
→ name="quantity" size="5" />
<br />
Discount: <input type="text"
→ name="discount" size="5" />
<br />
Tax: <input type="text" name="tax"
→ size="3" />
<br />
```

HTML has no input type for numbers, so you create text boxes for these values. You might want to add text explaining the formatting for each field (no dollar signs, the tax as a percent, and so on).

Also remember that the names used for the inputs have to correspond to valid PHP variable names (letters, numbers, and the underscore only; doesn't start with a number, and so forth).

continues on next page

4. Add a field in which the user can select a shipping method:

```
Shipping method:
→ <select name="shipping">
<option value="5.00">
→ Slow and steady</option>
<option value="8.95">
→ Put a move on it.</option>
<option value="19.36">
→ I need it yesterday!</option>
</select>
<br />
```

The shipping method uses a drop-down menu. The value of the selected option is the cost for that option. Therefore, if the user selects, for example, the *Put a move on it.* option, the value of `$shipping` (or `$_POST['shipping']`) in `handle_calc.php` will be *8.95*.

5. Complete the HTML form:

```
Number of payments to make: <input type=
→ "text" name="payments" size="3" />
<br />
<input type="submit" name="submit"
→ value="Calculate!" />
</form>
```

The final two input types take a number for how many payments are required and then create a submit button (labeled *Calculate!*). The closing form tag marks the end of the form section of the page.

6. Complete the HTML page:

```
<!-- Script 4.1 - calculator.html -->
</body>
</html>
```

7. Save your script as `calculator.html` and view it in your Web browser (**Figure 4.1**).

Because this is an HTML page, you can view it directly in a Web browser.

Figure 4.1 This form takes numbers from the user and sends them to the PHP page.

Script 4.2 This PHP script performs all the standard mathematical calculations using the numbers submitted from the form.

```
<!DOCTYPE html PUBLIC "-//W3C//DTD XHTML
1.0 Transitional//EN"
"http://www.w3.org/TR/xhtml1/DTD/xhtml1-
transitional.dtd">
<html
xmlns="http://www.w3.org/1999/xhtml">
<head>
    <meta http-equiv="content-type" content=
    "text/html; charset=iso-8859-1" />
    <title>Product Cost</title>
</head>
<body>
<?php // Script 4.2 - handle_calc.php

/* This script takes values from
calculator.html and performs
total cost and monthly payment
calculations. */

// Address error handing.
ini_set ('display_errors', 1);
error_reporting (E_ALL & ~E_NOTICE);

// In case register_globals is disabled.
$price = $_POST['price'];
$quantity = $_POST['quantity'];
$discount = $_POST['discount'];
$tax = $_POST['tax'];
$shipping = $_POST['shipping'];
$payments = $_POST['payments'];

// Calculate the total.
$total = $price * $quantity;
$total = $total + $shipping;
$total = $total - $discount;

// Determine the tax rate.
$taxrate = $tax/100;
$taxrate = $taxrate + 1;

// Factor in the tax rate.
$total = $total * $taxrate;

// Calculate the monthly payments.
$monthly = $total / $payments;

// Print out the results.
print "You have selected to purchase:<br />
```

(script continues on next page)

Adding, Subtracting, Multiplying, and Dividing

Just as you learned in grade school, basic mathematics involve the principles of addition, subtraction, multiplication, and division. These are accomplished in PHP using the most obvious operators:

- Addition (+)
- Subtraction (-)
- Multiplication (*)
- Division (/)

To demonstrate these principles, you'll create a PHP script that calculates the total cost for the sale of some widgets. This handling script could be the basis of a shopping-cart application—a very practical Web page feature (although in this case the relevant number values will come from `calculator.html`).

When you're writing this script, be sure to note the use of comments (**Script 4.2**) to illuminate the different steps and the reasoning behind them.

To create your sales-cost calculator:

1. Open your text editor and create a new document (Script 4.2):

```
<!DOCTYPE html PUBLIC "-//W3C//
→ DTD XHTML 1.0 Transitional//EN"
"http://www.w3.org/TR/xhtml1/DTD/
→ xhtml1-transitional.dtd">
<html xmlns="http://www.w3.org/1999/
→ xhtml">
<head>
   <meta http-equiv="content-type"
   → content="text/html; charset=
   → iso-8859-1" />
   <title>Product Cost</title>
</head>
<body>
```

continues on next page

2. Insert the PHP tags and address error reporting, if desired:

```
<?php // Script 4.2 - handle_calc.php
ini_set ('display_errors', 1);
error_reporting (E_ALL & ~E_NOTICE);
```

These lines may or may not be necessary, depending on your PHP configuration. The meaning behind them was discussed in detail in Chapter 3, "HTML Forms and PHP."

3. Address the need for global variables:

```
$price = $_POST['price'];
$quantity = $_POST['quantity'];
$discount = $_POST['discount'];
$tax = $_POST['tax'];
$shipping = $_POST['shipping'];
$payments = $_POST['payments'];
```

If the PHP configuration has `register_globals` enabled, then the script will automatically receive variables called `$price`, `$quantity`, and so forth. If `register_globals` is disabled, then you must use the `$_POST` variable to access the form data. Assigning the `$_POST` values to variables in the script may be the easiest and most secure method of addressing this potential problem.

Regardless of whether `register_globals` is enabled, this system works. If you're using a version of PHP prior to 4.1, replace each instance of `$_POST` with `$HTTP_POST_VARS`. (The reasoning behind this step will make more sense in Chapter 7, "Using Arrays.")

4. Begin calculating the total cost:

```
$total = $price * $quantity;
$total = $total + $shipping;
$total = $total - $discount;
```

Script 4.2 *continued*

```
<b>$quantity</b> widget(s) at <br />
$<b>$price</b> price with a <br />
$<b>$shipping</b> shipping cost and a <br />
<b>$tax</b> percent tax rate.<br />
After your $<b>$discount</b> discount, the total cost is
$<b>$total</b>.<br />
Divided over <b>$payments</b> monthly payments, that would be $<b>$monthly</b> each.";

?>

</body>
</html>
```

The asterisk (*) indicates multiplication in PHP, so the total is first calculated as the number of items purchased (`$quantity`) multiplied by the price. Then the shipping cost is added to the total value (remember that the shipping cost correlates to the `value` attribute of the shipping drop-down menu), and the discount is subtracted.

Note that it's perfectly acceptable to determine a variable's value in part by using that variable's existing value (as you do in the last two lines).

5. Calculate the tax rate and the new total:

```
$taxrate = $tax/100;
$taxrate = $taxrate + 1;
$total = $total * $taxrate;
```

The tax rate should be entered as a percent—for example, 8 or 5.75. This number is then divided by 100 to get the decimal equivalent of the percent (.08 or .0575). Finally, you calculate how much something costs with tax by adding 1 to the percent and then multiplying that new rate by the total. This is the mathematical equivalent of multiplying the decimal tax rate times the total and then adding this result to the total (for example, a 5 percent tax on $100 is $5, making the total $105, which is the same as multiplying $100 times 1.05).

6. Calculate the monthly payment:

```
$monthly = $total / $payments;
```

As an example of division, assume that the widget(s) can be paid for over the course of many months. Hence, you divide the total by the number of payments to find the monthly payment.

continues on next page

7. Print the results:

```
print "You have selected to purchase:
→ <br />
<b>$quantity</b> widget(s) at <br />
$<b>$price</b> price with a <br />
$<b>$shipping</b> shipping cost and a
→ <br />
<b>$tax</b> percent tax rate.<br />
After your $<b>$discount</b> discount,
→ the total cost is
$<b>$total</b>.<br />
Divided over <b>$payments</b>
→ monthly payments, that would be $
→ <b>$monthly</b> each.";
```

The `print()` statement sends every value to the Web browser along with some text. To make it easier to read, `<br />` tags are added to format the browser result; in addition, the `print()` function operates over multiple lines to make the PHP code cleaner. Each variable's value is highlighted in the browser thanks to the HTML bold tags.

8. Close the PHP section and complete the HTML page.

```
?>
</body>
</html>
```

9. Save your script as `handle_calc.php` and upload it to your server (or onto your PHP-enabled computer), in the same directory as `calculator.html`.

10. Test the script in your Web browser (**Figures 4.2** and **4.3**).

You can experiment with these values (even omitting variables completely, as in **Figure 4.4**) to see how effectively your calculator works.

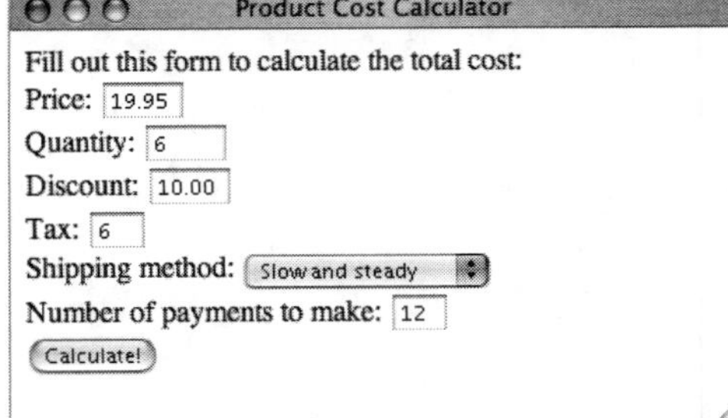

Figure 4.2 The HTML form...

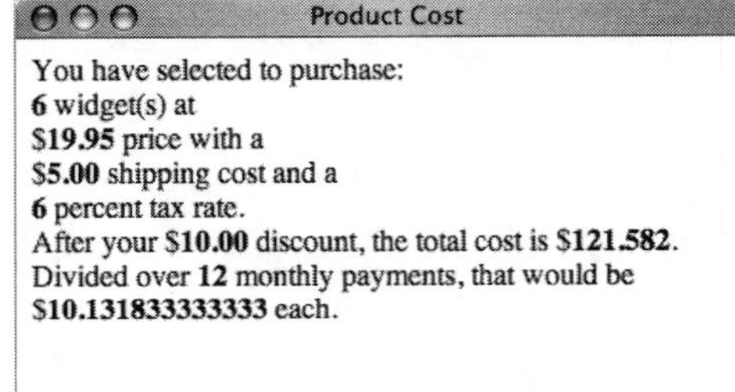

Figure 4.3 ...and the resulting calculations.

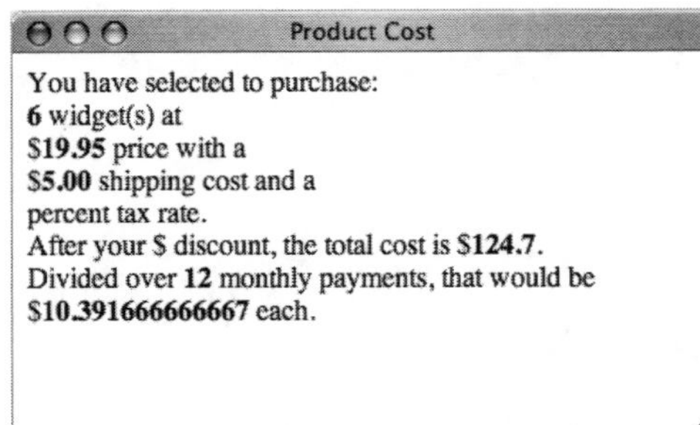

Figure 4.4 You can omit or change any value and rerun the calculator. Here I've omitted the tax and discount values.

✔ Tips

- As you'll certainly notice, the calculator comes up with numbers that don't correspond well to real dollar values (see Figures 4.3 and 4.4). In the next section, "Formatting Numbers," you'll learn how to compensate for this result.
- If you want to print the value of the total before tax or before the discount (or both), you can do so two ways. You can insert the appropriate `print()` statements immediately after the proper value has been determined but before the `$total` variable has been changed again. Or, you can use new variables to contain the values of the subsequent calculations (for example, `$total_with_tax` and `$total_less_discount`).
- You can use two methods to print a figure such as $2000.00: put a space (or HTML tags, as you do here) between the dollar sign and the variable name or escape the first dollar sign (`print "\$$total";`). You can't use `$$variable`, because the combination of two dollar signs creates a type of variable that's too complex to discuss in this book.
- This script performs differently based on whether the various fields are submitted. The only truly problematic field is the number of monthly payments: If this is omitted, you'll see a division-by-zero warning.

Formatting Numbers

Although the calculator is on its way to being practical, it still has one legitimate problem: You can't ask someone to make a monthly payment of $10.13183333. To create more usable numbers, you need to format them.

There are two appropriate functions for this purpose. The first, `round()`, rounds a value to a specified number of decimal places. For example:

```
round (4.30); // 4
round (4.289, 2); // 4.29
$num = 236.26985;
round ($num); // 236
```

The function's first argument is the number to be rounded. This can be either a number or a variable with a number value. The second argument is optional; it represents the number of decimal places to round to. (This feature was added in version 4 of PHP.)

The other function you can use in this situation is `number_format()`. It works like `round()` in that it takes a number (or a number-valued variable) and an optional decimal limiter. This function has the added benefit of formatting the number with commas, the way it would commonly be written:

```
number_format (428.4959, 2); // 428.50
number_format (428, 2); // 428.00
number_format (123456789); // 123,456,789
```

Let's rewrite the PHP script to format the numbers appropriately.

Script 4.3 The `number_format()` function gives the values of the number variables a more natural format.

```
<!DOCTYPE html PUBLIC "-//W3C//DTD XHTML 1.0 Transitional//EN"
"http://www.w3.org/TR/xhtml1/DTD/xhtml1-transitional.dtd">
<html xmlns="http://www.w3.org/1999/xhtml">
<head>
    <meta http-equiv="content-type" content="text/html; charset=iso-8859-1" />
    <title>Product Cost</title>
</head>
<body>
<?php // Script 4.3 - handle_calc.php (second version after Script 4.2)

/* This script takes values from calculator.html and performs
total cost and monthly payment calculations. */

// Address error handing.
ini_set ('display_errors', 1);
error_reporting (E_ALL & ~E_NOTICE);

// In case register_globals is disabled.
$price = $_POST['price'];
$quantity = $_POST['quantity'];
$discount = $_POST['discount'];
$tax = $_POST['tax'];
$shipping = $_POST['shipping'];
$payments = $_POST['payments'];

// Calculate the total.
$total = $price * $quantity;
$total = $total + $shipping;
$total = $total - $discount;

// Determine the tax rate.
$taxrate = $tax/100;
$taxrate = $taxrate + 1;

// Factor in the tax rate.
$total = $total * $taxrate;

// Calculate the monthly payments.
$monthly = $total / $payments;

// Apply the proper formatting.
```

(script continues on next page)

Script 4.3 *continued*

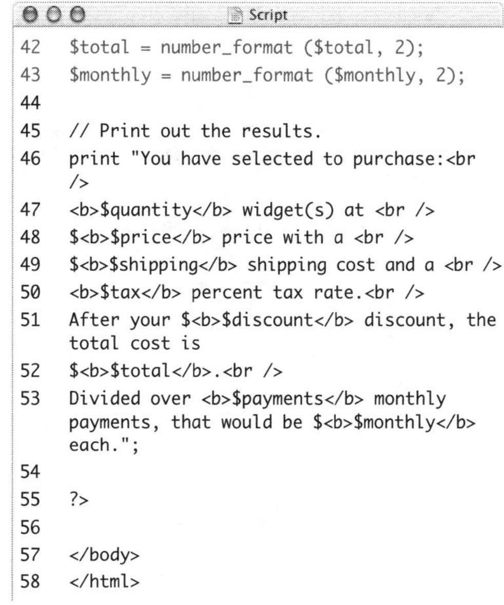

```
$total = number_format ($total, 2);
$monthly = number_format ($monthly, 2);

// Print out the results.
print "You have selected to purchase:<br
/>
<b>$quantity</b> widget(s) at <br />
$<b>$price</b> price with a <br />
$<b>$shipping</b> shipping cost and a <br />
<b>$tax</b> percent tax rate.<br />
After your $<b>$discount</b> discount, the
total cost is
$<b>$total</b>.<br />
Divided over <b>$payments</b> monthly
payments, that would be $<b>$monthly</b>
each.";

?>

</body>
</html>
```

Product Cost Calculator

Fill out this form to calculate the total cost:
Price: 99.00
Quantity: 4
Discount: 25.00
Tax: 5.5
Shipping method: Put a move on it.
Number of payments to make: 24
Calculate!

Figure 4.5 Another execution of the form.

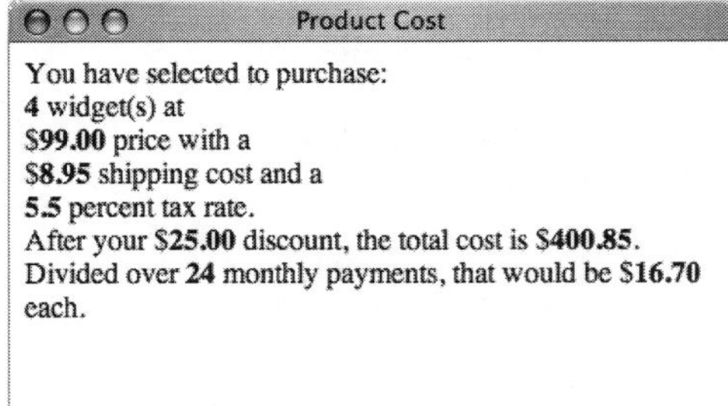

Figure 4.6 The updated version of the script returns more appropriate number values thanks to the `number_format()` function.

To format numbers:

1. Open `handle_calc.php` in your text editor (Script 4.2).
2. After all the calculations but before the `print()` statement, add the following (**Script 4.3**):

   ```
   $total = number_format ($total, 2);
   $monthly = number_format ($monthly, 2);
   ```

   To format the numbers, you apply this function after every calculation has been made but before they're sent to the Web browser. The second argument (the 2) indicates that the resulting number should have exactly two decimal places; this setting rounds the numbers and adds zeros at the end, as necessary.
3. Save the file, upload it to your server, and test in your browser (**Figures 4.5** and **4.6**).

✔ Tips

- Another, much more complex, way to format numbers is to use the `printf()` and `sprintf()` functions. Due to their tricky syntax, they're not discussed in this book; see the PHP manual for more information.
- For complicated reasons, the `round()` function rounds exact halves (.5, .05, .005, and so on) down half the time and up half the time.
- The `number_format()` function takes two other optional arguments that let you specify what characters to use to indicate a decimal point and break up thousands. This is useful, for example, for cultures that write *1,000.89* as *1.000,89*. See the PHP manual for the proper syntax, if you want to use this option.

Using Multiple Operators

Inevitably, after a discussion of the different sorts of mathematical operators comes the discussion of precedence. *Precedence* refers to the order in which a series of calculations are executed. For example, what is the value of the following variable?

```
$number = 10 - 4 / 2;
```

Is `$number` worth 3 (10 minus 4 equals 6, divided by 2 equals 3) or 8 (4 divided by 2 equals 2, subtracted from 10 equals 8)? The answer here is 8, because division takes precedence over subtraction.

Appendix B, "Resources," shows the complete list of operator precedence for PHP (including operators that haven't been covered yet). However, instead of attempting to memorize a large table of peculiar characters, you should bypass the whole concept by using parentheses. Parentheses always take precedence over any other operator. Thus:

```
$number = (10 - 4) / 2; // 3
$number = 10 - (4 / 2); // 8
```

Using parentheses in your calculations ensures that you never obtain peculiar results due to precedence issues. Parentheses also allow you to perform multiple calculations in fewer lines of code. Let's rewrite the `handle_calc.php` script, combining multiple lines into one while maintaining accuracy by using parentheses.

To use parentheses to establish precedence:

1. Open `handle_calc.php` in your text editor (Script 4.3).

2. Change the way the total is first calculated (**Script 4.4**):

   ```
   $total = (($price * $quantity) +
   → $shipping) - $discount;
   ```

Script 4.4 By using parentheses, you trim the multiple calculation lines (see Script 4.3) without affecting the script's mathematical accuracy.

Script

```
<!DOCTYPE html PUBLIC "-//W3C//DTD XHTML 1.0 Transitional//EN"
"http://www.w3.org/TR/xhtml1/DTD/xhtml1-transitional.dtd">
<html xmlns="http://www.w3.org/1999/xhtml">
<head>
    <meta http-equiv="content-type" content="text/html; charset=iso-8859-1" />
    <title>Product Cost</title>
</head>
<body>
<?php // Script 4.3 - handle_calc.php (third version of Scripts 4.2 and 4.3)

/* This script takes values from calculator.html and performs
total cost and monthly payment calculations. */

// Address error handing.
ini_set ('display_errors', 1);
error_reporting (E_ALL & ~E_NOTICE);

// In case register_globals is disabled.
$price = $_POST['price'];
$quantity = $_POST['quantity'];
$discount = $_POST['discount'];
$tax = $_POST['tax'];
$shipping = $_POST['shipping'];
$payments = $_POST['payments'];

// Calculate the total.
$total = (($price * $quantity) + $shipping) - $discount;

// Determine the tax rate.
$taxrate = ($tax/100) + 1;

// Factor in the tax rate.
$total = $total * $taxrate;

// Calculate the monthly payments.
$monthly = $total / $payments;

// Apply the proper formatting.
$total = number_format ($total, 2);
$monthly = number_format ($monthly, 2);
```

(script continues on next page)

Script 4.4 *continued*

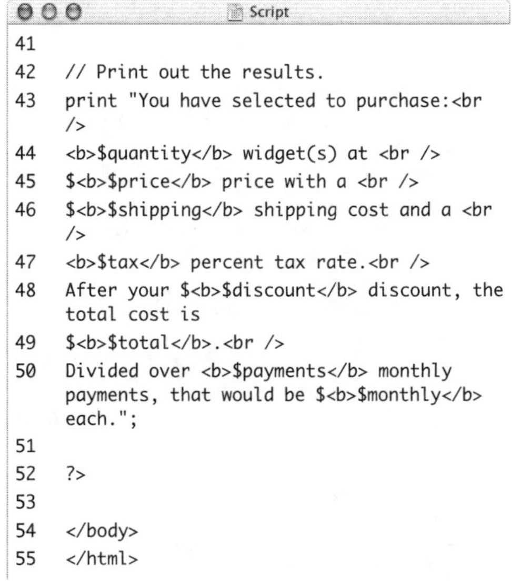

```
// Print out the results.
print "You have selected to purchase:<br
/>
<b>$quantity</b> widget(s) at <br />
$<b>$price</b> price with a <br />
$<b>$shipping</b> shipping cost and a <br
/>
<b>$tax</b> percent tax rate.<br />
After your $<b>$discount</b> discount, the
total cost is
$<b>$total</b>.<br />
Divided over <b>$payments</b> monthly
payments, that would be $<b>$monthly</b>
each.";

?>

</body>
</html>
```

Product Cost Calculator

Fill out this form to calculate the total cost:
Price: 1.50
Quantity: 250
Discount: 0
Tax: 6
Shipping method: I need it yesterday!
Number of payments to make: 2
Calculate!

Figure 4.7 Testing the form one more time.

Product Cost

You have selected to purchase:
250 widget(s) at
$**1.50** price with a
$**19.36** shipping cost and a
6 percent tax rate.
After your $**0** discount, the total cost is $**418.02**.
Divided over **2** monthly payments, that would be $**209.01** each.

Figure 4.8 Even though the calculations have been condensed, the math works out the same. If you see different results or get an error message, double-check your parentheses for balance (an equal number of opening and closing parentheses).

There's no reason not to make all the calculations in one step, as long as you use parentheses to ensure that the math works properly. The other option is to memorize PHP's rules of precedence for multiple operators, but using parentheses is a lot easier.

3. Change how the tax is calculated:

   ```
   $taxrate = ($tax/100) + 1;
   ```

   Again, the tax calculations can be made in one line instead of two separate ones.

4. Save your script, upload it to the server, and test it in your browser (**Figures 4.7** and **4.8**).

✔ Tips

- Be sure that you match your parentheses consistently as you create your formulas (every opening parenthesis requires a closing parenthesis). Failure to do so will cause parse errors.
- Granted, using the methods applied here, you could combine all the total calculations into just one line of code (instead of three)—but there is such a thing as oversimplifying.

Incrementing and Decrementing a Number

PHP, like Perl and most other programming languages, includes some shortcuts that let you avoid ugly constructs such as

```
$tax = $tax + 1;
```

When you need to increase the value of a variable by 1 (called an *incremental* adjustment) or decrease the value of a variable by 1 (a *decremental* adjustment), you can use ++ or --, respectively:

```
$var = 20; // 20
$var++; // 21
$var++; // 22
$var--; // 21
```

Solely for the sake of testing this concept, you'll rewrite the `handle_calc.php` script one last time.

To increment the value of a variable:

1. Open `handle_calc.php` in your text editor (Script 4.4).
2. Change the tax rate calculation from Script 4.3 to read as follows (**Script 4.5**):
   ```
   $taxrate = $tax/100;
   $taxrate++;
   ```
   The first line calculates the tax rate as the `$tax` value divided by 100. The second line increments this value by 1 so that it can be multiplied by the total to determine the total with tax.

Script 4.5 Incrementing or decrementing a number is a common operation using ++ or --, respectively.

```
<!DOCTYPE html PUBLIC "-//W3C//DTD XHTML 1.0 Transitional//EN"
"http://www.w3.org/TR/xhtml1/DTD/xhtml1-transitional.dtd">
<html xmlns="http://www.w3.org/1999/xhtml">
<head>
    <meta http-equiv="content-type" content="text/html; charset=iso-8859-1" />
    <title>Product Cost</title>
</head>
<body>
<?php // Script 4.5 - handle_calc.php (fourth version of Scripts 4.2, 4.3 and 4.4)

/* This script takes values from calculator.html and performs
total cost and monthly payment calculations. */

// Address error handing.
ini_set ('display_errors', 1);
error_reporting (E_ALL & ~E_NOTICE);

// In case register_globals is disabled.
$price = $_POST['price'];
$quantity = $_POST['quantity'];
$discount = $_POST['discount'];
$tax = $_POST['tax'];
$shipping = $_POST['shipping'];
$payments = $_POST['payments'];

// Calculate the total.
$total = (($price * $quantity) + $shipping) - $discount;

// Determine the tax rate.
$taxrate = $tax/100;
$taxrate++;

// Factor in the tax rate.
$total = $total * $taxrate;

// Calculate the monthly payments.
$monthly = $total / $payments;

// Apply the proper formatting.
$total = number_format ($total, 2);
$monthly = number_format ($monthly, 2);
```

(script continues on next page)

Script 4.5 *continued*

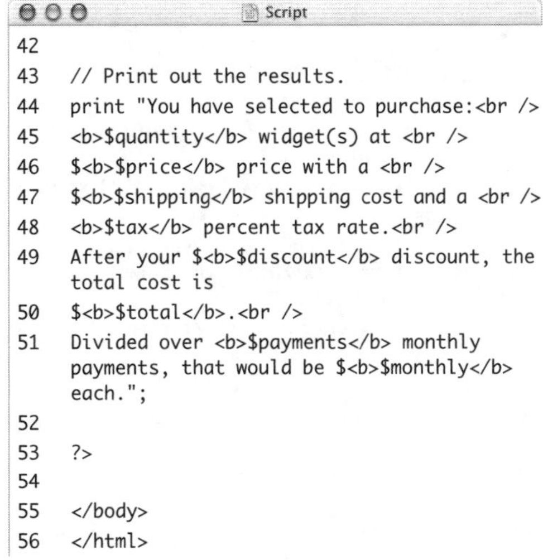

```
// Print out the results.
print "You have selected to purchase:<br />
<b>$quantity</b> widget(s) at <br />
$<b>$price</b> price with a <br />
$<b>$shipping</b> shipping cost and a <br />
<b>$tax</b> percent tax rate.<br />
After your $<b>$discount</b> discount, the total cost is
$<b>$total</b>.<br />
Divided over <b>$payments</b> monthly payments, that would be $<b>$monthly</b> each.";

?>

</body>
</html>
```

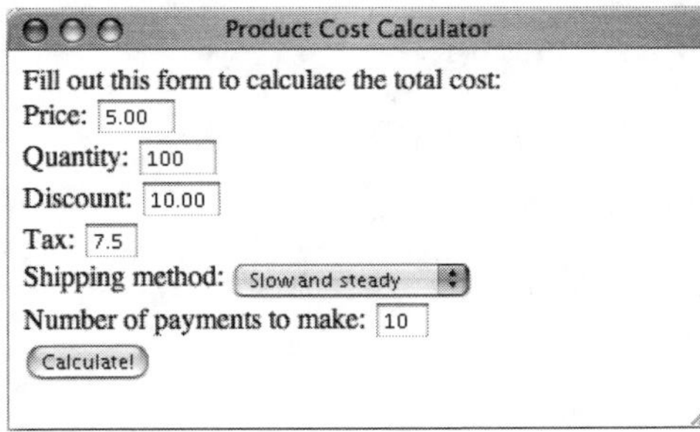

Figure 4.9 The last execution of the form.

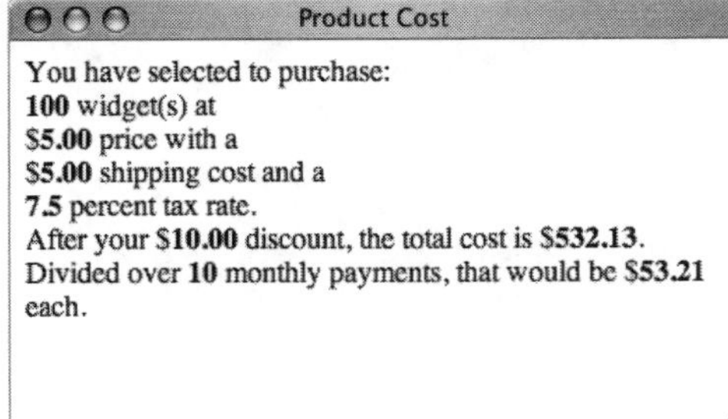

Figure 4.10 It won't affect your calculations if you use the long or short version of incrementing a variable (compare Scripts 4.4 and 4.5).

3. Save your script, upload it to the server, and test it in your browser (**Figures 4.9** and **4.10**).

✔ Tips

- Although functionally it doesn't matter whether you code `$taxrate = $taxrate + 1;` or the abbreviated `$taxrate++`, the latter method (using the increment operator) is more professional and common.

- In Chapter 6, "Control Structures," you'll see how the increment operator is commonly used in conjunction with loops.

- PHP also supports a combination of mathematical and assignment operators. These are `+=`, `-=`, `*=`, and `/=`. Each will assign a value to a variable by performing a calculation upon it. For example:

```
$tax = 5;
$tax /= 100; // Now $tax is .05
$tax += 1; // 1.05
```

Creating Random Numbers

The last function you'll learn about here is `rand()`, a random-number generator:

```
$n = rand(); // 31
$n = rand(); // 87
```

The `rand()` function can also take minimum and maximum parameters, if you prefer to limit the generated number to a specific range:

```
$n = rand (0, 10);
```

These values are inclusive, so in this case 0 and 10 are feasible returned values.

As an example of generating random numbers, let's create a simple "Lucky Numbers" script.

To generate random numbers:

1. Begin a new document in your text editor (**Script 4.6**):

```
<!DOCTYPE html PUBLIC "-//W3C//DTD XHTML 1.0 Transitional//EN"
"http://www.w3.org/TR/xhtml1/DTD/xhtml1-transitional.dtd">
<html xmlns="http://www.w3.org/1999/xhtml">
<head>
   <meta http-equiv="content-type" content="text/html; charset=iso-8859-1" />
   <title>Lucky Numbers</title>
</head>
<body>
```

2. Include the PHP tags and address error management:

```
<?php // Script 4.6 - random.php
ini_set ('display_errors', 1);
error_reporting (E_ALL & ~E_NOTICE);
```

Script 4.6 The `rand()` function generates random numbers.

```
<!DOCTYPE html PUBLIC "-//W3C//DTD XHTML
1.0 Transitional//EN"
"http://www.w3.org/TR/xhtml1/DTD/xhtml1-
transitional.dtd">
<html xmlns="http://www.w3.org/1999/xhtml">
<head>
    <meta http-equiv="content-type"
    content="text/html; charset=
    iso-8859-1" />
    <title>Lucky Numbers</title>
</head>
<body>
<?php // Script 4.6 - random.php

/* This script generates 3 random
numbers. */

// Address error handing.
ini_set ('display_errors', 1);
error_reporting (E_ALL & ~E_NOTICE);

$n1 = rand (1, 99);
$n2 = rand (1, 99);
$n3 = rand (1, 99);

// Print out the numbers.
print "Your lucky numbers are:<br />
<pre>$n1    $n2    $n3</pre>";

?>

</body>
</html>
```

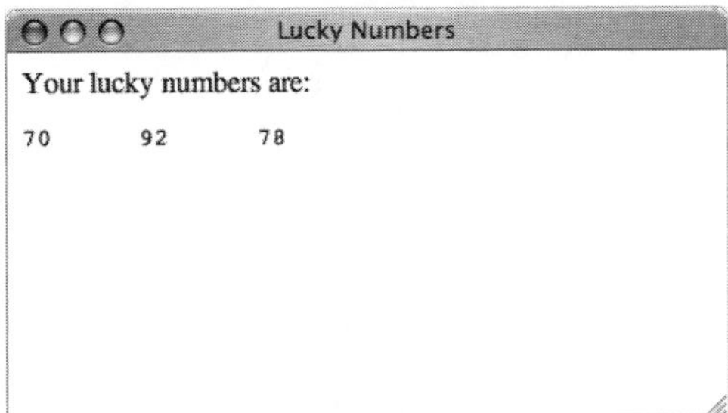

Figure 4.11 The rand() function creates random numbers.

Figure 4.12 Running the script again produces different results.

3. Create three random numbers:

```
$n1 = rand (1, 99);
$n2 = rand (1, 99);
$n3 = rand (1, 99);
```

This script prints out a person's lucky numbers, like those found on the back of a fortune cookie's fortune. These numbers are generated by calling the rand() function three separate times and assigning each result to a variable.

4. Print out the numbers:

```
print "Your lucky numbers are:<br />
<pre>$n1	$n2	$n3</pre>";
```

The print() statement is fairly simple. The numbers are printed with tabs between them. By placing the tab-separated numbers in the HTML <pre> tags, you put some space between the printed numbers in the Web browser. The <pre> tags tell the browser to abide by the existing formatting, which, in this case, means the browser should honor the tabs. (Web browsers normally ignore tabs.)

5. Close the PHP code and the HTML page:

```
?>
</body>
</html>
```

6. Save the file as random.php, upload it to your Web server, and test in your Web browser (**Figures 4.11** and **4.12**).

continues on next page

✔ Tips

- In versions of PHP prior to 4.2, you had to use the `srand()` function prior to calling `rand()` in order to generate random numbers. This is no longer a requirement, but you might still see this in older scripts.
- The `getrandmax()` function returns the largest possible random number that can be created using `rand()`. This value differs by operating system.
- PHP has a second function that generates random numbers: `mt_rand()`. It works similarly to (but, arguably, better than) `rand()` and is the smarter choice for sensitive situations like cryptography.

Other Mathematical Functions

PHP has a number of built-in functions for manipulating mathematical data. This chapter introduced `round()`, `number_format()`, and `rand()`.

PHP has broken `round()` into two other functions. The first, `ceil()`, rounds every number to the next highest integer. The second, `floor()`, rounds every number to the next lowest integer.

Another function the calculator page could make good use of is `abs()`, which returns the absolute value of a number. In case you don't remember your absolute values, the function works like this:

```
$number = abs(-23); // 23
$number = abs(23); // 23
```

In layman's terms, the absolute value of a number is always a positive number.

Beyond these functions, PHP supports all the trigonometry, exponent, base conversion, and logarithm functions you'll ever need. See the PHP manual for more information.

5

USING STRINGS

As introduced in Chapter 2, "Variables," the second category of variables used by PHP is *strings*—a collection of characters enclosed within either single or double quotation marks. A string variable may consist of a single letter, a word, a sentence, a paragraph, HTML code, or even a jumble of nonsensical letters, numbers, and symbols (which might represent a password). Strings may be the most common variable type used in PHP.

Passwords, names, email addresses, comments, and similar input from HTML forms all become strings in your PHP script. You witnessed this behavior when you used the `feedback.html` and `handle_form.php` pages in Chapter 3, "HTML Forms and PHP."

This chapter covers PHP's most basic built-in functions for manipulating string data, regardless of whether the string originates from a form. Some common techniques will be introduced—trimming strings, joining strings together, and encoding strings. Other uses for strings will be illustrated in subsequent chapters.

Creating the HTML Form

As in Chapter 3, let's begin by creating an HTML form that sends different values—in the form of string variables—to a PHP script. The example being used is an online bulletin board or forum where users can post a message, their email address, and their first and last names.

To create an HTML form:

1. Create a new HTML document in your text editor (**Script 5.1**):

```
<!DOCTYPE html PUBLIC "-//W3C//DTD
→ XHTML 1.0 Transitional//EN"
"http://www.w3.org/TR/xhtml1/DTD/
→ xhtml1-transitional.dtd">
<html xmlns="http://www.w3.org/1999/
→ xhtml">
<head>
    <meta http-equiv="content-type"
    → content="text/html; charset=
    → iso-8859-1" />
    <title>Forum Posting</title>
</head>
<body>
Please complete this form to submit
your posting: <br />
```

2. Create the initial form tag:

```
<form action="handle_post.php"
→ method="post">
```

This form will send its data to a `handle_post.php` script and will use the POST method.

Script 5.1 This form sends string data to a PHP script.

```
<!DOCTYPE html PUBLIC "-//W3C//DTD XHTML 1.0 Transitional//EN"
        "http://www.w3.org/TR/xhtml1/DTD/xhtml1-transitional.dtd">
<html xmlns="http://www.w3.org/1999/xhtml">
<head>
    <meta http-equiv="content-type" content="text/html; charset=iso-8859-1" />
    <title>Forum Posting</title>
</head>
<body>
Please complete this form to submit your posting: <br />
<form action="handle_post.php" method="post">

First Name: <input type="text" name="first_name" size="20" />
<br />
Last Name: <input type="text" name="last_name" size="20" />
<br />
Email Address: <input type="text" name="email" size="20" />
<br />
Posting: <textarea name="posting" rows="3" cols="30"></textarea>
<br />
<input type="submit" name="submit" value="Send My Posting" />

</form>

<!-- Script 5.1 - posting.html -->
</body>
</html>
```

3. Add inputs for the first name, last name, and email address:

```
First Name: <input type="text"
→ name="first_name" size="20" />
<br />
Last Name: <input type="text"
→ name="last_name" size="20" />
<br />
Email Address: <input type="text"
→ name="email" size="20" />
<br />
```

These are all basic text input types, which were covered back in Chapter 3. Remember that the various inputs' `name` values should adhere to the rules of PHP variable names (no spaces; must not begin with a number; consists only of letters, numbers, and the underscore). The HTML breaks are added to make each input appear on its own line in the browser window.

4. Add an input for the posting:

```
Posting: <textarea name="posting"
→ rows="3" cols="30"></textarea>
<br />
```

The posting field is a textarea, which is a larger type of text input box.

5. Create a submit button and close the form:

```
<input type="submit" name="submit"
→ value="Send My Posting" />
</form>
```

Every form must have a submit button (or a submit image).

You should mark the end of the form with a closing form tag.

continues on next page

6. Complete the HTML page:

```
<!-- Script 5.1 - posting.html -->
</body>
</html>
```

7. Save the file as `posting.html`, upload it to your server (or save it to the appropriate directory on your computer if you have PHP installed), and view it in your Web browser (**Figure 5.1**).

   This is an HTML page, so it doesn't have to be on a PHP-enabled server in order for you to view it. But because it will eventually send data to a PHP script, it's best to go ahead and place the file on your server.

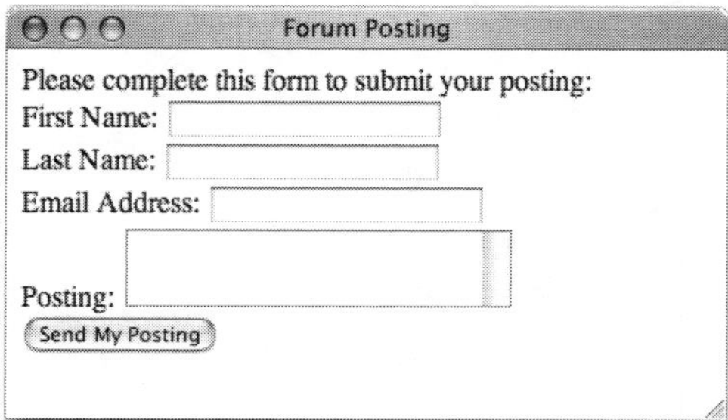

Figure 5.1 This HTML form is the basis for most of the examples in this chapter.

✔ Tips

- Many forum systems written in PHP are freely available for your use. For this reason this book doesn't cover how to write one yourself, but it points you in the right direction in case you decide that you want to do so.
- This book's Web site has a forum where readers can post questions and other readers (and the author) answer questions. You can find it at `www.DMCInsights.com/phorum/` → `list.php?f=10`.

Connecting Strings (Concatenation)

Concatenation is an unwieldy term but a useful concept. It refers to the process of linking items together. Specifically, in programming, you concatenate strings. The period (`.`) is the operator for performing this action, and it's used like so:

```
$s1 = 'Hello, ';
$s2 = 'world!';
$greeting = $s1 . $s2;
```

The end result of this concatenation is that the `$greeting` variable has a value of *Hello, world!*.

Due to the way PHP deals with variables, the same effect could be accomplished using

```
$greeting = "$s1 $s2";
```

(although that approach adds an extra space in this example). Variables used within double quotation marks are replaced with their value when handled by PHP. However, the formal method of using the period to concatenate strings is more commonly used and is recommended (it will be more obvious what's occurring in your code).

The `posting.html` script sends several string variables to the `handle_post.php` page. Of those variables, the first and last names could logically be concatenated. It's quite common and even recommended to take a user's first and last name as separate inputs, as you did with this form. On the other hand, it would be advantageous to be able to refer to the two together as one name. You'll write the PHP script with this in mind.

To use concatenation:

1. Create a new PHP script by beginning with the HTML head (**Script 5.2**):

```
<!DOCTYPE html PUBLIC "-//W3C//DTD
→ XHTML 1.0 Transitional//EN"
"http://www.w3.org/TR/xhtml1/DTD/
→ xhtml1-transitional.dtd">
<html xmlns="http://www.w3.org/1999/
→ xhtml">
<head>
   <meta http-equiv="content-type"
   → content="text/html;
   → charset=iso-8859-1" />
   <title>Your Forum Posting</title>
</head>
<body>
```

2. Create the initial PHP tag, and address PHP's error handling, if necessary:

```
<?php // Script 5.2 - handle_post.php
ini_set ('display_errors', 1);
error_reporting (E_ALL & ~E_NOTICE);
```

These lines won't be necessary for some users, but they're included here just in case. You can always refer back to Chapter 3 for more information on when, why, and how to use these lines.

3. Address the `register_globals` issue, if necessary:

```
$first_name = $_POST['first_name'];
$last_name = $_POST['last_name'];
$posting = $_POST['posting'];
```

As introduced in Chapter 3, if `register_globals` is disabled in your PHP configuration, you'll need to include these lines in order to access the `$first_name`, `$last_name`, and `$posting` variables. All of this will be made clear in Chapter 7, "Using Arrays".

This example doesn't have a line for the email address because you won't be using it yet, but you can duplicate this code to include it as well.

Script 5.2 This PHP script demonstrates concatenation, one of the most common manipulations of a string variable. Think of it as addition for strings.

```
<!DOCTYPE html PUBLIC "-//W3C//DTD XHTML 1.0 Transitional//EN"
        "http://www.w3.org/TR/xhtml1/DTD/xhtml1-transitional.dtd">
<html xmlns="http://www.w3.org/1999/xhtml">
<head>
    <meta http-equiv="content-type" content="text/html; charset=iso-8859-1" />
    <title>Your Forum Posting</title>
</head>
<body>
<?php // Script 5.2 - handle_post.php

// Address error handing.
ini_set ('display_errors', 1);
error_reporting (E_ALL & ~E_NOTICE);

// In case register_globals is disabled.
$first_name = $_POST['first_name'];
$last_name = $_POST['last_name'];
$posting = $_POST['posting'];

// Create a name variable.
$name = $first_name . ' ' . $last_name;

// Print the message.
print "Thank you, $name, for your posting:<br />
<p>$posting</p>";


?>
</body>
</html>
```

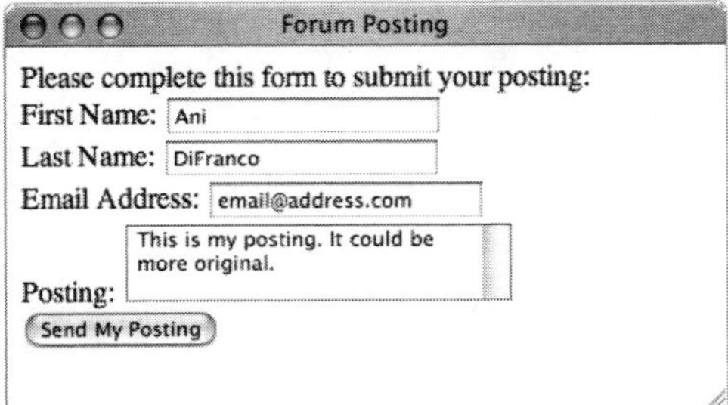

Figure 5.2 The HTML form in use...

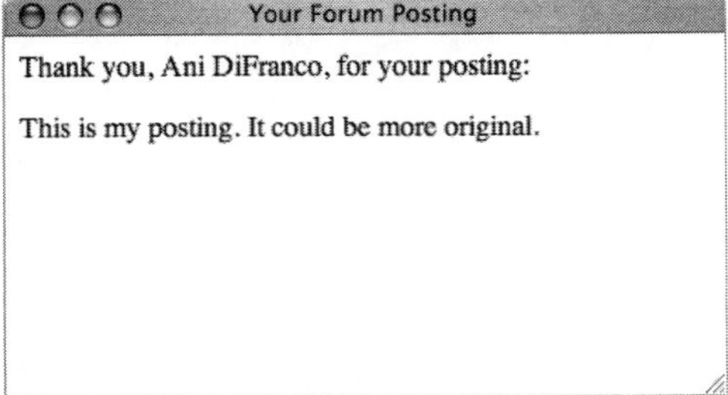

Figure 5.3 ...and the resulting PHP page.

4. Create a new `$name` variable using concatenation:

   ```
   $name = $first_name . ' ' .
   $last_name;
   ```

   This act of concatenation takes two variables plus a space and joins them all together to create a new variable, called `$name`. Assuming you entered *`Elliott`* and *`Smith`* as the names, then `$name` would be equal to *Elliott Smith*.

5. Print out the message to the user:

   ```
   print "Thank you, $name, for your
   → posting:<br />
   <p>$posting</p>";
   ```

   This message reports back to the user what was entered in the form.

6. Close the PHP section and complete the HTML code:

   ```
   ?>
   </body>
   </html>
   ```

7. Save your script as `handle_post.php`, upload it to your Web server (in the same directory as `posting.html`), and test both the form and the script in your Web browser (**Figures 5.2** and **5.3**).

continues on next page

✔ Tips

- If you used quotation marks of any kind in your form and saw extraneous slashes in the printed result, read the next section of this chapter to find out why.
- As a reminder, it's very important to know the difference between single and double quotation marks in PHP. Characters within single quotation marks are treated literally; characters within double quotation marks are *interpreted* (for example, a variable's name will be replaced by its value). See Chapter 3 for a refresher.
- You can link as many strings as you want using concatenation. You can even join numbers to strings:

  ```
  $new_string = $s1 . $s2 . $number;
  ```

  This works because PHP is *weakly typed*, meaning that its variables aren't locked in to one particular format. Here, the `$number` variable will be turned into a string and appended to the value of the `$new_string` variable.
- In this example you could also have written

  ```
  $first_name = $first_name . ' ' .
  → $last_name;
  ```

  but there are two reasons not to. First, doing so would overwrite the original value of the `$first_name` variable. Second, `$first_name` would no longer be an appropriate description of the variable's value. You should always try to maintain valid variable names as you program.
- Concatenation can be used in many ways, even when you're feeding arguments to a function. An uncommon but functional example would be

  ```
  print 'Hello, ' . $first_name . '!';
  ```

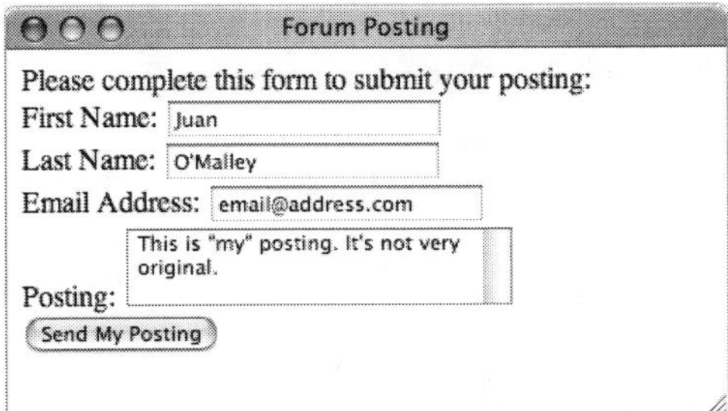

Figure 5.4 Quotation marks entered in the form...

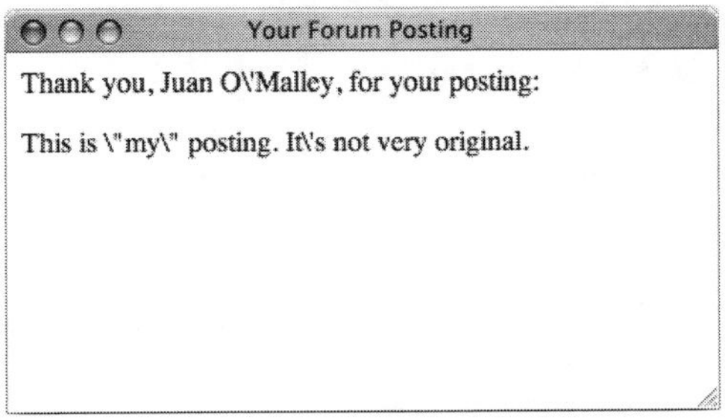

Figure 5.5 ...are escaped by Magic Quotes if this feature is enabled.

Combating Magic Quotes

Chapter 3 discussed three different PHP settings that affect the results of your PHP scripts: `register_globals`, `display_errors`, and `error_reporting`. A final PHP setting (or feature) of which you should be aware is *Magic Quotes*. When enabled, Magic Quotes automatically escapes problematic characters. Normally this means that single and double quotation marks in strings are preceded by a backslash.

There are three types of Magic Quotes:

- *GPC* Magic Quotes affect data transmitted via the GET or POST method and data stored in cookies.
- *Runtime* Magic Quotes affect data retrieved from databases and command-line actions.
- *Sybase* Magic Quotes are a special type and are less of an issue.

By default, all three Magic Quotes settings are turned off. However, if Magic Quotes GPC is enabled, then quotes in your form (**Figure 5.4**) will create unusual results in the PHP page (**Figure 5.5**).

To combat this behavior, you can use the `stripslashes()` function to remove the escapes:

```
$string = stripslashes ($string);
```

The following task rewrites `handle_post.php` with this potential problem in mind.

To work with Magic Quotes:

1. Open `handle_post.php` (Script 5.2) in your text editor.
2. After the `$name` variable is created but before the `print()` statement, add

   ```
   $name = stripslashes ($name);
   $posting = stripslashes ($posting);
   ```

   To undo the effect of Magic Quotes (if they're enabled), you apply the `stripslashes()` function to these two variables, removing any backslashes used to escape certain characters.
3. Save the file, upload it to your Web server, and test it again in your Web browser (**Figure 5.6**).

   If the Magic Quotes feature is enabled, the PHP script now behaves more appropriately.

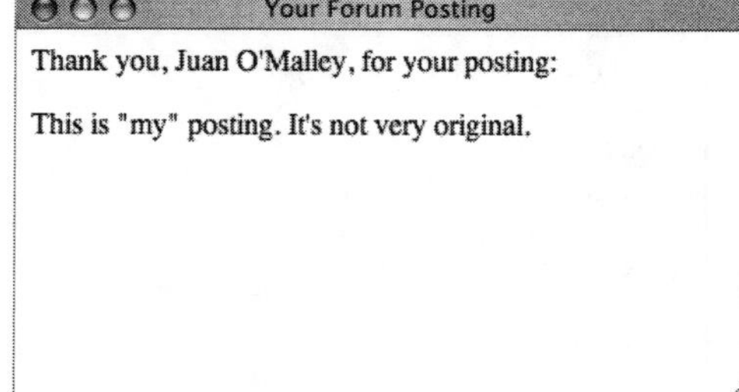

Figure 5.6 The form data entered in Figure 5.4 no longer creates weird results.

✔ Tips

- If Magic Quotes isn't turned on in your PHP configuration, this script strips out any slashes the user entered (although presumably that wouldn't occur with this example).
- In Chapter 11, "Files and Directories," you'll learn a trick with the `ini_get()` function that applies the `stripslashes()` function only if Magic Quotes is enabled.
- You can also modify the script by changing the initial variable lines to something like

  ```
  $posting = stripslashes
  → ($_POST['posting']);
  ```
- There's no point in using the `ini_set()` function to adjust the Magic Quotes setting the way you've been using it to affect `display_errors`. The `ini_set()` change would take effect after the data already arrived at the page, and therefore wouldn't change things.
- To escape problematic characters manually, use `addslashes()`:

  ```
  $string = addslashes ($string);
  ```

  You might want to use this function if you're inserting data into a database (where quotation marks are a major problem) and the Magic Quotes feature is disabled.

HTML and PHP

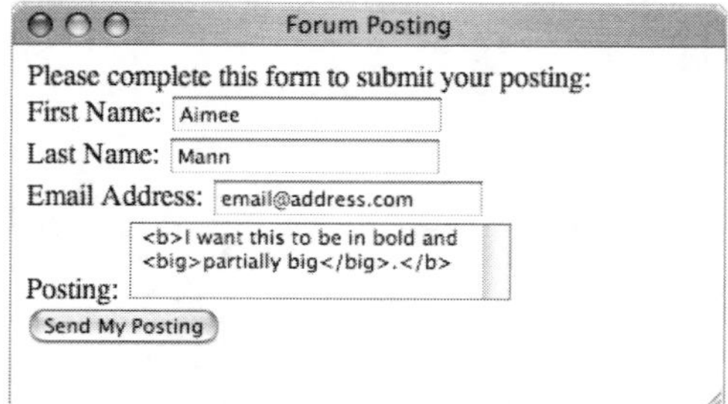

Figure 5.7 If the user enters HTML code in the posting...

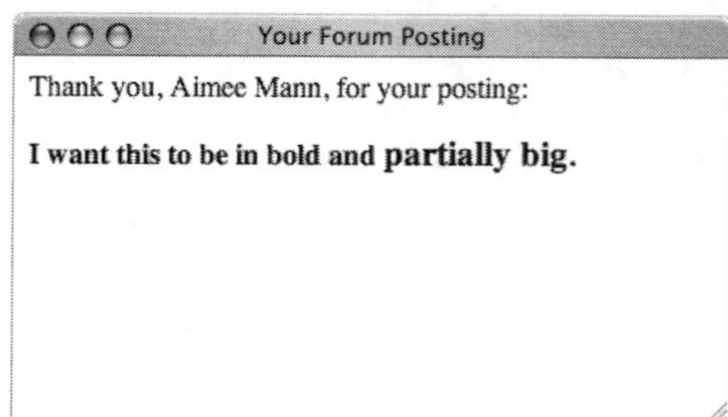

Figure 5.8 ...it's rendered by the Web browser.

As you should understand by this point, PHP is a server-side technology that's frequently used to send data to the Web browser. This data can be in the form of plain text, HTML code, or both.

In this chapter's example, data is entered in an HTML form and then printed back to the Web browser with PHP. A potential problem is that the user can enter HTML characters in the form, which will throw off the resulting page's formatting (**Figures 5.7** and **5.8**)—or, worse, cause security problems.

Because of the relationship between HTML and PHP, you can use many PHP functions to manipulate HTML tags within PHP string variables:

- `htmlspecialchars()` turns certain HTML tags into an entity version.
- `htmlentities()` turns all HTML tags into their entity versions.
- `nl2br()` converts newlines (created when the user presses the Enter key) into HTML `<br />` tags.
- `strip_tags()` removes all HTML and PHP tags.

The first two functions turn an HTML tag (for example, `<b>`) into an entity version like `<b>`. The entity version appears in the output but isn't rendered. The fourth function, `strip_tags()` removes HTML and PHP characters entirely.

This task rewrites `handle_post.php` to demonstrate how these functions work.

To work with HTML and PHP:

1. Open `handle_post.php` (**Script 5.3**) in your text editor.

continues on next page

Script 5.3 The `stripslashes()` function combats the effect of magic quotes.

```
<!DOCTYPE html PUBLIC "-//W3C//DTD XHTML 1.0 Transitional//EN"
        "http://www.w3.org/TR/xhtml1/DTD/xhtml1-transitional.dtd">
<html xmlns="http://www.w3.org/1999/xhtml">
<head>
    <meta http-equiv="content-type" content="text/html; charset=iso-8859-1" />
    <title>Your Forum Posting</title>
</head>
<body>
<?php // Script 5.3 - handle_post.php - second version after Script 5.2

// Address error handing.
ini_set ('display_errors', 1);
error_reporting (E_ALL & ~E_NOTICE);

// In case register_globals is disabled.
$first_name = $_POST['first_name'];
$last_name = $_POST['last_name'];
$posting = $_POST['posting'];

// Create a name variable.
$name = $first_name . ' ' . $last_name;

// Adjust for Magic Quotes.
$name = stripslashes ($name);
$posting = stripslashes ($posting);

// Print the message.
print "Thank you, $name, for your posting:<br />
<p>$posting</p>";

?>
</body>
</html>
```

2. After you add the `stripslashes()` function before the `print()` statement, add the following lines (**Script 5.4**):

   ```
   $post1 = htmlentities ($posting);
   $post2 = strip_tags ($posting);
   ```

   To clarify the difference between how these two functions work, you apply them both to the posting, creating two new variables in the process.

Script 5.4 This version of the PHP script addresses HTML tags in two different ways.

```
<!DOCTYPE html PUBLIC "-//W3C//DTD XHTML 1.0 Transitional//EN"
        "http://www.w3.org/TR/xhtml1/DTD/xhtml1-transitional.dtd">
<html xmlns="http://www.w3.org/1999/xhtml">
<head>
    <meta http-equiv="content-type" content="text/html; charset=iso-8859-1" />
    <title>Your Forum Posting</title>
</head>
<body>
<?php // Script 5.4 - handle_post.php - third version after Scripts 5.2 and 5.3

// Address error handing.
ini_set ('display_errors', 1);
error_reporting (E_ALL & ~E_NOTICE);

// In case register_globals is disabled.
$first_name = $_POST['first_name'];
$last_name = $_POST['last_name'];
$posting = $_POST['posting'];

// Create a name variable.
$name = $first_name . ' ' . $last_name;

// Adjust for Magic Quotes.
$name = stripslashes ($name);
$posting = stripslashes ($posting);

// Adjust for HTML tags.
$post1 = htmlentities ($posting);
$post2 = strip_tags ($posting);

// Print the message.
print "Thank you, $name, for your posting:<br />
<p>$posting</p>
<p>$post1</p>
<p>$post2</p>
";

?>
</body>
</html>
```

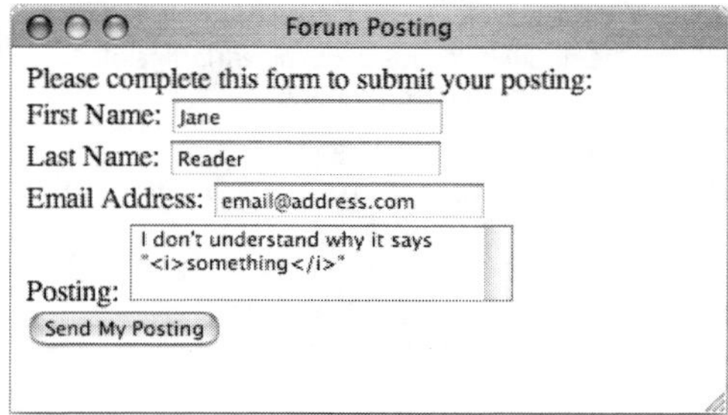

Figure 5.9 The HTML characters you enter as part of a posting are addressed by PHP.

Your Forum Posting

Thank you, Jane Reader, for your posting:

I don't understand why it says "*something*"

I don't understand why it says "<i>something</i>"

I don't understand why it says "something"

Figure 5.10 The resulting PHP page shows the original post as it would look if printed without modification, the effect of `htmlentities()`, and the effect of `strip_tags()`.

3. Alter the print statement to read as follows:

```
print "Thank you, $name, for your
→ posting:<br />
<p>$posting</p>
<p>$post1</p>
<p>$post2</p>
";
```

To highlight the different results, you print out the three different versions of the postings. First is the original posting as it was entered, followed by the `htmlentities()` version of the posting. It will show the HTML tags without rendering them. Finally, the `strip_tags()` version will be printed; it doesn't include any HTML (or PHP) tags.

4. Save the file, upload it to your Web server, and test again in your Web browser (**Figures 5.9** and **5.10**).

✔ Tips

- The `html_entity_decode()` function does just the opposite of `htmlentities()`, turning HTML entities into their respective HTML code.
- Another useful function for outputting strings in the Web browser is `word_wrap()`. This function wraps a string to a certain number of characters.

Encoding and Decoding Strings

At the end of Chapter 3, the section "Manually Sending Data to a Page" demonstrated how to use the thinking behind the GET method to send data to a page by appending it to the URL. At that time, you used this technique to send a variable with a single word value. But what if you want to pass several words as one variable value?

In these instances you can use the `urlencode()` function. As its name implies, this function takes a string and *encodes* it (changes its format) so that it can properly be passed as part of a URL. The function replaces spaces with plus signs (+) and translates special characters (for example, the apostrophe) into less problematic versions. The syntax for this function is

```
$string = urlencode ($string);
```

To demonstrate one use of this function, you'll rewrite the `handle_post.php` page, adding a link that passes the user's name and email address to a third page.

To use urlencode():

1. Open `handle_post.php` (Script 5.4) in your text editor.

2. If you want, delete the `htmlentities()` and `strip_tags()` lines added in the previous task. You can also revert to the older version of the `print()` statement.

3. After the `print()` statement, add the following (**Script 5.5**):

   ```
   $name = urlencode ($name);
   $email = urlencode ($_POST['email']);
   ```

   This script will pass these two variables to a second page. In order for it to do so, they must both be encoded.

Script 5.5 This script encodes two variables before adding them to a link. This way, the variables are successfully passed to the other page.

```
<!DOCTYPE html PUBLIC "-//W3C//DTD XHTML 1.0 Transitional//EN"
        "http://www.w3.org/TR/xhtml1/DTD/xhtml1-transitional.dtd">
<html xmlns="http://www.w3.org/1999/xhtml">
<head>
    <meta http-equiv="content-type" content="text/html; charset=iso-8859-1" />
    <title>Your Forum Posting</title>
</head>
<body>
<?php // Script 5.5 - handle_post.php - fourth version after Scripts 5.2, 5.3 and 5.4

// Address error handing.
ini_set ('display_errors', 1);
error_reporting (E_ALL & ~E_NOTICE);

// In case register_globals is disabled.
$first_name = $_POST['first_name'];
$last_name = $_POST['last_name'];
$posting = $_POST['posting'];

// Create a name variable.
$name = $first_name . ' ' . $last_name;

// Adjust for Magic Quotes.
$name = stripslashes ($name);
$posting = stripslashes ($posting);

// Print the message.
print "Thank you, $name, for your posting: <br />
<p>$posting</p>
";

// Make a link to another page.
$name = urlencode ($name);
$email = urlencode ($_POST['email']);
print "Click <a href=\"thanks.php?name=$name&email=$email\">here</a> to continue.";

?>
</body>
</html>
```

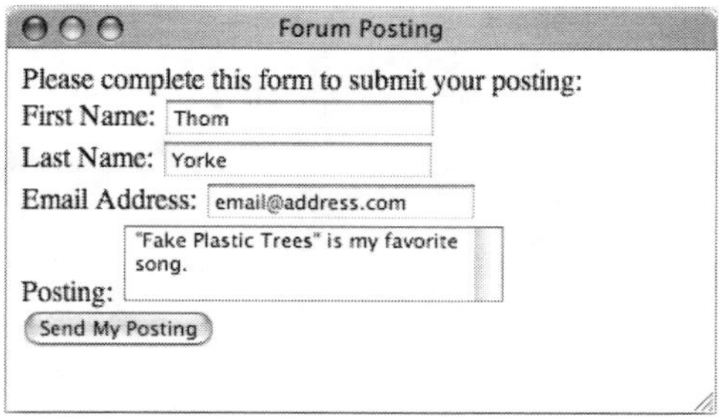

Figure 5.11 Another use of the form.

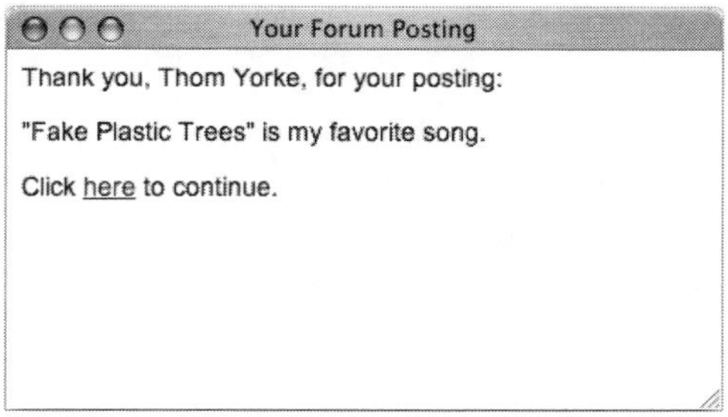

Figure 5.12 The handling page now displays a link to another page.

Because you haven't previously referred to or used the `$email` variable, the second line both retrieves the `$email` value from the `$_POST` array and encodes it in one step. This is the same as having these two separate lines:

```
$email = $_POST['email'];
$email = urlencode ($email);
```

4. Add another print statement that creates the link:

```
print "Click <a href=\"thanks.php?
→ name=$name&email=$email\">here</a>
→ to continue.";
```

The core purpose of this `print()` statement is to create an HTML link in the Web page, the source code of which would be something like

```
<a href="thanks.php?name=Larry+
→ Ullman&email=phpvqs2%40DMCInsights.
→ com">here</a>
```

To accomplish this you begin by hard-coding most of the HTML and then include the appropriate variable names. Because the HTML code requires that the URL for the link be in double quotation marks—and the `print()` statement already uses double quotation marks—you must escape them in order for them to be printed.

5. Save the file, upload it to your Web server, and test again in your Web browser (**Figures 5.11** and **5.12**).

continues on next page

6. View the HTML source code of the handling page to see the resulting link in the HTML form (**Figure 5.13**).

✔ Tips

- The `urldecode()` function does just the opposite of `urlencode()`—it takes an encoded URL and turns it back into a standard form. You'll use it less frequently, though, as PHP will automatically decode most values it receives.

- Since you can use concatenation with functions, the new `print()` statement could be written as follows:

  ```
  print 'Click <a href="thanks.php?
  → name=' . $name . '
  → &email=' . $email . '">
  → here</a> to continue.';
  ```

  This method has two added benefits. First, it uses single quotation marks to start and stop the statement, meaning you don't need to escape the double quotation marks. Second, the variables used are more obvious—they aren't buried in a lot of other code.

Source of http://localhost/handle_post.php

```
<!DOCTYPE html PUBLIC "-//W3C//DTD XHTML 1.0 Transitional//EN"
        "http://www.w3.org/TR/xhtml1/DTD/xhtml1-transitional.dtd">
<html xmlns="http://www.w3.org/1999/xhtml">
<head>
     <meta http-equiv="content-type" content="text/html; charset=iso-8859-1" />
     <title>Your Forum Posting</title>
</head>
<body>
Thank you, Thom Yorke, for your posting:<br />
<p>"Fake Plastic Trees" is my favorite song.</p>
Click <a href="thanks.php?name=Thom+Yorke&email=email%40address.com">here</a> to continue.</body>
</html>
```

Figure 5.13 Check the page's HTML source code to confirm that the link is as it should be.

Script 5.6 The thanks.php script prints a greeting based on two values it receives in the URL.

```
<!DOCTYPE html PUBLIC "-//W3C//DTD XHTML 1.0 Transitional//EN"
        "http://www.w3.org/TR/xhtml1/DTD/xhtml1-transitional.dtd">
<html xmlns="http://www.w3.org/1999/xhtml">
<head>
    <meta http-equiv="content-type" content="text/html; charset=iso-8859-1" />
    <title>Thanks!</title>
</head>
<body>
<?php // Script 5.6 - thanks.php
// This is the page the user sees after clicking on the link in handle_post.php (Script 5.5).
// This page receives $name and $email variables in the URL.

// Address error handing.
ini_set ('display_errors', 1);
error_reporting (E_ALL & ~E_NOTICE);

// In case register_globals is disabled.
$name = $_GET['name'];
$email = $_GET['email'];

// Print the message.
print "Thank you, $name. We will contact you at $email.";

?>
</body>
</html>
```

Just in case it's not clear, let's quickly write the thanks.php page to which users are directed when they click the link in handle_post.php (see Figure 5.12).

To write thanks.php:

1. Begin with a new HTML header (**Script 5.6**):
```
<!DOCTYPE html PUBLIC "-//W3C//DTD XHTML 1.0 Transitional//EN"
"http://www.w3.org/TR/xhtml1/DTD/xhtml1-transitional.dtd">
<html xmlns="http://www.w3.org/1999/xhtml">
<head>
   <meta http-equiv="content-type" content="text/html; charset=iso-8859-1" />
   <title>Thanks!</title>
</head>
<body>
```

2. Create the initial PHP tag:
```
<?php // Script 5.6 - thanks.php
```

3. If necessary, address register_globals and error handling:
```
ini_set ('display_errors', 1);
error_reporting (E_ALL & ~E_NOTICE);
$name = $_GET['name'];
$email = $_GET['email'];
```
Because the variable values will come from the URL and not from an HTML form with the POST method, you use $_GET instead of $_POST.

4. Print out a simple message:
```
print "Thank you, $name. We will contact you at $email.";
```

continues on next page

5. Complete the PHP code and the HTML page:

```
?>
</body>
</html>
```

6. Save the page as `thanks.php`, upload it to your Web server (in the same directory as `posting.html` and `handle_post.php`), and test it in your Web browser by clicking the link in the handling page (**Figure 5.14**).

✔ Tip

- Remember that values sent directly from a form are automatically URL-encoded prior to being sent and decoded upon arrival at the receiving script. You only need the `urlencode()` function to manually encode data (as in the example).

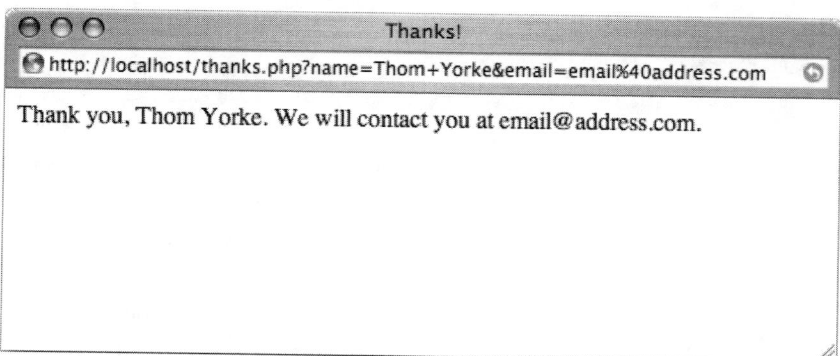

Figure 5.14 The handling page prints a message based on values it receives as part of the URL.

Script 5.7 This version of the handling script replaces uses of *badword* with a bunch of Xs.

```
<!DOCTYPE html PUBLIC "-//W3C//DTD XHTML 1.0 Transitional//EN"
        "http://www.w3.org/TR/xhtml1/DTD/xhtml1-transitional.dtd">
<html xmlns="http://www.w3.org/1999/xhtml">
<head>
    <meta http-equiv="content-type" content="text/html; charset=iso-8859-1" />
    <title>Your Forum Posting</title>
</head>
<body>
<?php // Script 5.7 - handle_post.php - fifth version after Scripts 5.2, 5.3, 5.4 and 5.5

// Address error handing.
ini_set ('display_errors', 1);
error_reporting (E_ALL & ~E_NOTICE);

// In case register_globals is disabled.
$first_name = $_POST['first_name'];
$last_name = $_POST['last_name'];
$posting = $_POST['posting'];

// Create a name variable.
$name = $first_name . ' ' . $last_name;

// Adjust for Magic Quotes.
$name = stripslashes ($name);
$posting = stripslashes ($posting);

// Take out the bad words.
$posting = str_replace ('badword', 'XXXXX', $posting);

// Print the message.
print "Thank you, $name, for your posting:<br />
<p>$posting</p>
";

// Make a link to another page.
$name = urlencode ($name);
$email = urlencode ($_POST['email']);
print "Click <a href=\"thanks.php?name=$name&email=$email\">here</a> to continue.";

?>
</body>
</html>
```

Replacing Parts of a String

As you can probably tell by now, you can do many different things with strings because PHP has dozens of built-in functions to manipulate them. The last two sections of this chapter cover a smattering of different tools so that you'll have a better sense of the possibilities.

You can replace *substrings* (parts of strings) with new values using the `str_replace()` function:

```
$string = str_replace ($needle,
→ $replacement, $haystack);
```

This function replaces every occurrence of `$needle` found in `$haystack` with `$replacement`. For example:

```
$me = 'Larry E. Ullman';
$me = str_replace ('E.', 'Edward', $me);
```

The `$me` variable now has a value of *Larry Edward Ullman.*

You can also use this function to strip bad words out of a string, as demonstrated in the following task.

To use str_replace():

1. Open `handle_post.php` (Script 5.5) in your text editor.
2. Before the `print()` statement, add the following (**Script 5.7**):
   ```
   $posting = str_replace ('badword',
   → 'XXXXX', $posting);
   ```
   This example flags the use of a bad word in a posting by crossing it out. Rather than an actual curse word, the code uses *badword*. (You can use whatever you want, of course.)

continues on next page

If you'd like to catch many bad words, you can use multiple lines, like so:

```
$posting = str_replace ('badword1',
→ 'XXXXX', $posting);
$posting = str_replace ('badword2',
→ 'XXXXX', $posting);
$posting = str_replace ('badword3',
→ 'XXXXX', $posting);
```

3. Save the file, upload it to your Web server, and test again in your Web browser (**Figures 5.15** and **5.16**).

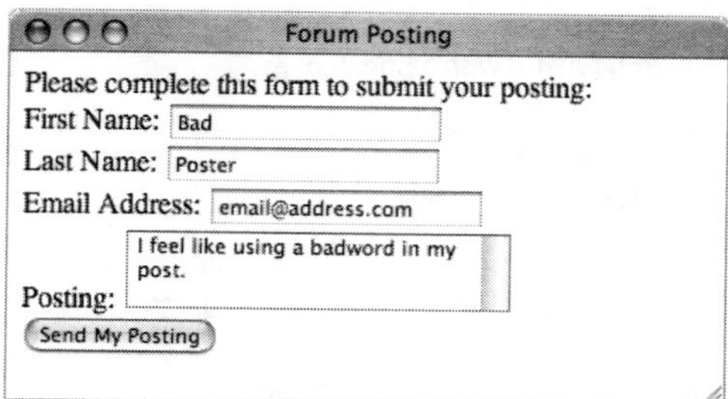

Figure 5.15 If a user enters a word you'd prefer they not use...

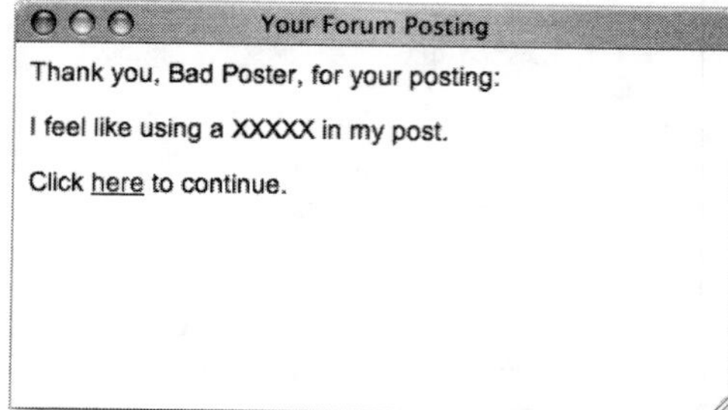

Figure 5.16 ...you can have PHP replace it.

✔ Tips

- The `str_replace()` function will even catch bad words in context. For example, if you entered *I feel like using badwords*, the result would be *I feel like using XXXXXs*.
- The `str_replace()` function can also take an array of needle terms, an array of replacement terms, and even an array as the haystack. Because you may not know what an array is yet, this technique isn't demonstrated here.
- The `strlen()` function returns the number of characters (including spaces and punctuation) contained within a given string. For example, `strlen ('Hello, world!');` returns the number 13.
- New to PHP 5 is the `str_ireplace()` function, a case-insensitive version of `str_replace()`.
- The `str_word_count()` function, which was added to PHP in version 4.3, returns the number of words in a given string (using spaces as the delimiter).
- If you want to check whether a string matches a certain format—for example, to see if it's a valid email address—you need to use regular expressions. *Regular expressions* are an advanced concept in which you define patterns and then see if a value fits the mold. (See Chapter 13, "Regular Expressions," for more information.)

Tokenizing, Searching, and Comparing Strings

PHP has a few functions you can use to pull apart strings, search through them, and do comparisons. If you don't understand conditionals, loops, and other control structures, these functions will do you little good. So, they're mentioned here, and later chapters use them more formally.

Earlier in this chapter you learned how to join strings using concatenation. Besides making larger strings out of smaller pieces, you can also extract subsections of a string (which is to say, *tokenize* them). The trick to using any method to pull out a subsection of a string is that you must know something about the string itself in order to do so effectively.

The `strtok()` function creates a substring, referred to as a *token*, from a larger string based on a predetermined separator (such as a comma or a space). For example, if you have users enter their full name in one field (presumably with their first and last names separated by a space), you can ascertain their first name with this code: `$first_name = strtok ($name, ' ');`

This line tells PHP to pull out everything from `$name` until it finds a blank space.

If you have users enter their full name in the format *Surname, First*, you can find their surname by writing: `$last_name = strtok ($name, ',');`

A second way to pull out sections of a string is by referring to the *indexed position* of the characters within the string. The *index* of a string is the numerical location of a character, counting from the beginning. However, PHP—like most programming languages—begins all indexes with the number 0. For example, to index the string *Larry*, you begin with the *L* at position 0, followed by *a* at 1, *r* at 2, the second *r* at 3, and *y* at 4. Even though the string length of *Larry* is 5, its index goes from 0 to 4.

With this in mind, you can utilize the `substr()` function to create a substring based on the index position of the substring's characters, like this: `$sub = substr ($string,0,10);`

First, you must enter the master string from which your substring will be derived. Second, you indicate where the substring begins, as its indexed position (0 means that you want to start with the first character). Third, from that starting point, you determine how many characters the substring is composed of (10). In this case, if `$string` isn't 10 characters long, the resulting `$sub` will end with the end of `$string`.

To search through a string (finding a needle in a haystack), you'll use these functions:

- `strstr()` returns the haystack from the first occurrence of a needle to the end.
- `strpos()` searches through a haystack and returns the numeric location of a particular needle.

Both of these functions also have a case-insensitive alternative: `stristr()` and `stripos()`, respectively.

To compare two strings, you can always use the equality operator, which you'll learn about in the next chapter. Otherwise you can use these functions:

- `strcmp()` indicates how two strings compare by returning a whole number.
- `strnatcmp()` is similar but linguistically more precise.

These also have case-insensitive companions, `strcasecmp()` and `strnatcasecmp()`.

Other String Functions

It's quite common for extra spaces to be added to a string variable, either because a user enters information carelessly or due to sloppy HTML code. For purposes of clarity, data integrity, and Web design, it's worth your while to delete those spaces from the strings before you use them. Extra spaces sent to the Web browser could make the page appear oddly, and those sent to a database or cookie could have unfortunate consequences at a later date (for example, if a password has a superfluous space, it might not match when it's entered without the space).

The `trim()` function automatically strips away any extra spaces from both the beginning and the end of a string (but not the middle). The format for using `trim()` is as follows:

```
$string = " extra space before and after
→ text ";
$string = trim ($string);
// $string is now equal to "extra space
→ before and after text".
```

Along with `trim()`, PHP provides a few functions you can use to tweak strings:

- `ucfirst()` capitalizes the first letter of the string.
- `ucwords()` capitalizes the first letter of words in a string.
- `strtoupper()` makes an entire string uppercase.
- `strtolower()` makes an entire string lowercase.

Script 5.8 The final version of `handle_post.php` trims extraneous white space from submissions and alters the case of the person's name.

Script

```
<!DOCTYPE html PUBLIC "-//W3C//DTD XHTML 1.0 Transitional//EN"
        "http://www.w3.org/TR/xhtml1/DTD/xhtml1-transitional.dtd">
<html xmlns="http://www.w3.org/1999/xhtml">
<head>
    <meta http-equiv="content-type" content="text/html; charset=iso-8859-1" />
    <title>Your Forum Posting</title>
</head>
<body>
<?php // Script 5.8 - handle_post.php - sixth version after Scripts 5.2, 5.3, 5.4, 5.5 and 5.7

// Address error handing.
ini_set ('display_errors', 1);
error_reporting (E_ALL & ~E_NOTICE);

// In case register_globals is disabled.
// Strip out extra spaces using trim().
$first_name = trim ($_POST['first_name']);
$last_name = trim ($_POST['last_name']);
$posting = trim ($_POST['posting']);

// Create a name variable.
$name = $first_name . ' ' . $last_name;

// Adjust for Magic Quotes.
$name = stripslashes ($name);
$posting = stripslashes ($posting);

// Change the capitalization of the name.
$name = ucwords ( strtolower ($name) );

// Take out the bad words.
$posting = str_replace ('badword', 'XXXXX', $posting);

// Print the message.
print "Thank you, $name, for your posting:<br />
<p>$posting</p>
";

```

(script continues on next page)

Script 5.8 *continued*

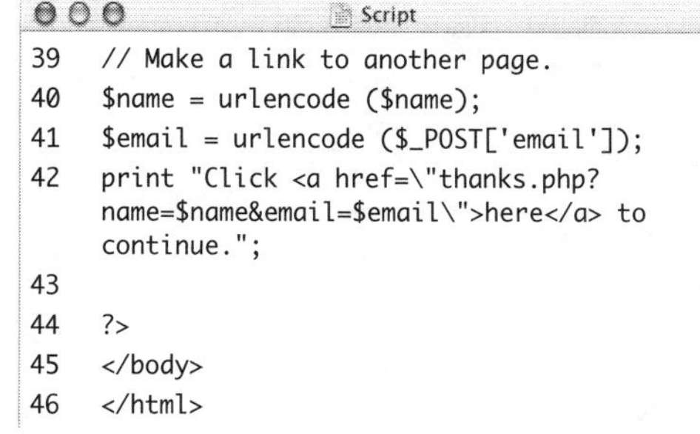

```
// Make a link to another page.
$name = urlencode ($name);
$email = urlencode ($_POST['email']);
print "Click <a href=\"thanks.php?
name=$name&email=$email\">here</a> to
continue.";

?>
</body>
</html>
```

This task demonstrates two of these functions by (you guessed it) altering `handle_post.php` for the final time. Before you witness this example, remember that the Web browser handles spaces in odd ways. A single space in the HTML source code will create a single space in the Web browser. But multiple spaces, tabs, and new lines will normally only create a single space or possibly none at all. For this reason, the best way to see the effect of the `trim()` function is to view the resulting HTML source code.

To use other string functions:

1. Open `handle_post.php` (Script 5.7) in your text editor.

2. Alter the initial `register_global` lines so that the values are trimmed (**Script 5.8**):

   ```
   $first_name = trim
   → ($_POST['first_name']);
   $last_name = trim
   → ($_POST['last_name']);
   $posting = trim ($_POST['posting']);
   ```

   Because you're creating `$first_name` and the other variables by referring to the `$_POST` equivalents, you can apply the `trim()` function at the same time. You could also write

   ```
   $first_name = $_POST['first_name'];
   $first_name = trim ($first_name);
   ```

   If you want, you can apply this to the email address as well by changing

   ```
   $email = urlencode ($_POST['email']);
   ```

   to

   ```
   $email = urlencode ( trim
   → ($_POST['email']) );
   ```

continues on next page

3. Before the main `print()` statement, where the name is printed, add

   ```
   $name = ucwords (strtolower($name));
   ```

   You can ensure that all posts use a consistent formatting scheme for names. To do so, you first make the entire name lowercase; then you capitalize the words in the name, which should be the first and last names. To save space, you nest the two functions so that the result returned by `strtolower()` is fed as the argument to `ucwords()`. This is the same as writing

   ```
   $name = strtolower ($name);
   $name = ucwords ($name);
   ```

4. Save the file, upload it to your Web server, and test again in your Web browser (**Figures 5.17** and **5.18**).

5. View the HTML source code of the handling page to see how the `trim()` function affects the posting (**Figure 5.19**).

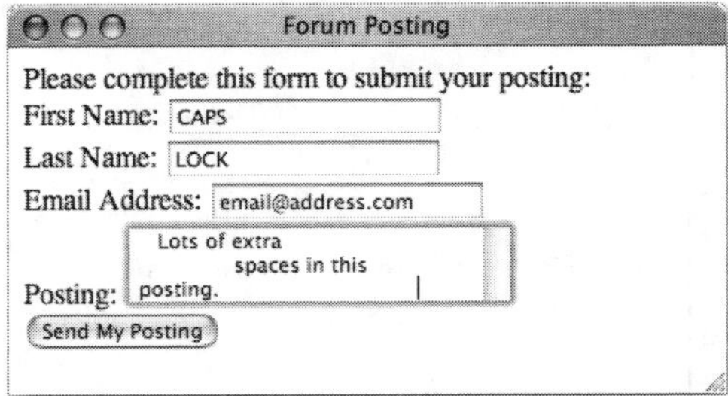

Figure 5.17 The last execution of the form uses all caps for the name and adds spaces to the posting.

Your Forum Posting

Thank you, Caps Lock, for your posting:

Lots of extra spaces in this posting.

Click here to continue.

Figure 5.18 The PHP result (see Figure 5.17), with a formatted name and trimmer posting (although you'll need to view the HTML source, Figure 5.19, to really appreciate this).

Source of http://localhost/handle_post.php

```
<!DOCTYPE html PUBLIC "-//W3C//DTD XHTML 1.0 Transitional//EN"
        "http://www.w3.org/TR/xhtml1/DTD/xhtml1-transitional.dtd">
<html xmlns="http://www.w3.org/1999/xhtml">
<head>
    <meta http-equiv="content-type" content="text/html; charset=iso-8859-1" />
    <title>Your Forum Posting</title>
</head>
<body>
Thank you, Caps Lock, for your posting:<br />
<p>Lots of extra
                spaces in this
posting.</p>
Click <a href="thanks.php?name=Caps+Lock&email=">here</a> to continue.</body>
</html>
```

Figure 5.19 The HTML source of the page shows how the spaces at the beginning and end of the posting are removed (or else they'd appear before and after the P tags).

✔ Tips

- This example of `strtolower()` and `ucwords()` isn't ideal because it will wreck first names like *C.J.* and last names like *McElhatton*. Due to the variance in people's names around the globe, there's really no flawless way to format names with PHP.
- If you need to trim excess spaces from the beginning or the end of a string but not both, PHP breaks the `trim()` function into two more specific functions: `rtrim()` removes spaces found at the end of a string variable, and `ltrim()` handles those at the beginning. They're both used just like `trim()`:

  ```
  $string = rtrim ($string);
  $string = ltrim ($string);
  ```
- The `levenshtein()` function calculates the *levenshtein* difference between any two strings: how many letters you need to change in the one to create the other. It's difficult to think of a use for this function, yet it's still nice to know that it exists!

Encrypting and Decrypting Strings

For security reasons, encryption and decryption are a necessary aspect of most Web sites, especially those that deal with e-commerce. Frequently, in order to protect data, programmers *encrypt* it—alter its state by transforming it to a form that's more difficult, if not virtually impossible, to discern. Passwords are an example of a variable you might want to encrypt. Depending on the level of security you want to establish, usernames, email addresses, and phone numbers are likely candidates for encryption, too. PHP has three primary encryption and decryption functions: `crypt()`, `encrypt()`, and `decrypt()`.

You can use the `crypt()` function to encrypt data, but be aware that no decryption option is available (it's known as *one-way* encryption). So, a password may be encrypted using it and then stored, but the decrypted value of the password can never be determined. Using this function in a Web application, you might encrypt a user's password upon registration; then, when the user logged in, the password they entered at that time would also be encrypted, and the two protected versions of the password would be compared. The syntax for using `crypt()` is

```
$data = crypt ($data);
```

This will be demonstrated with a password in Chapter 11.

A second encryption function is `encrypt()`, which can be decrypted using the appropriately named `decrypt()` function (note that `crypt()` and `encrypt()` are two different functions). Unfortunately, in order for you to be able to use these two functions, the Mcrypt extension must be installed with the PHP module. Don't be surprised if these functions aren't available and you're therefore limited to just `crypt()` encryption without the possibility of decryption.

Most PHP programmers encrypt values using functions built into the database application (for example, MySQL, PostgreSQL, Oracle, or SQL Server) where the data is stored. Depending on the technology you're using, it most likely provides both one-way and two-way encryption tools.

6 Control Structures

Now that you understand the basics of the variable types (aside from arrays, which will be discussed in Chapter 7, "Using Arrays"), let's get into the real meat of programming—*control structures* (conditionals and loops). In the process, this chapter finishes the discussion of PHP's various operators. (You've already seen the arithmetic and assignment operators in the previous chapters.)

Conditional structures are a staple of programming languages. PHP includes two general conditionals—`if` and `switch`—both of which you'll begin using in this chapter. They allow you to define a question and then perform actions based on the answer. This functionality gives you the ability to make your Web sites even more dynamic. The discussion of `if` conditionals will introduce two last categories of operators: comparison and logical. You'll commonly use these in your conditionals along with the concepts of TRUE and FALSE.

Finally, you'll begin programming with loops, which allow you to repeat an action for a specified number of iterations. Loops can save you programming time and help you get the most functionality out of arrays, as you'll see in the next chapter.

Creating the HTML Form

As with the previous chapters, the examples in this chapter are based on an HTML form that sends data to a PHP page. In this case, the form is a simple registration page that requests the following information:

- First name
- Last name
- Email address
- Password
- Date of birth
- Favorite color

The following task writes this form before getting into the PHP code.

To create the HTML form:

1. Begin a new HTML document in your text editor (**Script 6.1**):

```
<!DOCTYPE html PUBLIC "-//W3C//DTD
→ XHTML 1.0 Transitional//EN"
"http://www.w3.org/TR/xhtml1/DTD/
→ xhtml1-transitional.dtd">
<html xmlns="http://www.w3.org/1999/
→ xhtml">
<head>
   <meta http-equiv="content-type"
   → content="text/html; charset=
   → iso-8859-1" />
   <title>Register</title>
</head>
<body>
<!-- Script 6.1 - register.html -->
<p>Please complete this form to
→ register: </p>
```

Script 6.1 This pseudo-registration form is the basis for the examples in this chapter.

```
<!DOCTYPE html PUBLIC "-//W3C//DTD XHTML 1.0 Transitional//EN"
        "http://www.w3.org/TR/xhtml1/DTD/xhtml1-transitional.dtd">
<html xmlns="http://www.w3.org/1999/xhtml">
<head>
    <meta http-equiv="content-type" content="text/html; charset=iso-8859-1" />
    <title>Register</title>
</head>
<body>

<!-- Script 6.1 - register.html -->

<p>Please complete this form to register:</p>

<form action="handle_reg.php" method="post">

<p>First Name: <input type="text" name="first_name" size="20" /></p>

<p>Last Name: <input type="text" name="last_name" size="20" /></p>

<p>Email Address: <input type="text" name="email" size="20" /></p>

<p>Password: <input type="password" name="password" size="20" /></p>

<p>Confirm Password: <input type="password" name="confirm" size="20" /></p>

<p>Date Of Birth:
<select name="month">
<option value="">Month</option>
<option value="1">January</option>
<option value="2">February</option>
<option value="3">March</option>
<option value="4">April</option>
<option value="5">May</option>
<option value="6">June</option>
<option value="7">July</option>
<option value="8">August</option>
<option value="9">September</option>
<option value="10">October</option>
<option value="11">November</option>
<option value="12">December</option>
```

(script continues on next page)

Script 6.1 *continued*

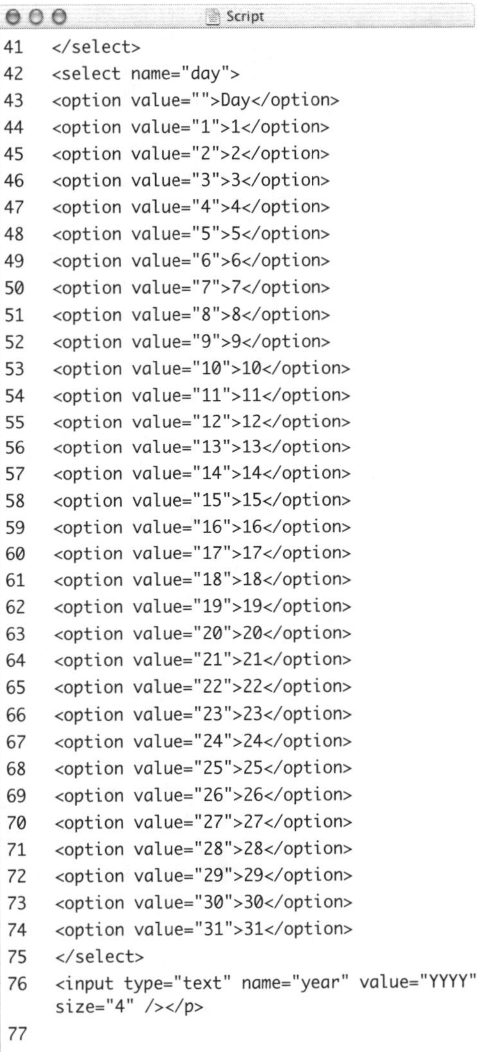

```
</select>
<select name="day">
<option value="">Day</option>
<option value="1">1</option>
<option value="2">2</option>
<option value="3">3</option>
<option value="4">4</option>
<option value="5">5</option>
<option value="6">6</option>
<option value="7">7</option>
<option value="8">8</option>
<option value="9">9</option>
<option value="10">10</option>
<option value="11">11</option>
<option value="12">12</option>
<option value="13">13</option>
<option value="14">14</option>
<option value="15">15</option>
<option value="16">16</option>
<option value="17">17</option>
<option value="18">18</option>
<option value="19">19</option>
<option value="20">20</option>
<option value="21">21</option>
<option value="22">22</option>
<option value="23">23</option>
<option value="24">24</option>
<option value="25">25</option>
<option value="26">26</option>
<option value="27">27</option>
<option value="28">28</option>
<option value="29">29</option>
<option value="30">30</option>
<option value="31">31</option>
</select>
<input type="text" name="year" value="YYYY" size="4" /></p>

```

(script continues on next page)

Password: ••••••••

Figure 6.1 A password input type, as it's being filled out.

2. Create the initial form tag:

```
<form action="handle_reg.php"
→ method="post">
```

As with many of the previous examples, this page uses the POST method. The handling script, identified by the `action` attribute, will be `handle_reg.php`.

3. Create inputs for the first name, last name, email address, and password:

```
<p>First Name: <input type="text"
→ name="first_name" size="20" /></p>
<p>Last Name: <input type="text"
→ name="last_name" size="20" /></p>
<p>Email Address: <input type="text"
→ name="email" size="20" /></p>
<p>Password: <input type="password"
→ name="password" size="20" /></p>
<p>Confirm Password: <input type=
→ "password" name="confirm"
→ size="20" /></p>
```

These lines should be self-evident. You wrap each line in HTML <p></p> tags to improve the spacing in the Web browser. Also, note that you create two password inputs—the second is used to confirm the text entered in the first. Password input types don't reveal what the user types (**Figure 6.1**), so it's a good insurance policy to make them type it again.

continues on next page

4. Begin making the inputs for the date of birth:

```
<p>Date Of Birth:
<select name="month">
<option value="">Month</option>
<option value="1">January</option>
<option value="2">February</option>
<option value="3">March</option>
<option value="4">April</option>
<option value="5">May</option>
<option value="6">June</option>
<option value="7">July</option>
<option value="8">August</option>
<option value="9">September</option>
<option value="10">October</option>
<option value="11">November</option>
<option value="12">December</option>
</select>
```

The date of birth will be broken into three separate inputs—month, day, and year—rather than have the user enter it all at once (for example, *10/23/1970* or *January 26, 1974*). This approach gives you more control over the format of the information submitted.

5. Create a drop-down menu for the birthday:

```
<select name="day">
<option value="">Day</option>
<option value="1">1</option>
<option value="2">2</option>
<option value="3">3</option>
<option value="4">4</option>
<option value="5">5</option>
<option value="6">6</option>
<option value="7">7</option>
<option value="8">8</option>
<option value="9">9</option>
<option value="10">10</option>
<option value="11">11</option>
```

Script 6.1 *continued*

Script

```
<p>Favorite Color:
<select name="color">
<option value="">Pick One</option>
<option value="red">Red</option>
<option value="yellow">Yellow</option>
<option value="green">Green</option>
<option value="blue">Blue</option>
</select></p>

<p><input type="submit" name="submit"
value="Register" /></p>

</form>

</body>
</html>
```

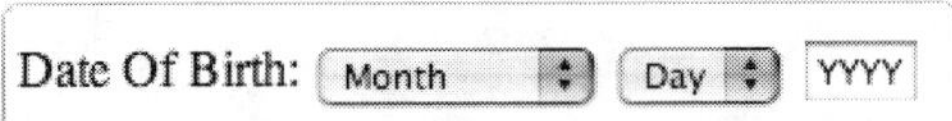

Figure 6.2 The year input, with a preset value.

```
<option value="12">12</option>
<option value="13">13</option>
<option value="14">14</option>
<option value="15">15</option>
<option value="16">16</option>
<option value="17">17</option>
<option value="18">18</option>
<option value="19">19</option>
<option value="20">20</option>
<option value="21">21</option>
<option value="22">22</option>
<option value="23">23</option>
<option value="24">24</option>
<option value="25">25</option>
<option value="26">26</option>
<option value="27">27</option>
<option value="28">28</option>
<option value="29">29</option>
<option value="30">30</option>
<option value="31">31</option>
</select>
```

6. Create a text input for the birth year:

```
<input type="text" name="year"
→ value="YYYY" size="4" /></p>
```

Rather than use a drop-down menu that displays 50 or 100 years, you have the user enter their birth year in a text box. By presetting the value of the input, you make the text box indicate the proper format for the year (**Figure 6.2**). Also, just to clarify, the closing </p> tag completes the paragraph begun in step 4.

continues on next page

7. Create a drop-down menu for the favorite color:

```
<p>Favorite Color:
<select name="color">
<option value="">Pick One</option>
<option value="red">Red</option>
<option value="yellow">Yellow</option>
<option value="green">Green</option>
<option value="blue">Blue</option>
</select></p>
```

As another way to identify a particular registrant, you have them select their favorite color from the list. Naturally, you can add as many colors as you want here.

8. Add a submit button and close the form:

```
<p><input type="submit" name="submit"
→ value="Register" /></p>
</form>
```

9. Complete the HTML page:

```
</body>
</html>
```

10. Save the file as `register.html`, upload it to your Web server (or save it to the appropriate directory of your PHP-enabled computer), and load the page in your Web browser (**Figure 6.3**).

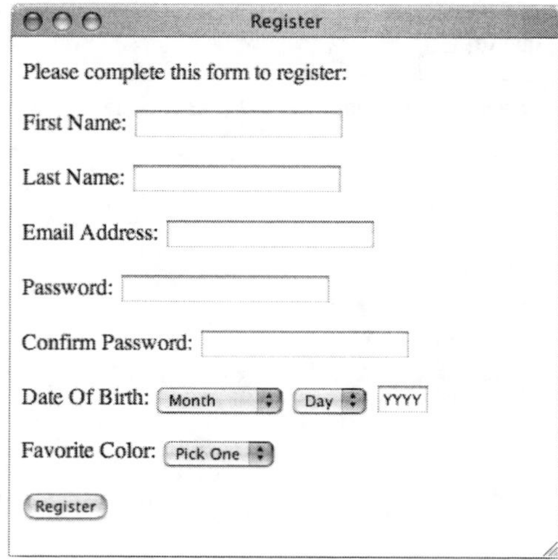

Figure 6.3 The whole HTML form.

✔ Tips

- Registration pages should always have users confirm their password and possibly their username or email address (whatever information will be used to log in).

- Most registration pages use either a nickname or an email address for the username. If you use the email address as a username, it's easier for your users to remember their registration information (a user may have only a few email addresses but a gazillion usernames for different sites around the Web). Furthermore, email addresses are, by their nature, unique.

The if Conditional

The basic programming conditional is the standard `if` (what used to be called an `if-then` conditional—the `then` is now implied). The syntax for this kind of conditional is very simple:

```
if (condition) {
   statement(s);
}
```

The *condition* must go within parentheses; then you begin the ***statement(s)*** area after a curly brace. You place executable commands in the ***statement(s)*** section of the conditional (for example, printing a string or adding two numbers together). Each separate statement (or command) must have its own semicolon indicating the end of the command line, but there is no limit on the number of statements that can result from a conditional. You then close the ***statement(s)*** section with another curly brace.

Programmers commonly indent these statements from the initial `if` line to indicate that they're the result of a conditional, but that format isn't syntactically required. You'll also see people use this syntax:

```
if (condition)
{
   statement(s);
}
```

Failure to use a semicolon after each statement, forgetting an opening or closing parenthesis or curly brace, or using a semicolon after either of the braces will cause errors to occur. So, be mindful of your syntax as you code with conditionals.

PHP uses the concepts of TRUE and FALSE when determining whether to execute the statements. If the condition is TRUE, the statements are executed; if it's FALSE, they are not executed.

Validation Functions

PHP has dozens of functions that are commonly used to validate form data. These are listed in the "Variable Functions" section of the manual. Of these functions, three are used in this chapter's examples.

First up is the `empty()` function, which checks to see if a given variable has a value other than 0 or an empty string. It returns TRUE if the variable doesn't have a value (or has a value of 0 or an empty string) and FALSE otherwise:

```
$v1 = 0;
$v2 = 'Prior';
empty ($v); // TRUE
empty ($v1); // TRUE
empty ($v2); // FALSE
```

This function is perfect for making sure that text boxes in forms have been filled out. For example, if the Name input in a form was skipped, then the `$name` value would be empty (because its value is an empty string).

Next is the `isset()` function, which is almost the opposite of `empty()`, albeit with a slight difference. The `isset()` function returns TRUE if a variable has a value (including 0 or an empty string) or FALSE otherwise. For example:

```
$v1 = 0;
$v2 = 'Prior';
isset ($v); // FALSE
isset ($v1); // TRUE
isset ($v2); // TRUE
```

Finally, the `is_numeric()` function returns TRUE if the submitted variable has a valid numerical value and FALSE otherwise. Integers, decimals, and even strings (if they're a valid number) can all pass the `is_numeric()` test:

```
is_numeric (2309); // TRUE
is_numeric ('80.23'); // TRUE
is_numeric ('Cubs'); // FALSE
```

The PHP manual lists other functions similar to `is_numeric()`, such as `is_array()`, `is_string()`, and `is_integer()`. However, the `is_numeric()` function is preferable for values coming from a form, because they're passed to the PHP page as a string type (even if that string contains only numbers).

Script 6.2 Using `if` conditionals and the `empty()` function, this PHP script begins checking whether the form was properly completed.

```
<!DOCTYPE html PUBLIC "-//W3C//DTD XHTML
1.0 Transitional//EN"
        "http://www.w3.org/TR/xhtml1/DTD/
        xhtml1-transitional.dtd">
<html xmlns="http://www.w3.org/1999/xhtml">
<head>
    <meta http-equiv="content-type"
    content="text/html; charset=iso-8859-
    1" />
    <title>Registration</title>
</head>
<body>
<?php // Script 6.2 - handle_reg.php

// Address error handling.
ini_set ('display_errors', 1);
error_reporting (E_ALL & ~E_NOTICE);

// In case register_globals is disabled.
$first_name = $_POST['first_name'];
$last_name = $_POST['last_name'];
$email = $_POST['email'];
$password = $_POST['password'];
$confirm = $_POST['confirm'];
$month = $_POST['month'];
$day = $_POST['day'];
$year = $_POST['year'];
$color = $_POST['color'];

print '<p>Registration Results:</p>';

```

(script continues on next page)

To begin working with the `if` conditional, you'll create the `handle_reg.php` script, which receives the data from `register.html`. Using one of the functions explained in the "Validation Functions" sidebar, you'll make sure the registration form is filled out correctly.

To create an if conditional:

1. Begin a new document with the default HTML header (**Script 6.2**):

   ```
   <!DOCTYPE html PUBLIC "-//W3C//DTD
   → XHTML 1.0 Transitional//EN"
   "http://www.w3.org/TR/xhtml1/DTD/
   → xhtml1-transitional.dtd">
   <html xmlns="http://www.w3.org/1999/
   → xhtml">
   <head>
      <meta http-equiv="content-type"
      → content="text/html; charset=
      → iso-8859-1" />
      <title>Registration</title>
   </head>
   <body>
   ```

2. Begin the PHP section and address error handling, if necessary:

   ```
   <?php // Script 6.2 - handle_reg.php
   ini_set ('display_errors', 1);
   error_reporting (E_ALL & ~E_NOTICE);
   ```

continues on next page

3. Assign all the form values to local variables, in case `register_globals` is disabled:

```
$first_name = $_POST['first_name'];
$last_name = $_POST['last_name'];
$email = $_POST['email'];
$password = $_POST['password'];
$confirm = $_POST['confirm'];
$month = $_POST['month'];
$day = $_POST['day'];
$year = $_POST['year'];
$color = $_POST['color'];
```

   To avoid complications resulting from `register_globals` begin turned off, you assign each `$_POST` variable to a new variable within the script. You use `$_POST` here because you used the POST method in the form (and remember that the capitalization of variables counts, so you can't use `$_post` or `First_Name`). (This will make more sense after you read the next chapter!)

4. Print an introductory message:

```
print '<p>Registration Results:</p>';
```

   In truth, the only purpose of this message is to avoid displaying a blank page when the form is filled out completely (as, in that case, no error messages will be printed).

5. Validate the first name value:

```
if (empty ($first_name)) {
   print '<p>Please enter your first
   → name.</p>';
}
```

   This `if` conditional uses the code `empty ($first_name)` as its condition. If the `$first_name` variable is empty, meaning it has no value, a value of 0, or a value of an empty string, the conditional is TRUE, and the `print()` statement is executed. If the `$first_name` variable isn't empty, then the conditional is FALSE, and the `print()` function is never called.

Script 6.2 *continued*

```
// Validate the first name.
if (empty ($first_name)) {
    print '<p>Please enter your first
    name.</p>';
}

// Validate the last name.
if (empty ($last_name)) {
    print '<p>Please enter your last
    name.</p>';
}

// Validate the email address.
if (empty ($email)) {
    print '<p>Please enter your email
    address.</p>';
}

// Validate the password.
if (empty ($password)) {
    print '<p>Please enter your
    password.</p>';
}

?>
</body>
</html>
```

Figure 6.4 Filling out the HTML form completely...

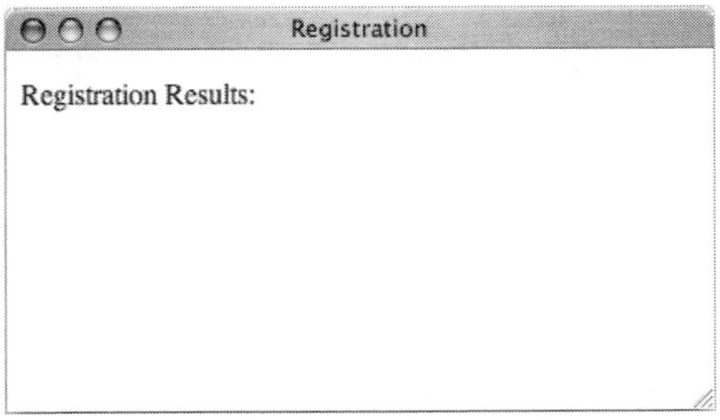

Figure 6.5 ...results in just this.

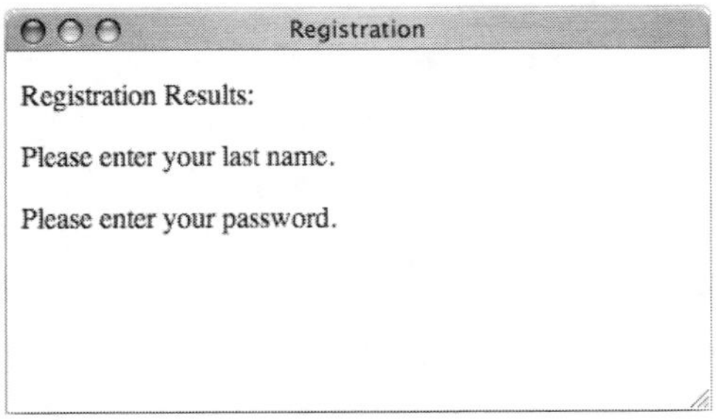

Figure 6.6 If you omit the first name, last name, email address, or password form input, you'll see messages like these.

6. Repeat the validation for the last name, email address, and password:

```
if (empty ($last_name)) {
   print '<p>Please enter your last
   → name.</p>';
}
if (empty ($email)) {
   print '<p>Please enter your email
   → address.</p>';
}
if (empty ($password)) {
   print '<p>Please enter your
   → password.</p>';
}
```

   Each of these is a repeat of the first name validation, but you switch the variable names and change the `print()` statements accordingly. You don't validate the other form inputs using this syntax for reasons you'll see as the chapter progresses.

7. Complete the PHP section and the HTML page:

```
?>
</body>
</html>
```

8. Save the file as `handle_reg.php`, upload it to your Web server (in the same directory as `register.html`), and test both in your Web browser (**Figures 6.4** and **6.5**).

9. Resubmit the form in different states of completeness to test the results some more (**Figure 6.6**).

continues on next page

✔ Tips

- If the *statement* area of your conditional is only one line long, you technically don't need the curly braces. In that case, you can place the whole conditional on one line, like so:

  ```
  if (condition) statement;
  ```

  You may run across code in this format. However, it's best to always use the multiline format (as demonstrated in the syntax introduction) to improve consistency and minimize errors.

- When you use functions within your conditionals, as you use `empty()` here, it's easy to forget a closing parenthesis and see a parse error. Be extra careful with your syntax when you're coding any control structure.

- One use of the `isset()` function is to avoid referring to a variable unless it exists. If PHP is set to report notices (see "Error Reporting" in Chapter 3), then, for example, using `$var` if it has not been defined will cause an error. You can avoid this by coding

  ```
  if (isset ($var)) {
     // Do whatever with $var.
  }
  ```

Script 6.3 By adding `if-else` conditionals, you can validate the date of birth and create a new variable in the process.

```
<!DOCTYPE html PUBLIC "-//W3C//DTD XHTML 1.0 Transitional//EN"
        "http://www.w3.org/TR/xhtml1/DTD/xhtml1-transitional.dtd">
<html xmlns="http://www.w3.org/1999/xhtml">
<head>
    <meta http-equiv="content-type" content="text/html; charset=iso-8859-1" />
    <title>Registration</title>
</head>
<body>
<?php // Script 6.3 - handle_reg.php - second version after Script 6.2

// Address error handling.
ini_set ('display_errors', 1);
error_reporting (E_ALL & ~E_NOTICE);

// In case register_globals is disabled.
$first_name = $_POST['first_name'];
$last_name = $_POST['last_name'];
$email = $_POST['email'];
$password = $_POST['password'];
$confirm = $_POST['confirm'];
$month = $_POST['month'];
$day = $_POST['day'];
$year = $_POST['year'];
$color = $_POST['color'];

print '<p>Registration Results:</p>';

// Validate the first name.
if (empty ($first_name)) {
    print '<p>Please enter your first name.</p>';
}

// Validate the last name.
if (empty ($last_name)) {
    print '<p>Please enter your last name.</p>';
}

```

(script continues on next page)

Using else

The next logical formation after an `if` conditional is the `if-else` (sometimes called the `if-then-else`) conditional. It allows you to establish a condition that indicates when one statement would be executed and then execute other statement(s) if that condition isn't met:

```
if (condition) {
    statement(s);
} else {
    other_statement(s);
}
```

The important thing to remember when using this construct is that unless the condition is explicitly met, the `else` statement will be executed. In other words, the statements after the `else` constitute the default action, whereas the statements after the `if` condition are the exception to the rule.

You can now rewrite the `handle_reg.php` page incorporating `if-else` conditionals.

To use else:

1. Open `handle_reg.php` in your text editor (Script 6.2).
2. After the existing conditionals, validate the month value (**Script 6.3**):

```
if (is_numeric ($month)) {
    $birthdate = $month . '-';
} else {
    print '<p>Please select the month you were born.</p>';
}
```

continues on next page

Because the `$month` variable should be a number, you can use the `is_numeric()` function to check its value, rather then `empty()`.

If `$month` has a numeric value (meaning that the conditional is TRUE), then a `$birthdate` variable is created, beginning with the `$month` value. Otherwise an error message is printed.

3. Repeat this structure to validate the day and year variables:

```
if (is_numeric ($day)) {
   $birthdate .= $day . '-';
} else {
   print '<p>Please select the day
   → you were born.</p>';
}
if (is_numeric ($year)) {
   $birthdate .= $year;
} else {
   print '<p>Please enter the year
   → you were born as four digits.
   → </p>';
}
```

The `$day` validation is identical to the `$month` validation. You also check whether `$year` has a numeric value using the `is_numeric()` function, even though its value comes from a text box and not a drop-down menu. If the user changed the default year value (*YYYY*, see Figure 6.2) to a number, this conditional is TRUE, and the `$year` is added to the `$birthdate` variable. Otherwise, an error message is printed.

Script 6.3 *continued*

```
// Validate the email address.
if (empty ($email)) {
    print '<p>Please enter your email address.</p>';
}

// Validate the password.
if (empty ($password)) {
    print '<p>Please enter your password.</p>';
}

// Validate the month.
if (is_numeric ($month)) {
    $birthdate = $month . '-';
} else {
    print '<p>Please select the month you were born.</p>';
}

// Validate the day.
if (is_numeric ($day)) {
    $birthdate .= $day . '-';
} else {
    print '<p>Please select the day you were born.</p>';
}

// Validate the year.
if (is_numeric ($year)) {
    $birthdate .= $year;
} else {
    print '<p>Please enter the year you were born as four digits.</p>';
}

print "You entered your birthday as $birthdate";

?>
</body>
</html>
```

Figure 6.7 Test the form again, omitting some of the date-of-birth information.

Registration

Registration Results:

Please select the month you were born.

Please select the day you were born.

Please enter the year you were born as four digits.

You entered your birthday as

Figure 6.8 If you skip any of the date-of-birth fields, error messages are printed.

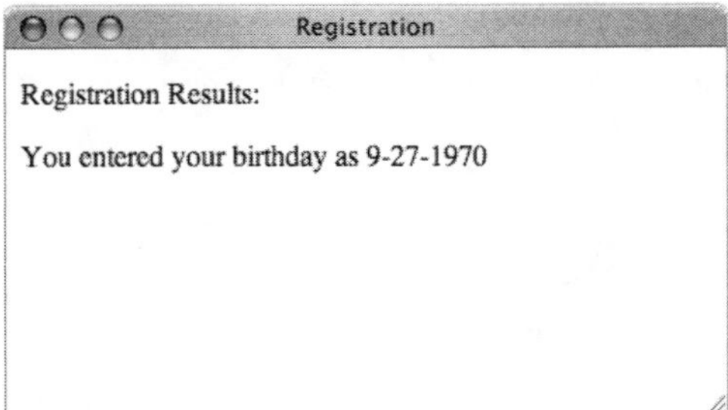

Figure 6.9 If the user completes the date-of-birth section properly, his or her birth date is printed in a new format.

4. Print out the value of the `$birthdate` variable at the end of the page:

```
print "You entered your birthday as
→ $birthdate";
```

5. Save your script, upload it to your server, and test in your Web browser (**Figures 6.7**, **6.8**, and **6.9**).

✔ Tips

- At this time, you could also add `else` clauses to the other conditionals. For example:

```
if (empty ($first_name)) {
   print '<p>Please enter your first
   → name.</p>';
} else {
   print '<p>You entered your first
   → name.</p>';
}
```

- Another good validation function is `checkdate()`, which you can use to confirm that a date exists (or existed in the past).

More Operators

Previous chapters discussed most of PHP's operators along with the variable types that use them. These operators include arithmetic for numbers: addition (+), subtraction (-), multiplication (*), and division (/), along with the incremental (++) and decremental (--) shortcuts for increasing or decreasing the value of a number by 1. Then there is the assignment operator (=), which is used to set the value of a variable, regardless of type. You've also learned about concatenation (.), which appends one string to another.

These operators are all handy for establishing the value of a variable, but they're of less use when it comes to conditionals. Now you'll explore comparison and logical operators that widen your conditional possibilities. **Table 6.1** lists a fuller assortment of PHP's operators.

PHP's Operators

<table>
<tr><th>Operator</th><th>Usage</th><th>Type</th></tr>
<tr><td>+</td><td>Addition</td><td>Arithmetic</td></tr>
<tr><td>-</td><td>Subtraction</td><td>Arithmetic</td></tr>
<tr><td>*</td><td>Multiplication</td><td>Arithmetic</td></tr>
<tr><td>/</td><td>Division</td><td>Arithmetic</td></tr>
<tr><td>%</td><td>Modulus (remainder of a division)</td><td>Arithmetic</td></tr>
<tr><td>++</td><td>Incrementation</td><td>Arithmetic</td></tr>
<tr><td>--</td><td>Decrementation</td><td>Arithmetic</td></tr>
<tr><td>=</td><td>Assigns a value to a variable</td><td>Assignment</td></tr>
<tr><td>==</td><td>Equality</td><td>Comparison</td></tr>
<tr><td>!=</td><td>Inequality</td><td>Comparison</td></tr>
<tr><td><</td><td>Less than</td><td>Comparison</td></tr>
<tr><td>></td><td>Greater than</td><td>Comparison</td></tr>
<tr><td><=</td><td>Less than or equal to</td><td>Comparison</td></tr>
<tr><td>>=</td><td>Greater than or equal to</td><td>Comparison</td></tr>
<tr><td>!</td><td>Negation</td><td>Logical</td></tr>
<tr><td>AND</td><td>And</td><td>Logical</td></tr>
<tr><td>&&</td><td>And</td><td>Logical</td></tr>
<tr><td>OR</td><td>Or</td><td>Logical</td></tr>
<tr><td>||</td><td>Or</td><td>Logical</td></tr>
<tr><td>XOR</td><td>Or not</td><td>Logical</td></tr>
<tr><td>.</td><td>Concatenation</td><td>String</td></tr>
<tr><td>.=</td><td>Concatenates to the value of a variable</td><td>Combined concatenation & assignment</td></tr>
<tr><td>+=</td><td>Adds to the value of a variable</td><td>Combined arithmetic & assignment</td></tr>
<tr><td>-=</td><td>Subtracts from the value of a variable</td><td>Combined arithmetic & assignment</td></tr>
</table>

Table 6.1 A listing of PHP's most commonly used operators.

Comparison

When the assignment operator (the equals sign) was first introduced in Chapter 2, "Variables," you learned that its meaning isn't exactly what you'd conventionally think it to be. The line `$variable = 5;` doesn't state that `$variable` *is equal to* 5 but that it *is assigned the value of* 5. This is an important distinction.

When you're writing conditionals, you'll often want to see if a variable is equal to a specific value (to match usernames or passwords, perhaps), which you can't do with the equals sign alone (because it's used for assigning a value, not equating values). For this purpose, you have the equals operator (==), which is created by using two equals signs together:

```
$variable = 5;
if ($variable == 5) { ...
```

Script 6.4 This version of the form-handling script uses comparison operators to validate the password and year values.

```
<!DOCTYPE html PUBLIC "-//W3C//DTD XHTML 1.0 Transitional//EN"
        "http://www.w3.org/TR/xhtml1/DTD/xhtml1-transitional.dtd">
<html xmlns="http://www.w3.org/1999/xhtml">
<head>
    <meta http-equiv="content-type" content="text/html; charset=iso-8859-1" />
    <title>Registration</title>
</head>
<body>
<?php // Script 6.4 - handle_reg.php - third version after Scripts 6.2 and 6.3

// Address error handling.
ini_set ('display_errors', 1);
error_reporting (E_ALL & ~E_NOTICE);

// In case register_globals is disabled.
$first_name = $_POST['first_name'];
$last_name = $_POST['last_name'];
$email = $_POST['email'];
$password = $_POST['password'];
$confirm = $_POST['confirm'];
$month = $_POST['month'];
$day = $_POST['day'];
$year = $_POST['year'];
$color = $_POST['color'];

print '<p>Registration Results:</p>';

// Validate the first name.
if (empty ($first_name)) {
    print '<p>Please enter your first name.</p>';
}

// Validate the last name.
if (empty ($last_name)) {
    print '<p>Please enter your last name.</p>';
}

// Validate the email address.
if (empty ($email)) {
    print '<p>Please enter your email address.</p>';
}
```

(script continues on next page)

Using these two lines of code together first establishes the value of `$variable` as 5, and then makes a TRUE conditional when you see whether `$variable` is equal to 5. This example demonstrates the significant difference one more equals sign makes in your PHP code and why you must distinguish carefully between the assignment and comparison operators.

The next comparison operator (not equal to) is represented by an exclamation mark coupled with an equals sign (`!=`). The remaining comparison operators are identical to their mathematical counterparts: less than (<), greater than (>), less than or equal to (<=), and greater than or equal to (>=).

As a demonstration of comparison operators, you'll make sure that the user's birth year is before 2004 and that the confirmed password matches the original password.

To use comparison operators:

1. Open `handle_reg.php` (Script 6.3) in your text editor.
2. After the password validation, check that the two passwords match (**Script 6.4**):

   ```
   if ( $password != $confirm ) {
      print '<p>Your confirmed password
      → does not match the original
      → password.</p>';
   }
   ```

   To compare these two string values, you use the not-equal-to operator. You could use one of the string comparison functions (see Chapter 5, "Using Strings"), but this will suffice.

continues on next page

3. After the year validation, check that the year is before 2004:

```
if ($year >= 2004) {
   print '<p>Either you entered your
   → birth year wrong or you come
   → from the future!</p>';
}
```

   If the user entered their year of birth as 2004 or later, it's presumably a mistake.

4. Save your script, upload it to the server, and test in your Web browser again (**Figures 6.10** and **6.11**).

Script 6.4 *continued*

```

// Validate the password.
if (empty ($password)) {
    print '<p>Please enter your
    password.</p>';
}

// Check the two passwords for equality.
if ( $password != $confirm ) {
    print '<p>Your confirmed password does
    not match the original password.</p>';
}

```

(script continues on next page)

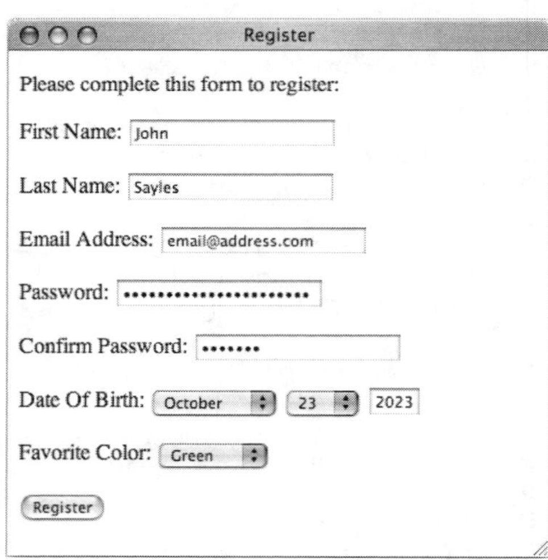

Figure 6.10 Run the form once again...

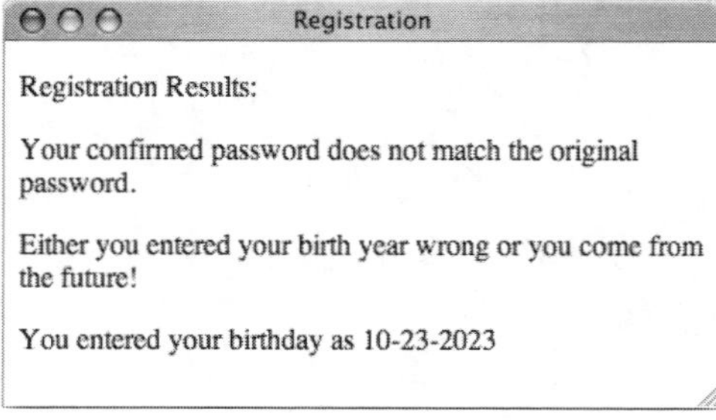

Figure 6.11 ...with two new validation checks in place.

Script 6.4 *continued*

```
// Validate the month.
if (is_numeric ($month)) {
    $birthdate = $month . '-';
} else {
    print '<p>Please select the month you
    were born.</p>';
}

// Validate the day.
if (is_numeric ($day)) {
    $birthdate .= $day . '-';
} else {
    print '<p>Please select the day you
    were born.</p>';
}

// Validate the year.
if (is_numeric ($year)) {
    $birthdate .= $year;
} else {
    print '<p>Please enter the year you
    were born as four digits.</p>';
}

// Check that they were born before 2004.
if ($year >= 2004) {
    print '<p>Either you entered your
    birth year wrong or you come from the
    future!</p>';
}

print "You entered your birthday as
$birthdate";

?>
</body>
</html>
```

✔ Tips

- Before you compare two string values that come from a form (like the password and confirmed password), it's a good idea to apply the `trim()` function to both, to get rid of any errant spaces. You don't do so here, so as not to overcomplicate matters, but this habit is recommended.
- Another method of checking that a text input type has been filled out (as opposed to using the `empty()` function) is this:

  ```
  if (strlen ($var) > 0 ) {
     // $var is okay.
  }
  ```

- In an `if` conditional, if you make the mistake of writing `$variable = 5` as opposed to `$variable == 5`, you'll see that the corresponding conditional statements are always executed. This happens because although the condition `$variable == 5` may or may not be TRUE, the condition `$variable = 5` is always TRUE.
- Some programmers advocate reverse conditionals—for example, writing `5 == $variable`. Although it looks awkward, if you inadvertently code `5 = $variable`, an error results (allowing you to catch the mistake more easily) because the number 5 can't be assigned another value.

Logical

Writing conditions in PHP comes down to identifying TRUE or FALSE situations. This can be accomplished using functions or comparative operators, as you've already seen. Logical operators—the final operator type discussed in this chapter—help you create more elaborate or apparent constructs.

In PHP, one example of a TRUE condition is simply a variable name that has a value that isn't zero or an empty string, such as

```
$variable = 5;
if ($variable) { ...
```

A condition is also TRUE if it makes logical sense:

```
if (5 >= 3) { ...
```

Your condition will be FALSE if it refers to a variable and that variable has no value (or a value of 0 or an empty string), or if you've created an illogical construct. The following conditional is always false:

```
if (5 <= 3) { ...
```

In PHP, the exclamation mark (`!`) is the `NOT` operator. You can use it to invert the TRUE/FALSE status of a statement. For example:

```
$var = 'value';
if ($var) {... // TRUE
if (! $var) {... // FALSE
isset ($var); // TRUE
! isset ($var); // FALSE
! empty ($var); // TRUE
```

Nesting Conditionals

Besides using logical operators to create more complex conditionals, you can use *nesting* for this purpose (the process of placing one conditional inside of another). The key to doing so is to place the interior conditional as the ***statement(s)*** section of the exterior conditional. For example:

```
if (condition1) {

   if (condition2) {
      2statement(s);
   } else { // condition2 else
      2other_statement(s);
   } // End of 2

} else{ // condition1 else

   1other_statement(s);

} // End of 1
```

As you can see from this example, you can cut down on the complexity of these structures by using extensive indentations and comments. As long as every conditional is syntactically correct, there are no rules as to how many levels of nesting you can have, whether you use an `else` clause, or even whether a subconditional is part of the `if` or the `else` section of the main conditional.

To go beyond simple one-part conditions, PHP supports five more types of logical operators: two versions of *and* (AND and &&), two versions of *or* (OR and ||—a character called the *pipe*, put together twice), and *or not* (XOR). When you have two options for one operator (as with *and* and *or*), they differ only in precedence. For almost every situation, you can use either version of *and* or either version of *or* interchangeably.

Using parentheses and logical operators, you can create even more complex `if` conditionals. For an AND conditional, every conjoined part must be TRUE in order for the whole conditional to be TRUE. With OR, at least one subsection must be TRUE to render the whole condition TRUE. These conditionals are TRUE:

```
if ( (5 <= 3) OR (5 >= 3) ) { ...
if ( (5 > 3) AND (5 < 10) ) { ...
```

These conditionals are FALSE:

```
if ( (5 != 5) AND (5 > 3) ) { ...
if ( (5 != 5) OR (5 < 3) ) { ...
```

As you construct your conditionals, remember two important things: first, in order for the statements that are the result of a conditional to be executed, the conditional must have a TRUE value; second, by using parentheses, you can ignore rules of precedence and ensure that your operators are addressed in the order of your choosing.

To demonstrate logical operators, you'll add two more conditionals to the `handle_reg.php` page. You'll also nest one of the `$year` conditionals inside another conditional (see the sidebar "Nesting Conditionals" for more).

To use logical operators:

1. Open `handle_reg.php` (Script 6.4) in your text editor.
2. Delete the existing `$year` validations (**Script 6.5**).

   You'll entirely rewrite these conditionals as one nested conditional, so it's best to get rid of the old version entirely.
3. Check that the `$year` variable is a four-digit number:

   ```
   if ( is_numeric ($year) AND strlen
   → ($year) == 4 ) {
   ```

   This conditional has two parts. The first you've already seen—it tests for a valid numeric value. The second part gets the length of the `$year` variable (using the `strlen()` function) and checks if this value is equal to 4. Because of the `AND`, this conditional is TRUE only if both conditions are met.

Script 6.5 Change the handling PHP script so that the year validation routine uses both multiple and nested conditions. The color conditional also uses a logical operator.

```
<!DOCTYPE html PUBLIC "-//W3C//DTD XHTML 1.0 Transitional//EN"
        "http://www.w3.org/TR/xhtml1/DTD/xhtml1-transitional.dtd">
<html xmlns="http://www.w3.org/1999/xhtml">
<head>
    <meta http-equiv="content-type" content="text/html; charset=iso-8859-1" />
    <title>Registration</title>
</head>
<body>
<?php // Script 6.5 - handle_reg.php - fourth version after Scripts 6.2, 6.3, and 6.4

// Address error handling.
ini_set ('display_errors', 1);
error_reporting (E_ALL & ~E_NOTICE);

// In case register_globals is disabled.
$first_name = $_POST['first_name'];
$last_name = $_POST['last_name'];
$email = $_POST['email'];
$password = $_POST['password'];
$confirm = $_POST['confirm'];
$month = $_POST['month'];
$day = $_POST['day'];
$year = $_POST['year'];
$color = $_POST['color'];

print '<p>Registration Results:</p>';

// Validate the first name.
if (empty ($first_name)) {
    print '<p>Please enter your first name.</p>';
}

// Validate the last name.
if (empty ($last_name)) {
    print '<p>Please enter your last name.</p>';
}

```

(script continues on next page)

Script 6.5 *continued*

```
// Validate the email address.
if (empty ($email)) {
    print '<p>Please enter your email address.</p>';
}

// Validate the password.
if (empty ($password)) {
    print '<p>Please enter your password.</p>';
}

// Check the two passwords for equality.
if ($password != $confirm) {
    print '<p>Your confirmed password does not match the original password.</p>';
}

// Validate the month.
if (is_numeric ($month)) {
    $birthdate = $month . '-';
} else {
    print '<p>Please select the month you were born.</p>';
}

// Validate the day.
if (is_numeric ($day)) {
    $birthdate .= $day . '-';
} else {
    print '<p>Please select the day you were born.</p>';
}

// Validate the year.
if ( is_numeric ($year) AND strlen ($year) == 4 ) {

    // Check that they were born before 2004.
    if ($year >= 2004) {
        print '<p>Either you entered your birth year wrong or you come from the future!</p>';
    } else {
        $birthdate .= $year;
    } // End of 2nd conditional.

```

(script continues on next page)

4. Create a subconditional to verify the `$year` value isn't after 2004:

```
if ($year >= 2004) {
   print '<p>Either you entered your birth year wrong or you come from the future!</p>';
} else {
   $birthdate .= $year;
}
```

This `if-else` conditional is the result of the main conditional being TRUE. It checks whether the `$year` variable is greater than or equal to 2004. If it is, an error message is printed. Otherwise, the `$year` value is appended to the `$birthdate` variable as before.

5. Complete the main `$year` conditional:

```
} else {
   print '<p>Please enter the year you were born as four digits.</p>';
}
```

This `else` section completes the `$year` conditional begun in step 3. If at least one of the conditions set forth there isn't TRUE, this message is printed.

continues on next page

6. Validate that a color was selected:

```
if (!$color) {
   print '<p>Please select your
   → favorite color.</p>';
}
```

The `$color` variable comes from the Favorite Color drop-down menu, whose first option—Pick One—has a value of `""`. If the user never changed this value, then the `$color` variable has the value of an empty string, which means the condition `!$color` is TRUE. In such a case, a message is printed.

7. Those are the only changes to the script, so you can now save it again, upload it to the server, and test in your Web browser (**Figures 6.12** and **6.13**).

8. If desired, change your year value to be in the future and submit the form again (**Figure 6.14**).

Script 6.5 *continued*

```
} else { // Else for 1st conditional.

    print '<p>Please enter the year you were born as four digits.</p>';

} // End of 1st conditional.

// Validate the color.
if (!$color) {
    print '<p>Please select your favorite color.</p>';
}

print "You entered your birthday as $birthdate";

?>
</body>
</html>
```

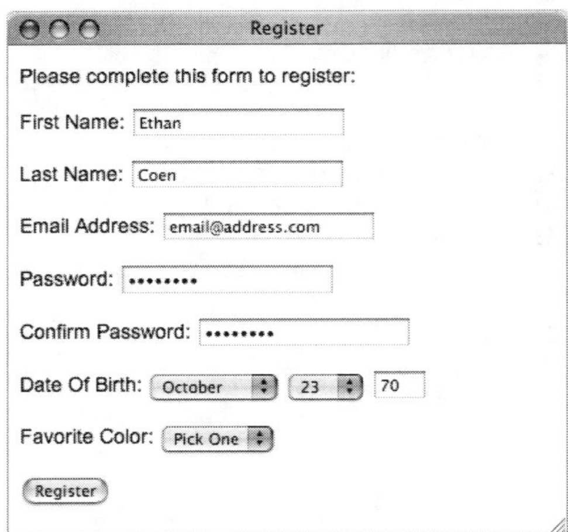

Figure 6.12 The PHP script now catches if a color isn't selected or if the year isn't a four-digit number, as will be the case with this form submission.

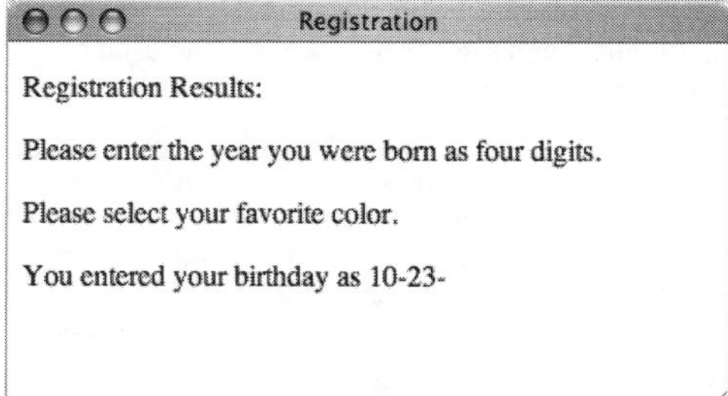

Figure 6.13 Error messages are printed if fields are incorrectly filled out.

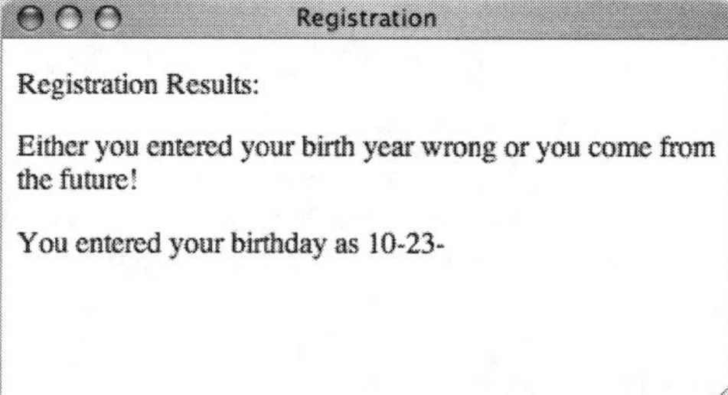

Figure 6.14 The year validation still checks that the date is before 2004.

✔ Tips

- It's another common programming convention—which is maintained in this book—to write the terms TRUE and FALSE in all capitals. This isn't a requirement of PHP, though. For example, the following conditional is TRUE:

  ```
  if (true) {...
  ```

- It's very easy in long, complicated conditionals to forget an opening or closing parenthesis or curly brace, which will produce either error messages or unexpected results. Find a system (like spacing out your conditionals and using comments) to help clarify your code. Another good technique is to create the entire conditional's structure first, and then go back to add the details.

- If you have problems getting your `if-else` statements to execute, print out the values of your variables to help debug the problem. A conditional may never be TRUE because a variable doesn't have the value you think it does.

Using elseif

Similar to the `if-else` conditional is `if-elseif` (or `if-elseif-else`). It acts like a running `if` statement and can be expanded to whatever length you require:

```
if (condition1) {
   statement(s);
} elseif (condition2) {
   other_statement(s);
}
```

Here's another example:

```
if (condition1) {
   statement(s);
} elseif (condition2) {
   other_statement(s);
} else {
   other_other_statement(s);
}
```

You must always make the `else` the last part of a conditional because it's executed unless one of the conditions to that point has been met (again, it represents the default behavior). You can, however, continue to use `elseif`s as many times as you want as part of one `if` conditional.

As an example, you'll create an elaborate conditional to find the registering user's astrological sign.

Script 6.6 This elaborate (and lengthy) nested conditional finds a user's horoscope sign based on the submitted birth month and day.

Script

```
<!DOCTYPE html PUBLIC "-//W3C//DTD XHTML 1.0 Transitional//EN"
        "http://www.w3.org/TR/xhtml1/DTD/xhtml1-transitional.dtd">
<html xmlns="http://www.w3.org/1999/xhtml">
<head>
    <meta http-equiv="content-type" content="text/html; charset=iso-8859-1" />
    <title>Registration</title>
</head>
<body>
<?php // Script 6.6 - handle_reg.php - fifth version after Scripts 6.2, 6.3, 6.4 and 6.5

// Address error handling.
ini_set ('display_errors', 1);
error_reporting (E_ALL & ~E_NOTICE);

// In case register_globals is disabled.
$first_name = $_POST['first_name'];
$last_name = $_POST['last_name'];
$email = $_POST['email'];
$password = $_POST['password'];
$confirm = $_POST['confirm'];
$month = $_POST['month'];
$day = $_POST['day'];
$year = $_POST['year'];
$color = $_POST['color'];

print '<p>Registration Results:</p>';

// Validate the first name.
if (empty ($first_name)) {
    print '<p>Please enter your first name.</p>';
}

// Validate the last name.
if (empty ($last_name)) {
    print '<p>Please enter your last name.</p>';
}

```

(script continues on next page)

Script 6.6 *continued*

```
// Validate the email address.
if (empty ($email)) {
    print '<p>Please enter your email address.</p>';
}

// Validate the password.
if (empty ($password)) {
    print '<p>Please enter your password.</p>';
}

// Check the two passwords for equality.
if ($password != $confirm) {
    print '<p>Your confirmed password does not match the original password.</p>';
}

// Validate the month.
if (is_numeric ($month)) {
    $birthdate = $month . '-';
} else {
    print '<p>Please select the month you were born.</p>';
}

// Validate the day.
if (is_numeric ($day)) {
    $birthdate .= $day . '-';
} else {
    print '<p>Please select the day you were born.</p>';
}

// Validate the year.
if ( is_numeric ($year) AND strlen ($year) == 4 ) {

    // Check that they were born before 2004.
    if ($year >= 2004) {
        print '<p>Either you entered your birth year wrong or you come from the future!</p>';
    } else {
        $birthdate .= $year;
    } // End of 2nd conditional.
```

(script continues on next page)

To use elseif:

1. Open `handle_reg.php` (Script 6.5) in your text editor.

2. After all the existing PHP code but before the closing PHP tag, begin a new conditional (**Script 6.6**):

   ```
   if ($month == 1) { // January
       if ($day <= 19) {
           $sign = 'Capricorn';
       } else {
           $sign = 'Aquarius';
       }
   ```

   In order to find the user's astrological sign, you need to use a combination of their birth month and day. To begin, you create one long `if-elseif` conditional to determine the month. Then, within each month, you check whether the `$day` variable is before or after a target date. Based on this second conditional, the proper sign name is assigned to the `$sign` variable.

3. Repeat the process for the second month:

   ```
   } elseif ($month == 2) {
       if ($day <= 18) {
           $sign = 'Aquarius';
       } else {
           $sign = 'Pisces';
       }
   ```

   The `elseif` continues the main `$month` conditional begun in step 2. The subconditional is a replication of the subconditional in step 2, using new sign and day values.

continues on next page

4. Complete the conditional for the rest of the year:

```
} elseif ($month == 3) {
   if ($day <= 20) {
      $sign = 'Pisces';
   } else {
      $sign = 'Aries';
   }
} elseif ($month == 4) {
   if ($day <= 19) {
      $sign = 'Aries';
   } else {
      $sign = 'Taurus';
   }
} elseif ($month == 5) {
   if ($day <= 20) {
      $sign = 'Taurus';
   } else {
      $sign = 'Gemini';
   }
} elseif ($month == 6) {
   if ($day <= 19) {
      $sign = 'Gemini';
   } else {
      $sign = 'Cancer';
   }
} elseif ($month == 7) {
   if ($day <= 22) {
      $sign = 'Cancer';
   } else {
      $sign = 'Leo';
   }
} elseif ($month == 8) {
   if ($day <= 22) {
      $sign = 'Leo';
   } else {
      $sign = 'Virgo';
   }
```


Script 6.6 *continued*

```
Script

} else { // Else for 1st conditional.

    print '<p>Please enter the year you
    were born as four digits.</p>';

} // End of 1st conditional.

// Validate the color.
if (!$color) {
    print '<p>Please select your favorite
    color.</p>';
}

print "You entered your birthday as
$birthdate";

// Get the horoscope sign.
if ($month == 1) { // January
    if ($day <= 19) {
        $sign = 'Capricorn';
    } else {
        $sign = 'Aquarius';
    }
} elseif ($month == 2) { // February
    if ($day <= 18) {
        $sign = 'Aquarius';
    } else {
        $sign = 'Pisces';
    }
} elseif ($month == 3) {
    if ($day <= 20) {
        $sign = 'Pisces';
    } else {
        $sign = 'Aries';
    }
} elseif ($month == 4) {
    if ($day <= 19) {
        $sign = 'Aries';
    } else {
        $sign = 'Taurus';
    }
} elseif ($month == 5) {
    if ($day <= 20) {
        $sign = 'Taurus';
    } else {
        $sign = 'Gemini';
    }
```

(script continues on next page)

Script 6.6 *continued*

```
} elseif ($month == 6) {
    if ($day <= 19) {
        $sign = 'Gemini';
    } else {
        $sign = 'Cancer';
    }
} elseif ($month == 7) {
    if ($day <= 22) {
        $sign = 'Cancer';
    } else {
        $sign = 'Leo';
    }
} elseif ($month == 8) {
    if ($day <= 22) {
        $sign = 'Leo';
    } else {
        $sign = 'Virgo';
    }
} elseif ($month == 9) {
    if ($day <= 22) {
        $sign = 'Virgo';
    } else {
        $sign = 'Libra';
    }
} elseif ($month == 10) {
    if ($day <= 22) {
        $sign = 'Libra';
    } else {
        $sign = 'Scorpio';
    }
} elseif ($month == 11) {
    if ($day <= 21) {
        $sign = 'Scorpio';
    } else {
        $sign = 'Sagittarius';
    }
} elseif ($month == 12) {
    if ($day <= 21) {
        $sign = 'Sagittarius';
    } else {
        $sign = 'Capricorn';
    }
}

print "<p>You are a(n) $sign.</p>";

?>
</body>
</html>
```

```
} elseif ($month == 9) {
   if ($day <= 22) {
      $sign = 'Virgo';
   } else {
      $sign = 'Libra';
   }
} elseif ($month == 10) {
   if ($day <= 22) {
      $sign = 'Libra';
   } else {
      $sign = 'Scorpio';
   }
} elseif ($month == 11) {
   if ($day <= 21) {
      $sign = 'Scorpio';
   } else {
      $sign = 'Sagittarius';
   }
} elseif ($month == 12) {
   if ($day <= 21) {
      $sign = 'Sagittarius';
   } else {
      $sign = 'Capricorn';
   }
}
```

Once you understand the main concept, it's just a matter of repeating the `elseifs` and subconditionals for each month.

continues on next page

5. Print out the user's sign:

```
print "<p>You are a(n) $sign.</p>";
```

6. Save the script, upload it to the server, and test in your Web browser using different birth date values (**Figures 6.15** and **6.16**).

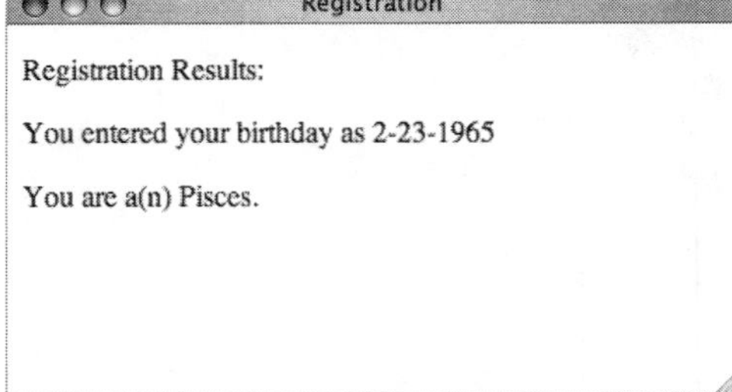

Figure 6.15 The script now determines the user's horoscope sign and prints out this value.

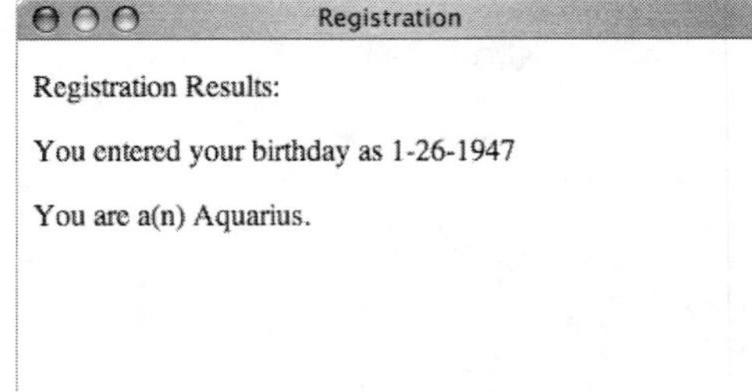

Figure 6.16 Each birthday returns its appropriate sign.

✔ Tips

- You could improve on this new conditional by changing each `$day else` to `elseif`. For example:

  ```
  if ($day <= 19) {
     $sign = 'Capricorn';
  } elseif ($day > 19) {
     $sign = 'Aquarius';
  }
  ```

  This slightly altered syntax compensates if the user didn't select a day value. As it stands, if the user selected a month but not a day, the script assumes that the day falls into the second part of the month.

- PHP also allows you to write `elseif` as two words, if you prefer:

  ```
  if (condition1) {
     statement(s);
  } else if (condition2) {
     2statement(s);
  }
  ```

The Switch Conditional

Once you get to the point where you have very elaborate `if-elseif-else` conditionals (as in the last example), you may find that you can save time and clarify your programming by using a `switch` conditional instead. The `switch` conditional takes only one possible condition, which is the value of a variable:

```
switch ($variable) {
   case "value1":
      1statement(s);
      break;
   case "value2":
      2statement(s);
      break;
   default:
      3statement(s);
      break;
}
```

It's critical that you comprehend how a `switch` conditional works in order to use it properly. Starting at the beginning, once PHP finds the case that matches the value of the conditional variable, it continues to execute those statements until it either comes to the end of the `switch` conditional (the closing curly brace) or hits a `break` statement, at which point it exits the `switch` construct. Thus, it's imperative that you close every case (even the default case, for consistency's sake) with a `break`.

This previous `switch` conditional is like a rewrite of this:

```
if ($variable == 'value1') {
   1statement(s);
} elseif ($variable == 'value2') {
   2statement(s)2;
} else {
   3statement(s);
}
```

Because the switch conditional uses the value of *$variable* as its condition, it first checks to see if *$variable* is equal to *value1* and, if so, executes *1statement(s)*. If not, it checks to see if *$variable* is equal to *value2* and, if so, executes *2statement(s)*. If neither condition is met, the default action of the switch condition is to execute *3statement(s)*.

With this in mind, let's rewrite the horoscope conditional as a switch.

To use a switch conditional:

1. Open handle_reg.php (Script 6.6) in your text editor.

2. Delete the extended horoscope conditional (**Script 6.7**).

3. Begin the switch:

   ```
   switch ($month) {
   ```

   As mentioned earlier, a switch conditional takes only one condition: a variable's name. In this case, it's $month.

Script 6.7 Switch conditionals can simplify complicated if-elseif conditionals.

```
<!DOCTYPE html PUBLIC "-//W3C//DTD XHTML 1.0 Transitional//EN"
        "http://www.w3.org/TR/xhtml1/DTD/xhtml1-transitional.dtd">
<html xmlns="http://www.w3.org/1999/xhtml">
<head>
    <meta http-equiv="content-type" content="text/html; charset=iso-8859-1" />
    <title>Registration</title>
</head>
<body>
<?php // Script 6.7 - handle_reg.php - sixth version after Scripts 6.2, 6.3, 6.4, 6.5 and 6.6

// Address error handling.
ini_set ('display_errors', 1);
error_reporting (E_ALL & ~E_NOTICE);

// In case register_globals is disabled.
$first_name = $_POST['first_name'];
$last_name = $_POST['last_name'];
$email = $_POST['email'];
$password = $_POST['password'];
$confirm = $_POST['confirm'];
$month = $_POST['month'];
$day = $_POST['day'];
$year = $_POST['year'];
$color = $_POST['color'];

print '<p>Registration Results:</p>';

// Validate the first name.
if (empty ($first_name)) {
    print '<p>Please enter your first name.</p>';
}

// Validate the last name.
if (empty ($last_name)) {
    print '<p>Please enter your last name.</p>';
}

// Validate the email address.
if (empty ($email)) {
    print '<p>Please enter your email address.</p>';
}
```

(script continues on next page)

Script 6.7 *continued*

```
// Validate the password.
if (empty ($password)) {
    print '<p>Please enter your password.</p>';
}

// Check the two passwords for equality.
if ($password != $confirm) {
    print '<p>Your confirmed password does not match the original password.</p>';
}

// Validate the month.
if (is_numeric ($month)) {
    $birthdate = $month . '-';
} else {
    print '<p>Please select the month you were born.</p>';
}

// Validate the day.
if (is_numeric ($day)) {
    $birthdate .= $day . '-';
} else {
    print '<p>Please select the day you were born.</p>';
}

// Validate the year.
if ( is_numeric ($year) AND strlen ($year) == 4 ) {

    // Check that they were born before 2004.
    if ($year >= 2004) {
        print '<p>Either you entered your birth year wrong or you come from the future!</p>';
    } else {
        $birthdate .= $year;
    } // End of 2nd conditional.

} else { // Else for 1st conditional.

    print '<p>Please enter the year you were born as four digits.</p>';

} // End of 1st conditional.
```

(script continues on next page)

4. Create the first case:

   ```
   case 1:
      if ($day <= 19) {
         $sign = 'Capricorn';
      } else {
         $sign = 'Aquarius';
      }
      break;
   ```

   The first `case` checks to see if `$month` has a value of 1. Because this is a numeric value (as opposed to a string), it doesn't need to be quoted. If `$month` is equal to 1, then you run through the same conditional on the `$day` value as used previously. Finally, you include a `break` statement to exit the switch.

5. Repeat the process for February:

   ```
   case 2:
      if ($day <= 18) {
         $sign = 'Aquarius';
      } else {
         $sign = 'Pisces';
      }
      break;
   ```

continues on next page

6. Repeat the switch for the remaining months:

```
case 3:
    if ($day <= 20) {
        $sign = 'Pisces';
    } else {
        $sign = 'Aries';
    }
    break;
case 4:
    if ($day <= 19) {
        $sign = 'Aries';
    } else {
        $sign = 'Taurus';
    }
    break;
case 5:
    if ($day <= 20) {
        $sign = 'Taurus';
    } else {
        $sign = 'Gemini';
    }
    break;
case 6:
    if ($day <= 19) {
        $sign = 'Gemini';
    } else {
        $sign = 'Cancer';
    }
    break;
case 7:
    if ($day <= 22) {
        $sign = 'Cancer';
    } else {
        $sign = 'Leo';
    }
    break;
case 8:
    if ($day <= 22) {
```

Script 6.7 *continued*

```
// Validate the color.
if (!$color) {
    print '<p>Please select your favorite color.</p>';
}

print "You entered your birthday as $birthdate";

// Get the horoscope sign.
switch ($month) {
    case 1:
        if ($day <= 19) {
            $sign = 'Capricorn';
        } else {
            $sign = 'Aquarius';
        }
        break;
    case 2:
        if ($day <= 18) {
            $sign = 'Aquarius';
        } else {
            $sign = 'Pisces';
        }
        break;
    case 3:
        if ($day <= 20) {
            $sign = 'Pisces';
        } else {
            $sign = 'Aries';
        }
        break;
    case 4:
        if ($day <= 19) {
            $sign = 'Aries';
        } else {
            $sign = 'Taurus';
        }
        break;
    case 5:
        if ($day <= 20) {
            $sign = 'Taurus';
        } else {
            $sign = 'Gemini';
        }
        break;
    case 6:
        if ($day <= 19) {
            $sign = 'Gemini';
        } else {
```

(script continues on next page)

Script 6.7 *continued*

Script

```
            $sign = 'Cancer';
        }
        break;
    case 7:
        if ($day <= 22) {
            $sign = 'Cancer';
        } else {
            $sign = 'Leo';
        }
        break;
    case 8:
        if ($day <= 22) {
            $sign = 'Leo';
        } else {
            $sign = 'Virgo';
        }
        break;
    case 9:
        if ($day <= 22) {
            $sign = 'Virgo';
        } else {
            $sign = 'Libra';
        }
        break;
    case 10:
        if ($day <= 22) {
            $sign = 'Libra';
        } else {
            $sign = 'Scorpio';
        }
        break;
    case 11:
        if ($day <= 21) {
            $sign = 'Scorpio';
        } else {
            $sign = 'Sagittarius';
        }
        break;
    case 12:
        if ($day <= 21) {
            $sign = 'Sagittarius';
        } else {
            $sign = 'Capricorn';
        }
        break;
} // End of switch.

print "<p>You are a(n) $sign.</p>";

?>
</body>
</html>
```

```
            $sign = 'Leo';
        } else {
            $sign = 'Virgo';
        }
        break;
    case 9:
        if ($day <= 22) {
            $sign = 'Virgo';
        } else {
            $sign = 'Libra';
        }
        break;
    case 10:
        if ($day <= 22) {
            $sign = 'Libra';
        } else {
            $sign = 'Scorpio';
        }
        break;
    case 11:
        if ($day <= 21) {
            $sign = 'Scorpio';
        } else {
            $sign = 'Sagittarius';
        }
        break;
    case 12:
        if ($day <= 21) {
            $sign = 'Sagittarius';
        } else {
            $sign = 'Capricorn';
        }
        break;
} // End of switch.
```

continues on next page

7. Save the script, upload it to the server, and test in your Web browser (**Figures 6.17** and **6.18**).

✔ Tips

- A default case isn't required in your `switch` conditional (you could set it up so that if the value isn't explicitly met by one of the cases, nothing happens), but if it's used, it must be listed as the last case.
- If you're using a string in your `switch` conditional as the case value, keep in mind that it's case sensitive, meaning that *Value* won't match *value*.

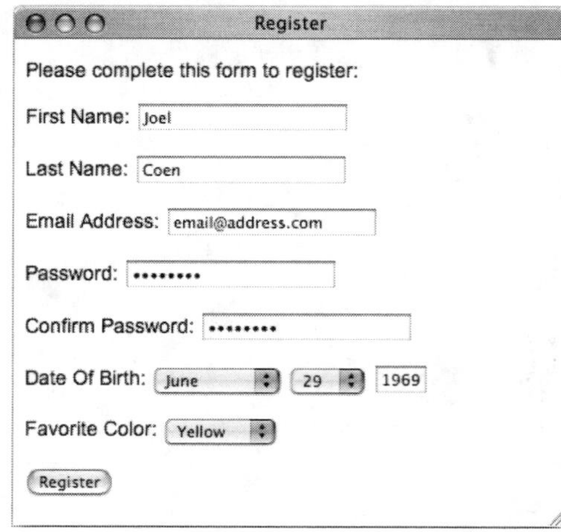

Figure 6.17 The form has remained the same...

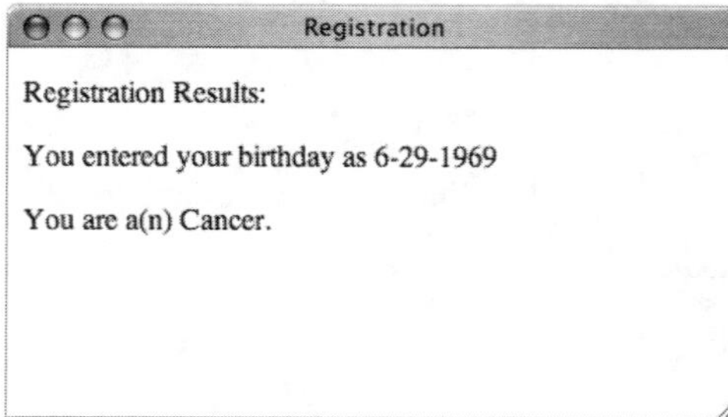

Figure 6.18 ...but the handling script now uses a `switch` conditional that creates the same results.

The for Loop

Loops are the final type of control structure discussed in this chapter. As suggested earlier, you use loops to execute a section of code repeatedly. You may want to create a drop-down menu consisting of the days of the month (print the numbers 1 through 31). Or, you may want to print out each value of an array. For either of these cases, and many more, you can use a loop (The latter example is demonstrated in the next chapter.)

PHP supports three kinds of loops: `for`, `while`, and `foreach`. The `while` loop is similar to `for`, but it's used most frequently when retrieving values from a database. `Foreach` is related to using arrays and is introduced in the next chapter.

The `for` loop is designed to perform specific statements for a determined number of iterations (unlike `while`, which runs until the condition is FALSE—similar, but significantly different, concepts). You normally use a dummy variable in the loop for this purpose:

```
for (initial expression; condition;
→ closing expression) {
   statement(s);
}
```

The initial expression is executed once, the first time the loop is called. Then the condition is used to determine whether to execute the statements. The closing expression is executed each time the condition is found to be TRUE, but only after the statements are executed.

It will make more sense to view a sample for loop as it would be syntactically executed. Here's a simple loop that prints out the numbers 1 through 10:

```
for ($v = 1; $v <= 10; $v++) {
   print "$v ";
}
```

This might make more sense rewritten as follows (assuming PHP had a GOTO method):

```
$v = 1; // initial expression
if ($v <= 10) { // condition
   print "$v "; // statements(s)
}
$var++; // closing expressions
// Go back to condition as long as the
→ condition is TRUE.
```


The while Loop

The second of the three types of loops that exist in PHP—the while loop—is designed to continue working as long as the condition you establish is TRUE. Like the for loop, it checks the value of the condition before each iteration. Once the condition becomes FALSE, the while loop is exited:

```
while (condition) {
   statement(s);
}
```

The main difference between for and the while is that while doesn't include a system for setting initial conditions or for executing closing expressions

You also have the option of using the do...while loop, which guarantees that the statements are executed at least once (this isn't necessarily true of the while loop):

```
do {
statement(s);
} while (condition);
```

Although there is a fair amount of overlap regarding when you can use the two major loop constructs (while and for), you'll discover as you program that sometimes one is more logical than the other. The while loop is frequently used in the retrieval of data from a database (see Chapter 12, "Introduction to Databases").

Script 6.8 You use a PHP `for` loop to dynamically generate the day of the month drop-down menu.

```
<!DOCTYPE html PUBLIC "-//W3C//DTD XHTML 1.0 Transitional//EN"
        "http://www.w3.org/TR/xhtml1/DTD/xhtml1-transitional.dtd">
<html xmlns="http://www.w3.org/1999/xhtml">
<head>
    <meta http-equiv="content-type" content="text/html; charset=iso-8859-1" />
    <title>Register</title>
</head>
<body>

<!-- Script 6.8 - register.php -->

<p>Please complete this form to register:</p>

<form action="handle_reg.php" method="post">

<p>First Name: <input type="text" name="first_name" size="20" /></p>

<p>Last Name: <input type="text" name="last_name" size="20" /></p>

<p>Email Address: <input type="text" name="email" size="20" /></p>

<p>Password: <input type="password" name="password" size="20" /></p>

<p>Confirm Password: <input type="password" name="confirm" size="20" /></p>

<p>Date Of Birth:
<select name="month">
<option value="">Month</option>
<option value="1">January</option>
<option value="2">February</option>
<option value="3">March</option>
<option value="4">April</option>
<option value="5">May</option>
<option value="6">June</option>
<option value="7">July</option>
<option value="8">August</option>
<option value="9">September</option>
<option value="10">October</option>
<option value="11">November</option>
<option value="12">December</option>
```

(script continues on next page)

To practice with the `for` loop, you'll use it to create the day drop-down menu in the HTML form.

To write a for loop:

1. Open `register.html` (Script 6.1) in your text editor.
2. Delete all the lines between `<option value="">Day</option>` and `</select>` (lines 44–74 of the original script), which create the different drop-down options (**Script 6.8**).
3. Create a new PHP section:

   ```
   <?php
   ```

   Because PHP can be embedded within HTML, you'll use it to populate the drop-down menu. You begin with the standard PHP tag.
4. Create a `for` loop to print out 31 days as menu options:

   ```
   for ($d = 1; $d <= 31; $d++) {
     print "<option value=\"$d\">$d
     → </option>\n";
   }
   ```

   The loop begins with creating a dummy variable called `$d`. On the first use of the loop, this variable is set to 1. Then, as long as `$d` is less than or equal to 31, the contents of the loop are executed. These contents are the `print()` statement, which creates code like `<option value="1">1</option>`, followed by a return (created with `\n`). After this statement is executed, the `$d` variable is incremented by one. Then the condition (`$d <= 31`) is checked again, and the process is repeated.

continues on next page

5. Close the PHP section:

   ?>

6. Save the file as `register.php`.

   You must save the file with the `.php` extension now, in order for the PHP code to be executed.

7. Upload the file to your server and test in your Web browser (**Figure 6.19**).

8. If desired, view the HTML source code (**Figure 6.20**).

Script 6.8 *continued*

```
</select>
<select name="day">
<option value="">Day</option>
<?php

// Print out 31 days.
for ($d = 1; $d <= 31; $d++) {
    print "<option value=\"$d\">$d</option>\n";
}

?>
</select>
<input type="text" name="year" value="YYYY" size="4" /></p>

<p>Favorite Color:
<select name="color">
<option value="">Pick One</option>
<option value="red">Red</option>
<option value="yellow">Yellow</option>
<option value="green">Green</option>
<option value="blue">Blue</option>
</select></p>

<p><input type="submit" name="submit" value="Register" /></p>

</form>

</body>
</html>
```


Break, Exit, Die, and Continue

PHP includes many language constructs: tools that aren't functions but still do something in your scripts. The first of these is `break`, which you saw demonstrated in the `switch`. `Break` exits the current structure, be it a switch, an `if-else` conditional, or a loop.

Similar to this is `continue`, which terminates the current iteration of the loop. Any remaining statements within the loop aren't executed, and the loop's condition is checked again to see if the loop should be entered.

`Exit` and `die` are more potent versions of `break` (and they're synonymous). Instead of exiting the current structure, these two language constructs terminate the execution of the PHP script. Therefore, all PHP code after a use of `exit` or `die` is never executed. For that matter, any HTML after these constructs is never sent to the Web browser. You'll see `die` used most frequently in code that accesses files and databases. `Exit` is often used in conjunction with the `header()` function.

Register

Please complete this form to register:

First Name:

Last Name:

Email Address:

Password:

Confirm Password:

Date Of Birth: Month Day YYYY

Favorite Color: Pick One

Register

Figure 6.19 The form looks exactly as it did before, even though PHP created some of the HTML.

Source of http://localhost/register.php

```
<p>Confirm Password: <input type="password" name="confirm" size="20" /></p>

<p>Date Of Birth:
<select name="month">
<option value="">Month</option>
<option value="1">January</option>
<option value="2">February</option>
<option value="3">March</option>
<option value="4">April</option>
<option value="5">May</option>
<option value="6">June</option>
<option value="7">July</option>
<option value="8">August</option>
<option value="9">September</option>
<option value="10">October</option>
<option value="11">November</option>
<option value="12">December</option>
</select>
<select name="day">
<option value="">Day</option>
<option value="1">1</option>
<option value="2">2</option>
<option value="3">3</option>
<option value="4">4</option>
<option value="5">5</option>
<option value="6">6</option>
<option value="7">7</option>
<option value="8">8</option>
<option value="9">9</option>
<option value="10">10</option>
<option value="11">11</option>
<option value="12">12</option>
<option value="13">13</option>
<option value="14">14</option>
<option value="15">15</option>
<option value="16">16</option>
<option value="17">17</option>
<option value="18">18</option>
<option value="19">19</option>
<option value="20">20</option>
<option value="21">21</option>
<option value="22">22</option>
<option value="23">23</option>
<option value="24">24</option>
<option value="25">25</option>
<option value="26">26</option>
<option value="27">27</option>
<option value="28">28</option>
<option value="29">29</option>
<option value="30">30</option>
<option value="31">31</option>
</select>
<input type="text" name="year" value="YYYY" size="4" /></p>

<p>Favorite Color:
```

Figure 6.20 If you view the HTML source code for the form, you'll see the data generated by the `for` loop.

✔ Tips

- Just as you can write the `if` conditional on one line if you have only one statement, you can do the same with the `while` and `for` loops. Again, though, this isn't recommended.
- Loops can be nested inside each other. You can also place conditionals within loops, loops within conditionals, and so forth.
- Pay close attention to your loop's condition so that the loop ends at some point. Otherwise you'll create an infinite loop, and the script will run and run and run.

7

Using Arrays

The next variable type you'll learn about in this book is arrays. Arrays are significantly different than either numbers or strings, and you can't make the most of programming in PHP without comprehending them.

Because of their unique nature, this chapter will cover arrays more deliberately and slowly than the other variable types. The chapter begins with a thorough introduction to the concept, along with the basics of creating and using arrays. Then it covers some of the array-related functions and concludes with multidimensional arrays.

What Is an Array?

Arrays constitute a complicated but very useful notion. Whereas numbers and strings are *scalar* variables (meaning they only ever have a single value), an array is a collection of multiple values assembled into one overriding variable. An array can consist of numbers and/or strings (and/or other arrays), which allows this one variable to hold exponentially more information than a simple string or number can. For example, if you wanted to create a grocery list using strings, your code would look something like this:

```
$item1 = 'apples';
$item2 = 'bananas';
$item3 = 'oranges';
```

For each added item, you'd need to create a new string. This approach is cumbersome, and it makes it difficult to refer back to the entire list or any specific value later in your code. You can greatly simplify matters by placing your entire list into one array (say, `$items`), which contains everything you need (**Table 7.1**).

As an array, your list can be added to, sorted, searched, and so forth. With this context in mind, let's look into the syntax of arrays.

Grocery List Array

Item Number	Item
1	apples
2	bananas
3	oranges

Table 7.1 A sample array of multiple items.

Syntactical rules for arrays

The other variable types you've dealt with—numbers and strings—have a variable name and a corresponding value (for example, `$first_name` could be equal to *Larry*). Arrays also have a name, derived using the same conventions, they:

- Begin with a dollar sign.
- Continue with a letter or underscore.
- Finish with any combination of letters, numbers, or the underscore.

But arrays differ in that they contain what this book will refer to as multiple *elements* (think of each row in Table 7.1 as an element). An element consists of an *index* or *key* (the two words can be used interchangeably) and a value. In Table 7.1, the Item Number is the key, and the Item is the value.

An array's index is used as a reference point to the values. An array can have either numbers or strings as its keys (or both), depending on how you set it up.

Generally, when you use an array it looks the same as any other variable, except that you include a key in square brackets (`[]`) when referring to particular values. So, `$items` refers to the array as a whole, but `$items[1]` points to a specific element in the array (in this example, *apples*).

Superglobals and You

Throughout this book, you've already dealt with some arrays: `$_GET` and `$_POST`. These are called the *superglobals*, and they were introduced in version 4.1 of PHP.

The `$_POST` array receives all the data sent from a form using the POST method. Its indexes are the names of the form inputs, and its values are the values for those form inputs. Therefore, `$_POST['first_name']` refers to the value typed in a form input created by the code
`<input type="text" name="first_name" />`

Similarly, `$_GET` refers to data sent from a form using the GET method or from data otherwise passed in the URL.

As you may have already seen, if `register_globals` is disabled in your PHP configuration, you'll need to use, for example, `$_POST['first_name']` instead of `$first_name`. Not only can using superglobals be a requirement in some setups, but it's also more secure. The security concern has to do with the fact that the variable `$first_name` could refer to similarly named form input, URL input, cookies, or session data. If you use `$_POST['first_name']` instead, you're more precise about where a value comes from.

You'll encounter other superglobals, including `$_COOKIE`, `$_SESSION`, and `$_SERVER`. If you're using a version of PHP prior to 4.1, you'll have to use the slightly different `$HTTP_POST_VARS` instead of `$_POST`, `$HTTP_GET_VARS` instead of `$_GET`, and `$HTTP_COOKIE_VARS` instead of `$_COOKIE`.

Creating an Array

The formal method of creating an array is to use the `array()` function. Its syntax follows the form shown here:

```
$list = array ('apples', 'bananas',
→ 'oranges');
```

In this example—which doesn't specify an index for the elements—the first item, *apples*, is automatically indexed at 0, the second item at 1, and the third at 2. Arrays automatically begin their indexing at 0, unless otherwise indicated.

You can assign the index when using `array()`:

```
$list = array (1 => 'apples',
→ 2 => 'bananas', 3 => 'oranges');
```

Because PHP is very liberal when it comes to blank space in your scripts, you can make this structure easier to read by writing it over multiple lines:

```
$list = array (
1 => 'apples',
2 => 'bananas',
3 => 'oranges'
);
```

Finally, the index value you specify doesn't have to be a number—you can use words as well. This indexing technique is practical for making more meaningful lists. As an example, you could create an array that records the soup of the day for each day of the week, as in the following script.

Script 7.1 The $soups array contains three elements and uses strings for its keys.

```
<!DOCTYPE html PUBLIC "-//W3C//DTD XHTML 1.0 Transitional//EN"
        "http://www.w3.org/TR/xhtml1/DTD/xhtml1-transitional.dtd">
<html xmlns="http://www.w3.org/1999/xhtml">
<head>
    <meta http-equiv="content-type" content="text/html; charset=iso-8859-1" />
    <title>No Soup for You!</title>
</head>
<body>
Mmmmm...soups:<br />
<?php // Script 7.1 - soups1.php

// Address error handling.
ini_set ('display_errors', 1);
error_reporting (E_ALL & ~E_NOTICE);

// Create the array.
$soups = array (
'Monday' => 'Clam Chowder',
'Tuesday' => 'White Chicken Chili',
'Wednesday' => 'Vegetarian'
);

// Try to print the array.
print "<p>$soups</p>";

// Print the contents of the array.
print_r ($soups);

?>
</body>
</html>
```

To create an array:

1. Create a new PHP document in your text editor.

2. Write the standard HTML header (**Script 7.1**):

```
<!DOCTYPE html PUBLIC "-//W3C//DTD XHTML 1.0 Transitional//EN"
"http://www.w3.org/TR/xhtml1/DTD/xhtml1-transitional.dtd">
<html xmlns="http://www.w3.org/1999/xhtml">
<head>
    <meta http-equiv="content-type" content="text/html; charset=iso-8859-1" />
    <title>No Soup for You!</title>
</head>
<body>
Mmmmm...soups:<br />
```

3. Begin the PHP section of the script and address error handling, if necessary:

```
<?php // Script 7.1 - soups1.php
ini_set ('display_errors', 1);
error_reporting (E_ALL & ~E_NOTICE);
```

4. Use the `array()` function to create an array:

```
$soups = array (
'Monday' => 'Clam Chowder',
'Tuesday' => 'White Chicken Chili',
'Wednesday' => 'Vegetarian'
);
```

This is the proper format for initializing (creating and assigning a value to) an array in PHP, using strings as the indices. Because both the keys and values are strings, you surround them with single quotation marks.

continues on next page

Do not inadvertently add a comma after the final array element (*Wednesday*) as this will cause a parse error.

5. Print the array to the Web browser:
```
print "<p>$soups</p>";
```
As you'll soon see, arrays are also different in that they can't be printed the way you'd print other (scalar) variables.

6. Use the `print_r()` function to print out the array differently:
```
print_r ($soups);
```
In Chapter 2, "Variables," you learned how to use the `print_r()` and `var_dump()` functions to show the contents and structure of any variable. You use the former here so that you can see the difference between the way this function and `print()` work with arrays.

7. Close the PHP and the HTML sections:
```
?>
</body>
</html>
```

8. Save your document as `soups1.php`, upload it to your server, and test in your Web browser (**Figure 7.1**).

✔ Tips

- The practice of beginning any index at 0 is standard in PHP and most other programming languages. As unnatural as this counting system may seem, it's here to stay, so you have two possible coping techniques. First, manually start all of your arrays indexed at position 1. Second, unlearn a lifetime of counting from 1. You can decide which is easier, but most programmers just get used to this odd construct.

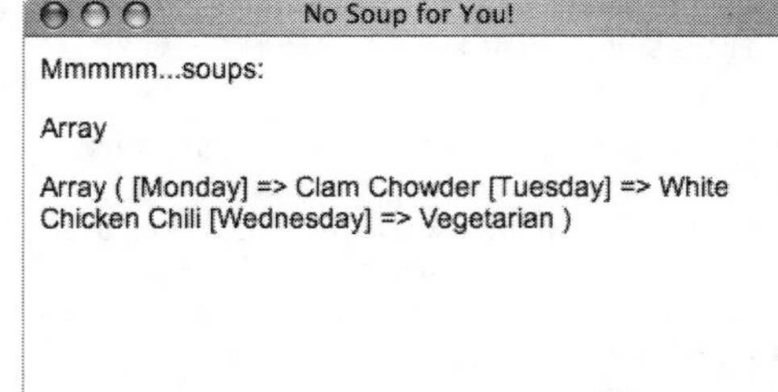

Figure 7.1 Because an array is structured differently than other variable types, a request to print an array results in the word *Array*. On the other hand, the `print_r()` function prints the array's contents and structure.

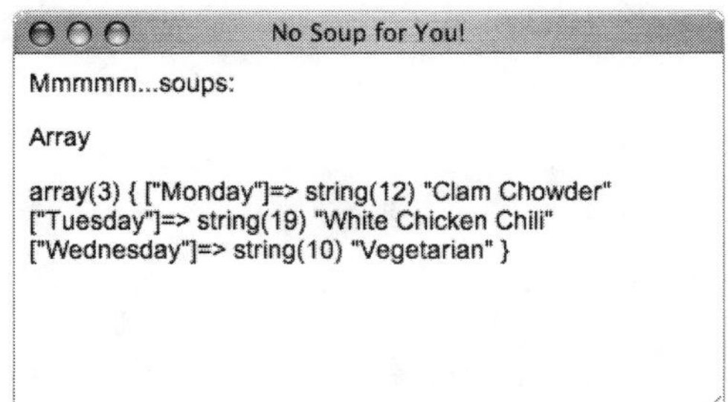

Figure 7.2 The `var_dump()` function (used with Script 7.1 instead of the `print_r()` function) shows how many elements are in an array and how long each string value is.

- You must refer to an array's elements using the same index used to create the array. In the `$soups` example, `$soups[0]` has no value even though the array obviously has a first element (the first element being indexed at 0 numerically).
- If you use the `array()` function to define an index, you can associate the first index, and the others will follow sequentially. For example:

```
$list = array (1 => 'apples',
→ 'bananas', 'oranges');
```

- The `range()` function can also be used to create an array of items based on a range of values. Here are two examples:

```
$ten = range (1, 10);
$alphabet = range ('a', 'z');
```

- As of PHP version 5, the `range()` function includes a step parameter that lets you specify increments:

```
$evens = range (0, 100, 2);
```

- If you use the `var_dump()` function in your script in lieu of `print_r()`, it shows not only the contents of the array but also its structure in a more detailed format (**Figure 7.2**).
- An array whose keys are numbers is called an *indexed* array. If the keys are strings, it's referred to as an *associative* array.

Adding Items to an Array

In PHP, once an array exists, you can add extra elements to the array with the assignment operator (the equals sign), in a way similar to how you assign a value to a string or a number. When doing so, you can either specify the key of the added element or not, but in either case, you must refer to the array with the square brackets. To add two items to the `$list` array, you'd write

```
$list[] = 'pears';
$list[] = 'tomatoes';
```

If you don't specify the key, each element is appended to the existing array, indexed with the next sequential number. Assuming this is the same array from the previous section, which was indexed at 1, 2, and 3, *pears* is now located at 4 and *tomatoes* at 5.

If you do specify the index, the value is assigned at that location. Any existing value already indexed at that point are overwritten, like so:

```
$list[3] = 'pears';
$list[4] = 'tomatoes';
```

Now, the value of the element in the fourth position of the array is *tomatoes*, and no element of `$list` is equal to *oranges* (this value was overwritten by *pears*). With this in mind, unless you intend to overwrite any existing data, you'll be better off not including a specific key when adding values to your arrays. However, if the array uses strings for indices, you'll probably want to specify keys so you don't end up with an odd combination of string and number keys.

To test this process, in the following task you'll rewrite `soups1.php` to add more elements to the array. In order to see the difference adding more elements makes, you'll print out the number of elements in the array before and after the new additions.

Deleting Arrays and Array Elements

You won't need to delete an individual item from an array frequently, but it's possible to do so by using the `unset()` function:

```
unset ($array[4]);
unset ($array['name']);
```

This function eliminates a variable and frees up the memory it used. When applied to an array element, that element is deleted; if you apply `unset()` to an entire array or any other variable type, the whole variable is deleted:

```
unset ($array);
unset ($string);
```

You can also *reset* an array (empty it without deleting the variable altogether) using the `array()` function:

```
$array = array();
```

This has the effect of initializing the variable: making it exist and defining its type without assigning a value.

Script 7.2 You can directly add elements to an array one at a time by assigning each element a value with the assignment operator. The `count()` function will help you keep track of how many elements the array contains.

```
<!DOCTYPE html PUBLIC "-//W3C//DTD XHTML 1.0 Transitional//EN"
        "http://www.w3.org/TR/xhtml1/DTD/xhtml1-transitional.dtd">
<html xmlns="http://www.w3.org/1999/xhtml">
<head>
    <meta http-equiv="content-type" content="text/html; charset=iso-8859-1" />
    <title>No Soup for You!</title>
</head>
<body>
Mmmmm...soups:<br />
<?php // Script 7.2 - soups2.php

// Address error handing.
ini_set ('display_errors', 1);
error_reporting (E_ALL & ~E_NOTICE);

// Create the array.
$soups = array (
'Monday' => 'Clam Chowder',
'Tuesday' => 'White Chicken Chili',
'Wednesday' => 'Vegetarian'
);

// Count and print the current number of elements.
$number1 = count ($soups);
print "<p>The soups array originally had $number1 elements.</p>";

// Add three items to the array.
$soups['Thursday'] = 'Chicken Noodle';
$soups['Friday'] = 'Tomato';
$soups['Saturday'] = 'Cream of Broccoli';

// Count and print the number of elements again.
$number2 = count ($soups);
print "<p>After adding 3 more soups, the array now has $number2 elements.</p>";

print_r ($soups);

?>
</body>
</html>
```

Just as you can find the length of a string—how many characters it contains—using `strlen()`, you can determine the number of elements in an array, using `count()`:

```
$how_many = count ($array);
```

To add elements to an array:

1. Open `soups1.php` in your text editor, if it isn't already open.

2. After the array is initialized using `array()`, add the following (**Script 7.2**):

   ```
   $number1 = count ($soups);
   print "<p>The soups array originally had $number1 elements.</p>";
   ```

   The `count()` function determines how many elements are in `$soups`. By assigning that value to a variable, you can easily print it out.

3. Add three more elements to the array:

   ```
   $soups['Thursday'] = 'Chicken Noodle';
   $soups['Friday'] = 'Tomato';
   $soups['Saturday'] = 'Cream of Broccoli';
   ```

   This code adds three more soups—indexed at *Thursday*, *Friday*, and *Saturday*—to the existing array.

4. Recount how many elements are in the array, and print this value.

   ```
   $number2 = count ($soups);
   print "<p>After adding 3 more soups, the array now has $number2 elements.</p>";
   ```

   This second `print()` statement is a repetition of the first, letting you know how many elements the array now contains.

continues on next page

5. If you want to, delete the `print "<p>$soups</p>";` line.

   This line isn't needed anymore, so you can get rid of it (you now know that you can't print an array that easily).

6. Save your script as `soups2.php`, upload it to your server, and test in your Web browser (**Figure 7.3**).

No Soup for You!

Mmmmm...soups:

The soups array originally had 3 elements.

After adding 3 more soups, the array now has 6 elements.

Array ([Monday] => Clam Chowder [Tuesday] => White Chicken Chili [Wednesday] => Vegetarian [Thursday] => Chicken Noodle [Friday] => Tomato [Saturday] => Cream of Broccoli)

Figure 7.3 A direct way to ensure that the new elements were successfully added to the array is to count the number of elements before and after you make the additions.

✔ Tips

- Be very careful when you directly add elements to an array. There's a correct way to do it (`$array[] = "Add This";` or `$array[1] = "Add This";`) and an incorrect way (`$array = "Add This";`). If you forget to use the brackets, the added value will replace the entire existing array, leaving you with a simple string or number.
- The code

  ```
  $array[] = 'Value';
  ```

  creates the `$array` variable if it doesn't yet exist.
- While working with these arrays, you're using single quotation marks to enclose both the keys and the values. Nothing needs to be interpolated (like a variable), so double quotation marks aren't required. It's perfectly acceptable to use double quotation marks, though, if you want to.
- You don't (and, in fact, shouldn't) quote your keys if they're numbers, variables, or constants (you'll learn about constants in Chapter 8, "Creating Web Applications"). For example:

  ```
  $day = 'Sunday';
  $soups[$day] = 'Mushroom';
  ```
- The `sizeof()` function is an alias to `count()`. It also returns the number of elements in an array.

Merging Arrays

PHP has a function that allows you to append one array onto another. Think of it as concatenation for arrays. The function, `array_merge()`, works like so:

```
$new_array = array_merge ($array1,
→ $array2);
```

You could also write the `soups2.php` page using this function:

```
$soups2 = array (
'Thursday' => 'Chicken Noodle',
'Friday' => 'Tomato',
'Saturday' => 'Cream of Broccoli',
);
$soups = array_merge ($soups, $soups2);
```

You could even accomplish this result with the plus sign (thus adding two arrays together):

```
$soups = $soups + $soups2;
```

or

```
$soups += $soups2;
```

Accessing Array Elements

Regardless of how you establish your array, there's only one way to retrieve a specific element (or value) from it, and that is to refer to its index:

```
print "The total of your order comes to
→ $array[0]";
```

When you print from an array, you must adjust for the quotation marks you'd normally use around the index, because they conflict with the `print()` statement. This line will cause problems:

```
print "The total of your order comes to
→ $array['total']";
```

To combat this issue, you can wrap the whole array construct within curly braces, as you've already seen:

```
print "The total of your order comes to
→ {$array['total']}";
```

Ironically, the feature that makes arrays so useful—being able to store multiple values in one variable—also gives it a limitation the other variable types don't have: You must know the keys of the array in order to access its elements. If the array was set using strings, like the `$soups` array, then referring to `$soups[1]` points to nothing. For that matter, because variables are case sensitive, `$soups['monday']` is worthless because you indexed *Clam Chowder* at `$soups['Monday']`.

The fastest and easiest way to access all the values of an array is to use a `foreach` loop. This construct loops through every element of an array:

```
foreach ($array as $key => $value) {
   print "Key is $key. Value is $value";
}
```

You can now write a new soups script to use this knowledge. Instead of merely being able to print out how many elements are in an array (as you've done to this point), you can access the actual values.

To print the values of any array:

1. Create a new PHP document in your text editor.

2. Write the standard HTML header (**Script 7.3**):

```
<!DOCTYPE html PUBLIC "-//W3C//DTD
→ XHTML 1.0 Transitional//EN"
"http://www.w3.org/TR/xhtml1/DTD/
→ xhtml1-transitional.dtd">
<html xmlns="http://www.w3.org/1999/
→ xhtml">
<head>
   <meta http-equiv="content-type"
   → content="text/html; charset=
   → iso-8859-1" />
   <title>No Soup for You!</title>
</head>
<body>
<b>Soup of the Day:</b><p>
```

3. Start the PHP section of the page and address error handling:

```
<?php // Script 7.3 - soups3.php
ini_set ('display_errors', 1);
error_reporting (E_ALL & ~E_NOTICE);
```

4. Create the `$soups` array:

```
$soups = array (
'Monday' => 'Clam Chowder',
'Tuesday' => 'White Chicken Chili',
'Wednesday' => 'Vegetarian',
'Thursday' => 'Chicken Noodle',
'Friday' => 'Tomato',
'Saturday' => 'Cream of Broccoli'
);
```

Here you create the entire array at once, although you could use the same method (creating the array in steps) as in the previous script.

Script 7.3 A `foreach` loop is the easiest way to access every element in an array.

```
<!DOCTYPE html PUBLIC "-//W3C//DTD XHTML 1.0 Transitional//EN"
        "http://www.w3.org/TR/xhtml1/DTD/xhtml1-transitional.dtd">
<html xmlns="http://www.w3.org/1999/xhtml">
<head>
    <meta http-equiv="content-type" content="text/html; charset=iso-8859-1" />
    <title>No Soup for You!</title>
</head>
<body>
<b>Soup of the Day:</b><p>
<?php // Script 7.3 - soups3.php

// Address error handing.
ini_set ('display_errors', 1);
error_reporting (E_ALL & ~E_NOTICE);

// Create the array.
$soups = array (
'Monday' => 'Clam Chowder',
'Tuesday' => 'White Chicken Chili',
'Wednesday' => 'Vegetarian',
'Thursday' => 'Chicken Noodle',
'Friday' => 'Tomato',
'Saturday' => 'Cream of Broccoli'
);

// Print each key and value.
foreach ($soups as $day => $soup) {
    print "$day: $soup<br />\n";
}

?>
</p>
</body>
</html>
```

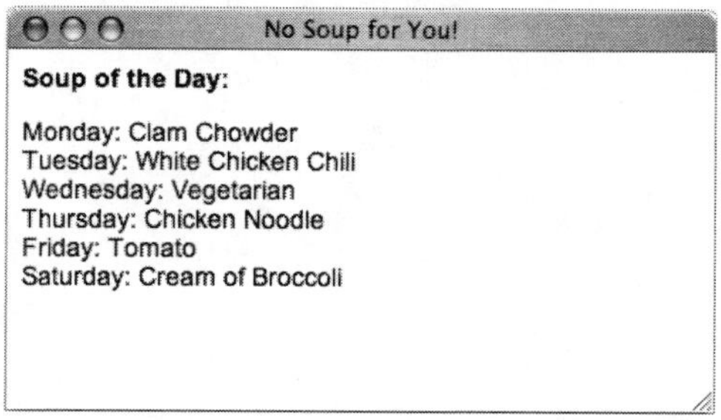

No Soup for You!

Soup of the Day:

Monday: Clam Chowder
Tuesday: White Chicken Chili
Wednesday: Vegetarian
Thursday: Chicken Noodle
Friday: Tomato
Saturday: Cream of Broccoli

Figure 7.4 The execution of the loop for every element in the array generates this page. The `foreach` construct allows the script to access each key and value without prior knowledge of what they were.

5. Create a `foreach` loop to print out each day's soup:

```
foreach ($soups as $day => $soup) {
   print "$day: $soup<br />\n";
}
```

   The `foreach` loop iterates through every element of the `$soups` array, assigning each index to `$day` and each value to `$soup`. These values are then printed out along with an HTML break tag and a new line character (created by `\n`, which affects the HTML source code of the page).

6. Close the PHP section and the HTML page:

```
?>
</p>
</body>
</html>
```

   In case you're wondering, the closing `</p>` tag here completes the paragraph begun in Step 2.

7. Save the page as `soups3.php`, upload it to your server, and test in your Web browser (**Figure 7.4**).

continues on next page

✔ Tips

- One option for handling arrays is to assign a specific element's value to a separate variable using the assignment operator:

  ```
  $total = $array[1];
  ```

  By doing this, you can preserve the original value in the array and still manipulate it separately as a variable.

- If you only need to access an array's values (and not its keys), you can use this `foreach` structure:

  ```
  foreach ($array as $value) {
     // Do whatever.
  }
  ```

- Remember that the curly braces are used to avoid errors when printing array values that have strings for keys. Here's an example where using quotation marks isn't problematic, so the curly braces aren't required:

  ```
  $name = trim ($array['Name']);
  ```

- Another common way to access all of an array's elements is to use a `for` loop:

  ```
  for ($n = 0; $n < count ($array);
  → $n++) {
     print "The value is $array[$n]";
  }
  ```

Creating Multidimensional Arrays

Multidimensional arrays are both simple and complicated at the same time. The structure and concept may be somewhat difficult to grasp, but creating and accessing multidimensional arrays in PHP is surprisingly easy.

A multidimensional array is used so that you can create an array containing more information than a standard array. This is accomplished by using other arrays for values instead of just strings and numbers. For example:

```
$fruits = array ('apples', 'bananas',
→ 'oranges');
$meats = array ('steaks', 'hamburgers',
→ 'pork chops');
$groceries = array (
'fruits' => $fruits,
'meats' => $meats,
'other' => 'peanuts',
'cash' => 30.00
);
```

This array, `$groceries`, now consists of one string (*peanuts*), one floating-point number (*30.00*), and two arrays (`fruits` and `meats`).

Pointing to an element in an array within an array is tricky. The key (pardon the pun) is to continue adding indices in square brackets as necessary. So in this example, *bananas* is at `$groceries['fruits'][1]`.

First, you point to the element (in this case, an array) in the `$groceries` array, by using `['fruits']`. Then, you point to the element in that array based on its position—it's the second item, so you use the index `[1]`.

In this task you'll write a script that provides another example. You'll create a multidimensional array containing the chapters for three books.

To use multidimensional arrays:

1. Open your text editor and create a new PHP document, starting with the standard HTML head (**Script 7.4**):

```
<!DOCTYPE html PUBLIC "-//W3C//DTD
→ XHTML 1.0 Transitional//EN"
"http://www.w3.org/TR/xhtml1/DTD/
→ xhtml1-transitional.dtd">
<html xmlns="http://www.w3.org/1999/
→ xhtml">
<head>
   <meta http-equiv="content-type"
   content="text/html; charset=
   → iso-8859-1" />
   <title>My Books and Chapters</title>
</head>
<body>
```

2. Create the initial PHP tags, and address error handling:

```
<?php // Script 7.4 - books.php
ini_set ('display_errors', 1);
error_reporting (E_ALL & ~E_NOTICE);
```

3. Create the first array:

```
$phpvqs = array (1 => 'Getting
→ Started', 'Variables', 'HTML Forms
→ and PHP', 'Using Numbers');
```

To build up the multidimensional array, you'll create three standard arrays and then use them as the values for the larger array. This array (called `$phpvqs`, which is short for *PHP for the World Wide Web: Visual QuickStart Guide*) uses numbers for the keys and strings for the values. The numbers begin with 1 and correspond to the chapter numbers. The values are the chapter titles.

Script 7.4 The multidimensional `$books` array stores a lot of information in one big variable.

```
<!DOCTYPE html PUBLIC "-//W3C//DTD XHTML 1.0 Transitional//EN"
        "http://www.w3.org/TR/xhtml1/DTD/xhtml1-transitional.dtd">
<html xmlns="http://www.w3.org/1999/xhtml">
<head>
    <meta http-equiv="content-type" content="text/html; charset=iso-8859-1" />
    <title>My Books and Chapters</title>
</head>
<body>
<?php // Script 7.4 - books.php

// Address error handing.
ini_set ('display_errors', 1);
error_reporting (E_ALL & ~E_NOTICE);

// Create the first array.
$phpvqs = array (1 => 'Getting Started', 'Variables', 'HTML Forms and PHP', 'Using Numbers');

// Create the second array.
$phpadv = array (1 => 'Advanced PHP Programming', 'Object-Oriented Programming', 'Databases', 'Security');

// Create the third array.
$phpmysql = array (1 => 'Introduction to PHP', 'Programming with PHP', 'Creating Dynamic Web Sites', 'Introduction to SQL and MySQL');

// Create the multidimensional array.
$books = array (
'PHP VQS' => $phpvqs,
'PHP Advanced VQP' => $phpadv,
'PHP and MySQL VQP' => $phpmysql
);

// Print out some values.
print "<p>The third chapter of my first book is <i>{$books['PHP VQS'][3]}</i>.</p>";
print "<p>The first chapter of my second book is <i>{$books['PHP Advanced VQP'][1]}</i>.</p>";
print "<p>The fourth chapter of my fourth book is <i>{$books['PHP and MySQL VQP'][4]}</i>.</p>";
```

(script continues on next page)

Script 7.4 *continued*

```
// See what happens with foreach.
foreach ($books as $key => $value) {
    print "<p>$key: $value</p>\n";
}

?>
</body>
</html>
```

4. Create the next two arrays:

```
$phpadv = array (1 => 'Advanced PHP
→ Programming', 'Object-Oriented
→ Programming', 'Databases',
→ 'Security');
$phpmysql = array (1 => 'Introduction
→ to PHP', 'Programming with PHP',
→ 'Creating Dynamic Web Sites',
→ 'Introduction to SQL and MySQL');
```

For each array, you add only the books' first four chapters for simplicity's sake.

5. Create the main, multidimensional array:

```
$books = array (
'PHP VQS' => $phpvqs,
'PHP Advanced VQP' => $phpadv,
'PHP and MySQL VQP' => $phpmysql
);
```

The `$books` array is the master array for this script. It uses strings for keys (which are shortened versions of the book titles) and arrays for values. You use the `array()` function to create it, as you would any other array.

6. Print out the name of the third chapter of the *PHP Visual QuickStart Guide* book:

```
print "<p>The third chapter of my
→ first book is <i>{$books['PHP VQS']
→ [3]}</i>.</p>";
```

Following the rules stated earlier, all you need to do to access any individual chapter name is to begin with `$books`, follow that with the first index (`['PHP VQS']`), and follow that with the next index (`[3]`). Because you're placing this in a `print()` statement, you enclose the whole construct in curly braces to avoid parse errors.

continues on next page

7. Print out two more examples:

```
print "<p>The first chapter of my
→ second book is <i>{$books['PHP
→ Advanced VQP'][1]}</i>.</p>";
print "<p>The fourth chapter of my
→ fourth book is <i>{$books['PHP and
→ MySQL VQP'][4]}</i>.</p>";
```

8. Run the `$books` array through a `foreach` loop to see the results:

```
foreach ($books as $key => $value) {
    print "<p>$key: $value</p>\n";
}
```

The `$key` variable stores each abbreviated book title, and the `$value` variable ends up containing each chapter array.

9. Close the PHP section and complete the HTML page:

```
?>
</body>
</html>
```

10. Save the file as `books.php`, upload it to your Web server, and test it in your browser (**Figure 7.5**).

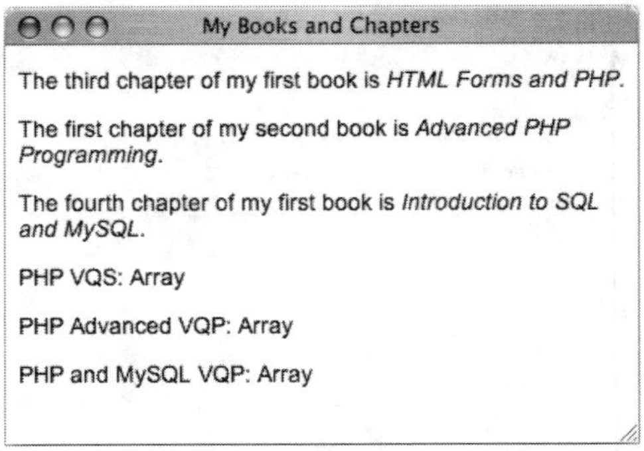

My Books and Chapters

The third chapter of my first book is *HTML Forms and PHP*.

The first chapter of my second book is *Advanced PHP Programming*.

The fourth chapter of my first book is *Introduction to SQL and MySQL*.

PHP VQS: Array

PHP Advanced VQP: Array

PHP and MySQL VQP: Array

Figure 7.5 The first three lines are generated by `print()` statements. The last three show the results of the `foreach` loop.

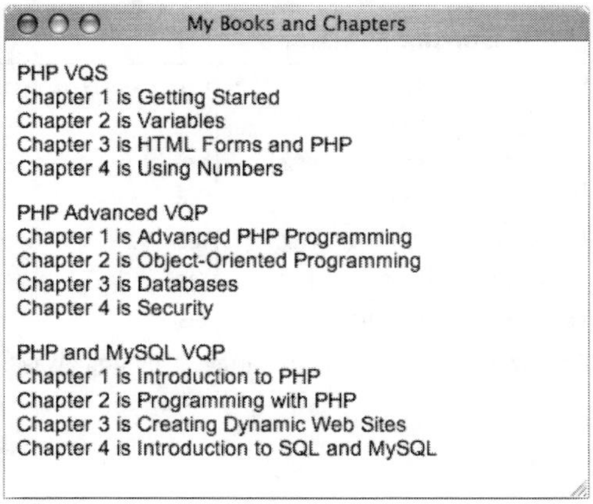

My Books and Chapters

PHP VQS
Chapter 1 is Getting Started
Chapter 2 is Variables
Chapter 3 is HTML Forms and PHP
Chapter 4 is Using Numbers

PHP Advanced VQP
Chapter 1 is Advanced PHP Programming
Chapter 2 is Object-Oriented Programming
Chapter 3 is Databases
Chapter 4 is Security

PHP and MySQL VQP
Chapter 1 is Introduction to PHP
Chapter 2 is Programming with PHP
Chapter 3 is Creating Dynamic Web Sites
Chapter 4 is Introduction to SQL and MySQL

Figure 7.6 One foreach loop within another can access every element of a multidimensional array.

My Books and Chapters

```
array(3) {
  ["PHP VQS"]=>
  array(4) {
    [1]=>
    string(15) "Getting Started"
    [2]=>
    string(9) "Variables"
    [3]=>
    string(18) "HTML Forms and PHP"
    [4]=>
    string(13) "Using Numbers"
  }
  ["PHP Advanced VQP"]=>
  array(4) {
    [1]=>
    string(24) "Advanced PHP Programming"
    [2]=>
    string(27) "Object-Oriented Programming"
    [3]=>
    string(9) "Databases"
    [4]=>
    string(8) "Security"
  }
  ["PHP and MySQL VQP"]=>
  array(4) {
    [1]=>
    string(19) "Introduction to PHP"
    [2]=>
    string(20) "Programming with PHP"
    [3]=>
    string(26) "Creating Dynamic Web Sites"
    [4]=>
    string(29) "Introduction to SQL and MySQL"
  }
}
```

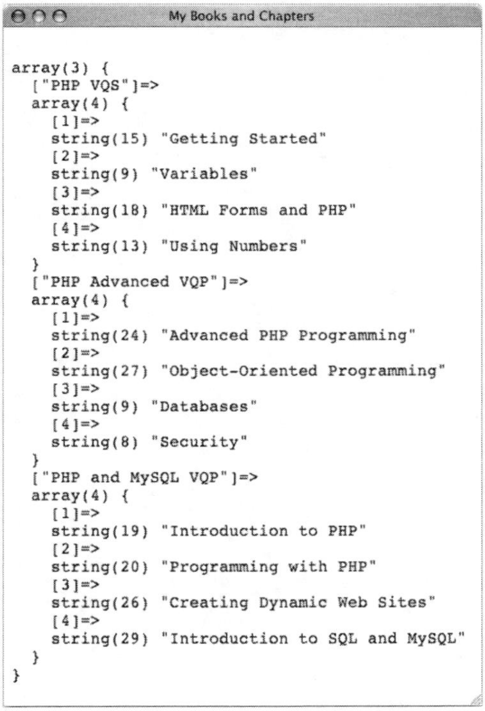

Figure 7.7 The var_dump() function shows the structure and contents of the $books array.

✔ Tips

- To access every element of every array, you can nest two foreach loops like this (**Figure 7.6**):

```
foreach ($books as $title =>
$chapters) {
   print "<p>$title";
   foreach ($chapters as $number =>
   → $chapter) {
      print "<br />Chapter $number is
      → $chapter";
   }
   print '</p>';
}
```

- Using the print_r() or var_dump() function (preferably enclosed in HTML <pre> tags for better formatting), you can view an entire multidimensional array (**Figure 7.7**).
- You can create a multidimensional array in one statement by using a series of nested array() calls (instead of using several steps as in this example). However, doing so isn't recommended, because it's all too easy to make syntactical errors as a statement becomes more and more nested.
- Although all the sub-arrays in this example have the same structure (numbers for indexes and four elements), that isn't required with multidimensional arrays.
- To learn about the greater "Larry Ullman collection" beyond the three books referenced here, go to this book's Web site: www.DMCInsights.com/phpvqs2.

Sorting Arrays

PHP supports a variety of ways to sort an array (*sort* refers to an alphabetical sort if the values being sorted are strings, or a numerical sort if the values being sorted are numbers). When you're sorting an array, you must keep in mind that an array consists of pairs of keys and values. Thus, an array can be sorted based on the keys or the values. This is further complicated by the fact that you can sort the values and keep the corresponding keys aligned, or you can sort the values and have them be assigned new keys.

To sort the values without regard to the keys, you use `sort()`. To sort these values (again, without regard to the keys) in reverse order, you use `rsort()`. The syntax for every sorting function is:

```
function ($array);
```

So, `sort()` and `rsort()` are used as follows:

```
sort ($array);
rsort ($array);
```

To sort the values while maintaining the correlation between each value and its key, you use `asort()`. To sort the values in reverse while maintaining the key correlation, you use `arsort()`.

To sort by the keys while maintaining the correlation between the key and its value, you use `ksort()`. Conversely, `krsort()` sorts the keys in reverse. **Table 7.2** lists all these functions.

Last, `shuffle()` randomly reorganizes the order of an array.

As an example of sorting arrays, you'll create a list of students and the grades they received on a test, and then sort this list first by grade and then by name.

Array Sorting Functions

Function	Sorts By	Maintains Key-Values?
sort()	Values	No
rsort()	Values (inverse)	No
asort()	Values	Yes
arsort()	Values (inverse)	Yes
ksort()	Keys	Yes
krsort()	Keys (inverse)	Yes

Table 7.2 These functions sort arrays in different ways.

Script 7.5 PHP provides a number of different functions for sorting arrays, including `arsort()` and `ksort()` (used here).

```
Script
<!DOCTYPE html PUBLIC "-//W3C//DTD XHTML 1.0 Transitional//EN"
        "http://www.w3.org/TR/xhtml1/DTD/xhtml1-transitional.dtd">
<html xmlns="http://www.w3.org/1999/xhtml">
<head>
    <meta http-equiv="content-type" content="text/html; charset=iso-8859-1" />
    <title>My Little Gradebook</title>
</head>
<body>
<?php // Script 7.5 - sort.php

// Address error handing.
ini_set ('display_errors', 1);
error_reporting (E_ALL & ~E_NOTICE);

// Create the array.
$grades = array(
'Richard' => 95,
'Sherwood' => 82,
'Toni' => 98,
'Franz' => 87,
'Melissa' => 75,
'Roddy' => 85
);

// Print the original array.
print "<p>Originally the array looks like this: <br />";
foreach ($grades as $student => $grade) {
    print "$student: $grade<br />\n";
}
print "</p>";

// Sort by value in reverse order, then print again.
arsort ($grades);
print "<p>After sorting the array by value using arsort(), the array looks like this: <br />";
foreach ($grades as $student => $grade) {
    print "$student: $grade<br />\n";
}
print "</p>";
```

(script continues on next page)

To sort an array:

1. Open your text editor and create a new PHP document.

2. Begin with the standard HTML code (**Script 7.5**):

```
<!DOCTYPE html PUBLIC "-//W3C//DTD
→ XHTML 1.0 Transitional//EN"
"http://www.w3.org/TR/xhtml1/DTD/
→ xhtml1-transitional.dtd">
<html xmlns="http://www.w3.org/1999/
→ xhtml">
<head>
    <meta http-equiv="content-type"
    → content="text/html; charset=
    → iso-8859-1" />
    <title>My Little Gradebook</title>
</head>
<body>
```

3. Begin the PHP section, and address error handling, if desired:

```
<?php // Script 7.5 - sort.php
ini_set ('display_errors', 1);
error_reporting (E_ALL & ~E_NOTICE);
```

4. Create the array:

```
$grades = array(
'Richard' => 95,
'Sherwood' => 82,
'Toni' => 98,
'Franz' => 87,
'Melissa' => 75,
'Roddy' => 85
);
```

The `$grades` array consists of six students' names along with their corresponding grades. Because the grades are number values, they don't need to be quoted when assigning them.

continues on next page

5. Print a caption, and then print each element of the array using a `foreach` loop:

```
print "<p>Originally the array looks
→ like this: <br />";
foreach ($grades as $student =>
→ $grade) {
   print "$student: $grade<br />\n";
}
print "</p>";
```

The caption tells you what point in the script you're at. At first, it prints the array in the original order. To do that, you use a `foreach` loop, where each index (the student's name) is assigned to `$student`, and each value (the student's grade) is assigned to `$grade`. The final `print()` statement closes the HTML paragraph.

6. Sort the array in reverse order by value to determine who has the highest grade:

```
arsort ($grades);
```

Because you're determining who has the highest grade, you need to use `arsort()` instead of `asort()`. The latter, which sorts the array in numeric order, would order the grades 75, 82, 85, and so on, rather than the desired 98, 95, 87.

You also must use `arsort()` and not `rsort()` in order to maintain the key-value relationship (`rsort()` would eliminate the student's name associated with each grade).

7. Print the array again (with a caption), using another loop:

```
print "<p>After sorting the array by
→ value using arsort(), the array
→ looks like this: <br />";
foreach ($grades as $student =>
→ $grade) {
   print "$student: $grade<br />\n";
}
print "</p>";
```

Script 7.5 *continued*

```

// Sort by key, then print again.
ksort ($grades);
print "<p>After sorting the array by key using ksort(), the array looks like this: <br />";
foreach ($grades as $student => $grade) {
    print "$student: $grade<br />\n";
}
print "</p>";

?>
</body>
</html>
```

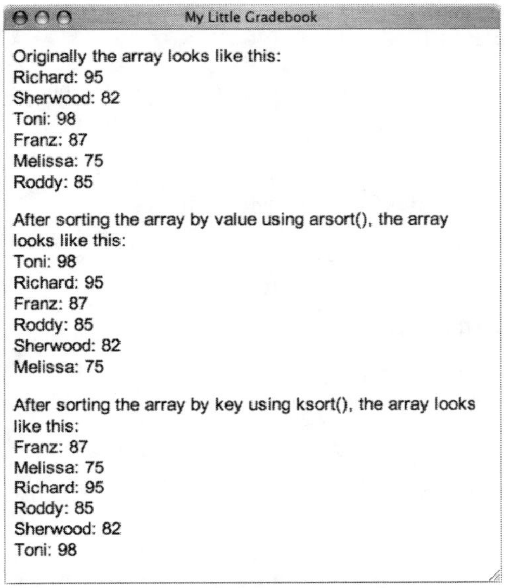

My Little Gradebook

Originally the array looks like this:
Richard: 95
Sherwood: 82
Toni: 98
Franz: 87
Melissa: 75
Roddy: 85

After sorting the array by value using arsort(), the array looks like this:
Toni: 98
Richard: 95
Franz: 87
Roddy: 85
Sherwood: 82
Melissa: 75

After sorting the array by key using ksort(), the array looks like this:
Franz: 87
Melissa: 75
Richard: 95
Roddy: 85
Sherwood: 82
Toni: 98

Figure 7.8 You can sort an array in a number of ways with varied results. Pay close attention to whether you want to maintain your key-value association when choosing a sort function.

8. Sort the array by key to put the array in alphabetical order by student name:

```
ksort ($grades);
```

The `ksort()` function organizes the array by key (in this case, alphabetically) while maintaining the key-value correlation.

9. Print a caption and the array one last time:

```
print "<p>After sorting the array by
key using ksort(), the array looks
→ like this: <br />";
foreach ($grades as $student =>
→ $grade) {
   print "$student: $grade<br />\n";
}
print "</p>";
```

10. Close the script with the standard PHP and HTML tags:

```
?>
</body>
</html>
```

11. Save your script as `sort.php`, upload it to the server, and test in your Web browser (**Figure 7.8**).

✔ Tips

- The `$grades` array could have been created using the grades as the keys and the names of the students as values. It works either way.
- The `natsort()` and `natcasesort()` functions sort a string (without maintaining key-value associations) using *natural order*. The most obvious example of natural order sorting is that it places *name2* before *name12*, whereas `sort()` orders them *name12* and then *name2*.
- The `usort()`, `uasort()`, and `ursort()` functions let you sort an array using a user-defined comparison function. These functions are most often used with multidimensional arrays.

More Array Functions

PHP 4 really brought arrays to the forefront, creating dozens of new functions for your every array need. You can find these functions in the PHP manual online at www.php.net/manual/en/ref.array.php.

Of the available array-related functions, two are particularly useful: `extract()` and `list()`.

The `extract()` function takes an associative array (where the keys are strings) and creates variables from it. For example:

```
$me = array ('first' => 'Larry', 'last' => 'Ullman');
extract ($me);
print $first; // Larry
print $last; // Ullman
```

The `list()` function is similar (in that it allows you to turn array elements in to variables) but requires a little more effort:

```
$date = array ('Thursday', 23, 'October');
list ($weekday, $day, $month) = $date;
```

Now there is a `$weekday` variable with a value of *Thursday*, a `$day` variable with a value of *23*, and a `$month` variable with a value of *October*. Whereas `extract()` works on associative arrays, `list()` only works on numerically indexed arrays. Also, when you're using the `list()` function, you must acknowledge each array element. So, you can write

```
list ($weekday, , $month) = $date;
```

or

```
list (, , $month) = $date;
```

but not

```
list ($month) = $date;
```

The `extract()` function can be used as a good debugging tool or as a shortcut to access array values. The `list()` function is often used when retrieving values from a database.

Transforming Between Strings and Arrays

Now that you understand both strings and arrays, this section introduces two functions for switching between the two formats. The first, `implode()`, turns an array into a string. The second, `explode()`, does just the opposite. Here are some reasons to use these functions:

- To turn an array into a string in order to pass that value appended to a URL (which you can't do as easily with an array)
- To turn an array into a string in order to store that information in a database
- To turn a string into an array to convert a comma-delimited text field (say a keyword search area of a form) into its separate parts

The syntax for using `explode()` is as follows:

```
$array = explode ($separator, $string);
```

The *separator* refers to whatever character(s) define where one array element ends and another begins. Commonly this is a comma, a tab, or a blank space. Thus your code might be

```
$array = explode (',', $string);
```

or

```
$array = explode (' ', $string);
```

To go from an array to a string, you need to define what the separator (a k a the *glue*) should be, and PHP does the rest:

```
$string = implode ($glue, $array);
$string = implode (',', $array);
```

or

```
$string = implode (' ', $array);
```

To demonstrate how to use `explode()` and `implode()`, you'll create an HTML form that takes a space-delimited string of names from the user. The PHP will then turn the string into an array so that it can sort the list. Finally, the code will create and return the alphabetized string.

To convert between strings and arrays:

1. Create a new HTML document in your text editor.

2. Write the standard HTML header (**Script 7.6**):

```
<!DOCTYPE html PUBLIC "-//W3C//DTD XHTML 1.0 Transitional//EN"
"http://www.w3.org/TR/xhtml1/DTD/xhtml1-transitional.dtd">
<html xmlns="http://www.w3.org/1999/xhtml">
<head>
   <meta http-equiv="content-type" content="text/html; charset=iso-8859-1" />
   <title>I Must Sort This Out!</title>
</head>
<body>
```

3. Create an HTML form with a text input:

```
Enter the words you want alphabetized with each individual word separated by a space: <br />
<form action="handle_list.php" method="post">
<input type="text" name="words" size="60" />
```

It's important in cases like this to instruct the user. For example, if they enter a comma-delimited list, you won't be able to handle the string properly (after completing both scripts, try using commas in lieu of spaces and see what happens).

Script 7.6 This is a simple HTML form where a user can submit a list of words. Including detailed instructions for how the form should be used is a prudent Web design policy.

```
<!DOCTYPE html PUBLIC "-//W3C//DTD XHTML 1.0 Transitional//EN"
        "http://www.w3.org/TR/xhtml1/DTD/xhtml1-transitional.dtd">
<html xmlns="http://www.w3.org/1999/xhtml">
<head>
    <meta http-equiv="content-type" content="text/html; charset=iso-8859-1" />
    <title>I Must Sort This Out!</title>
</head>
<body>
Enter the words you want alphabetized with each individual word separated by a space: <br />

<form action="handle_list.php" method="post">
<input type="text" name="words" size="60" />
<br />
<input type="submit" name="submit" value="Alphabetize!" />
</form>

<!-- Script 7.6 - list.html -->
</body>
</html>
```

Script 7.7 Because the `explode()` and `implode()` functions are so simple and powerful, you can quickly and easily sort a submitted list of words (of practically any length) in just a couple of lines.

```
Script
<!DOCTYPE html PUBLIC "-//W3C//DTD XHTML 1.0 Transitional//EN"
        "http://www.w3.org/TR/xhtml1/DTD/xhtml1-transitional.dtd">
<html xmlns="http://www.w3.org/1999/xhtml">
<head>
    <meta http-equiv="content-type" content="text/html; charset=iso-8859-1" />
    <title>I Have This Sorted Out</title>
</head>
<body>
<?php // Script 7.7 - handle_list.php

// Address error handing.
ini_set ('display_errors', 1);
error_reporting (E_ALL & ~E_NOTICE);

// Turn the incoming string into an array.
$words_array = explode (' ', $_POST['words']);

// Sort the array.
sort ($words_array);

// Turn the array back into a string.
$string_words = implode ('<br />', $words_array);

// Print the results.
print "<p>An alphabetized version of your list is: <br />$string_words</p>";

?>
</body>
</html>
```

4. Create a submit button, and then close the form and the HTML page:

```
<br />
<input type="submit" name="submit"
→ value="Alphabetize!" />
</form>
<!-- Script 7.6 - list.html -->
</body>
</html>
```

5. Save your script as `list.html` and upload it to your server.

   Now you'll write the `handle_list.php` page to process the data generated by `list.html`.

6. Create a new HTML document in your text editor.

7. Write the standard HTML header and then open the PHP section of the page (**Script 7.7**):

```
<!DOCTYPE html PUBLIC "-//W3C//DTD
→ XHTML 1.0 Transitional//EN"
"http://www.w3.org/TR/xhtml1/DTD/
→ xhtml1-transitional.dtd">
<html xmlns="http://www.w3.org/1999/
→ xhtml">
<head>
   <meta http-equiv="content-type"
   → content="text/html; charset=
   → iso-8859-1" />
   <title>I Have This Sorted Out
   → </title>
</head>
<body>
<?php // Script 7.7 - handle_list.php
ini_set ('display_errors', 1);
error_reporting (E_ALL & ~E_NOTICE);
```

continues on next page

8. Turn the incoming string, `$_POST['words']`, into an array:

```
$words_array = explode (' ', $_POST
→ ['words']);
```

This line of code creates a new array, `$words_array`, out of the string `$_POST['words']`. Each space between the words in `$_POST['words']` indicates that the next word should be a new array element. Hence the first word becomes `$words_array[0]`, then there is a space in `$_POST['words']`, then the second word becomes `$words_array[1]`, and so forth, until the end of `$_POST['words']`.

9. Sort the array alphabetically:

```
sort ($words_array);
```

Because you don't need to maintain key-value associations in the `$words_array`, you can use `sort()` instead of `asort()` (which you used before).

10. Create a new string out of the sorted array:

```
$string_words = implode ('<br />',
→ $words_array);
```

Arrays don't print as easily as strings, so you turn `$words_array` into a string called `$string_words`. The resulting string starts with the value of `$words_array[0]`, followed by the HTML `<br />` tag, the value of `$words_array[1]`, and so on. Using `<br />` instead of a space or comma gives the list a more readable format when it's printed to the browser.

11. Print the new string to the browser:

```
print "<p>An alphabetized version of
→ your list is: <br />$string_words
→ </p>";
```

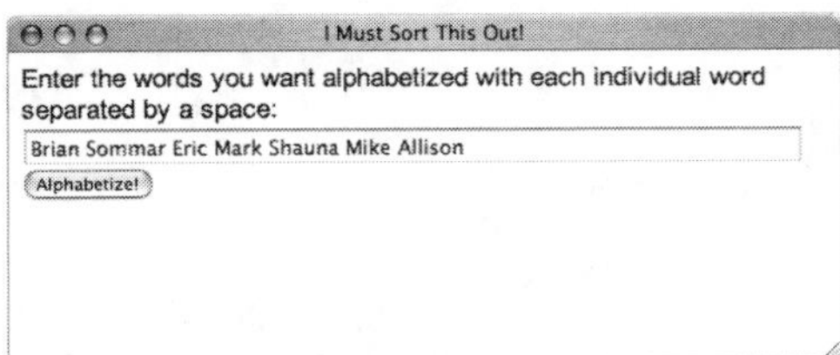

Figure 7.9 This HTML form takes a list of words, which is then alphabetized in the `handle_list.php` script (Figure 7.10).

I Have This Sorted Out

An alphabetized version of your list is:
Allison
Brian
Eric
Mark
Mike
Shauna
Sommar

Figure 7.10 Here's the same list, alphabetized for the user. This process is quick and easy to code, but doing so would be impossible without arrays.

12. Close the PHP section and the HTML page:

```
?>
</body>
</html>
```

13. Save your page as `handle_list.php`, upload it to the server (in the same directory as `list.html`), and test both scripts in your Web browser (**Figures 7.9** and **7.10**).

✔ Tips

- The conversion from `$words_array` back to `$string_words` was more of an example than a requirement. You could print out `$words_array` using a `foreach` loop.
- You'll also run across code written using the `join()` function, which is identical to `implode()`.

Creating an Array from a Form

Throughout this chapter, you've established arrays entirely from within a PHP page. You can, however, send an array of data to a PHP script via an HTML form. In fact, every time you use $_POST, this is the case. But you can take this one step further by creating arrays with an HTML form, which are then a part of the greater $_POST array.

The most logical use of this capability is in dealing with check boxes, where users might need to select multiple options from a category (**Figure 7.11**). The HTML source code for a check box is as follows:

```
<input type="checkbox" name="some_input"
→ value="some_value" />
```

The problem is that you must name each input differently in order to receive multiple values. The workaround is to use an array.

To create an array with an HTML form:

1. Create a new HTML document in your text editor.
2. Create the standard HTML header (**Script 7.8**):

```
<!DOCTYPE html PUBLIC "-//W3C//DTD
→ XHTML 1.0 Transitional//EN"
"http://www.w3.org/TR/xhtml1/DTD/
→ xhtml1-transitional.dtd">
<html xmlns="http://www.w3.org/1999/
→ xhtml">
<head>
   <meta http-equiv="content-type"
   → content="text/html; charset=
   → iso-8859-1" />
   <title>Add an Event</title>
</head>
<body>
```

Script 7.8 This HTML form has an array for the check box input names.

```
<!DOCTYPE html PUBLIC "-//W3C//DTD XHTML 1.0 Transitional//EN"
        "http://www.w3.org/TR/xhtml1/DTD/xhtml1-transitional.dtd">
<html xmlns="http://www.w3.org/1999/xhtml">
<head>
    <meta http-equiv="content-type" content="text/html; charset=iso-8859-1" />
    <title>Add an Event</title>
</head>
<body>

<form action="handle_event.php" method="post">
<p>Event Name: <input type="text" name="name" size="30" /></p>
<p>Week Days:
<input type="checkbox" name="weekdays[]" value="Sunday" /> S
<input type="checkbox" name="weekdays[]" value="Monday" /> M
<input type="checkbox" name="weekdays[]" value="Tuesday" /> T
<input type="checkbox" name="weekdays[]" value="Wednesday" /> W
<input type="checkbox" name="weekdays[]" value="Thursday" /> T
<input type="checkbox" name="weekdays[]" value="Friday" /> F
<input type="checkbox" name="weekdays[]" value="Saturday" /> S
</p>
<input type="submit" name="submit" value="Add the Event!" />
</form>

<!-- Script 7.8 - event.html -->
</body>
</html>
```

Week Days: S M T W T F S

Figure 7.11 Check boxes in an HTML form.

3. Begin the HTML form:

```
<form action="handle_event.php"
→ method="post">
```

4. Create a text input for an event name:

```
<p>Event Name: <input type="text"
→ name="name" size="30" /></p>
```

This example allows the user to enter an event name and the days of the week when it takes place.

5. Create the weekday check boxes:

```
<p>Week Days:
<input type="checkbox" name=
→ "weekdays[]" value="Sunday" /> S
<input type="checkbox" name=
→ "weekdays[]" value="Monday" /> M
<input type="checkbox" name=
→ "weekdays[]" value="Tuesday" /> T
<input type="checkbox" name=
→ "weekdays[]" value="Wednesday" /> W
<input type="checkbox" name=
→ "weekdays[]" value="Thursday" /> T
<input type="checkbox" name=
→ "weekdays[]" value="Friday" /> F
<input type="checkbox" name=
→ "weekdays[]" value="Saturday" /> S
</p>
```

All of these check boxes use `weekdays[]` as the `name` value, which creates a `$weekdays` (or `$_POST['weekdays']`) array in the PHP script. The `value` attributes differ for each check box, corresponding to the day of the week.

6. Complete the HTML form:

```
<input type="submit" name="submit"
→ value="Add the Event!" />
</form>
```

continues on next page

7. Complete the HTML page:

```
<!-- Script 7.8 - event.html -->
</body>
</html>
```

8. Save your page as `event.html` and upload it to your server.

   You also need to write a `handle_event.php` page to handle this HTML form.

9. Create a new PHP document in your text editor, beginning with the standard HTML header (**Script 7.9**):

```
<!DOCTYPE html PUBLIC "-//W3C//DTD
→ XHTML 1.0 Transitional//EN"
"http://www.w3.org/TR/xhtml1/DTD/
→ xhtml1-transitional.dtd">
<html xmlns="http://www.w3.org/1999/
→ xhtml">
<head>
   <meta http-equiv="content-type"
   → content="text/html; charset=
   → iso-8859-1" />
   <title>Add an Event</title>
</head>
<body>
```

10. Create the initial PHP tag, address error handling, and print an introductory message:

```
<?php // Script 7.9 -
handle_event.php
ini_set ('display_errors', 1);
error_reporting (E_ALL & ~E_NOTICE);
print "<p>You want to add an event
→ called <b>{$_POST['name']}</b>
→ which takes place on: <br />";
```

The `print()` statement prints out the value of the event's name. If you wanted to, you could add a conditional to check that a value was entered (see Chapter 6, "Control Structures").

Script 7.9 It doesn't matter to the PHP whether it receives a number of strings from an HTML form or from an array, as it does here. However, using an array leaves you with fewer variables to manage.

Script

```
<!DOCTYPE html PUBLIC "-//W3C//DTD XHTML 1.0 Transitional//EN"
        "http://www.w3.org/TR/xhtml1/DTD/xhtml1-transitional.dtd">
<html xmlns="http://www.w3.org/1999/xhtml">
<head>
    <meta http-equiv="content-type" content="text/html; charset=iso-8859-1" />
    <title>Add an Event</title>
</head>
<body>
<?php // Script 7.9 - handle_event.php

// Address error handing.
ini_set ('display_errors', 1);
error_reporting (E_ALL & ~E_NOTICE);

// Print an introductory text.
print "<p>You want to add an event called <b>{$_POST['name']}</b> which takes place on: <br />";

// Print each weekday.
if (is_array ($_POST['weekdays'])) {

    foreach ($_POST['weekdays'] as $day) {
        print "$day<br />\n";
    }

} else {
    print 'Please select at least one weekday for this event!';
}

// Complete the paragraph:
print '</p>';

?>
</body>
</html>
```

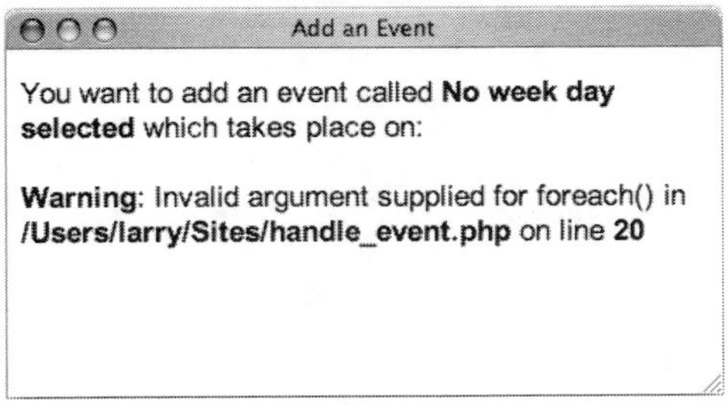

Add an Event

You want to add an event called **No week day selected** which takes place on:

Warning: Invalid argument supplied for foreach() in **/Users/larry/Sites/handle_event.php** on line **20**

Figure 7.12 The result if you try to apply a `foreach` loop to a variable that isn't an array.

11. Begin a conditional to check that at least one weekday was selected:

```
if (is_array ($_POST['weekdays'])) {
```

The `foreach` loop will create an error (**Figure 7.12**) if it receives a variable that isn't an array. To avoid this result, you put the `foreach` loop in a conditional. The `is_array()` function returns TRUE if the submitted variable is an array.

12. Print each selected weekday:

```
foreach ($_POST['weekdays'] as $day)
{
   print "$day<br />\n";
}
```

To print out each checked weekday, you run the `$_POST['weekdays']` array through a `foreach` loop (you could also use `$weekdays`, if `register_globals` is enabled, although doing so is less ideal). The array contains the values (from the HTML form inputs, for example, *Monday*, *Tuesday*, and so on) for every box that was selected.

13. Complete the `is_array()` conditional:

```
} else {
   print 'Please select at least
   → one weekday for this event!';
}
```

If no weekday was selected, then the `is_array()` condition is FALSE, and this message is printed.

continues on next page

14. Complete the main paragraph, the PHP section, and the HTML page:

```
print '</p>';
?>
</body>
</html>
```

15. Save the page as `handle_event.php`, upload it to your server (in the same directory as `event.html`), and test both pages in your Web browser (**Figures 7.13** and **7.14**).

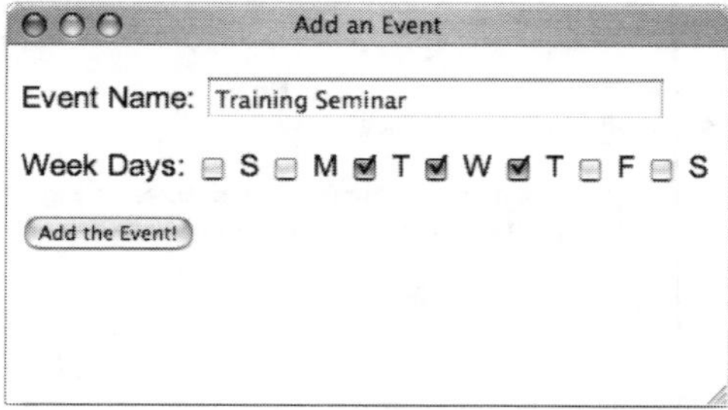

Figure 7.13 The HTML form with its check boxes.

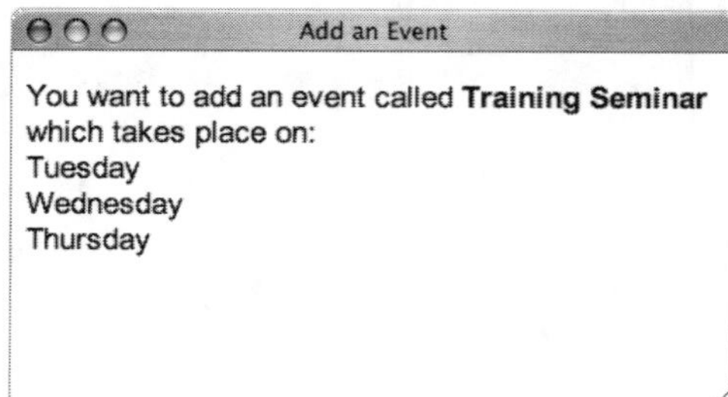

Figure 7.14 The results of the HTML form.

8

Creating Web Applications

Now that you've learned the fundamentals of programming with PHP, it's time to begin tying it all together into professional-caliber Web applications. In this chapter, you'll learn about a number of functions and techniques that you can utilize to make your Web sites more professional, feature-rich, and easier to maintain.

First, you'll begin learning how to use external files to break your Web pages into individual pieces (allowing you to separate the logic from the formatting, to a degree). Then you'll tinker with constants, a special data type in PHP. After that, you'll be introduced to some of the date- and time-related functions built into PHP.

The next two topics reveal useful programming methods: having the same page both display and handle an HTML form, and having a form remember user-submitted values. Quickly thereafter, you'll see how easy it can be to send email from PHP. Finally, the chapter concludes with the slightly more advanced topics of output buffering and using HTTP headers.

Creating Templates

Up to this point, you've written one-page scripts that handle HTML forms, sort arrays, or perform calculations. However, as you begin to develop multiple-page Web sites (which is to say *Web applications*), it quickly becomes impractical to repeat common elements over the course of several pages.

Certain features, such as the HTML design, will be used by every page within the site. You can put these elements into each individual page, but when you need to make a change, you'll be required to make that change over and over again. You can save time by creating templates that separate out the repeating content from the page-specific materials. For example, a Web site may have navigation, copyright, and other features that repeat across multiple pages (**Figures 8.1** and **8.2**).

The key to using templates is to create a prototype and then divide it into parts. Using the PHP functions you'll learn in the next section of this chapter, the repeating parts can be easily included in each page while the new content is generated on a page-by-page basis. You'll first learn how to develop the template files.

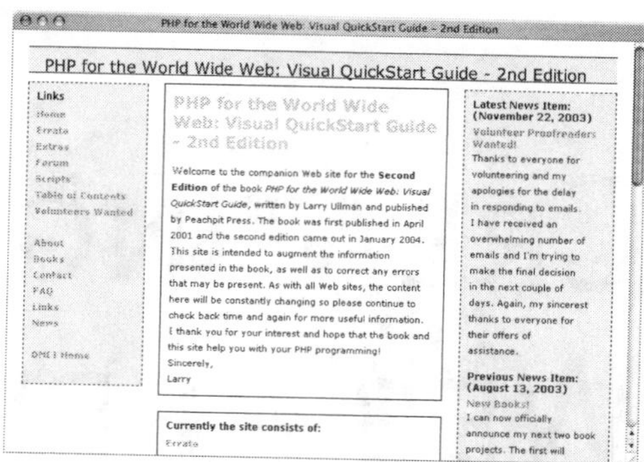

Figure 8.1 The book's home page has its page-specific content in the middle column.

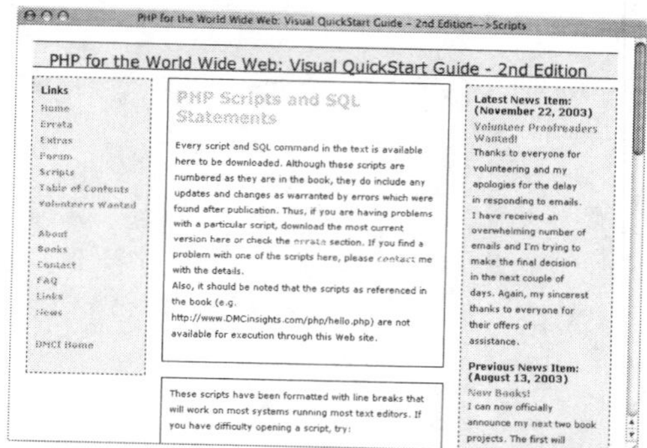

Figure 8.2 The book's "scripts" page uses the same left and right columns as the home page (Figure 8.1), thanks to the templates.

The Three-Second Guide to CSS

Cascading Style Sheets (CSS) have been an increasingly important part of the World Wide Web for some time. Their initial usage was focused on cosmetics (font sizes, colors, and so on), but now CSS are frequently used in lieu of tables to control the layout of pages. The Web application in this chapter uses this approach.

This example defines two areas of the page—*leftcontent* and *rightcontent*. The leftcontent area changes for each page. The rightcontent contains standard items, such as navigation links, that appear on each page of the application.

Just to be clear: There is no relationship between PHP and CSS other than the fact that you can use PHP to generate CSS, just as you'd use PHP to generate HTML. In this example, though, the CSS is hard-coded into the head section of the HTML document.

The example used in this chapter is based on one of the many CSS examples displayed at glish.com (`http://glish.com/css`). This specific example, in turn, comes from the excellent site A List Apart (`www.alistapart.com`).

Script 8.1 This script represents the end result you're looking for with the template system.

```
<!DOCTYPE html PUBLIC "-//W3C//DTD XHTML
1.0 Transitional//EN"
        "http://www.w3.org/TR/xhtml1/DTD/
        xhtml1-transitional.dtd">
<html xmlns="http://www.w3.org/1999/xhtml">
<head>
    <meta http-equiv="content-type"
    content="text/html; charset=
    iso-8859-1" />
    <title>Elliott Smith Fan Club</title>

<style type="text/css">

    body {
        margin:0px 0px 0px 0px;
        background: #9F9;
        }

    #leftcontent {
        float:left;
        width:67%;
        background:#fff;
        border-right:2px solid #000;
        border-bottom:2px solid #000;
        margin-right:15px;
        padding-bottom:20px;
        }

    p,h1,pre {
        margin:0px 30px 10px 30px;
        }

    h1 {
        font-size:14px;
        padding-top:10px;
        }

    #rightcontent p {
        font-size:14px;
        margin-left:0px;
        }

</style>
</head>
<body>

```

(script continues on next page)

To create the layout model:

1. Begin a new HTML document in your text or WYSIWYG editor (**Script 8.1**):

```
<!DOCTYPE html PUBLIC "-//W3C//DTD
→ XHTML 1.0 Transitional//EN"
"http://www.w3.org/TR/xhtml1/DTD/
→ xhtml1-transitional.dtd">
<html xmlns="http://www.w3.org/1999/
→ xhtml">
<head>
    <meta http-equiv="content-type"
    → content="text/html; charset=
    → iso-8859-1" />
    <title>Elliott Smith Fan Club
    → </title>
```

   The first step in developing any template system is to create a model document—an example of what the resulting PHP page should look like. Once you've created this, you can break it down into its parts.

2. Generate the CSS code:

```
<style type="text/css">
    body {
        margin:0px 0px 0px 0px;
        background: #9F9;
        }
    #leftcontent {
        float:left;
        width:67%;
        background:#fff;
        border-right:2px solid #000;
        border-bottom:2px solid #000;
        margin-right:15px;
        padding-bottom:20px;
        }
    p,h1,pre {
        margin:0px 30px 10px 30px;
        }
```

continues on next page

```
h1 {
    font-size:14px;
    padding-top:10px;
    }
  #rightcontent p {
    font-size:14px;
    margin-left:0px;
    }
</style>
```

This example uses CSS for most of the formatting and layout controls. See the sidebar for a quick introduction to the topic, if you're unfamiliar with it.

3. Close the HTML head, begin the body, and mark the start of the changeable content:

```
</head>
<body>
<!-- BEGIN CHANGEABLE CONTENT. -->
```

Everything up until this point will remain the same for every page in the Web application. To indicate this, you include an HTML comment.

Script 8.1 *continued*

```
<!-- BEGIN CHANGEABLE CONTENT. -->
<div id="leftcontent">
    <h1>Welcome to the Elliott Smith Fan Club!</h1>
    <p>Here's a whole lotta text. Here's a whole lotta text. Here's a whole lotta text. Here's a whole lotta text. Here's a whole lotta text. Here's a whole lotta text. Here's a whole lotta text. Here's a whole lotta text. Here's a whole lotta text. </p>
    <p>Here's a whole lotta text. Here's a whole lotta text. Here's a whole lotta text. Here's a whole lotta text. Here's a whole lotta text. Here's a whole lotta text. Here's a whole lotta text. Here's a whole lotta text. Here's a whole lotta text. </p>
</div>
<!-- END CHANGEABLE CONTENT. -->

<div id="rightcontent">
    <h1>Navigation</h1>
    <p>
    <a href="index.php">Home</a><br />
    <a href="albums.php">Discography</a><br />
    <a href="login.php">Login</a><br />
    <a href="register.php">Register</a><br />
    </p>

</div>

<!-- Script 8.1 - layout.html -->
</body>
</html>
```

4. Create the page's content:

```
<div id="leftcontent">
    <h1>Welcome to the Elliott Smith
    Fan Club!</h1>
    <p>Here's a whole lotta text.
    → Here's a whole lotta text.
    → Here's a whole lotta text.
    → Here's a whole lotta text.
    → Here's a whole lotta text.
    → Here's a whole lotta text.
    → Here's a whole lotta text.
    → Here's a whole lotta text.
    → Here's a whole lotta text.
    → Here's a whole lotta text. </p>
    <p>Here's a whole lotta text.
    → Here's a whole lotta text.
    → Here's a whole lotta text.
    → Here's a whole lotta text.
    → Here's a whole lotta text.
    → Here's a whole lotta text.
    → Here's a whole lotta text.
    → Here's a whole lotta text.
    → Here's a whole lotta text.
    → Here's a whole lotta text. </p>
</div>
```

The *leftcontent* area is defined in the CSS code and is the main content part of the page. For the example, it contains a header and a whole lot of text.

5. Mark the end of the changeable content:

```
<!-- END CHANGEABLE CONTENT. -->
```

The code in Step 4 is the only text that will change on a page-by-page basis. Just as you indicated where that section starts (using an HTML comment), you also indicate where it ends.

continues on next page

6. Create the navigation area:

```
<div id="rightcontent">
   <h1>Navigation</h1>
   <p>
   <a href="index.php">Home</a><br />
   <a href="albums.php">Discography
   → </a><br />
   <a href="login.php">Login</a><br />
   <a href="register.php">Register</a>
   → <br />
   </p>
</div>
```

The *rightcontent* area (also defined in the CSS code) contains links to the other pages in the Web application.

7. Finish the HTML page:

```
<!-- Script 8.1 - layout.html -->
</body>
</html>
```

8. Save the file as `layout.html` and test in your Web browser (**Figure 8.3**).

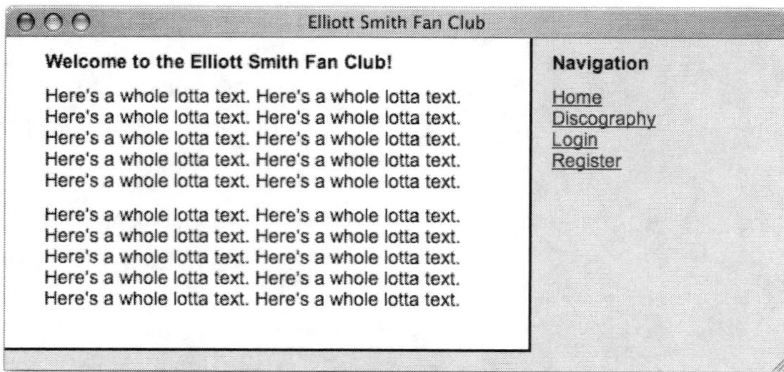

Figure 8.3 Although this isn't very fancy, it gives you a model to work toward with your PHP templates.

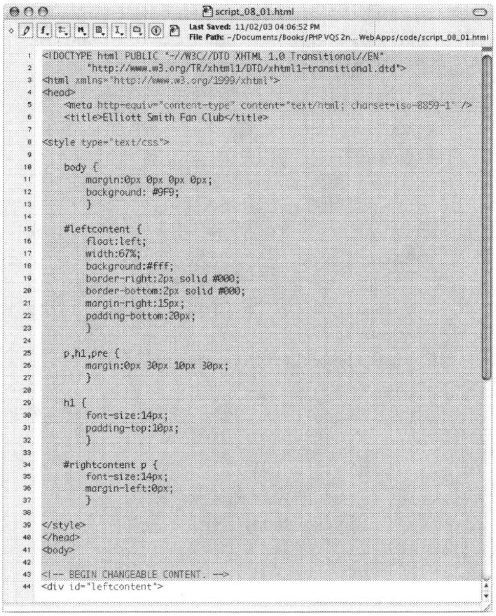

script_08_01.html

Last Saved: 11/02/03 04:06:52 PM
File Path: ~/Documents/Books/PHP VQS 2n... WebApps/code/script_08_01.html

```
<!DOCTYPE html PUBLIC "-//W3C//DTD XHTML 1.0 Transitional//EN"
        "http://www.w3.org/TR/xhtml1/DTD/xhtml1-transitional.dtd">
<html xmlns="http://www.w3.org/1999/xhtml">
<head>
    <meta http-equiv="content-type" content="text/html; charset=iso-8859-1" />
    <title>Elliott Smith Fan Club</title>

<style type="text/css">

    body {
        margin:0px 0px 0px 0px;
        background: #9F9;
        }

    #leftcontent {
        float:left;
        width:67%;
        background:#fff;
        border-right:2px solid #000;
        border-bottom:2px solid #000;
        margin-right:15px;
        padding-bottom:20px;
        }

    p,h1,pre {
        margin:0px 30px 10px 30px;
        }

    h1 {
        font-size:14px;
        padding-top:10px;
        }

    #rightcontent p {
        font-size:14px;
        margin-left:0px;
        }

</style>
</head>
<body>

<!-- BEGIN CHANGEABLE CONTENT. -->
<div id="leftcontent">
```

Figure 8.4 Using the example file, select and copy the initial lines of code to create the header.

Once you've completed a model that you like, you can break it into its various parts to generate the template system.

To create the header file:

1. Open `layout.html` (Script 8.1) in your text editor, if it isn't already open.
2. Select everything from the initial HTML code to the `<!-- BEGIN CHANGEABLE CONTENT -->` HTML comment (**Figure 8.4**).

   Part of the benefit of identifying the start of the page-specific content with an HTML comment is that it simplifies breaking the model into its parts.
3. Copy this code.

   Using your Edit menu or keyboard shortcut (Ctrl+C on Windows, Command+C on the Macintosh), copy all of the highlighted code to your computer's temporary memory (which is to say, the clipboard).
4. Create a new, blank document in your text editor.

continues on next page

5. Paste the copied text into the document (**Script 8.2**).

   Using your Edit menu or keyboard shortcut (Ctrl+V on Windows, Command+V on the Macintosh), paste all of the highlighted code into this new document.

6. Save the file as `header.html`.

Script 8.2 This is a basic header file that creates the HTML head information (including the CSS) and begins the body.

```
<!DOCTYPE html PUBLIC "-//W3C//DTD XHTML
1.0 Transitional//EN"
        "http://www.w3.org/TR/xhtml1/DTD/
        xhtml1-transitional.dtd">
<html xmlns="http://www.w3.org/1999/xhtml">
<head>
    <meta http-equiv="content-type"
    content="text/html; charset=
    iso-8859-1" />
    <title>Elliott Smith Fan Club</title>

<style type="text/css">

    body {
        margin:0px 0px 0px 0px;
        background: #9F9;
        }

    #leftcontent {
        float:left;
        width:67%;
        background:#fff;
        border-right:2px solid #000;
        border-bottom:2px solid #000;
        margin-right:15px;
        padding-bottom:20px;
        }

    p,h1,pre {
        margin:0px 30px 10px 30px;
        }

    h1 {
        font-size:14px;
        padding-top:10px;
        }

    #rightcontent p {
        font-size:14px;
        margin-left:0px;
        }

</style>
</head>
<body>

<!-- BEGIN CHANGEABLE CONTENT. -->
<!-- Script 8.2 - header.html -->
```

Script 8.3 This is a basic footer file that creates the navigation column and concludes the HTML page.

```
<!-- END CHANGEABLE CONTENT. -->

<div id="rightcontent">
    <h1>Navigation</h1>
    <p>
    <a href="index.php">Home</a><br />
    <a href="albums.php">Discography</a>
    <br />
    <a href="login.php">Login</a><br />
    <a href="register.php">Register</a>
    <br />
    </p>

</div>

<!-- Script 8.3 - footer.html -->
</body>
</html>
```

```
text. </p>
</div>
<!-- END CHANGEABLE CONTENT. -->

<div id="rightcontent">
    <h1>Navigation</h1>
    <p>
    <a href="index.php">Home</a><br />
    <a href="albums.php">Discography</a><br />
    <a href="login.php">Login</a><br />
    <a href="register.php">Register</a><br />
    </p>

</div>

<!-- Script 8.1 - layout.html -->
</body>
</html>
```

Figure 8.5 Again using the example file, select and copy the concluding lines of code for the footer.

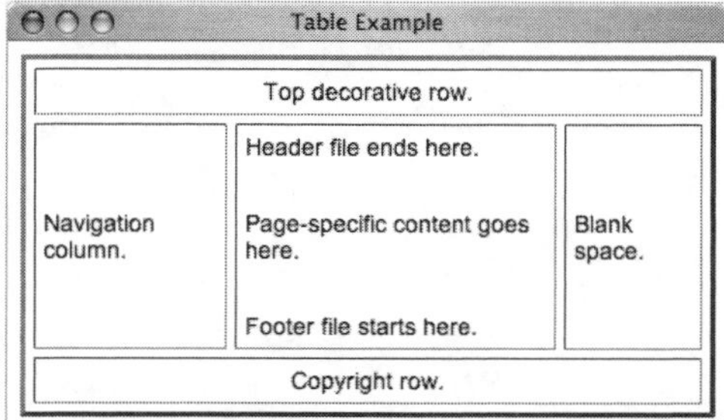

Figure 8.6 This mundane example shows how a table is used with template files to create a design.

Now that the header file has been created, you'll make the footer file using the same process.

To create the footer file:

1. Open `layout.html` (Script 8.1) in your text editor, if it isn't already open.
2. Select everything from the `<!-- END CHANGEABLE CONTENT -->` HTML comment to the end of the script (**Figure 8.5**).
3. Copy this code.
4. Create a new, blank document in your text editor.
5. Paste the copied text into the document (**Script 8.3**).
6. Save the file as `footer.html`.

✔ Tips

- There are many far more complex template systems you can use in PHP to separate the design from the logic. These include Smarty (`http://smarty.php.net`) and TemplateTamer (`www.templatetamer.com`).
- Although this example used CSS for its layout, you can certainly use tables instead (**Figure 8.6**). Your header file might begin the HTML page and the table. Each content page would then create its own specific content, and the footer file would complete the table and the HTML page. To turn this into a template, copy all of the code up to *Page-specific content goes here.* into a header file and everything after that into a footer file.

Using External Files

As the previous section said, you can save time by creating separate pages for particular elements and then bringing them into the main PHP pages using specific functions. These functions are `include()` and `require()`:

```
include ('file.php');
require ('file.html');
```

Both functions work the same way, with one relatively insignificant difference. If the `include()` function fails, the PHP script generates a warning (**Figure 8.7**) but continues to run. Conversely, if `require()` fails, it terminates the execution of the script (**Figure 8.8**).

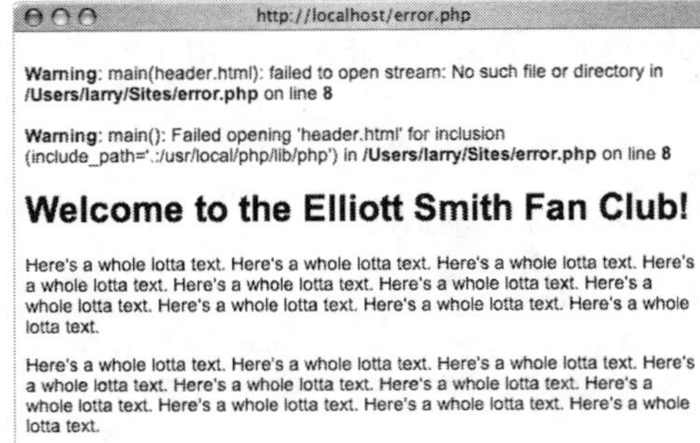

Figure 8.7 When an `include()` fails, warnings are issued, but the script continues to execute.

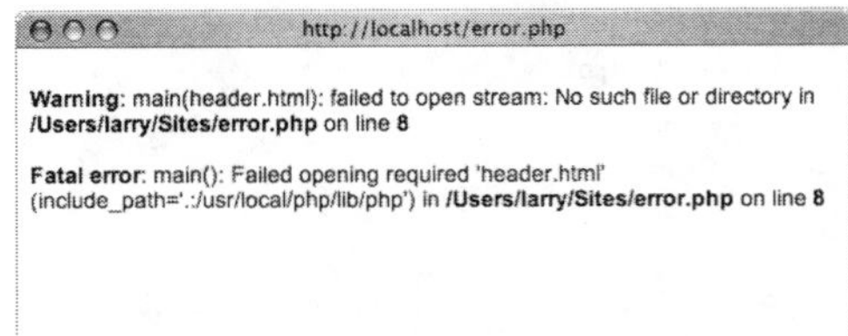

Figure 8.8 When a `require()` function call fails, warnings and errors are issued, and the script stops running.

But what do these two functions do? Both `include()` and `require()` incorporate the file referenced into the main file (for clarity's sake, this chapter refers to the file that has the `include()` or `require()` line as the *parent* file). Any code within the included file is treated as HTML unless it's within the PHP tags in the included file itself. This way, included files behave exactly as if you were running them in the Web browser.

There are any number of reasons to use included files. You could put your own defined functions into a common file (see Chapter 10, "Creating Functions," for information on writing your own functions). You might also want to place your database access information into a configuration file (see Chapter 12, "Introduction to Databases"). First, however, let's include the template files created in the previous section of the chapter in order to make pages abide by a consistent design.

File Navigation, File Extensions, and Site Structure

To be able to use external files, you need to understand file navigation on your computer or server. Just as you'd refer to other pages in HTML links or images in Web sites, you must properly point your parent file to the included scripts.

You can do this using *absolute* or *relative* paths. An absolute path is a specific address, like the following:

```
require ('C:\inetpub\wwwfiles\file.php');
require ('/Users/larry/Sites/file.php');
```

As long as the included files aren't moved (within the computer or from one computer to another), an absolute path will always work.

A relative path indicates where the included file is in relation to the parent file. These examples assume both are within the same directory:

```
require ('file.php');
require ('./file.php');
```

The included file can also be in a directory below the parent one:

```
require('otherfiles/file.php');
```

(In other words, the parent file and the `otherfiles` directory are in the same folder, and `file.php` is located within `otherfiles`.)

Or, the included file could be in the directory above the parent:

```
require('../file.php');
```

As part of this discussion of how you refer to files, let's revisit the topic of file extensions. As you know, you need to use `.php` for any file containing PHP, so the Web server will treat it properly. If it has no PHP, you can use `.html` (this is generally true, although it can vary from server to server). The file extension matters less for your included files, because the files aren't intended to be accessed directly in the Web browser.

As a general rule of thumb, you'll be safe using `.html` for an included file containing only or mostly HTML (in which case the extension indicates it's an HTML-related file) and `.php` for included files containing only or mostly PHP. Some programmers use an `.inc` extension (for *include*), but security risks can be associated with this practice. In fact, the most important rule is to use the `.php` extension for any file containing sensitive information (like database access parameters).

Finally, a note on site structure. Once you divvy your Web application into multiple pieces, you should begin thinking about arranging the files in appropriate folders. Complex sites might have the main folder, another for images, one for administration files, and a special directory for templates and included files. As long as you properly reference the files in your `include()` statements, structuring your applications will work fine and give the added benefit of making them easier to maintain.

To use external files:

1. Create a new PHP document in your text editor.

2. Start with the initial PHP tags and add any comments (**Script 8.4**):

```
<?php // Script 8.4 - index.php
// This is the home page. It uses
→ templates.
```

   Notice that, with the template system, the very first line of the script is the PHP tag. There's no need to begin with the initial HTML stuff, because it's now stored in the `header.html` file.

3. Address error handling, if necessary:

```
ini_set ('display_errors', 1);
error_reporting (E_ALL & ~E_NOTICE);
```

4. Include the header file:

```
require ('templates/header.html');
```

   To use the template system, you include the header file here using the `require()` function. Because the header file contains only HTML, all of its contents will be immediately sent to the Web browser as if they were part of this file. You use a relative path to refer to the included file (see the sidebar) and assume it's stored in the `templates` directory.

5. Close the PHP section and create the page-specific content:

```
?>
<div id="leftcontent">
   <h1>Welcome to the Elliott Smith
   → Fan Club!</h1>
   <p>Here's a whole lotta text.
   → Here's a whole lotta text.
   → Here's a whole lotta text.
   → Here's a whole lotta text.
   → Here's a whole lotta text.
   → Here's a whole lotta text.
   → Here's a whole lotta text.
   → Here's a whole lotta text. </p>
```

Script 8.4 Once the two included files have been created, the `require()` function incorporates them into the parent file to create the entire page on the fly.

```
<?php // Script 8.4 - index.php
// This is the home page. It uses templates.

// Address error handing.
ini_set ('display_errors', 1);
error_reporting (E_ALL & ~E_NOTICE);

require ('templates/header.html'); // Need the header.

// Leave the PHP section to display lots of HTML.
?>

<div id="leftcontent">
    <h1>Welcome to the Elliott Smith Fan Club!</h1>
    <p>Here's a whole lotta text. Here's a whole lotta text. Here's a whole lotta text. Here's a whole lotta text. Here's a whole lotta text. Here's a whole lotta text. Here's a whole lotta text. Here's a whole lotta text. Here's a whole lotta text. </p>
    <p>Here's a whole lotta text. Here's a whole lotta text. Here's a whole lotta text. Here's a whole lotta text. Here's a whole lotta text. Here's a whole lotta text. Here's a whole lotta text. Here's a whole lotta text. Here's a whole lotta text. </p>
</div>

<?php // Return to PHP.
require ('templates/footer.html'); // Need the footer.
?>
```

```
    <p>Here's a whole lotta text.
    → Here's a whole lotta text.
    → Here's a whole lotta text.
    → Here's a whole lotta text.
    → Here's a whole lotta text.
    → Here's a whole lotta text.
    → Here's a whole lotta text.
    → Here's a whole lotta text.
    → Here's a whole lotta text.
    → Here's a whole lotta text. </p>
</div>
```

Because the bulk of this page is standard HTML, you exit out of the PHP section and then type the HTML (rather than using `print()` to send it to the Web browser).

6. Create another PHP section and require the footer file:

   ```
   <?php
   require ('templates/footer.html');
   ?>
   ```

   To conclude the page, you need to include the footer file (which displays the navigation and closes the HTML code). To do this, you create a new section of PHP—you can have multiple sections of PHP code within a script—and call the `require()` function again.

7. Save the file as `index.php`.

8. Create a folder called `templates` within the main Web document directory (on your PHP-enabled computer or Web server).

   To further separate the design elements from the main content, the header and footer files go within their own directory.

9. Upload `index.php`, `header.html`, and `footer.html` to your Web browser (or place them in the proper directory on your PHP-enabled computer).

   The index file should be in the same directory as the `templates` folder, and the header and footer files should go within `templates`.

continues on next page

10. Run `index.php` in your Web browser (**Figure 8.9**).

    The resulting page should look exactly like the original layout (Figure 8.3).

11. View the page's source code in your Web browser (**Figure 8.10**).

    The source code should be exactly like the source code of the `layout.html` script (Script 8.1), aside from the altered and added comments for the script names and numbers.

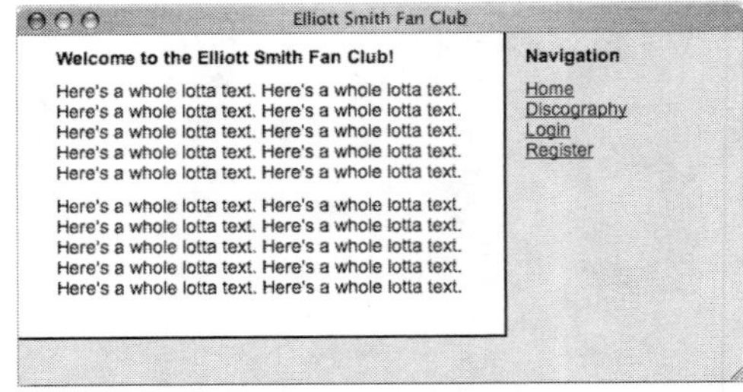

Figure 8.9 This page has been dynamically generated using included files.

Source of http://127.0.0.1/temp/

```
        }

    p,h1,pre {
        margin:0px 30px 10px 30px;
        }

    h1 {
        font-size:14px;
        padding-top:10px;
        }

    #rightcontent p {
        font-size:14px;
        margin-left:0px;
        }

</style>
</head>
<body>

<!-- BEGIN CHANGEABLE CONTENT. -->
<!-- Script 8.2 - header.html -->
<div id="leftcontent">
    <h1>Welcome to the Elliott Smith Fan Club!</h1>
    <p>Here's a whole lotta text. Here's a whole lotta text. Here's a whole lotta text. Here's a
whole lotta text. Here's a whole lotta text. Here's a whole lotta text. Here's a whole lotta text.
Here's a whole lotta text. Here's a whole lotta text. Here's a whole lotta text. </p>
    <p>Here's a whole lotta text. Here's a whole lotta text. Here's a whole lotta text. Here's a
whole lotta text. Here's a whole lotta text. Here's a whole lotta text. Here's a whole lotta text.
Here's a whole lotta text. Here's a whole lotta text. Here's a whole lotta text. </p>
</div>

<!-- END CHANGEABLE CONTENT. -->

<div id="rightcontent">
    <h1>Navigation</h1>
    <p>
    <a href="index.php">Home</a><br />
    <a href="albums.php">Discography</a><br />
    <a href="login.php">Login</a><br />
    <a href="register.php">Register</a><br />
    </p>

</div>

<!-- Script 8.3 - footer.html -->
</body>
</html>
```

Figure 8.10 Nothing in the page's source indicates that this was compiled on the fly (OK, the comments do, but you understand). You can see how the two included files are brought in as if they were a part of the parent file.

✔ Tips

- The `require()` and `include()` functions can be used with or without parentheses:

```
require 'filename.html';
require $filename;
```

- Prior to version 4.0.2 of PHP, regardless of where the `require()` function was within your script, it was always called, even if it was the result of a conditional that was never true! The `include()` function, conversely, took effect only if the function was called. This significant difference between the two functions has since been dropped.
- Both `include()` and `require()` have variations: `include_once()` and `require_once()`. Each is identical to its counterpart except that it allows the same file to be included only one time (in a parent script).
- If you see error messages like those in Figures 8.7 and 8.8, the parent script can't locate an included file. This problem is most likely caused by a misspelled included filename or an error in the path (for example, using `header.html` instead of `templates/header.html`).
- Another good use of an external file is to place your error settings code there so that the settings changes are applied to every page in the Web site.

Using Constants

Constants are a specific data type in PHP. Unlike variables, they retain their initial value throughout the course of a script. You can't change the value of a constant once it has been set.

To create a constant, you use the `define()` function instead of the assignment operator (=) used for variables:

```
define ('CONSTANT_NAME', 'constant
→ value');
```

Notice that—as a rule of thumb—constants are named using all capital letters, although this isn't required. Most important, constants don't use the initial dollar sign as variables do (because constants are not variables).

Referring to constants is generally straightforward:

```
print CONSTANT_NAME;
some_function ( CONSTANT_NAME );
```

But using constants within quotation marks is more complicated. You can't print constants within single or double quotation marks, like this:

```
print "Hello, FIRST_NAME";
print 'Hello, FIRST_NAME';
```

In both cases, the literal text *Hello, FIRST_NAME* will be sent to the Web browser. Instead, you use concatenation or multiple `print()` statements:

```
print 'Hello, ' . FIRST_NAME;
```

or

```
print 'Hello, ';
print FIRST_NAME;
```

Script 8.5 This script uses the same template system as `index.php` (Script 8.4) but also uses a constant to identify the page's title.

```
<?php // Script 8.5 - albums.php
// This page lists Elliott Smith's discography.

// Address error handing.
ini_set ('display_errors', 1);
error_reporting (E_ALL & ~E_NOTICE);

// Set the page title and include the header file.
define ('TITLE', 'Records by Elliott Smith');
require ('templates/header.html');

// Leave the PHP section to display lots of HTML.
?>

<div id="leftcontent">
    <h1>Elliott Smith's Albums</h1>
    <p>
    <ul>
        <li>Roman Candle</li>
        <li>Elliott Smith</li>
        <li>Either/Or</li>
        <li>XO</li>
        <li>Figure 8</li>
    </ul>
    </p>
</div>

<?php // Return to PHP.
require ('templates/footer.html'); // Need the footer.
?>
```

Not to confuse you, but along with the `define()` function for making constants is the `defined()` function, which returns TRUE if the submitted constant has been defined:

```
defined ('CONSTANT_NAME'); // TRUE
defined ('OOPS'); //FALSE
```

As an example of working with constants, you'll give the example application the ability to display a different title (which appears at the top of the browser window) for each page. To accomplish this, you'll define a constant in the parent script that's printed by the header file. This technique works because any variable or constants that exist in the parent document before the `include()` or `require()` call are available to the included file (it's as if the included file was part of the parent file).

To use constants:

1. Create a new PHP document in your text editor, beginning with the initial PHP tag (**Script 8.5**):

   ```
   <?php // Script 8.5 - albums.php
   ```

2. Address error handling, if necessary:

   ```
   ini_set ('display_errors', 1);
   error_reporting (E_ALL & ~E_NOTICE);
   ```

continues on next page

3. Define the page title as a constant:

```
define ('TITLE', 'Records by Elliott
→ Smith');
```

Here you define one constant, TITLE, and give it the value *Records by Elliott Smith.*

4. Include the header file:

```
require ('templates/header.html');
```

This script uses the same header file as all the others, although you'll modify it shortly to take the constant into account.

5. Close the PHP section and create the HTML:

```
?>
<div id="leftcontent">
   <h1>Elliott Smith's Albums</h1>
   <p>
   <ul>
      <li>Roman Candle</li>
      <li>Elliott Smith</li>
      <li>Either/Or</li>
      <li>XO</li>
      <li>Figure 8</li>
   </ul>
   </p>
</div>
```

The content here is simple but serves the page's purpose nicely.

6. Create a new PHP section that includes the footer file:

```
<?php
require ('templates/footer.html');
?>
```

7. Save the file as albums.php.

Script 8.6 Modify the `header.html` file so that it can set the page title value based on the existence and value of a constant.

```
Script
1    <!DOCTYPE html PUBLIC "-//W3C//DTD XHTML 1.0 Transitional//EN"
2            "http://www.w3.org/TR/xhtml1/DTD/xhtml1-transitional.dtd">
3    <html xmlns="http://www.w3.org/1999/xhtml">
4    <head>
5        <meta http-equiv="content-type" content="text/html; charset=iso-8859-1" />
6        <title>
7        <?php // Print the page title.
8        if (defined ('TITLE')) { // Is the title defined?
9            print TITLE;
10       } else { // The title is not defined.
11           print 'Elliott Smith Fan Club';
12       }
13       ?>
14   </title>
15
16   <style type="text/css">
17
18       body {
19           margin:0px 0px 0px 0px;
20           background: #9F9;
21           }
22
23       #leftcontent {
24           float:left;
25           width:67%;
26           background:#fff;
27           border-right:2px solid #000;
28           border-bottom:2px solid #000;
29           margin-right:15px;
30           padding-bottom:20px;
31           }
32
33       p,h1,pre {
34           margin:0px 30px 10px 30px;
35           }
36
37       h1 {
38           font-size:14px;
39           padding-top:10px;
40           }
41
```

(script continues on next page)

To take advantage of the constant, you now need to rewrite the `header.html` file.

To print out a constant:

1. Open `header.html` (Script 8.2) in your text editor.
2. Delete the *Elliott Smith Fan Club* text that appears between the `title` tags (line 6).

   Now that the page title will be determined on a page-by-page basis, you don't need it to be hard-coded into the page.
3. In the place of the deleted text (between the `title` tags), add the following (**Script 8.6**):

   ```
   <?php
   if (defined ('TITLE')) {
     print TITLE;
   } else {
     print 'Elliott Smith Fan Club';
   }
   ?>
   ```

   To have PHP create the page title, you need to begin by starting a section of PHP code between the `title` tags. Then you use a conditional to see if the `TITLE` constant has been defined. If it has, you print its value as the page title. If `TITLE` hasn't been defined, you print a default title.
4. Save the file as `header.html`.
5. Upload `albums.php` and `header.html` to your Web server (`albums.php` should be in the same directory as `index.php`; `header.html` should replace the previous version, in the same directory—`templates`—as `footer.html`).

continues on next page

6. Run `albums.php` in your Web browser (**Figure 8.11**).

7. View `index.php` (the home page) in your Web browser (**Figure 8.12**).

8. If you want, add the constant definition line to `index.php`.

✔ Tips

- The formal rules for naming constants are exactly like those for variables except for the omission of a dollar sign. Constant names must begin with a letter; can contain any combination of letters, numbers, and the underscore; and are case-sensitive.

- To be frank, this is a trivial use of a constant (a variable would have worked just as well for setting the page title), but it was time to present the idea to you. A good use of constants is for establishing your database connection information.

- PHP runs with several predefined constants. These include `PHP_VERSION` (the version of PHP running) and `PHP_OS` (the operating system of the server).

- In Chapter 9, "Cookies and Sessions," you'll learn about another constant, `SID` (which stands for *session ID*).

- An added benefit of using constants is that they're global in scope. This concept will mean more to you after you read the "Understanding Variable Scope" section of Chapter 10.

- Not only can the value of a constant never be changed, a constant can't be deleted. Also, unlike arrays, a constant can only ever contain a single value, like a string or a number variable.

Script 8.6 *continued*

```
	#rightcontent p {
		font-size:14px;
		margin-left:0px;
		}

</style>
</head>
<body>

<!-- BEGIN CHANGEABLE CONTENT. -->
<!-- Script 8.6 - header.html -->
```

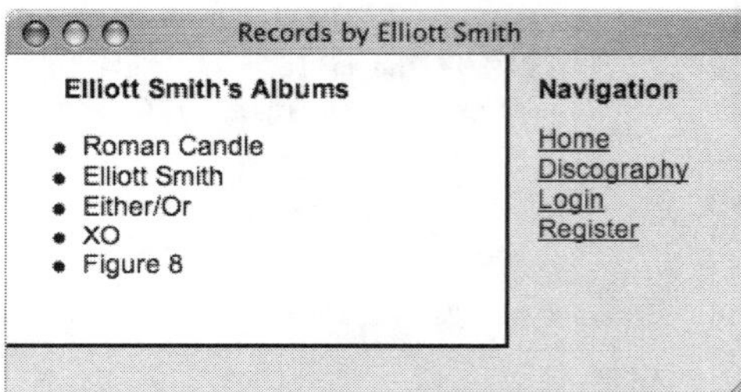

Figure 8.11 The albums page uses a PHP constant to create its title.

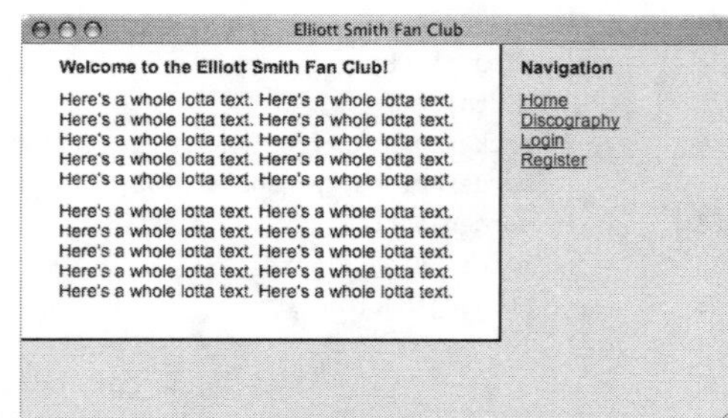

Figure 8.12 Because the index page didn't have a `TITLE` constant defined in it, the default page title is used (thanks to the conditional in Script 8.6).

Date() Function Formatting

CHARACTER	MEANING	EXAMPLE
Y	Year as 4 digits	2004
y	Year as 2 digits	04
n	Month as 1 or 2 digits	2
m	Month as 2 digits	02
F	Month	February
M	Month as 3 letters	Feb
j	Day of the month as 1 or 2 digits	8
d	Day of the month as 2 digits	08
l (lowercase L)	Day of the week	Monday
D	Day of the week as 3 letters	Mon
w	Day of the week as a single digit	0 (Sunday)
z	Day of the year: 0 to 365	189
t	Number of days in the given month	31
S	English ordinal suffix for a day, as 2 characters	rd
g	Hour; 12-hour format as 1 or 2 digits	6
G	Hour; 24-hour format as 1 or 2 digits	18
h	Hour; 12-hour format as 2 digits	06
H	Hour; 24-hour format as 2 digits	18
i	Minutes	45
s	Seconds	18
a	am or pm	am
A	AM or PM	PM
U	Seconds since the epoch	1048623008

Table 8.1 The list of formatting possibilities for the `date()` function is long and not easy to remember. You should keep a copy of this list close at hand while you program.

Working with the Date and Time

PHP has a few functions for working with the date and time, the most important of which is `date()`. The only thing the `date()` function does is return date and time information in a format based on the arguments it's fed, but you'd be surprised how useful that can be! The basic usage of the `date()` function is just

```
date ('formatting');
```

A long list of possible options is available for formatting, as indicated in **Table 8.1**. These parameters can also be combined—for example, `date ('l F j, Y');` returns *Friday January 26, 2004*.

The `date()` function can take another argument called a *timestamp*. A timestamp is a number representing how many seconds have passed since midnight on January 1, 1970—a moment referred to as the *epoch*. The `time()` function returns the timestamp for the current moment. The `mktime()` function can return a timestamp for a particular time and date:

```
mktime (hour, minute, second, month,
→ day, year);
```

So the code

```
$timestamp = mktime (12, 30, 0, 11, 5,
→ 2003);
```

assigns to `$timestamp` the number of seconds from the epoch to 12:30 on November 5, 2003. That number can then be fed into the `date()` function like so:

```
date ('D', $timestamp);
```

This returns *Wed*, which is the three-letter format for that day of the week.

To demonstrate the `date()` function, you'll add today's date and time to the footer file.

To use date():

1. Open `footer.html` (Script 8.3) in your text editor.

2. Before the closing `</div>` tag, add the following (**Script 8.7**):

```
<p><em>
<?php
```

   The initial HTML tags format the date and time slightly, putting them in italics (thanks to the emphasis tag). Then you open a PHP section so that you can call the `date()` function.

3. Use the `date()` function to print out today's date and time:

```
print date ( 'g:i a l F j' );
```

   Using the formatting parameters from Table 8.1, the `date()` function will return a value like *4:15 pm Sunday February 22*. This value will immediately be printed.

4. Close the PHP section and finish the HTML code:

```
?>
</p></em>
```

5. Save the file as `footer.html`, upload it to your Web server, and test it in your Web browser (**Figure 8.13**).

✔ Tip

- Because PHP is a server-side technology, these functions reflect the date and time on the server. To get the time on the client (in other words, on the computer where the Web browser viewing the page is located), you must use JavaScript.

Script 8.7 The modified `footer.html` file uses the `date()` function to print the current date and time.

```
<!-- END CHANGEABLE CONTENT. -->

<div id="rightcontent">
    <h1>Navigation</h1>
    <p>
    <a href="index.php">Home</a><br />
    <a href="albums.php">Discography</a>
    <br />
    <a href="login.php">Login</a><br />
    <a href="register.php">Register</a>
    <br />
    </p>

    <p><em>
    <?php
    print date ( 'g:i a l F j' );
    ?>
    </p></em>

</div>

<!-- Script 8.7 - footer.html (second
version after script 8.3) -->
</body>
</html>
```

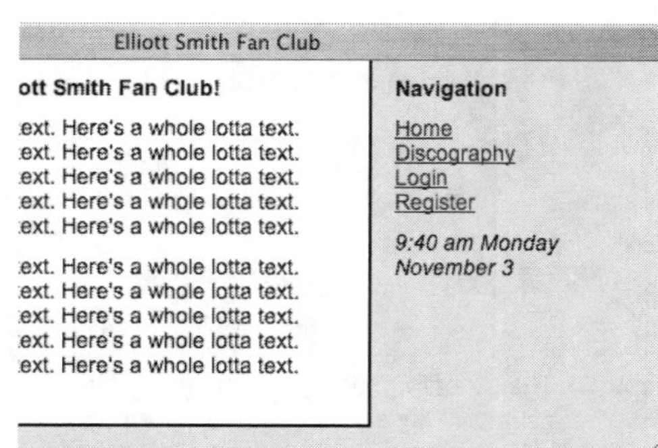

Figure 8.13 The Web site now displays the date and time in the sidebar, thanks to the `date()` function.

Handling HTML Forms with PHP, Revisited

All the examples in this book so far have used two separate scripts for handling HTML forms: one that displayed the form and another that received and processed the form's data. There's certainly nothing wrong with this method, but there are advantages to having the entire process in one script. To make a page both display and handle a form, use a conditional:

```
if (/* form has been submitted */) {
   // Handle the form.
} else {
   // Display the form.
}
```

To determine if the form has been submitted, you can check whether the `submit` variable is set (which means the submit button has been clicked). For example:

```
if (isset ($_POST['submit'])) { …
```

If you want a page to handle a form and then immediately display the form again, do this:

```
if (isset ($_POST['submit'])) {
   // Handle the form.
}
// Display the form.
```

As an example, you'll create the basics of a log-in form.

To use one page to display and handle a form:

1. Begin a new PHP document in your text editor (**Script 8.8**):

```
<?php // Script 8.8 - login.php
ini_set ('display_errors', 1);
error_reporting (E_ALL & ~E_NOTICE);
```

Script 8.8 The log-in page serves two purposes. It displays the log-in form (Figure 8.14) and handles its submission (Figures 8.15, 8.16, and 8.17).

```
<?php // Script 8.8 - login.php
// This page lets people log into the site.

// Address error handling.
ini_set ('display_errors', 1);
error_reporting (E_ALL & ~E_NOTICE);

// Set the page title and include the header file.
define ('TITLE', 'Login');
require ('templates/header.html');

// Basic HTML formatting stuff.
print '<div id="leftcontent">
    <h1>Login Form</h1>
    <p>Users who are logged in can take advantage of certain features like this, that, and the
    other thing.</p>';

// Check if the form has been submitted.
if ( isset ($_POST['submit'])) {

    // Handle the form.
    if ( (!empty ($_POST['username'])) && (!empty ($_POST['password'])) ) {

        if ( ($_POST['username'] == 'testing') && ($_POST['password'] == 'testpass') ) { // Okay.

            print '<p>You are now logged in!<br />Now you can blah, blah, blah...</p>';

        } else { // Not okay.

            print '<p>The submitted username and password do not match those on file!<br />Go back
            and try again.</p>';

        }

    } else { // Forgot a field.

        print '<p>Please make sure you enter both a username and a password!<br />Go back and try
        again.</p>';
```

(script continues on next page)

Script 8.8 *continued*

```

    }

} else {

    // Display the form.
    print '<form action="login.php" method="post"><p>
    Username: <input type="text" name="username" size="20" /><br />
    Password: <input type="password" name="password" size="20" /><br />
    <input type="submit" name="submit" value="Log In!" /></p>
    </form>';

} // End of main conditional.

// Complete the HTML formatting stuff.
print '</div>';

require ('templates/footer.html'); // Need the footer.
?>
```

2. Define the page title as a constant and include the header file:

```
define ('TITLE', 'Login');
require ('templates/header.html');
```

Using the constant system developed earlier in the chapter, you give this page its own unique page title.

3. Add some HTML text and formatting:

```
print '<div id="leftcontent">
  <h1>Login Form</h1>
  <p>Users who are logged in can
  → take advantage of certain
  → features like this, that, and
  → the other thing.</p>';
```

This text, which appears outside of the main conditional, will always show in the Web browser, whether the form is being displayed or has been submitted. Because the core of this script revolves around a PHP conditional, you print out the HTML from PHP rather than exit out of the PHP code as you did in the previous two examples (`index.php` and `albums.php`).

4. Begin the conditional to check whether the form has been submitted:

```
if ( isset ($_POST['submit'])) {
```

To test whether the form has been submitted, you check whether the `$_POST['submit']` variable has a value (is set). Alternatively, you could use the trick developed in Chapter 7, "Using Arrays," where you start the script with

```
$submit = $_POST['submit'];
```

and then use

```
if ( isset ($submit)) {
```

here.

continues on next page

5. Create a nested pair of conditionals to process the form data:

```
if ( (!empty ($_POST['username'])) &&
→ (!empty ($_POST['password'])) ) {
   if ( ($_POST['username'] ==
   → 'testing') && ($_POST['password']
   → == 'testpass') ) {
      print '<p>You are now logged in!
      → <br />Now you can blah, blah,
      → blah... </p>';
   } else {
      print '<p>The submitted
      → username and password do not
      → match those on file!<br />
      → Go back and try again. </p>';
   }
} else {
   print '<p>Please make sure you
   → enter both a username and a
   → password!<br />Go back and try
   → again. </p>';
}
```

These conditionals handle the form data. First, one conditional checks that both the username and password variables have values. If they don't, a message is displayed (*Please make sure...*). Within that, another conditional checks whether the username is equal to *testing* and the password is equal to *testpass*. If so, let's say the user is logged in (it would be too advanced at this juncture to store and retrieve user information). Otherwise, a message indicates that the wrong values were entered.

Be certain to use the equals operator (==) here and not the assignment operator (=), a common mistake.

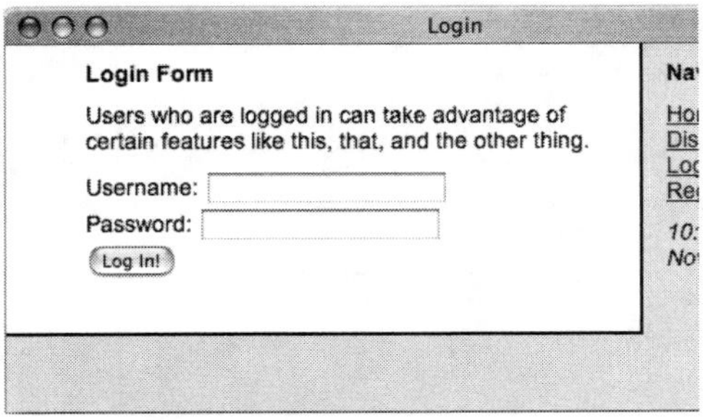

Figure 8.14 This simple log-in page takes a username and password.

6. Complete the main conditional:

```
} else {
   print '<form action="login.php"
   → method="post"><p>
   Username: <input type="text" name=
   → "username" size="20" /><br />
   Password: <input type="password"
   → name="password" size="20" /><br />
   <input type="submit" name="submit"
   → value="Log In!" /></p>
   </form>';
}
```

   This concludes the main conditional, which checks whether the form has been submitted. If it hasn't been, then the form is displayed. The form itself is very simple (**Figure 8.14**).

   In order for this process to work—where the same page both handles and displays the form—the `name` attribute of your submit button must exactly match the name of the variable used as the conditional (and it's case-sensitive, remember).

7. Complete the HTML:

```
print '</div>';
```

   This concludes the *leftcontent* `div` started in Step 3.

continues on next page

8. Require the footer file and complete the PHP page:

```
require ('templates/footer.html');
?>
```

9. Save the file as `login.php`, upload it to your Web server, and test it in your Web browser (**Figures 8.15**, **8.16**, and **8.17**).

✔ Tips

- Alternatively, you can check whether a form has been submitted by testing for the presence of another variable, like a hidden input.
- If you use an image for your form submission button, you can't use the `isset($_POST['submit'])` code, because the submit variable won't have a value.

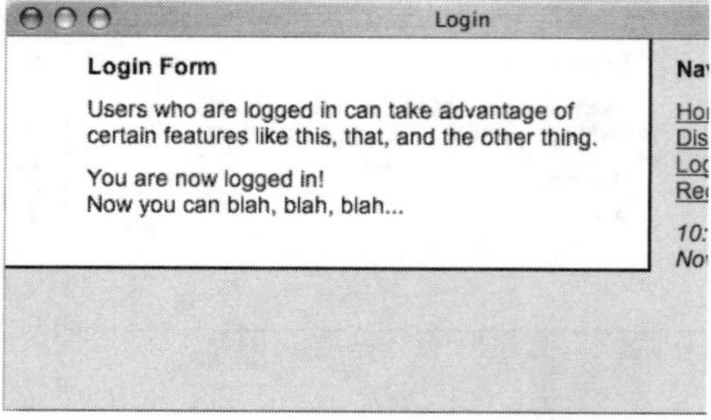

Figure 8.15 Upon successfully logging in, the user sees this message.

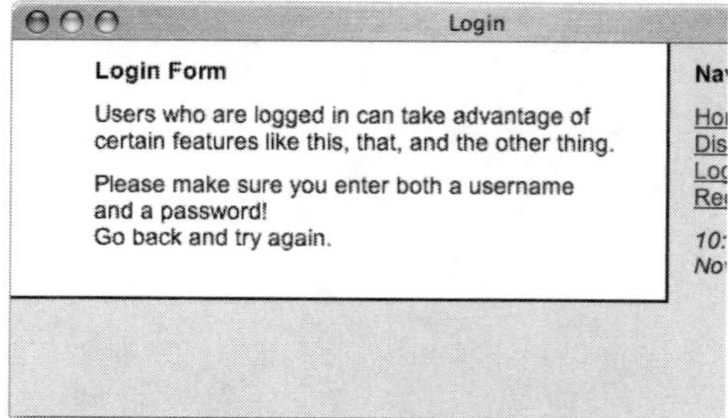

Figure 8.16 Failure to submit either a username or a password results in this message.

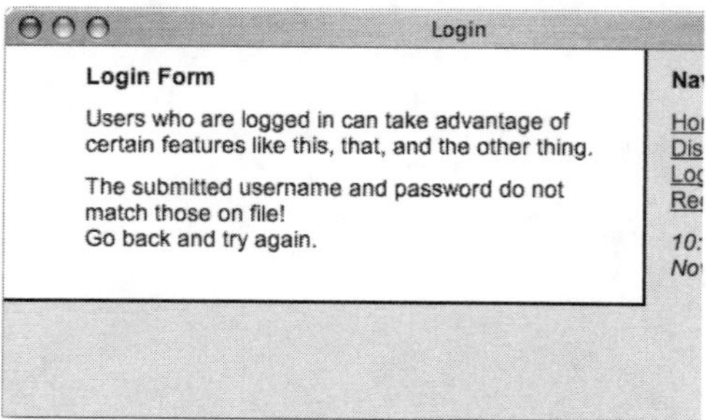

Figure 8.17 If either the username or the password doesn't match that in the script, the user sees this error message.

Making Forms Sticky

A *sticky* form remembers values entered into it. A common example is the Google search engine, which always displays your terms in the search box, even after you click on the Google Search button. You might also want to use sticky forms on occasions where the user failed to complete a form accurately and therefore must complete it again.

From a technological standpoint, sticky forms work by having your form inputs' values predetermined. You can do this by setting the value input when you create the form:

```
<input type="text" name="first_name"
→ size="20" value="Stephanie" />
```

To have PHP preset that value, print the appropriate variable between the quotation marks:

```
<input type="text" name="first_name"
→ size="20" value="<?php print
→ $first_name; ?>" />
```

The first time the form is run, the PHP code prints nothing (because the variable has no value). If the form is displayed again after submission, values that the user originally entered in the form input will be displayed there automatically. To demonstrate, you'll create the shell of a registration form.

To make a sticky form:

1. Create a new PHP script in your text editor (**Script 8.9**):

   ```
   <?php // Script 8.9 - register.php
   ini_set ('display_errors', 1);
   error_reporting (E_ALL & ~E_NOTICE);
   ```

2. Set the page title and include the HTML header:

   ```
   define ('TITLE', 'Register');
   require ('templates/header.html');
   ```

3. Add some HTML formatting:

   ```
   print '<div id="leftcontent">
      <h1>Registration Form</h1>
      <p>Register so that you can take advantage of certain features like this, that, and the other thing.</p>';
   ```

4. Check whether the form has been submitted:

   ```
   if ( isset ($_POST['submit'])) {
   ```

   Like the log-in page, this script both displays and handles the registration form. You don't have to use this method to make a sticky form, but it makes the process significantly easier.

   Again, you use the `$_POST` superglobal array to access the form values. You can also use `$submit` if `register_globals` is enabled or `$HTTP_POST_VARS['submit']` if you have an earlier version of PHP.

5. Create a flag variable:

   ```
   $problem = FALSE;
   ```

   The `$problem` variable is used to indicate whether a problem occurred. Specifically, you want to make sure that every form input has been filled out before you formally register the user. Initially, this variable is set to FALSE, because no problems have occurred.

Script 8.9 The registration form uses a so-called *sticky* feature so that it recalls the values entered into it.

```
<?php // Script 8.9 - register.php
// This page lets people register for the site (sort of).

// Address error handling.
ini_set ('display_errors', 1);
error_reporting (E_ALL & ~E_NOTICE);

// Set the page title and include the header file.
define ('TITLE', 'Register');
require ('templates/header.html');

// Basic HTML formatting stuff.
print '<div id="leftcontent">
    <h1>Registration Form</h1>
    <p>Register so that you can take advantage of certain features like this, that, and the other thing.</p>';

// Check if the form has been submitted.
if ( isset ($_POST['submit'])) {

    $problem = FALSE; // No problems so far.

    // Check for each value.
    if (empty ($_POST['username'])) {
        $problem = TRUE;
        print '<p>Please enter a username!</p>';
    }

    if (empty ($_POST['first_name'])) {
        $problem = TRUE;
        print '<p>Please enter your first name!</p>';
    }

    if (empty ($_POST['last_name'])) {
        $problem = TRUE;
        print '<p>Please enter your last name!</p>';
    }

    if (empty ($_POST['email'])) {
        $problem = TRUE;
        print '<p>Please enter your email address!</p>';
    }
```

(script continues on next page)

Script 8.9 *continued*

```
Script

    if (empty ($_POST['password1'])) {
        $problem = TRUE;
        print '<p>Please enter a password!
        </p>';
    }

    if ($_POST['password1'] != $_POST
    ['password2']) {
        $problem = TRUE;
        print '<p>Your password did not
        match your confirmed
        password!</p>';
    }

    if (!$problem) { // If there weren't
    any problems...

        print '<p>You are now registered!
        <br />Okay, you are not really
        registered but...</p>';

    } else { // Forgot a field.

        print '<p>Please try again!</p>';

    }

} // End of handle form IF.

// Display the form.
print '<form action="register.php"
method="post"><p>';

print 'Username: <input type="text"
name="username" size="20" value="' .
$_POST['username'] . '" /><br />';

print 'First Name: <input type="text"
name="first_name" size="20" value=
"' . $_POST['first_name'] . '" /><br />
Last Name: <input type="text"
name="last_name" size="20" value=
"' . $_POST['last_name'] . '" /><br />
Email Address: <input type="text"
name="email" size="20" value=
"' . $_POST['email'] . '" /><br />';

```

(script continues on next page)

6. Check that a username was entered:

```
if (empty ($_POST['username'])) {
    $problem = TRUE;
    print '<p>Please enter a username!
    → </p>';
}
```

As a simple test to determine whether the user has entered a username value, you check that the variable isn't empty. (This technique was first discussed in Chapter 6, "Control Structures.") If the variable is empty, then you indicate a problem by setting that variable to TRUE and print an error message.

7. Repeat the validation for the first name, last name, and email address:

```
if (empty ($_POST['first_name'])) {
    $problem = TRUE;
    print '<p>Please enter your first
    → name!</p>';
}
if (empty ($_POST['last_name'])) {
    $problem = TRUE;
    print '<p>Please enter your last
    → name!</p>';
}
if (empty ($_POST['email'])) {
    $problem = TRUE;
    print '<p>Please enter your email
    → address!</p>';
}
```

Each of these checks is a variation on the username validation routine.

continues on next page

8. Validate the passwords:

```
if (empty ($_POST['password1'])) {
   $problem = TRUE;
   print '<p>Please enter a password! </p>';
}
if ($_POST['password1'] != $_POST['password2']) {
   $problem = TRUE;
   print '<p>Your password did not match your confirmed password! </p>';
}
```

The password validation requires two conditionals. The first checks whether the `$password1` variable is empty. The second checks whether the `$password1` variable isn't equal to the `$password2` variable. You don't need to see if `$password2` is empty because if it is and `$password1` isn't, the second conditional will catch it. If `$password2` and `$password1` are both empty, the first conditional will catch that.

9. Check whether a problem occurred, and complete the main conditional:

```
   if (!$problem) {
      print '<p>You are now registered! <br />Okay, you are not really registered but...</p>';
   } else {
      print '<p>Please try again!</p>';
   }
}
```

If there were no problems, the `$problem` variable is still FALSE, and the initial condition here is TRUE (the condition being that `$problem` has a value of FALSE). In that case, the registration process would take place. The formal registration process, where the data is stored in a file or database, has not yet been developed, so a simple message

Script 8.9 *continued*

```
print 'Password: <input type="password" name="password1" size="20" /><br />
Confirm Password: <input type="password" name="password2" size="20" /><br />
<input type="submit" name="submit" value="Register!" /></p>
</form>';

// Complete the HTML formatting stuff.
print '</div>';

require ('templates/footer.html'); // Need the footer.
?>
```

appears in its stead here. If a problem occurred, the user is asked to complete the form again.

10. Begin the HTML form:

```
print '<form action="register.php"
→ method="post"><p>';
```

Unlike the log-in example, this page always displays the form. Therefore, the form isn't part of any conditional.

Note that, to explain this process clearly, the example breaks the form creation into four separate `print()` statements. You could combine Steps 10, 11, 12, and 13 into one large `print()` statement instead.

11. Create the sticky username input:

```
print 'Username: <input type="text"
→ name="username" size="20" value=
→ "' . $_POST['username'] . '" />
→ <br />';
```

To make the username input sticky, you preset its `value` attribute by printing out the `$username` variable. The easiest way to do this is to concatenate a single-quoted `print()` statement with the variable name. Alternatively, you could code

```
print "Username: <input type=\"text\"
→ name=\"username\" size=\"20\"
→ value=\"{$_POST['username']}\" />
→ <br />";
```

You can use whichever syntax makes the most sense to you—just be careful, because it's easy to introduce parse errors in these situations.

continues on next page

12. Repeat the process for the first name, last name, and email address:

```
print 'First Name: <input type="text"
→ name="first_name" size="20"
→ value="' . $_POST['first_name'] . '" />
→ <br />
Last Name: <input type="text"
→ name="last_name" size="20"
→ value="' . $_POST['last_name'] . '" />
→ <br />
Email Address: <input type="text"
→ name="email" size="20"
→ value="' . $_POST['email'] . '" />
→ <br />';
```

These are variations on Step 11, switching the variable names as appropriate.

13. Add the rest of the form:

```
print 'Password: <input type=
→ "password" name="password1"
→ size="20" /><br />
Confirm Password: <input type=
→ "password" name="password2"
→ size="20" /><br />
<input type="submit" name="submit"
→ value="Register!" /></p>
</form>';
```

You can't preset a value for a password input, so there's no point in trying. Otherwise, this `print()` statement concludes the HTML form (**Figure 8.18**).

14. Complete the HTML formatting and the PHP page:

```
print '</div>';
require ('templates/footer.html');
?>
```

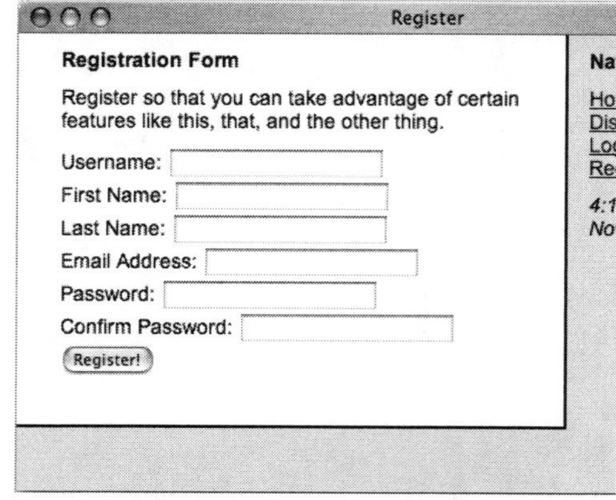

Figure 8.18 The registration form as the user first sees it.

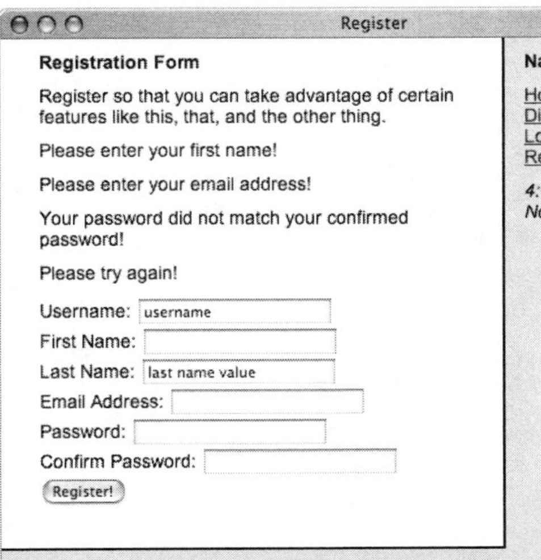

Figure 8.19 The registration form indicates any problems and retains the form values, except for the passwords.

Figure 8.20 The registration form after the user successfully fills it out.

15. Save the file as `register.php`, upload it to your Web server, and test it in your Web browser (**Figures 8.19** and **8.20**).

✔ Tips

- According to (X)HTML rules, you must quote all attributes in form inputs. Specifically, you should use double quotation marks. If you don't quote your values, any spaces in them mark the end of the value (for example, *Larry Ullman* will display as just *Larry* in the form input).

- To preset the status of radio buttons or check boxes as checked, add the code `checked="checked"` to their input tag:

```
<input type="checkbox"
→ name="interests[]" value="Skiing"
→ checked="checked" />
```

- To preselect a pull-down menu, use `selected="selected"`:

```
<select name="year">
<option value="2003">2003</option>
<option value="2004" selected=
→ "selected">2004</option>
</select>
```

- To preset the value of a textarea, place the value between the `textarea` tags:

```
<textarea name="comments" rows="10"
→ cols="50">preset value</textarea>
```

- If you don't want the form to retain the user-submitted values (in other words, it shouldn't be sticky after a successful use), add the line

```
$_POST = array();
```

  just after the successful registration message to reset this variable.

Making Forms Sticky

Sending Email

Among the numerous things you can do with great ease in PHP is send email. To do so, you use the `mail()` function. The `mail()` function uses the server's email application (such as sendmail on Unix or Mac OS X) or an SMTP (Simple Mail Transfer Protocol) server to send out the messages (see the sidebar):

```
mail ('mailto', 'subject', 'body');
```

The first argument is the email address (or addresses) the mail should be sent to. The second argument sets the message's subject line, and the third argument creates the text of the message.

This function can take another argument through which you can add more details (additional headers) to the email, including a *From* address, email priority, and carbon-copy addresses:

```
mail ('mailto', 'subject', 'body', 'From:
→ email@address.com');
```

As an example, you'll add a `mail()` function call to the registration page.

Configuring Your Server to Send Email

Sending email with PHP is easy, as long as your Web server (or computer) is set up to send email. If you're using a Web hosting service or your own Unix computer (like Linux), this shouldn't be a problem. However, if you're running your own Windows or Mac OS X machine—as many of you probably are—this could be a sticking point.

You should try this example using a valid email address. If you don't receive the email, see Appendix A, "Installation and Configuration," for information about getting `mail()` to work. Just so you're prepared, not everyone will be able to get their own computer to send out email.

Script 8.10 In PHP, you can send email with only one function—`mail()`.

Script

```
<?php // Script 8.10 - register.php (second version after Script 8.9)
// This page lets people register for the site (sort of).

// Address error handing.
ini_set ('display_errors', 1);
error_reporting (E_ALL & ~E_NOTICE);

// Set the page title and include the header file.
define ('TITLE', 'Register');
require ('templates/header.html');

// Basic HTML formatting stuff.
print '<div id="leftcontent">
    <h1>Registration Form</h1>
    <p>Register so that you can take advantage of certain features like this, that, and the other thing.</p>';

// Check if the form has been submitted.
if ( isset ($_POST['submit'])) {

    $problem = FALSE; // No problems so far.

    // Check for each value.
    if (empty ($_POST['username'])) {
        $problem = TRUE;
        print '<p>Please enter a username!</p>';
    }

    if (empty ($_POST['first_name'])) {
        $problem = TRUE;
        print '<p>Please enter your first name!</p>';
    }

    if (empty ($_POST['last_name'])) {
        $problem = TRUE;
        print '<p>Please enter your last name!</p>';
    }

    if (empty ($_POST['email'])) {
        $problem = TRUE;
        print '<p>Please enter your email address!</p>';
    }
```

(script continues on next page)

To send email with PHP:

1. Open `register.php` (Script 8.9) in your text editor.

2. After the registration message (line 55), add the following (**Script 8.10**):

   ```
   $body = "Thank you for registering with the Elliott Smith fan club!
   Your username is {$_POST['username']}.
   Your password is {$_POST['password1']}.";
   mail ($_POST['email'], 'Thank you for registering at the Elliott Smith Fan Club!', $body, 'From: admin@site.com');
   ```

   Sometimes the easiest way to use this function is to establish the body as a variable and then feed it into the `mail()` function. The message itself is sent to the address with which the user registered, with the subject *Thank you for registering at the Elliott Smith Fan Club!*, from the address admin@site.com.

continues on next page

Script 8.10 *continued*

Script

```
    if (empty ($_POST['password1'])) {
        $problem = TRUE;
        print '<p>Please enter a password!</p>';
    }

    if ($_POST['password1'] != $_POST['password2']) {
        $problem = TRUE;
        print '<p>Your password did not match your confirmed password!</p>';
    }

    if (!$problem) { // If there weren't any problems...

        print '<p>You are now registered!<br />Okay, you are not really registered but...</p>';

        // Send the email.
        $body = "Thank you for registering with the Elliott Smith fan club!
Your username is {$_POST['username']}. Your password is {$_POST['password1']}.";
        mail ($_POST['email'], 'Thank you for registering at the Elliott Smith Fan Club!', $body, 'From: admin@site.com');

    } else { // Forgot a field.

        print '<p>Please try again!</p>';

    }

} // End of handle form IF.

// Display the form.
print '<form action="register.php" method="post"><p>';

print 'Username: <input type="text" name="username" size="20" value="' . $_POST['username'] . '" /><br />';

print 'First Name: <input type="text" name="first_name" size="20" value="' . $_POST['first_name'] . '" /><br />
Last Name: <input type="text" name="last_name" size="20" value="' . $_POST['last_name'] . '" /><br />
Email Address: <input type="text" name="email" size="20" value="' . $_POST['email'] . '" /><br />';

print 'Password: <input type="password" name="password1" size="20" /><br />
Confirm Password: <input type="password" name="password2" size="20" /><br />
<input type="submit" name="submit" value="Register!" /></p>
</form>';

// Complete the HTML formatting stuff.
print '</div>';

require ('templates/footer.html'); // Need the footer.
?>
```

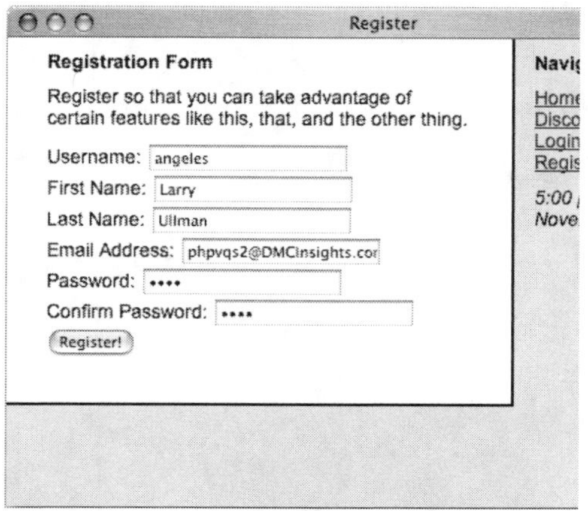

Figure 8.21 Testing the registration form again...

Registration Form

Register so that you can take advantage of certain features like this, that, and the other thing.

You are now registered!
Okay, you are not really registered but...

Username: angeles
First Name: Larry
Last Name: Ullman
Email Address: phpvqs2@DMCinsights.cor
Password:
Confirm Password:
Register!

Figure 8.22 ...and now you should receive an email confirming the registration process (Figure 8.23).

Thank you for registering at the Elliott Smith Fan Club!

From: admin@site.com
Subject: **Thank you for registering at the Elliott Smith Fan Club!**
Date: December 13, 2003 6:44:16 PM EST
To: phpvqs2@dmcinsights.com

Thank you for registering with the Elliott Smith fan club!
Your username is angeles. Your password is pass.

Figure 8.23 This email was sent by the PHP script.

3. Save the file, upload it to your Web server (or place it in the proper directory of your PHP- and email-enabled computer), and test it in your Web browser (**Figures 8.21** and **8.22**).

4. Check your email for the message (**Figure 8.23**).

✔ Tips

- It's possible to send email with attachments or HTML email, although doing so requires far more sophisticated coding (normally involving classes and objects). Fortunately, a number of programmers have already developed workable solutions that are available for use. See Appendix B, "Resources," for Web sites that may be of assistance.

- The `mail()` function returns a value (*1* or *0*) indicating its successful use. This value only indicates whether PHP was able to *attempt* to send the email (by using whatever email system is in place). There's no easy way to use PHP to tell whether an email address is valid or whether the end user received the message.

- To send an email to multiple addresses, either use the *CC* parameter or separate each *TO* address with a comma.

- To create new lines within the email body, either create the message over multiple lines, as in this example, or use the newline character (\n) within double quotation marks.

- If you want to send multiple headers in addition to the *From* address, separate them with a combination of \r\n:

```
mail ('phpvqs2@DMCInsights.com',
→ 'Testing', $body, "From:
→ email@address.com\r\nBcc:
→ hidden@address.com,
→ third@address.com");
```

Output Buffering

Output control (or output buffering) allows you to write and execute your scripts as normal but send data to the Web browser only at select points. The main benefit of this system is that you can call the `header()`, `setcookie()`, and `session_start()` functions—all of which you'll soon learn—at nearly any spot in your script without concern for the *headers already sent error messages*, (**Figure 8.24**). Although you haven't dealt with any of these functions yet, the chapter introduces output buffering now because it will greatly reduce errors as you begin using headers (in the next section of this chapter), cookies (in the next chapter), and sessions (also in the next chapter).

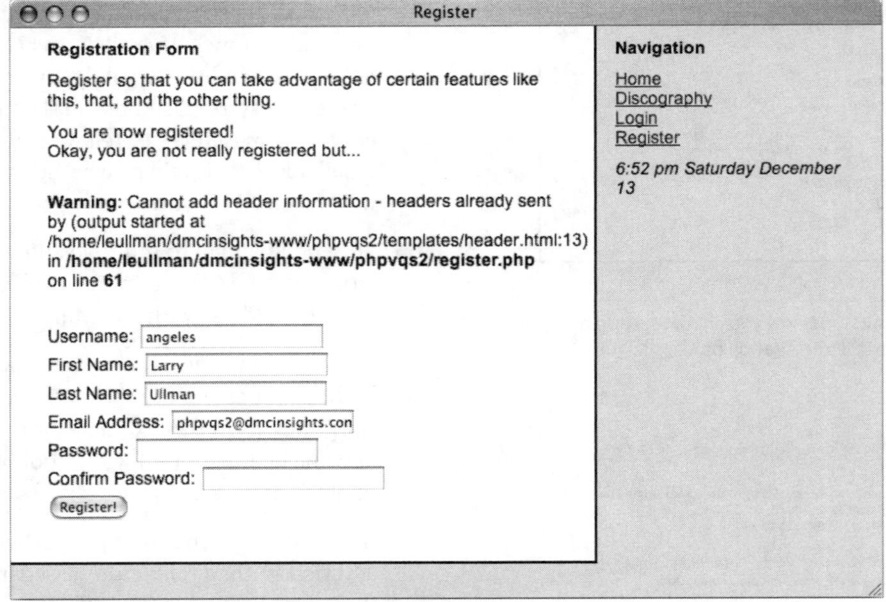

Figure 8.24 If the browser receives any HTML prior to a `header()` call, you'll see this error message.

Script 8.11 Add output buffering to the Web application by placing the `ob_start()` function at the top of the `header.html` script.

```
<?php // Script 8.11 - header.html (third version after Scripts 8.6 and 8.2)

// Turn on output buffering.
ob_start();

?>
<!DOCTYPE html PUBLIC "-//W3C//DTD XHTML 1.0 Transitional//EN"
        "http://www.w3.org/TR/xhtml1/DTD/xhtml1-transitional.dtd">
<html xmlns="http://www.w3.org/1999/xhtml">
<head>
    <meta http-equiv="content-type" content="text/html; charset=iso-8859-1" />
    <title>
    <?php // Print the page title.
    if (defined ('TITLE')) { // Is the title defined?
        print TITLE;
    } else { // The title is not defined.
        print 'Elliott Smith Fan Club';
    }
    ?>
</title>

<style type="text/css">

    body {
        margin:0px 0px 0px 0px;
        background: #9F9;
        }

    #leftcontent {
        float:left;
        width:67%;
        background:#fff;
        border-right:2px solid #000;
        border-bottom:2px solid #000;
        margin-right:15px;
        padding-bottom:20px;
        }

    p,h1,pre {
        margin:0px 30px 10px 30px;
        }

```

(script continues on next page)

To begin output buffering, use the `ob_start()` function at the very top of your page. Once you call it, every `print()` and similar function will send data to a memory buffer rather than to the Web browser. Conversely, HTTP calls (like `header()` and `setcookie()`) won't be buffered and will operate as usual.

At the conclusion of the script, call the `ob_end_flush()` function to send the accumulated buffer to the Web browser. Or, use the `ob_end_clean()` function to delete the buffered data without passing it along. Both functions turn off output buffering.

From a programmer's perspective, output buffering allows you to structure a script in a more linear form, without concern for HTTP headers. Let's remake `header.html` and `footer.html` so that every page uses output buffering. You won't appreciate the benefits yet, but the number of errors you won't see over the rest of this book will go a long way toward your programming sanity.

To use output buffering:

1. Open `header.html` (Script 8.6) in your text editor.

2. At the very top of the page, before any HTML code, add the following (**Script 8.11**):

   ```
   <?php // Script 8.11 - header.html
   ob_start();
   ?>
   ```

   The key to using output buffering is to call the `ob_start()` function as early as possible in a script. In this example, you create a special section of PHP prior to any HTML and call `ob_start()` there. By turning on output buffering in your header file and turning it off in your footer file, you buffer every page in the Web application.

continues on next page

3. Save the file.
4. Open `footer.html` (Script 8.7) in your text editor.
5. At the end of the script, after all the HTML, add this (**Script 8.12**):

```
<?php // Script 8.12 - footer.html
ob_end_flush();
?>
```

   This code turns off output buffering and sends the accumulated buffer to the Web browser. In other words, all the HTML is sent at this point.
6. Save the file.
7. Upload both files to the Web server (placing them in the `templates` directory) and test any page in your Web browser (**Figure 8.25**).

Script 8.11 *continued*

```
    h1 {
        font-size:14px;
        padding-top:10px;
        }

    #rightcontent p {
        font-size:14px;
        margin-left:0px;
        }

</style>
</head>
<body>

<!-- BEGIN CHANGEABLE CONTENT. -->
```

Script 8.12 Output buffering is completed at the end of the footer file using `ob_end_flush()`, which sends the accumulated buffer to the Web browser.

```
<!-- END CHANGEABLE CONTENT. -->

<div id="rightcontent">
    <h1>Navigation</h1>
    <p>
    <a href="index.php">Home</a><br />
    <a href="albums.php">Discography</a><br />
    <a href="login.php">Login</a><br />
    <a href="register.php">Register</a><br />
    </p>

    <p><em>
    <?php
    print date ( 'g:i a l F j' );
    ?>
    </em></p>

</div>

</body>
</html>
<?php // Script 8.12 - footer.html (third version after Scripts 8.7 and 8.3)

// Send the buffer to the browser and turn off buffering.
ob_end_flush();
?>
```

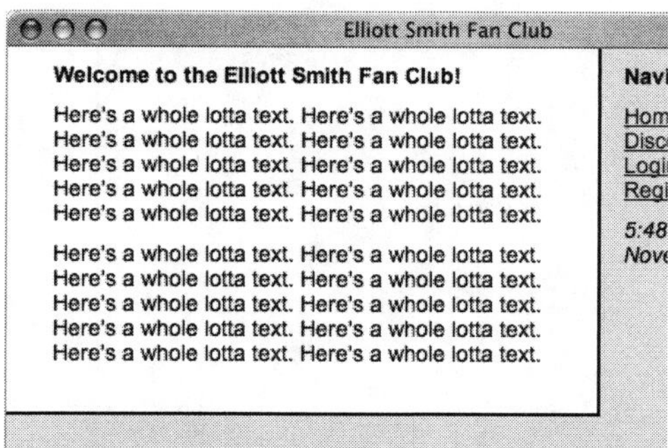

Figure 8.25 The site works the same as it did previously, but it will be easier to work with when you use HTTP headers later in this chapter.

✓ Tips

- You can set the maximum buffer size in the `php.ini` file. The default is 4,096 characters.
- You can send compressed output to browsers by starting output control with `ob_start('ob_gzhandler')`, minimizing the download size of your pages. The `ob_gzhandler()` function determines the appropriate type of compression to use (*gzip*, *deflate*, or *none*) based on what the browser can accept. Understand that compression is beneficial only on larger Web pages, and in order to use it, the `output_buffering` setting in the `php.ini` file must be set to *Off*.
- The `ob_get_length()` function returns the length (in number of characters) of the current buffer contents.
- The `ob_get_contents()` function returns the current buffer so that it can be assigned to a variable, should the need arise.
- The `ob_flush()` function—new as of PHP 4.2—sends the current contents of the buffer to the Web browser and then discards them, allowing a new buffer to be started. This function lets your scripts maintain more moderate buffer sizes.
- The `ob_clean()` function—also new as of PHP 4.2—deletes the current contents of the buffer without stopping the buffer process.
- PHP automatically runs `ob_end_flush()` at the conclusion of a script if it isn't otherwise done. But it's still a good idea to call it yourself.

Manipulating HTTP Headers

An HTTP (HyperText Transfer Protocol) header is used to send information back and forth between the server and the client (the Web browser). Normally this information is in the form of HTML, which is why the addresses for Web pages begin with `http://`.

But the subject of HTTP headers is complicated enough to warrant a little more attention. There are dozens of uses for HTTP headers, all of which you can take advantage of using PHP's `header()` function.

This section demonstrates the most frequently used purpose: redirecting the user from one page to another. To redirect the user's browser with PHP, you code

```
header ('Location: page.php');
```

Normally, the `header()` function is followed by `exit()`, to cancel the execution of the script (because the browser has been redirected to another page):

```
header ('Location: page.php');
exit();
```

The most important thing to understand about using `header()` is that the function must be called before anything else is sent to the Web browser—otherwise you'll see the all-too-common *Headers already sent* error message (Figure 8.24). If your Web page receives any HTML or even blank space, the `header()` function won't work.

Fortunately for you, the previous section introduced output buffering. Because output buffering is turned on in the Web application, nothing is sent to the Web browser until the very last line of the footer script (when `ob_end_flush()` is called). By using this method, you can avoid errors like those in Figure 8.24.

To demonstrate redirection, you'll rewrite the log-in page to take the user to a welcome page upon successful log-in.

To use the header() function:

1. Open `login.php` in your text editor (Script 8.8):
2. Delete the *You are now logged in...* `print()` statement (**Script 8.13**).

   Because the user is redirected to another page, there's no need to include this message.

continues on next page

Script 8.13 The new version of the log-in page redirects the user to another page using the `header()` function.

```
<?php // Script 8.13 - login.php (second version after Script 8.8)
// This page lets people log into the site.

// Address error handing.
ini_set ('display_errors', 1);
error_reporting (E_ALL & ~E_NOTICE);

// Set the page title and include the header file.
define ('TITLE', 'Login');
require ('templates/header.html');

// Basic HTML formatting stuff.
print '<div id="leftcontent">
    <h1>Login Form</h1>
    <p>Users who are logged in can take advantage of certain features like this, that, and the
    other thing.</p>';

// Check if the form has been submitted.
if ( isset ($_POST['submit'])) {

    // Handle the form.
    if ( (!empty ($_POST['username'])) && (!empty ($_POST['password'])) ) {

        if ( ($_POST['username'] == 'testing') && ($_POST['password'] == 'testpass') ) { // Okay.

            // Redirect the user to the welcome page!
            header ('Location: welcome.php');
            exit();

        } else { // Not okay.

```

(script continues on next page)

3. Where the `print()` statement was, add

```
header ('Location: welcome.php');
exit();
```

The first line redirects the user to `welcome.php`. The second line terminates the execution of the rest of the script.

4. Save the file.

Script 8.13 *continued*

```
            print '<p>The submitted username and password do not match those on file!<br />Go back and try again.</p>';

        }

    } else { // Forgot a field.

        print '<p>Please make sure you enter both a username and a password!<br />Go back and try again.</p>';

    }

} else {

    // Display the form.
    print '<form action="login.php" method="post"><p>
    Username: <input type="text" name="username" size="20" /><br />
    Password: <input type="password" name="password" size="20" /><br />
    <input type="submit" name="submit" value="Log In!" /></p>
    </form>';

}

// Complete the HTML formatting stuff.
print '</div>';

require ('templates/footer.html'); // Need the footer.
?>
```

Now you need to create the `welcome.php` page:

3. Create a new PHP document in your text editor (**Script 8.14**):

```
<?php // Script 8.14 - welcome.php
ini_set ('display_errors', 1);
error_reporting (E_ALL & ~E_NOTICE);
```

4. Define the page title and include the header:

```
define ('TITLE', 'Welcome to the
→ Elliott Smith Fan Club!');
require ('templates/header.html');
```

continues on next page

Script 8.14 The welcome page greets the user after they've logged in.

```
<?php // Script 8.14 - welcome.php
// This is the welcome page. It's used after the user logs in.

// Address error handing.
ini_set ('display_errors', 1);
error_reporting (E_ALL & ~E_NOTICE);

define ('TITLE', 'Welcome to the Elliott Smith Fan Club!');
require ('templates/header.html'); // Need the header.

// Leave the PHP section to display lots of HTML.
?>

<div id="leftcontent">
    <h1>Welcome to the Elliott Smith Fan Club!</h1>
    <p>You've successfully logged in and can now take advantage of everything the site has to
    offer.</p>
    <p>Here's a whole lotta text. Here's a whole lotta text. Here's a whole lotta text. Here's a
    whole lotta text. Here's a whole lotta text. Here's a whole lotta text. Here's a whole lotta
    text. Here's a whole lotta text. Here's a whole lotta text. Here's a whole lotta text. </p>
</div>

<?php // Return to PHP.
require ('templates/footer.html'); // Need the footer.
?>
```

5. Create the page content:

```
?>
<div id="leftcontent">
   <h1>Welcome to the Elliott Smith
   Fan → Club!</h1>
   <p>You've successfully logged in
   → and can now take advantage of
   → everything the site has to offer.
   → </p>
   <p>Here's a whole lotta text.
   → Here's a whole lotta text.
   → Here's a whole lotta text.
   → Here's a whole lotta text.
   → Here's a whole lotta text.
   → Here's a whole lotta text.
   → Here's a whole lotta text.
   → Here's a whole lotta text.
   → Here's a whole lotta text.
   → Here's a whole lotta text. </p>
</div>
```

6. Return to PHP and include the footer:

```
<?php
require ('templates/footer.html');
?>
```

7. Save the script as `welcome.php`, upload it to the server along with the new version of `login.php`, and test it in your Web browser (**Figures 8.26**, **8.27**, and **8.28**).

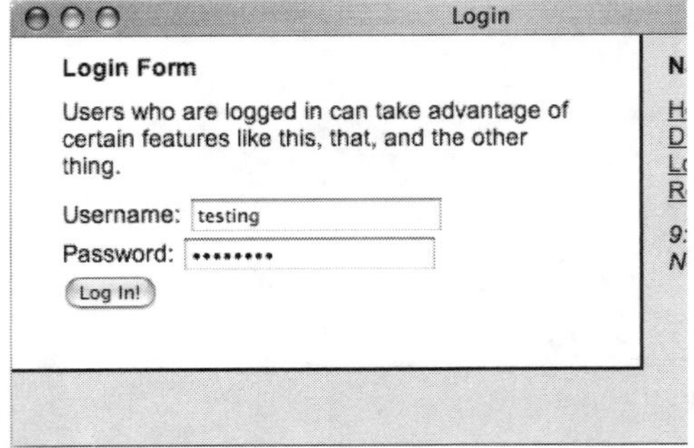

Figure 8.26 The log-in form...

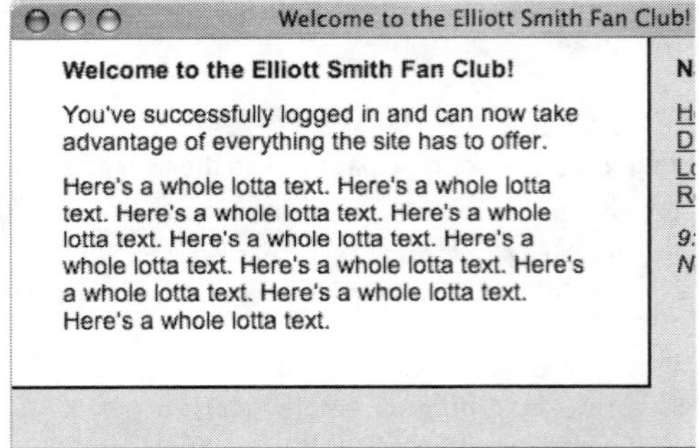

Figure 8.27 ...and the redirection if the user properly logged in.

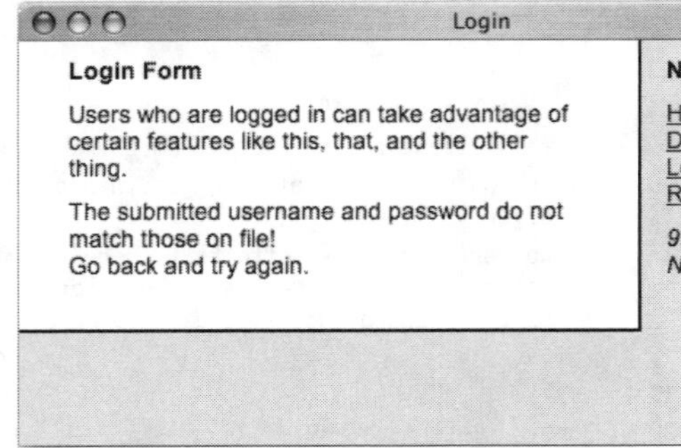

Figure 8.28 If the user didn't properly log in, they remain on the log-in page.

Using Absolute URLs with header()

You should ideally use an absolute URL with the header() function (for example, http://www.dmcinsights.com/site.php rather than just site.php). To do so in your scripts, you have two choices. First, you could hard-code the absolute URL using

```
header ('Location: http://
→ www.dmcinsights.com/admin/
→ page.php');
```

This method works unless the server configuration changes, the URL changes, or you move the script.

A more flexible method is to use the $_SERVER superglobal and the dirname() function (which returns the directory path of the current script). The PHP manual recommends the following code to redirect to a page located in the same directory as the current script:

```
header ('Location:  http://
→ ' . $_SERVER['HTTP_HOST'] .
→ dirname($_SERVER['PHP_SELF']) .
→ '/newpage.php');
```

This will effectively redirect the user to the current domain (www.dmcinsights.com), the current directory (admin), and the new page.

✔ Tips

- You can also use the header() function as an alternative to the setcookie() function, which you'll learn about in the next chapter.
- The headers_sent() function returns TRUE if the page has already received HTTP headers and the header() function can't be used.
- It would be a good idea to delete the accumulated page buffer using the ob_end_clean() function before you redirect the user (because the accumulated buffer won't be used).
- Using the GET method trick, you can pass values from one page to another using header():

  ```
  $var = urlencode ('Passing this text');
  header ("Location: page.php?message=
  → $var");
  ```

- The header() function should technically use a full path to the target page when redirecting. For example, it should be

  ```
  header ('Location: http://
  → www.dmcinsights.com/welcome.php');
  ```

  or

  ```
  header ('Location: http://localhost/
  → welcome.php');
  ```

  See the sidebar for a cool PHP trick to make this happen dynamically.

9 Cookies and Sessions

In the previous chapter, you learned a number of techniques for developing more complete Web applications. One of the problems you'll encounter as you begin to assemble a multi-page Web site is that the HyperText Transfer Protocol (HTTP) is a stateless technology. As a Web developer, this means you have no built-in method for tracking a user or remembering data from one page of an application to the next. This is a serious problem, because e-commerce applications, user registration and login systems, and other common online services rely on this functionality. Fortunately, maintaining state from one page to another is fairly simple using PHP.

This chapter discusses the two main methods for tracking data: cookies and sessions. You'll start by learning how to create, read, modify, and delete cookies. Then you'll see how easy it is to master sessions, a slightly more potent option for maintaining state.

What Are Cookies?

Cookies are one of the less understood and most maligned tools for today's World Wide Web. Many users have concerns about the security issues cookies are rumored to create, but few people realize what benefits cookies offer to the user.

Prior to the existence of cookies, traversing a Web site was a trip without a history. Although your browser tracks the pages you visit, allowing you to use the Back button to return to previously visited pages and indicating visited links in a different color, the server keeps no record of who has seen what. This is still true for sites that don't use cookies, as well as for users who have disabled cookies in their Web browsers (**Figure 9.1**).

Why is that a problem? If the server can't track a user, there can be no shopping carts for you to use to make purchases online. If cookies didn't exist (or if they're disabled in your Web browser), people wouldn't be able to use popular sites that require user registration.

Cookies are a way for a server to store information about the user (on the user's machine) so that the server can remember the user over the course of the visit or through several visits. Think of a cookie like a name tag: You tell the server your name, and it gives you a name tag. Then it can know who you are by referring back to the name tag.

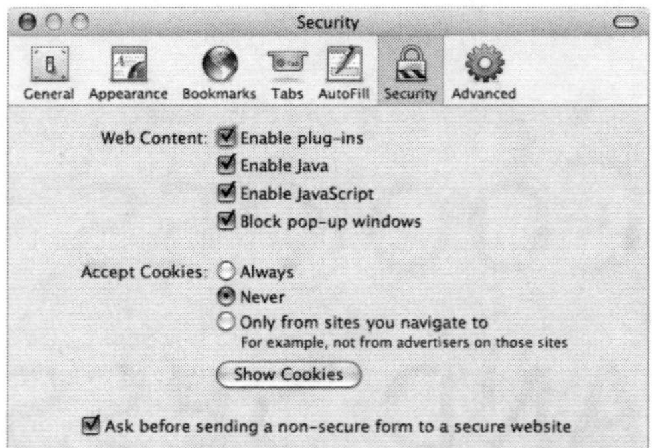

Figure 9.1 Most Web browsers let users set the cookie-handling preferences. This is Safari's Security tab.

This brings up another point about the security issues involved with cookies. Cookies have gotten a bad rap because users believe cookies allow a server to know too much about them. However, a cookie can only be used to store information that you give it, so it's as secure as you want it to be.

PHP has very good support for cookies. In this chapter, you'll learn how to set a cookie, retrieve information from a cookie, and then delete the cookie. You'll also see some of the optional parameters you can use to apply limits to a cookie's existence.

Debugging Cookies

When you begin working with cookies in PHP, you'll need to know how to debug your scripts when problems occur. Three areas might cause you concern:

- Sending the cookie with PHP
- Receiving the cookie in your Web browser
- Accessing a cookie in a PHP script

The first and last issues can be debugged by printing out the variable values in your PHP scripts (as you'll soon learn). The second issue requires that you know how to work with cookies in your Web browser. For debugging purposes, you'll want your Web browser to notify you when a cookie is being sent.

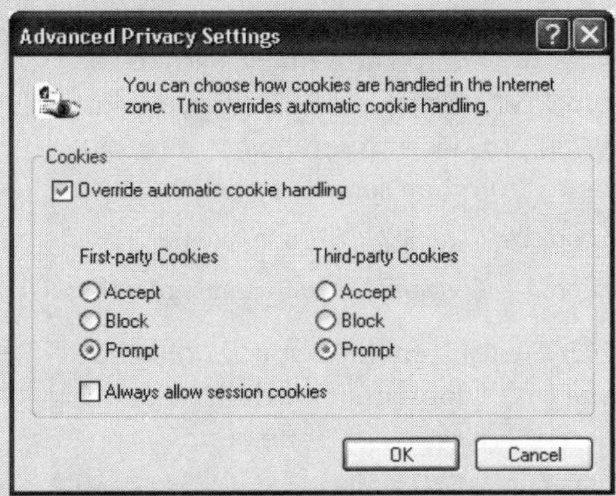

Figure 9.2 In Internet Explorer 6.0 (for Windows), you go through Tools > Internet Options > Privacy > Advanced to set your cookie preferences.

With Internet Explorer on Windows 2000 and XP, you can do this by choosing Internet Options under the Tools menu. Then click on the Privacy tab, followed by the Advanced button under Settings. Click "Override automatic cookie handling", and then choose Prompt for both First-party and Third-party Cookies (**Figure 9.2**). Other versions of Windows use different variations on this process.

Netscape and Mozilla users on any platform can control cookies through the Cookies subsection of the Privacy & Security area in the Preferences panel.

Some browsers also let you browse through the existing cookies to see their names and values. Doing so is a great asset in the debugging war.

Creating Cookies

The most important thing to understand about cookies is that they must be sent from the server to the client prior to any other information. Should the server attempt to send a cookie after the Web browser has already received HTML—even an extraneous white space—an error message will result and the cookie won't be sent (**Figure 9.3**). This is by far the most common cookie-related error.

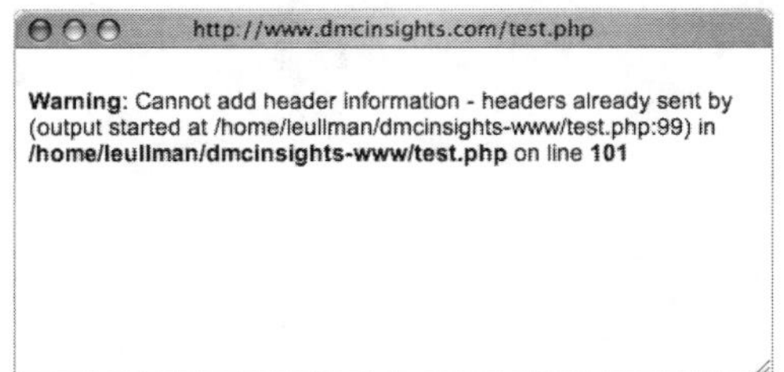

Figure 9.3 This friendly and informative message is what you'll see if the `setcookie()` function is called after anything, even a blank line, has already been sent to the Web browser.

Cookies are sent using the `setcookie()` function:

```
setcookie ('CookieName', 'This is the
→ cookie value.');
```

That line of code sends to the browser a cookie with the name *CookieName* and the value *This is the cookie value.* (**Figure 9.4**).

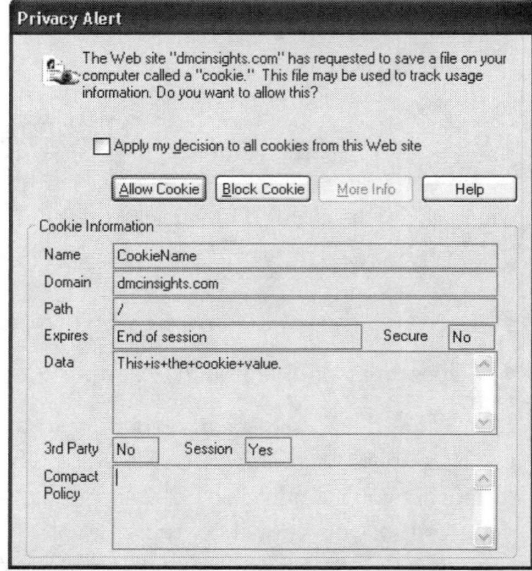

Figure 9.4 If the browser is set to prompt the user for cookies (see Figures 9.1 and 9.2), a message like this will appear for each cookie sent.

You can continue to send more cookies to the browser with subsequent uses of the `setcookie()` function, although you're limited by Web protocols to sending at most 20 cookies from one server to one user:

```
setcookie ('name2', 'some value');
setcookie ('name3', 'another value');
```

When creating cookies, you should use a name that's consistent with PHP's naming schemes for variables (for example, don't use spaces). You can also—as you'll see in this example—use a variable for the `name` or `value` attribute of your cookies:

```
setcookie($cookie_name, $cookie_value);
```

For an example of setting cookies, you'll create a page that allows the user to specify the text and background colors of a page. The page displays a form for choosing these values and then handles the form submission. A separate page, created in the next section of this chapter, will use these settings.

Script 9.1 Two cookies will be used to store the user's choices for the background and text colors. This page both displays and handles the form.

```
<?php // Script 9.1 - customize.php

// Address error handing.
ini_set ('display_errors', 1);
error_reporting (E_ALL & ~E_NOTICE);

$cookies = FALSE; // Cookies have not been sent.

// Handle the form if it has been submitted.
if (isset ($_POST['submit'])) {

    // Send the cookies.
    setcookie ('bg_color', $_POST['bg_color']);
    setcookie ('font_color', $_POST['font_color']);

    $cookies = TRUE; // Cookies have been sent.

} // End of submit IF.
?>
<!DOCTYPE html PUBLIC "-//W3C//DTD XHTML 1.0 Transitional//EN"
    "http://www.w3.org/TR/xhtml1/DTD/xhtml1-transitional.dtd">
<html xmlns="http://www.w3.org/1999/xhtml">
<head>
    <meta http-equiv="content-type" content="text/html; charset=iso-8859-1" />
    <title>Customize Your Settings</title>
</head>
<body>
<?php
// If the cookies were sent, print a message.
if ($cookies) {
    print '<p>Your settings have been entered! Click <a href="view_settings.php">here</a> to go back to the main page.</p>';
}
?>

<p>Use this form to set your preferences:</p>

```

(script continues on next page)

To send cookies:

1. Create a new PHP document in your text editor, beginning with the error-handling code (**Script 9.1**):

   ```
   <?php // Script 9.1 - customize.php
   ini_set ('display_errors', 1);
   error_reporting (E_ALL & ~E_NOTICE);
   ```

   The most critical issue with cookies is that they're created before anything is sent to the Web browser. To accomplish this, the script begins with a PHP section that handles the sending of cookies.

2. Set a flag variable indicating whether the cookies have been sent:

   ```
   $cookies = FALSE;
   ```

   As you'll soon see, the script will print a message to the user saying that their settings have been entered. Because you want this to happen only after the form has been submitted, you create this variable to track the status.

3. Check whether the form has been submitted:

   ```
   if (isset ($_POST['submit'])) {
   ```

   Using the technique described in the previous chapter, this page both displays and handles the form. If the form has been submitted, the `submit` variable is set and this condition will be TRUE.

4. Create the cookies:

   ```
   setcookie ('bg_color',
   → $_POST['bg_color']);
   setcookie ('font_color',
   → $_POST['font_color']);
   ```

   These two lines create two separate cookies. One is named *bg_color* and the other *font_color*. Their values will be based on the selected values from the HTML form, which are stored in the `$_POST['bg_color']` and `$_POST['font_color']` variables.

continues on next page

5. Set a flag variable indicating that the cookies have been sent, and complete the conditional and the PHP section:

```
$cookies = TRUE;
}
?>
```

When the form has been submitted, the cookies are sent and the `$cookies` variable is assigned a TRUE value. This variable will be used later in the script to print a message.

6. Create the HTML head and opening body tag:

```
<!DOCTYPE html PUBLIC "-//W3C//DTD
→ XHTML 1.0 Transitional//EN"
"http://www.w3.org/TR/xhtml1/DTD/
→ xhtml1-transitional.dtd">
<html xmlns="http://www.w3.org/1999/
→ xhtml">
<head>
   <meta http-equiv="content-type"
   content="text/html; charset=
   → iso-8859-1" />
   <title>Customize Your Settings
   → </title>
</head>
<body>
```

All of this code must come after the `setcookie()` lines. Not to overstate the fact, but no text, HTML, or blank spaces can be sent to the Web browser prior to the `setcookie()` calls.

7. Create another PHP section to report on the cookies' being sent:

```
<?php
if ($cookies) {
   print '<p>Your settings have been
   → entered! Click <a href=
   → "view_settings.php">here</a> to
   → go back to the main page.</p>';
}
?>
```

Script 9.1 *continued*

```
<form action="customize.php" method="post">
<select name="bg_color">
<option value="">Background Color</option>
<option value="#ffffff">White</option>
<option value="#00cc00">Green</option>
<option value="#0000ff">Blue</option>
<option value="#cc0000">Red</option>
<option value="#000000">Black</option>
</select>
<select name="font_color">
<option value="">Font Color</option>
<option value="#ffffff">White</option>
<option value="#00cc00">Green</option>
<option value="#0000ff">Blue</option>
<option value="#cc0000">Red</option>
<option value="#000000">Black</option>
</select>
<input type="submit" name="submit"
value="Set My Preferences" />
</form>

</body>
</html>
```

This section prints out a message if the cookies have been sent. The first time the user comes to the page, the cookies haven't been sent, so `$cookies` is FALSE and this `print()` statement never runs. Once the form has been submitted, `$cookies` is TRUE, so this conditional is TRUE.

8. Create the HTML form:

```
<p>Use this form to set your
→ preferences:</p>
<form action="customize.php" method=
→ "post">
<select name="bg_color">
<option value="">Background Color
→ </option>
<option value="#ffffff">White
→ </option>
<option value="#00cc00">Green
→ </option>
<option value="#0000ff">Blue</option>
<option value="#cc0000">Red</option>
<option value="#000000">Black
→ </option>
</select>
<select name="font_color">
<option value="">Font Color</option>
<option value="#ffffff">White</option>
<option value="#00cc00">Green
→ </option>
<option value="#0000ff">Blue</option>
<option value="#cc0000">Red</option>
<option value="#000000">Black
→ </option>
</select>
<input type="submit" name="submit"
→ value="Set My Preferences" />
</form>
```

continues on next page

The HTML form itself is very simple (**Figure 9.5**). The user is given one drop-down menu to select the background color and another to select the font color. The menus display the colors in text form, but the values are HTML color values.

Be certain that the name of your submit button (here, *submit*) exactly matches the key used in the conditional at the top of the script (`$_POST['submit']`). Otherwise the form will never be processed.

9. Complete the HTML page:

```
</body>
</html>
```

10. Save the file as `customize.php` and upload it to your server (or place it in the proper directory on your PHP-enabled computer).

11. Make sure you've set your Web browser to prompt for each cookie.

    To guarantee that the script is working, you want the browser to prompt you for each cookie. See the "Debugging Cookies" sidebar.

12. Run the script in your Web browser (**Figures 9.6**, **9.7**, and **9.8**).

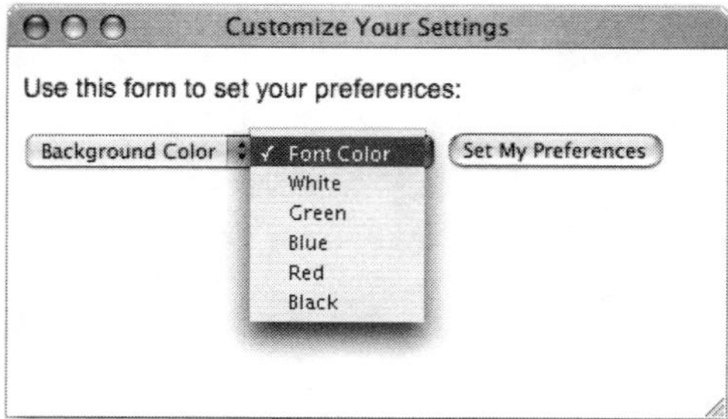

Figure 9.5 This form is used to select the background and font colors for another PHP page.

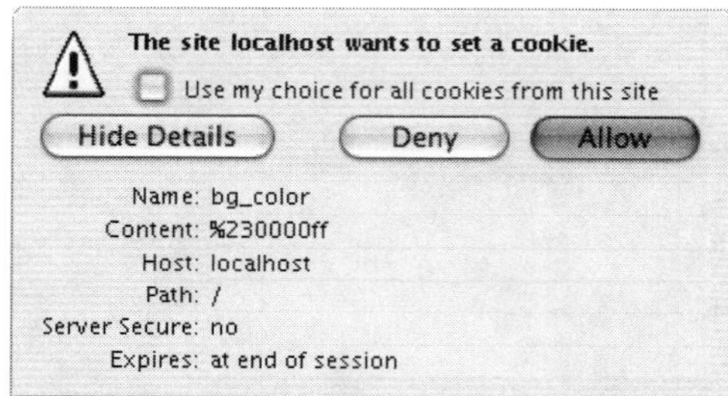

Figure 9.6 The user sees this message when the first `setcookie()` call is made, if they've opted to be prompted before accepting a cookie. This cookie is storing the value of *#0000ff* in a cookie named *bg_color*.

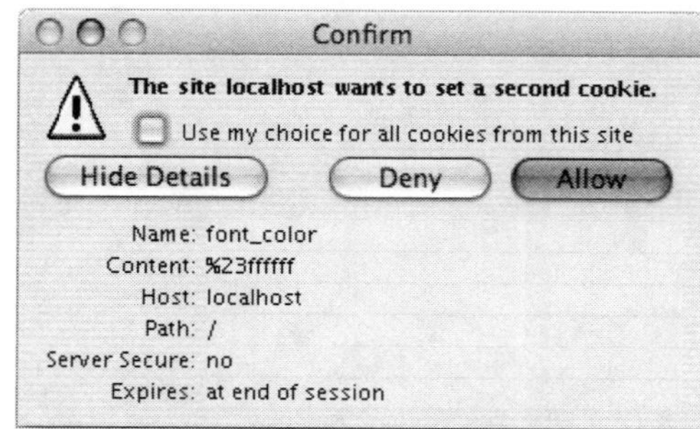

Figure 9.7 The second cookie that's sent is called *font_color* and has a value of *#ffffff* (*%23* is just an encoded form of *#*).

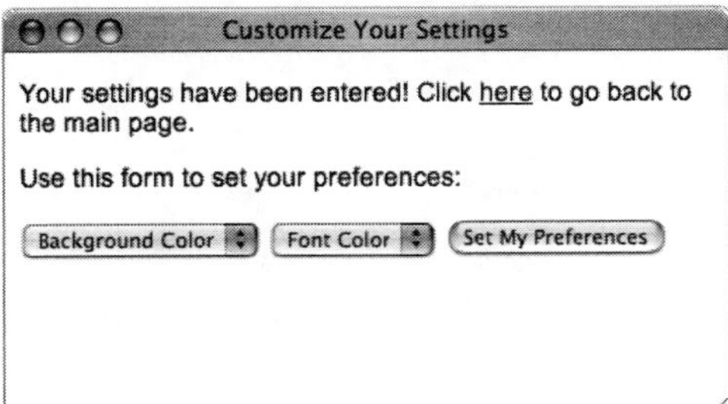

Figure 9.8 After submitting the form, the page shows a message and a link to another page (where the user's preferences are used).

✔ Tips

- Cookies are one of the few PHP tools that can behave differently from browser to browser or operating system to operating system. You should test your cookie-based applications on as many browsers and operating systems as you can.
- If you use the output buffering technique taught in Chapter 8, "Creating Web Applications," then you can place your `setcookie()` calls anywhere within the script (because the Web browser won't receive the data until the `ob_end_flush()` function is called).
- Cookies are limited to approximately 4 Kbytes of total data. This is more than sufficient for most applications.
- You can also create cookies using the `header()` function, because it uses the same HTTP header protocol.
- To test whether it's safe to send a cookie, use the `headers_sent()` function. It reports on whether HTTP headers have already been sent to the Web browser.

Reading from Cookies

Just as form data is stored in the $_POST array (assuming it used the POST method) and values passed to a script in the URL are stored in the $_GET array, the setcookie() function places cookie data in the $_COOKIE array. To retrieve a value from a cookie, you only need to refer to the cookie name as the index of this array. For example, to retrieve the value of the cookie established with the line

```
setcookie ('user', 'trout');
```

you would use the variable

```
$_COOKIE['user'].
```

Unless you change the cookie's parameters (as you'll see later in this chapter), the cookie will automatically be accessible to every other page in your Web application. You should understand, however, that a cookie is never accessible to a script that just sent it. You can't do this:

```
setcookie ('user', 'trout');
print $_COOKIE['user']; // No value.
```

To see how simple it is to access cookie values, let's write a script that uses the preferences set in customize.php to specify the background and text colors. The script relies on CSS to achieve this effect.

Script 9.2 This script sets the body background and font colors using the values stored in the cookies.

```
Script
<!DOCTYPE html PUBLIC "-//W3C//DTD XHTML
1.0 Transitional//EN"
        "http://www.w3.org/TR/xhtml1/DTD/
        xhtml1-transitional.dtd">
<html xmlns="http://www.w3.org/1999/xhtml">
<head>
    <meta http-equiv="content-type"
    content="text/html; charset=
    iso-8859-1" />
    <title>View Your Settings</title>
<style type="text/css">
    body {
<?php // Script 9.2 - view_settings.php

// Address error handling.
ini_set ('display_errors', 1);
error_reporting (E_ALL & ~E_NOTICE);

// Check for a bg_color value.
if (isset ($_COOKIE['bg_color'])) {
    print "\t\tbackground-color:
    {$_COOKIE['bg_color']};\n";
} else {
    print "\t\tbackground-color:
    #ffffff;\n";
}

// Check for a font_color value.
if (isset ($_COOKIE['font_color'])) {
    print "\t\tcolor: {$_COOKIE
    ['font_color']}; \n";
} else {
    print "\t\tcolor: #000000; \n";
}

?>
    }
</style>
</head>
<body>
<p><a href="customize.php">Customize Your
Settings</a></p>
<p><a href="reset.php">Reset Your
Settings</a></p>

```

(script continues on next page)

To retrieve cookie data with PHP:

1. Create a new PHP document in your text editor, starting with the standard HTML head (**Script 9.2**):

```
<!DOCTYPE html PUBLIC "-//W3C//DTD
→ XHTML 1.0 Transitional//EN"
"http://www.w3.org/TR/xhtml1/DTD/
→ xhtml1-transitional.dtd">
<html xmlns="http://www.w3.org/1999/
→ xhtml">
<head>
    <meta http-equiv="content-type"
    → content="text/html; charset=
    → iso-8859-1" />
    <title>View Your Settings</title>
```

2. Start the CSS section:

```
<style type="text/css">
    body {
```

The page will use CSS to enact the user's preferences. The aim is to create code like

```
body {
    background-color: #ffffff;
    color: #000000;
}
```

The two color values will differ based on what the user selected in the `customize.php` page. In this step, you create the initial CSS code.

3. Open a section of PHP code:

```
<?php // Script 9.2 - view_settings.php
ini_set ('display_errors', 1);
error_reporting (E_ALL & ~E_NOTICE);
```

The script will now use PHP to print out the remaining CSS, based on the cookies.

continues on next page

4. Use the background color cookie value, if it exists:

```
if (isset ($_COOKIE['bg_color'])) {
    print "\t\tbackground-color:
    → {$_COOKIE['bg_color']};\n";
} else {
    print "\t\tbackground-color:
    → #ffffff;\n";
}
```

   If the script can access a cookie named *bg_color*, it will print out that cookie's value as the background color. The `isset()` function is sufficient to see if the cookie exists. If no such cookie exists, PHP will print out a default color (white, represented by *#ffffff*).

   Just to clarify, each `print()` statement also creates two tabs (using `\t`) and one newline character (`\n`). The purpose of these is to give the CSS code some formatting, which will appear in the HTML source.

5. Repeat this process for the font color cookie:

```
if (isset ($_COOKIE['font_color'])) {
    print "\t\tcolor: {$_COOKIE
    → ['font_color']}; \n";
} else {
    print "\t\tcolor: #000000; \n";
}
```

6. Close the PHP section, complete the CSS code, and finish the HTML head:

```
?>
    }
</style>
</head>
```

Script 9.2 *continued*

```
<p>
yadda yadda yadda yadda yadda
yadda yadda yadda yadda yadda
yadda yadda yadda yadda yadda
yadda yadda yadda yadda yadda
yadda yadda yadda yadda yadda
</p>

</body>
</html>
```

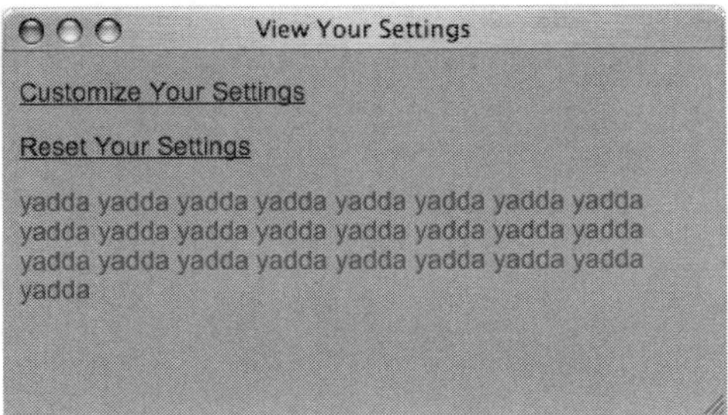

Figure 9.9 This page reflects the customized (and potentially ghastly) color choices you made using the other PHP script.

7. Start the HTML body and create links to two other pages:

```
<body>
<p><a href="customize.php">Customize
→ Your Settings</a></p>
<p><a href="reset.php">Reset Your
→ Settings</a></p>
```

   These two links take the user to two other PHP pages. The first, `customize.php`, has already been written and lets the user define their settings. The second, `reset.php`, will be written next and lets the user delete their customized settings.

8. Add some miscellaneous text:

```
<p>
yadda yadda yadda yadda yadda
yadda yadda yadda yadda yadda
yadda yadda yadda yadda yadda
yadda yadda yadda yadda yadda
yadda yadda yadda yadda yadda
</p>
```

9. Complete the HTML page:

```
</body>
</html>
```

10. Save the file as `view_settings.php`, upload it to your Web server—storing it in the same directory as `customize.php`—and test it in your Web browser (**Figure 9.9**).

continues on next page

11. View the source of the page to see the resulting CSS code (**Figure 9.10**).

12. Use the customize page to change your settings and return to this script (**Figure 9.11**).

Source of http://localhost/view_settings.php

```
<!DOCTYPE html PUBLIC "-//W3C//DTD XHTML 1.0 Transitional//EN"
        "http://www.w3.org/TR/xhtml1/DTD/xhtml1-transitional.dtd">
<html xmlns="http://www.w3.org/1999/xhtml">
<head>
    <meta http-equiv="content-type" content="text/html; charset=iso-8859-1" />
    <title>View Your Settings</title>
<style type="text/css">
    body {
        background-color: #0000ff;
        color: #ffffff;
    }
</style>
</head>
<body>
<p><a href="customize.php">Customize Your Settings</a></p>
<p><a href="reset.php">Reset Your Settings</a></p>

<p>
yadda yadda yadda yadda yadda
yadda yadda yadda yadda yadda
yadda yadda yadda yadda yadda
yadda yadda yadda yadda yadda
yadda yadda yadda yadda yadda
</p>

</body>
</html>
```

Figure 9.10 By viewing the source code of the page, you can also track how the color values change.

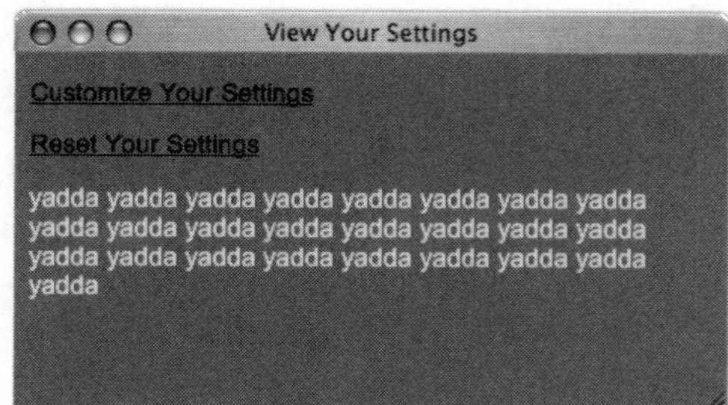

Figure 9.11 You can change your color settings to create new versions of the page.

✔ Tips

- The value of a cookie is automatically encoded when it's sent and decoded on being received by the PHP page. The same is true of values sent by HTML forms.
- One of the problems with relying on global variables (`$var` as opposed to `$_COOKIE['var']`) is that a variable's value can come from many places. For example, there's no way of knowing whether `$var` refers to a value passed in the URL, stored in a cookie or session, or submitted in a form using the POST method. For this reason, you should use the formal `$_GET`, `$_POST`, and `$_COOKIE` variables.
- If you want the `customize.php` page to also display the user's settings, you need to take into account the fact that the cookies aren't available immediately after they've been set. You'll use the `$_POST` values after the form has been submitted, the `$_COOKIE` values upon first arriving at the page (if the cookies exist), and the default values otherwise.

Adding Parameters to a Cookie

Although passing just the `name` and `value` arguments to the `setcookie()` function will suffice for most of your cookie uses, you ought to be aware of the other arguments available. The function can take up to four more parameters, each of which limits the operation of the cookie:

```
setcookie ('name', 'value', expiration,
→ 'path', 'domain', secure);
```

The *`expiration`* argument is used to set a specific length of time for a cookie to exist. If it isn't specified, the cookie will continue to be functional until the user closes their browser. Normally, you set the expiration time by adding a particular number of minutes or hours to the current time. This line of code sets the expiration time of the cookie to be one hour (60 seconds times 60 minutes) from the current moment:

```
setcookie ('name', 'value', time()+3600);
```

Because the expiration time will be calculated as the value of `time()` plus 3600, this particular argument isn't put in quotes (you don't want to literally pass *time() + 3600* as the expiration but rather the result of that calculation).

The *`path`* and *`domain`* arguments are used to limit a cookie to a specific folder in a Web site (the path) or to a specific domain (such as `www.site.com`). For example, you could limit the life of a cookie so it exists only while a user is in their folder of the domain:

```
setcookie ('name', 'value', time()+3600,
→ '/user/');
```

The *secure* value dictates that a cookie should only be sent over a secure HTTPS connection. A value of 1 indicates that a secure connection must be used, whereas 0 indicates that a secure connection isn't necessary. You should ensure a secure connection for e-commerce sites:

```
setcookie ('name', 'value', time()+
→ 3600, '', '', 1);
```

As with all functions that take arguments, you must pass all the values in order. In the previous example, you don't want to specify (or limit) the path and domain, so you use empty quotes. By doing so, you maintain the proper number of arguments and can still indicate that a HTTPS connection is necessary.

Let's add an expiration date to the existing `customize.php` page so that the user's preferences will remain even after they've closed their browser and then returned to the site later.

To set a cookie's expiration date:

1. Open `customize.php` (Script 9.1) in your text editor.
2. Change the two `setcookie()` lines to read as follows (**Script 9.3**):

```
setcookie ('bg_color',
→ $_POST['bg_color'],
→ time()+10000000, '/', '', 0);
setcookie ('font_color',
→ $_POST['font_color'],
→ time()+10000000, '/', '', 0);
```

continues on page 256

Script 9.3 By adding the expiration arguments to the two cookies, you make the cookies persist even after the user has closed out of and returned to their browser.

Script

```
<?php // Script 9.3 - customize.php (Second version after Script 9.1)

// Address error handling.
ini_set ('display_errors', 1);
error_reporting (E_ALL & ~E_NOTICE);

$cookies = FALSE; // Cookies have not been sent.

// Handle the form if it has been submitted.
if (isset ($_POST['submit'])) {

    // Send the cookies.
    setcookie ('bg_color', $_POST['bg_color'], time()+10000000, '/', '', 0);
    setcookie ('font_color', $_POST['font_color'], time()+10000000, '/', '', 0);

    $cookies = TRUE; // Cookies have been sent.

} // End of submit IF.
?>
<!DOCTYPE html PUBLIC "-//W3C//DTD XHTML 1.0 Transitional//EN"
        "http://www.w3.org/TR/xhtml1/DTD/xhtml1-transitional.dtd">
<html xmlns="http://www.w3.org/1999/xhtml">
<head>
    <meta http-equiv="content-type" content="text/html; charset=iso-8859-1" />
    <title>Customize Your Settings</title>
</head>
<body>
<?php
// If the cookies were sent, print a message.
if ($cookies) {
    print '<p>Your settings have been entered! Click <a href="view_settings.php">here</a> to go back to the main page.</p>';
}
?>

<p>Use this form to set your preferences:</p>

<form action="customize.php" method="post">
<select name="bg_color">
<option value="">Background Color</option>
<option value="#ffffff">White</option>
<option value="#00cc00">Green</option>
<option value="#0000ff">Blue</option>
<option value="#cc0000">Red</option>
<option value="#000000">Black</option>
</select>
<select name="font_color">
<option value="">Font Color</option>
<option value="#ffffff">White</option>
```

(script continues on next page)

To make these cookies persist for a long time (specifically, for a couple of months), you set the expiration time to be 10,000,000 seconds from now. While you're at it, you set the *path*, *domain*, and *secure* arguments, which improves the consistency of sending cookies across the various browsers.

Because the expiration date of the cookies is set months into the future, the user's preferences, which are stored in the cookies, will be valid even after the user has closed and reopened the browser. Without this expiration date, the user would see the default colors and have to reassign their preferences with every new browser session.

3. Save the file, upload it to your Web server, and test it again in your Web browser (**Figures 9.12** and **9.13**).

Script 9.3 *continued*

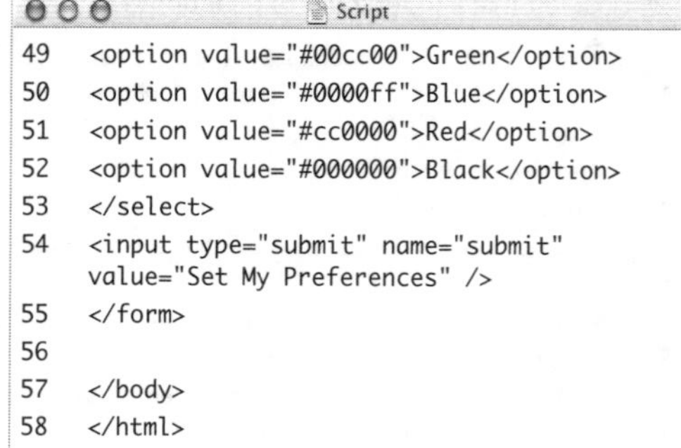

```
<option value="#00cc00">Green</option>
<option value="#0000ff">Blue</option>
<option value="#cc0000">Red</option>
<option value="#000000">Black</option>
</select>
<input type="submit" name="submit"
value="Set My Preferences" />
</form>

</body>
</html>
```

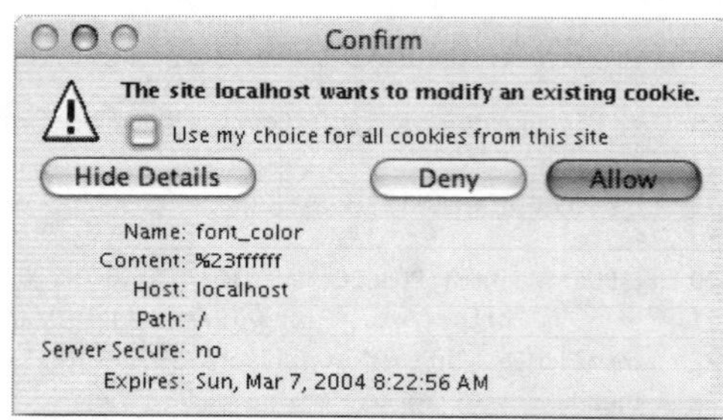

Figure 9.12 If you have your browser set to prompt you when receiving cookies, you'll see how the expiration time has been added (compare with Figure 9.6).

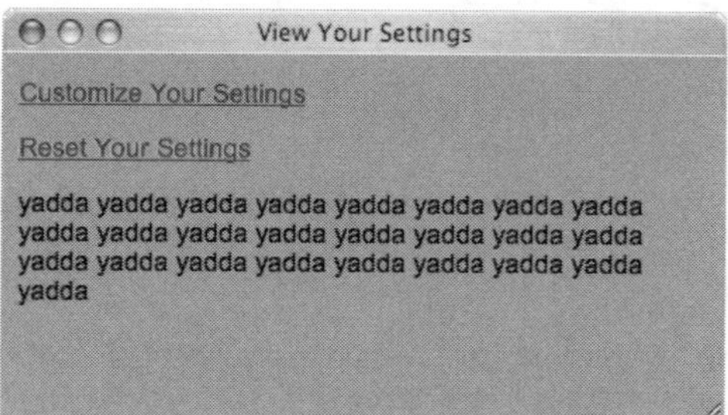

Figure 9.13 The new cookie parameters don't adversely affect the functionality of the application.

✔ Tips

- There's really no rule of thumb for what kind of expiration date to use with your cookies. Here are some general guidelines, though. If the cookie should last as long as the user browses through the site, don't set an expiration time. If the cookie should continue to exist after the user has closed and reopened their browser, set an expiration time that's months in the future. And if the cookie can constitute a security risk, set an expiration time of an hour or a fraction thereof so that the cookie doesn't continue to exist too long after a user has left their browser.
- There can be a big problem with cookie expirations if the server and the clients are in different time zones. The expiration time is set based on the server's time zone, but the browser may delete the cookie based on the client's time zone. Fortunately, some browsers do automatically correct for this.
- For security purposes, you can set a five- or ten-minute expiration time on a cookie and have the cookie re-sent with every new page the user visits. This way, the cookie will continue to persist as long as the user is active but will automatically die five or ten minutes after the user's last action.
- Setting the cookie's path to `'/'` makes the cookie accessible within an entire Web site.
- If your Web application involves sensitive information (such as online banking or e-commerce), you'll probably need to set up an SSL (Secure Sockets Layer) connection so that cookies can be sent securely.

Deleting a Cookie

The final thing to understand about using cookies is how to delete one. Although a cookie automatically expires when the user's browser is closed or when the expiration date/time is met, sometimes you'll want to manually delete the cookie as well. For example, Web sites that have registered users and login capabilities generally delete any cookies when the user logs out.

The `setcookie()` function can take up to six arguments, but only one is required—the name. If you send a cookie that consists of a name without a value, it will have the same effect as deleting the existing cookie of the same name. For example, to create the cookie *username*, you use this line:

```
setcookie('username', 'Larry');
```

To delete the *username* cookie, you code

```
setcookie('username', '');
```

As an added precaution, you can also set an expiration date that's in the past:

```
setcookie('username', '', time() - 60);
```

To demonstrate this feature, let's add a reset feature to the Web application that will destroy the sent cookies and display the default colors once again.

To delete a cookie:

1. Begin a new PHP script in your text editor (**Script 9.4**):

```
<?php // Script 9.4 - reset.php
ini_set ('display_errors', 1);
error_reporting (E_ALL & ~E_NOTICE);
```

Script 9.4 To reset all the values, send blank cookies with the same names as the existing cookies.

```
<?php // Script 9.4 - reset.php

// Address error handling.
ini_set ('display_errors', 1);
error_reporting (E_ALL & ~E_NOTICE);

// Delete the cookies.
setcookie ('bg_color', '', time()-60, '/', '', 0);
setcookie ('font_color', '', time()-60, '/', '', 0);

?>
<!DOCTYPE html PUBLIC "-//W3C//DTD XHTML 1.0 Transitional//EN"
        "http://www.w3.org/TR/xhtml1/DTD/xhtml1-transitional.dtd">
<html xmlns="http://www.w3.org/1999/xhtml">
<head>
    <meta http-equiv="content-type" content="text/html; charset=iso-8859-1" />
    <title>Reset Your Settings</title>
</head>
<body>

<p>Your settings have been reset! Click <a href="view_settings.php">here</a> to go back to the main page.</p>

</body>
</html>
```

2. Delete the existing cookies by sending blank cookies:

```
setcookie ('bg_color', '', time()-60,
→ '/', '', 0);
setcookie ('font_color', '', time()-
→ 60, '/', '', 0);
```

These two lines send cookies named *bg_color* and *font_color*, each with no value and an expiration time of one minute ago. As you did when creating cookies, you must call the `setcookie()` function before anything else is sent to the Web browser.

3. Complete the PHP code and create the HTML head:

```
?>
<!DOCTYPE html PUBLIC "-//W3C//DTD
→ XHTML 1.0 Transitional//EN"
"http://www.w3.org/TR/xhtml1/DTD/
→ xhtml1-transitional.dtd">
<html xmlns="http://www.w3.org/1999/
→ xhtml">
<head>
   <meta http-equiv="content-type"
   → content="text/html; charset=
   → iso-8859-1" />
   <title>Reset Your Settings</title>
</head>
```

continues on next page

4. Print the page's body:

```
<body>
<p>Your settings have been reset! Click
→ <a href="view_settings.php">here</a>
→ to go back to the main page.</p>
</body>
```

The body of this script merely tells the user that their settings have been reset. A link is then provided to return to the main page.

5. Complete the HTML:

```
</html>
```

6. Save the page as `reset.php`, upload it to your Web browser, and test it in your Web browser (**Figures 9.14**, **9.15**, and **9.16**).

✔ Tips

- Just as creating a cookie doesn't take effect until another page is loaded, deleting a cookie doesn't take effect until another page. This is to say that you can delete a cookie on a page but still access that cookie on it (because the cookie was received by the page before the delete cookie was sent).
- Just as creating cookies has mixed results using different browsers, the same applies to deleting them. Test your scripts on many browsers and play with the `setcookie()` settings to ensure the best all-around compatibility.
- The rest of the chapter will demonstrate how to use sessions to create a login/logout application. Using the cookie techniques demonstrated so far, you can modify the forthcoming scripts to easily make a cookie-based login/logout feature for your Web site.

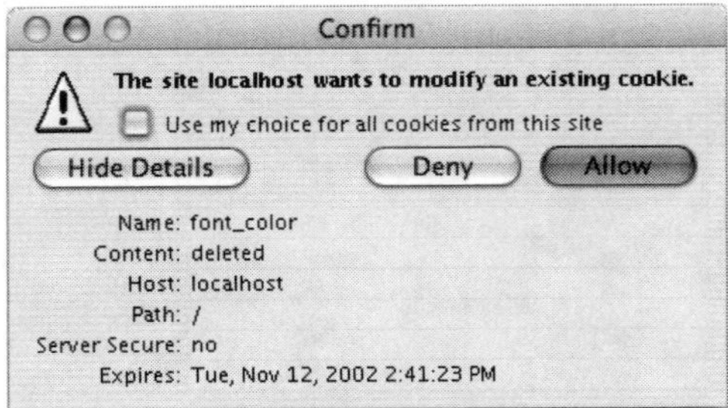

Figure 9.14 When the `setcookie()` function is used with a `name` but no `value`, the existing cookie of that name is deleted. The expiration date in the past also guarantees proper destruction of the existing cookie.

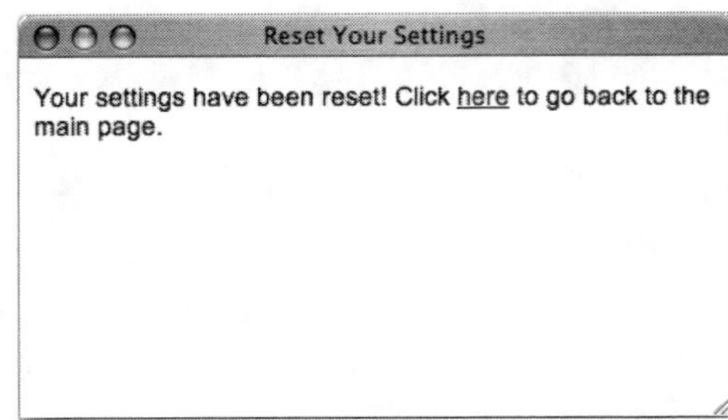

Figure 9.15 The reset page sends two blank cookies and then displays this message.

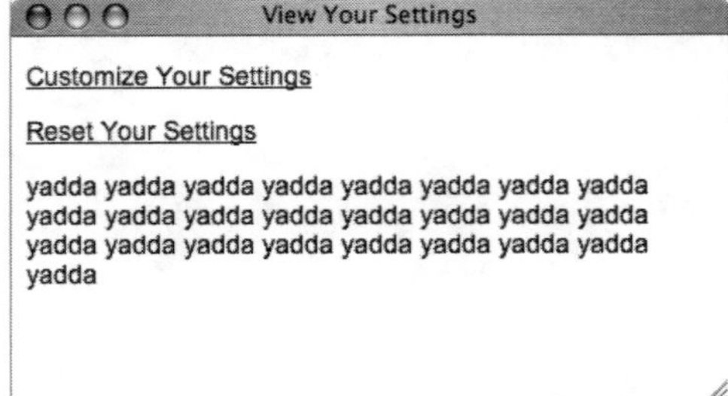

Figure 9.16 If the user has used the reset page, PHP destroys the cookies (Figure 9.14), which resets the main page to its default colors.

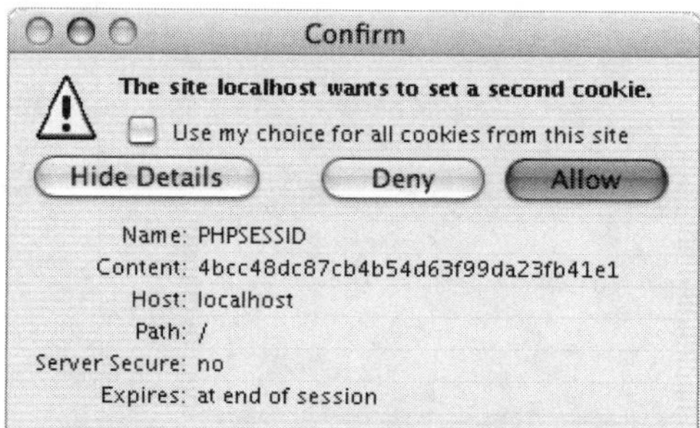

Figure 9.17 A session cookie is being sent to the Web browser.

Choosing between Sessions and Cookies

Sessions have many benefits over cookies, but there are still reasons why you would use the latter. Cookies have these advantages over sessions:

- Marginally easier to create and retrieve
- Require slightly less work from the server
- Normally persist over a longer period of time

As a rule of thumb, you should use cookies in situations where security is less of an issue and only a minimum of data is being stored. If security's a concern and there will be oodles of information to remember, you're best off with sessions. Understand, though, that using sessions may require a little more effort in writing your scripts.

What Are Sessions?

A session, like a cookie, provides a way for you to track data for a user over a series of pages. The difference between the two—and this is significant—is that a cookie stores the data on the client side (in the Web browser), whereas the session data is stored on the server. Because of this difference, sessions have numerous benefits over cookies:

- Sessions are more secure, because the data isn't transmitted back and forth between the client and server repeatedly.
- Sessions let you store more information than you can in a cookie.
- Sessions can be made to work even if the user doesn't accept cookies in their browser.

When you start a session, PHP generates a random session ID, a reference to that particular session and its stored data. By default, this session ID is sent to the Web browser as a cookie (**Figure 9.17**). Subsequent PHP pages will use this cookie to retrieve the session ID and access the session information.

Sessions were permanently added to PHP in version 4 of the language. Previously you had to use a whole library of code to achieve the same effect. Over the next few pages, you'll see just how easy sessions are to work with in PHP.

Creating a Session

Creating, accessing, or deleting a session begins with the `session_start()` function. This function will attempt to send a cookie the first time a session is started, so it absolutely must be called prior to any HTML or white space being sent to the Web browser. Therefore, on pages that use sessions, you should call the `session_start()` function as one of the very first lines in your script. Alternatively, you can use output buffering, as described in Chapter 8.

The first time a session is started, a random session ID is generated and a cookie is sent to the Web browser with a name of *PHPSESSID* (the session name) and a value like *4bcc48dc87cb4b54d63f99da23fb41e1*.

Once the session has been started, you can record data to it by assigning values to the `$_SESSION` array:

```
$_SESSION['first_name'] = 'John';
$_SESSION['age'] = 34;
```

Each time you do this, PHP writes that data to a temporary file stored on the server. To demonstrate, you'll rewrite the login script from Chapter 8, storing the username in a session.

Potential Session Problems

There are a few areas where you may have problems when it comes to working with sessions.

The first error message you may see is *headers already sent*. This is caused by calling the `session_start()` function after the Web page has received data.

Another problem you may come across is that the `$_SESSION` variable doesn't exist in your version of PHP. If you have a version prior to 4.1 but after 4.0, you'll need to use slightly different syntax. See the PHP manual's session chapter for more.

If you're running a Windows version of PHP, the first time you try to use sessions, you may see a message like

```
Warning: failed to write session data
→ (files).
```

To fix this problem, you need to open your `php.ini` file and change the `session.save_path` setting to a valid temporary directory on your server. Then restart your Web server, and you'll be good to go.

To create a session:

1. Open `login.php` (Script 8.13) in your text editor.

2. Before the `header()` line, add the following (**Script 9.5**):

```
session_start();
$_SESSION['username'] = 'testing';
$_SESSION['loggedin'] = time();
```

continues on next page

Script 9.5 This script stores two values in the session and then redirects the user to another page, where the session values are accessed.

```
<?php // Script 9.5 - login.php (third version after Scripts 8.8 and 8.13)
// This page lets people log into the site.

// Address error handling.
ini_set ('display_errors', 1);
error_reporting (E_ALL & ~E_NOTICE);

// Set the page title and include the header file.
define ('TITLE', 'Login');
require ('templates/header.html');

// Basic HTML formatting stuff.
print '<div id="leftcontent">
    <h1>Login Form</h1>
    <p>Users who are logged in can take advantage of certain features like this, that, and the
    other thing.</p>';

// Check if the form has been submitted.
if ( isset ($_POST['submit'])) {

    // Handle the form.
    if ( (!empty ($_POST['username'])) && (!empty ($_POST['password'])) ) {

        if ( ($_POST['username'] == 'testing') && ($_POST['password'] == 'testpass') ) { // Okay.

            // Do session stuff.
            session_start();
            $_SESSION['username'] = 'testing';
            $_SESSION['loggedin'] = time();

```

(script continues on next page)

To store two values in the session, begin by calling the `session_start()` function. Although you normally have to call this function first thing in your script (because it may attempt to send a cookie), that's not required here because the header file for this script begins output buffering.

The session stores a dummy username value and the time the user logged in, which is determined by calling the `time()` function. This function returns the number of seconds that have elapsed since the epoch (midnight on January 1, 1970).

Script 9.5 *continued*

```
            // Redirect the user to the welcome page!
            header ('Location: welcome.php');
            exit();

        } else { // Not okay.

            print '<p>The submitted username and password do not match those on file!<br />Go back and try again.</p>';

        }

    } else { // Forgot a field.

        print '<p>Please make sure you enter both a username and a password!<br />Go back and try again.</p>';

    }

} else {

    // Display the form.
    print '<form action="login.php" method="post"><p>
    Username: <input type="text" name="username" size="20" /><br />
    Password: <input type="password" name="password" size="20" /><br />
    <input type="submit" name="submit" value="Log In!" /></p>
    </form>';

}

// Complete the HTML formatting stuff.
print '</div>';

require ('templates/footer.html'); // Need the footer.
?>
```

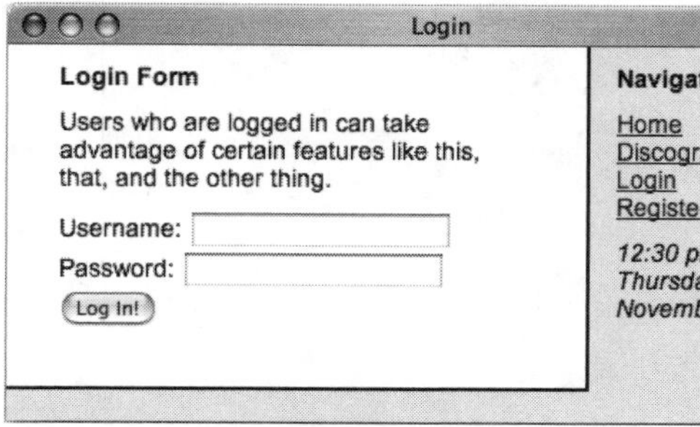

Figure 9.18 The login form.

3. Save the file as `login.php` and upload it to your Web server (or save it to the appropriate directory on your PHP-enabled computer) in the same directory as the other files from Chapter 8.

4. Load the form in your Web browser to ensure that it has no errors (**Figure 9.18**).

✔ Tips

- The `php.ini` configuration file includes many session-related settings that you can tinker with if you have administrative-level control over your server. Open the `php.ini` file in a text editor and see the manual for more information.

- You can also alter some of the session settings using the `ini_set()` function.

- The `session_name()` function lets you change the name of the session (instead of using the default *PHPSESSID*). It must be used before every `session_start()` call, like so:

```
session_name ('YourVisit');
session_start();
```

- The `session_set_cookie_params()` function alters the session cookie settings, like the expiration time, the path, and the domain.

- The constant `SID` stores a string in the format *name=ID*. For example:

```
PHPSESSID=4bcc48dc87cb4b54d63f99da23
→ fb41e1
```

- You can store any type of value—number, string, array, or object—or any combination thereof in your sessions.

Accessing Session Variables

Now that you've stored values in a session, you need to know how to access them. You must begin with the `session_start()` function, whether you're creating a new session or accessing an existing one. This function indicates to PHP that this particular script will use sessions.

From there it's simply a matter of referencing the `$_SESSION` variable as you would any other array. With this in mind, you'll write another welcome page—similar to the one from Chapter 8—that accesses the stored *username* and *loggedin* values.

To access session variables:

1. Create a new PHP document in your text editor (**Script 9.6**):
   ```
   <?php // Script 9.6 - welcome.php
   ini_set ('display_errors', 1);
   error_reporting (E_ALL & ~E_NOTICE);
   ```
2. Begin the session:
   ```
   session_start();
   ```
   Even when you're accessing session values, you should call the `session_start()` function before any data is sent to the Web browser.
3. Define a page title, and include the HTML header:
   ```
   define ('TITLE', 'Welcome to the
   → Elliott Smith Fan Club!');
   require ('templates/header.html');
   ```
   Because this page uses the same template system developed in Chapter 8, it also uses the same header system.

4. Greet the user by name:

```
print '<div id="leftcontent">
    <h1>Welcome to the Elliott Smith
    → Fan Club, ' .
    ucfirst($_SESSION['username']) .
    → '!</h1>';
```

To access the stored user's name, refer to `$_SESSION['username']`. You apply the `ucfirst()` function to it so that the value is printed with an initial capital letter.

continues on next page

Script 9.6 You can access stored session values using the `$_SESSION` array, as long as your script uses `session_start()` first.

```
<?php // Script 9.6 - welcome.php (second version after Script 8.14)
// This is the welcome page. It's used after the user logs in.

// Address error handling.
ini_set ('display_errors', 1);
error_reporting (E_ALL & ~E_NOTICE);

// Need the session.
session_start();

// Define a page title and include the header.
define ('TITLE', 'Welcome to the Elliott Smith Fan Club!');
require ('templates/header.html');

// Print a greeting.
print '<div id="leftcontent">
    <h1>Welcome to the Elliott Smith Fan Club, ' . ucfirst($_SESSION['username']) . '!</h1>';

// Print how long they've been logged in.
print '<p>You have been logged in since:<br /> ' . date ('g:i a', $_SESSION['loggedin']) . '</p>';

// Make a logout link.
print '<p><a href="logout.php">Click here to log out.</a></p>';

print '</div>';

require ('templates/footer.html'); // Need the footer.
?>
```

5. Show how long the user has been logged in:

```
print '<p>You have been logged in
→ since:<br /> ' . date ('g:i a',
→ $_SESSION['loggedin']) . '</p>';
```

To show how long the user has been logged in, refer to the `$_SESSION['loggedin']` variable. By using this as the second argument sent to the `date()` function, along with the appropriate formatting parameters, you make the PHP script create text like *11:22 pm*.

6. Complete the content:

```
print '<p><a href="logout.php">Click
→ here to log out.</a></p>';
print '</div>';
```

The next script will provide log-out functionality, so a link to it is added here.

7. Include the HTML footer, and complete the HTML page:

```
require ('templates/footer.html');
?>
```

8. Save the file as `welcome.php`, upload it to your Web server, and test it (starting with `login.php`, Script 9.5) in your Web browser (**Figure 9.19**).

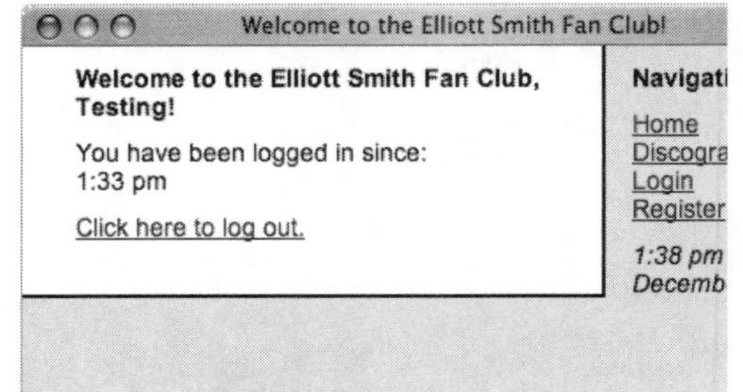

Figure 9.19 After successfully logging in (using *testing* and *testpass* in the form), the user is redirected to this page, which greets them using the session values.

✔ Tips

- To see whether a particular session variable exists, use `isset ($_SESSION['var'])` as you would to check if any other variable is set.
- If you're using a version of PHP prior to 4.1, you need to use `$HTTP_SESSION_VARS` instead.

Script 9.7 Deleting a session is a three-step process: start the session, delete the variable, and destroy the session data.

Script

```
<?php // Script 9.7 - logout.php
// This is the logout page. It destroys
the session information.

// Address error handling.
ini_set ('display_errors', 1);
error_reporting (E_ALL & ~E_NOTICE);

// Need the session.
session_start();

// Delete the session variable.
unset ($_SESSION);

// Destroy the session data.
session_destroy();

// Define a page title and include the
header.
define ('TITLE', 'Logout');
require ('templates/header.html');

?>
<div id="leftcontent">
    <h1>Welcome to the Elliott Smith Fan
    Club!</h1>
    <p>You are now logged out.</p>
    <p>Thank you for using this site.
    We hope that you liked it.<br />
    Blah, blah, blah...
    Blah, blah, blah...</p>
</div>

<?php
require ('templates/footer.html'); // Need
the footer.
?>
```

Deleting a Session

It's important to know how to delete a session, just as it's important to know how to delete a cookie: Sometimes you'll want to forget the data you've stored. Session data exists in two areas, so you'll need to delete both. But first you must begin with the `session_start()` function, as always:

```
session_start();
```

Then, you delete the session variables by resetting the `$_SESSION` array:

```
unset ($_SESSION);
```

Finally, you remove the session data from the server (where it's stored in temporary files). To do this, use

```
session_destroy();
```

With that in mind, let's write `logout.php`, which will delete the session, effectively logging out the user.

To delete a session:

1. Start a new PHP script in your text editor (**Script 9.7**).

   ```
   <?php // Script 9.7 - logout.php
   ini_set ('display_errors', 1);
   error_reporting (E_ALL & ~E_NOTICE);
   ```

2. Begin the session:

   ```
   session_start();
   ```

   Remember that you can't delete a session until you activate the session using this function.

3. Delete the session variable:

   ```
   unset ($_SESSION);
   ```

   You can use the `unset()` function to delete any variable, including `$_SESSION`. Doing so trashes any stored values.

continues on next page

4. Destroy the session data on the server:

```
session_destroy();
```

This step tells PHP to remove the actual session files on the server.

5. Include the HTML header, and complete this PHP section:

```
define ('TITLE', 'Logout');
require ('templates/header.html');
?>
```

6. Make the page content:

```
<div id="leftcontent">
    <h1>Welcome to the Elliott Smith
    → Fan Club!</h1>
    <p>You are now logged out.</p>
    <p>Thank you for using this site.
    → We hope that you liked it.<br />
    Blah, blah, blah...
    Blah, blah, blah...</p>
</div>
```

7. Include the HTML footer:

```
<?php
require ('templates/footer.html');
?>
```

8. Save the file as `logout.php`, upload it to your Web server, and test it in your Web browser by clicking on the link in `welcome.php` (**Figure 9.20**).

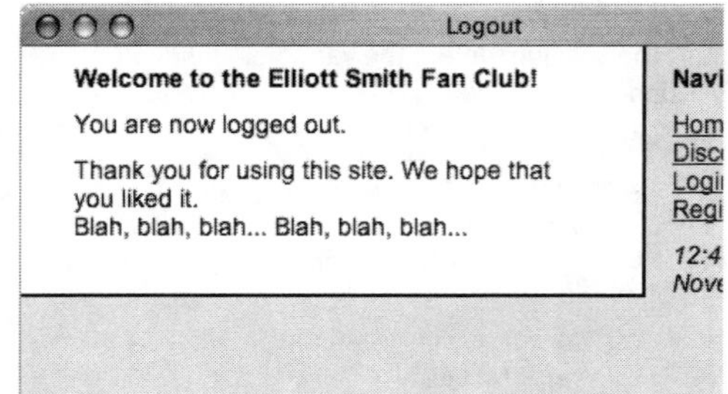

Figure 9.20 The log-out page destroys the session data.

✔ Tips

- To delete an individual session value, use `unset ($_SESSION['var']);`.
- The PHP module on the server will automatically perform *garbage collection* based on settings in its configuration. PHP uses garbage collection to manually delete session files from the server, with the assumption that they're no longer needed.
- You can have PHP use sessions without cookies, in which case the session ID must be appended to every link in your site (so that each page receives the session ID). If you enable the `enable_trans_side` setting (in the `php.ini` file), PHP will handle this for you.

Creating Functions

10

Throughout this book, you've used dozens of functions that provide much-needed functionality, such as `print()`, `setcookie()`, and `number_format()`. Whereas those functions have already been defined by PHP, here you'll be creating your own. However, once created, functions you've written and built-in PHP functions are used in the same manner.

Creating functions can save you oodles of time over the course of your programming life. In fact, they constitute a strong step in the process of creating Web applications and building a solid library of PHP code to use in future projects.

In this chapter, you'll see how to write your own functions that perform specific tasks. After that, you'll learn how to pass information to the function, use default values in a function, and have your function return a value. You'll also learn how functions and variables work together.

Creating and Using Simple Functions

As you program, you'll discover that you use certain sections of code frequently, either within a single script or over the course of several scripts. Placing these routines into a self-defined function can save you time and make your programming easier, especially as your Web sites become more complex. Once you create a function, the actions of that function take place each time the function is called, just as `print()` sends text to the browser with each use.

The syntax to create a user-defined function is

```
function function_name () {
    statement(s);
}
```

You can use roughly the same naming conventions for functions as you do for variables, just without the initial dollar sign. The most important rule is to remain consistent. Second to that is the suggestion that you creating meaningful function names, just as you ought to write representative variable names (`create_header` would be a better function name than `function1`). Remember not to use spaces, though—doing so constitutes two separate words for the function name, which will result in error messages (the underscore is a logical replacement for the space).

Any valid PHP code can go within the *`statement(s)`* area of the function, including calls to other functions. There is also no limit on the number of statements a function contains; but make sure each statement ends with a semicolon, just as you would within the rest of the PHP script.

The formatting of a function isn't important as long as the requisite elements are there. These elements include the word *function*, the function's name, the opening and closing parentheses, the opening and closing braces, and the statement(s). It's conventional to indent a function's statement(s) from the previous line, for clarity's sake, as you would with a loop or conditional. In any case, select a format style that you like (which is both syntactically correct and logically sound) and stick to it.

You call (or enact) the function by referring to it just as you do any built-in function. The line of code

```
function_name();
```

will cause the ***`statement(s);`*** part of the previously defined function to be executed.

Let's begin by creating a function that generates month, day, and year pull-down menus for a form.

To create and call a basic function:

1. Start a new PHP document in your text editor, beginning with the HTML head (**Script 10.1**):

```
<!DOCTYPE html PUBLIC "-//W3C//
→ DTD XHTML 1.0 Transitional//EN"
"http://www.w3.org/TR/xhtml1/DTD/
→ xhtml1-transitional.dtd">
<html xmlns="http://www.w3.org/1999/
→ xhtml">
<head>
   <meta http-equiv="content-type"
   → content="text/html; charset=
   → iso-8859-1" />
   <title>Date Menus</title>
</head>
<body>
```

continues on next page

Script 10.1 The function defined in this script creates three pull-down menus for a form.

```
<!DOCTYPE html PUBLIC "-//W3C//DTD XHTML 1.0 Transitional//EN"
        "http://www.w3.org/TR/xhtml1/DTD/xhtml1-transitional.dtd">
<html xmlns="http://www.w3.org/1999/xhtml">
<head>
    <meta http-equiv="content-type" content="text/html; charset=iso-8859-1" />
    <title>Date Menus</title>
</head>
<body>
<?php // Script 10.1 - menus1.php
// This script defines and calls a function.

// Address error handling.
ini_set ('display_errors', 1);
error_reporting (E_ALL & ~E_NOTICE);

// This function makes three pull-down menus for the months, days, and years.
function make_date_menus () {

    // Array to store the months.
    $months = array (1 => 'January', 'February', 'March', 'April', 'May', 'June', 'July',
    'August', 'September', 'October', 'November', 'December');

```

(script continues on next page)

2. Begin the PHP section:

```
<?php // Script 10.1 - menus1.php
ini_set ('display_errors', 1);
error_reporting (E_ALL & ~E_NOTICE);
```

3. Start defining a function:

```
function make_date_menus () {
```

The name of this function is `make_date_menus`, which is both descriptive of what the function does and easy to remember.

4. Create the month pull-down menu:

```
$months = array (1 => 'January',
→ 'February', 'March', 'April',
→ 'May', 'June', 'July', 'August',
→ 'September', 'October', 'November',
→ 'December');
print '<select name="month">';
foreach ($months as $key => $value) {
   print "\n<option value=\"$key\">
   → $value</option>";
}
print '</select>';
```

Script 10.1 *continued*

```
    // Make the month pull-down menu.
    print '<select name="month">';
    foreach ($months as $key => $value) {
        print "\n<option value=\"$key\">$value</option>";
    }
    print '</select>';

    // Make the day pull-down menu.
    print '<select name="day">';
    for ($day = 1; $day <= 31; $day++) {
        print "\n<option value=\"$day\">$day</option>";
    }
    print '</select>';

    // Make the year pull-down menu.
    print '<select name="year">';
    $start_year = date ('Y');
    for ($y = $start_year; $y <= ($start_year + 10); $y++) {
        print "\n<option value=\"$y\">$y</option>";

    }
    print '</select>';
} // End of function.

// Make the form.
print '<form action="" method="post">';
make_date_menus();
print '</form>';

?>
</body>
</html>
```

To generate a list of months, you first create an array of the month names, indexed numerically beginning at 1 for January. Because you specified the index for the first array element, the others will follow sequentially without the need to be explicit in naming them.

After the array has been created, the initial select tag is printed out. Then, a `foreach` loop runs through the `$months` array. For each element in the array, the HTML option tag is printed, using the array key (the numbers 1 through 12) as the option value and the array value (January through December) as the pull-down value. Each line is also preceded by a newline character (`\n`) so that each option ends up on its own line within the HTML source.

5. Create the day pull-down menu:

```
print '<select name="day">';
for ($day = 1; $day <= 31; $day++) {
   print "\n<option value=\"$day\">
   → $day</option>";
}
print '</select>';
```

   The day menu is a lot easier to create. To do so, you use a simple `for` loop, running through the numbers 1 through 31.

6. Create the year pull-down menu:

```
print '<select name="year">';
$start_year = date ('Y');
for ($y = $start_year; $y <=
→ ($start_year + 10); $y++) {
   print "\n<option value=\"$y\">
   → $y</option>";


}
print '</select>';
```

continues on next page

To create the year pull-down menu, you start by using the `date()` function to get the current year. Then you create options for this year plus the next 10, using a `for` loop.

7. Close the function:

```
} // End of function.
```

When you're creating functions, it's easy to create parse errors by forgetting the closing curly brace. You may want to add comments to help you remember this final step.

8. Make the form tags, and call the function:

```
print '<form action=""
method="post">';
make_date_menus();
print '</form>';
```

The `print()` statements are used to create the HTML form tags. Without those, the date pull-down menus won't appear properly in your script.

Once you've created your function, you simply have to call it by name (being careful to use the exact spelling) to make the function work. Be sure to include the parentheses as well.

9. Complete the PHP and HTML:

```
?>
</body>
</html>
```

10. Save the file as `menus1.php`, upload it to your Web server (or save it to your PHP-enabled computer), and run it in your Web browser (**Figure 10.1**).

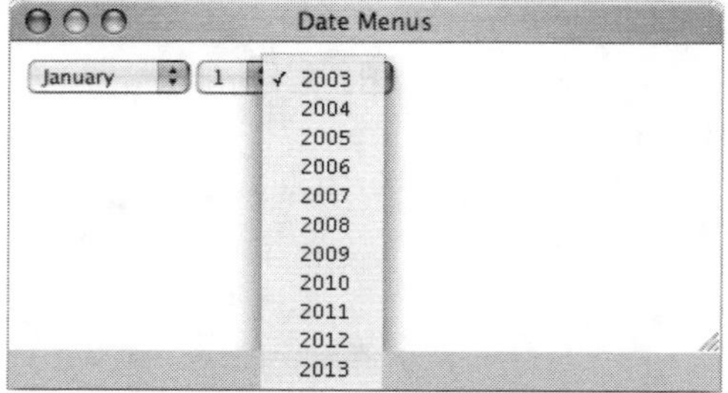

Figure 10.1 These pull-down menus were created by a user-defined function. This technique makes your code more portable without having an effect on the end result.

✔ Tips

- If you see a *Call to undefined function: some_function...* error message, it means you're trying to call a function that doesn't exist. Recheck your spelling in both the definition of the function and its usage to see if you made a mistake.

- The `function_exists()` function returns TRUE or FALSE based on whether a function exists in PHP. This applies to both user-defined functions and those that can be built into PHP:

  ```
  if (function_exists ('my_function'))
  → { …
  ```

- Although you aren't required in PHP 4 and 5 to define your functions before you call them, it's recommended that you habitually define your functions at the beginning of a script. The benefit of doing so is that it helps to separate this code from the main workings of the script.

- Names for the functions you create are case-insensitive, just as the names of existing PHP functions are case-insensitive. Therefore, it won't matter in your code if you use `make_date_menus` instead of the more formal `Make_Date_Menus`.

- Some people prefer this syntax for laying out their functions:

  ```
  function function_name ()
  {
     statement(s);
  }
  ```

- User-defined functions add extra memory requirements to your PHP scripts, so you should be judicious in using them. If you find that your function merely calls another PHP function or has but one line of code, it's probably not the best use of this capability.

Creating and Calling Functions that Take Arguments

Although being able to create a simple function is useful, writing one that takes input and does something with that input is even better. The input a function takes is called an *argument* (or sometimes a *parameter*). This is a concept you've seen before: the `print()` function takes a string as an argument, which it then sends to the browser.

The syntax for writing functions that take arguments is as follows:

```
function function_name ($argument1,
→ $argument2, ...) {
    statement(s);
}
```

The function's arguments are in the form of variables that are assigned the value sent to the function when you call it. Functions that take input are called much like those that don't—you just need to remember to pass along the necessary values. You can do this either by passing variables

```
function_name ($variable1, $variable2,
→ ...);
```

or by sending literal values, as in

```
function_name ('some value', 28.96,
→ ...);
```

or some combination thereof:

```
function_name ($variable1, 'value2',
→ ...);
```

The important thing to note is that arguments are passed quite literally: The first variable in the function is equal to the first value in the call line, the second function variable matches the second call value, and so forth. Functions aren't smart enough to intuitively understand how you meant the values to be associated. This is also true if you fail to pass a value, in which case the function will assume that value is null (*null* isn't the mathematical 0, which is actually a value, but closer to the idea of the word *nothing*). The same thing applies if a function takes four arguments and you pass three—the fourth will be null, which may create an error.

To demonstrate functions that take arguments, you'll rewrite the `make_date_menus()` function so that it takes a start year value and a number for how many years should be displayed. Then the function can easily create different year pull-down menus for different situations.

To create and call a function that takes an argument:

1. Open `menus1.php` in your text editor (Script 10.1).

2. Change the function definition line (line 17 in Script 10.1) so that it takes two arguments (**Script 10.2**):

   ```
   function make_date_menus
   → ($start_year, $num_years) {
   ```

   This function now takes two arguments, which will be assigned to the `$start_year` and `$num_years` variables.

continues on next page

Script 10.2 This version of the `make_date_menus()` function takes two arguments to dictate when the dates in the year pull-down menu begin and end.

```
<!DOCTYPE html PUBLIC "-//W3C//DTD XHTML 1.0 Transitional//EN"
        "http://www.w3.org/TR/xhtml1/DTD/xhtml1-transitional.dtd">
<html xmlns="http://www.w3.org/1999/xhtml">
<head>
    <meta http-equiv="content-type" content="text/html; charset=iso-8859-1" />
    <title>Date Menus</title>
</head>
<body>
<?php // Script 10.2 - menus2.php
// This script defines and calls a function that takes arguments.

// Address error handling.
ini_set ('display_errors', 1);
error_reporting (E_ALL & ~E_NOTICE);

// This function makes three pull-down menus for the months, days, and years.
// This function requires two arguments be passed to it:
    // A start year argument (the year the pull-down menu should begin)
    // The number of years to create
function make_date_menus ($start_year, $num_years) {

    // Array to store the months.
    $months = array (1 => 'January', 'February', 'March', 'April', 'May', 'June', 'July', 'August', 'September', 'October', 'November', 'December');

```

(script continues on next page)

3. Delete the `$start_year = date ('Y');` code (line 38 of the original script).

   Because the start year is being passed to the function, the function no longer needs to (or should) calculate this value for itself.

4. Rewrite the year `for` loop to use the passed arguments:

   ```
   for ($y = $start_year; $y <=
   → ($start_year + $num_years); $y++) {
   ```

   To use the received values, you just need to change the second part of the `for` loop (the condition the `for` loop checks against). Instead of having the loop execute 10 times, it executes for `$num_years` times.

5. Change the function call so that it passes two arguments:

   ```
   make_date_menus(2004, 20);
   ```

   The function now needs to be passed two values. The first value is the first year to display in the pull-down menu. The second value is how many years to display. Because these are both number values, they don't need to be placed within quotation marks.

Script 10.2 *continued*

```
    // Make the month pull-down menu.
    print '<select name="month">';
    foreach ($months as $key => $value) {
        print "\n<option value=\"$key\">$value</option>";
    }
    print '</select>';

    // Make the day pull-down menu.
    print '<select name="day">';
    for ($day = 1; $day <= 31; $day++) {
        print "\n<option value=\"$day\">$day</option>";
    }
    print '</select>';

    // Make the year pull-down menu.
    print '<select name="year">';
    for ($y = $start_year; $y <= ($start_year + $num_years); $y++) {
        print "\n<option value=\"$y\">$y</option>";
        $year++;
    }
    print '</select>';
} // End of function.

// Make the form.
print '<form action="" method="post">';
make_date_menus(2004, 20);
print '</form>';

?>
</body>
</html>
```

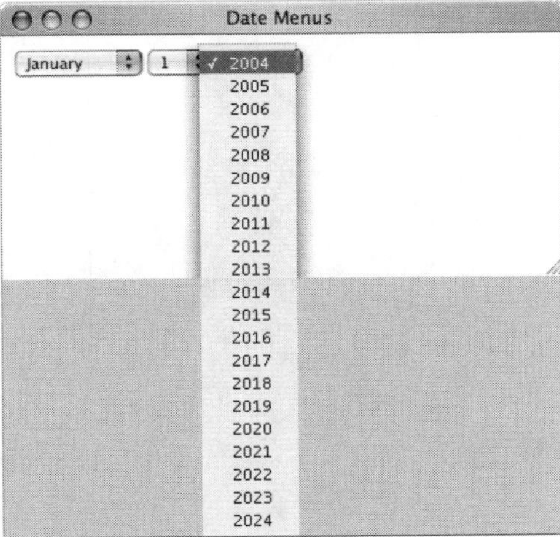

Figure 10.2 A slightly different variation on the original function (see Script 10.1 and Figure 10.1) lets you create different pull-down menus with ease.

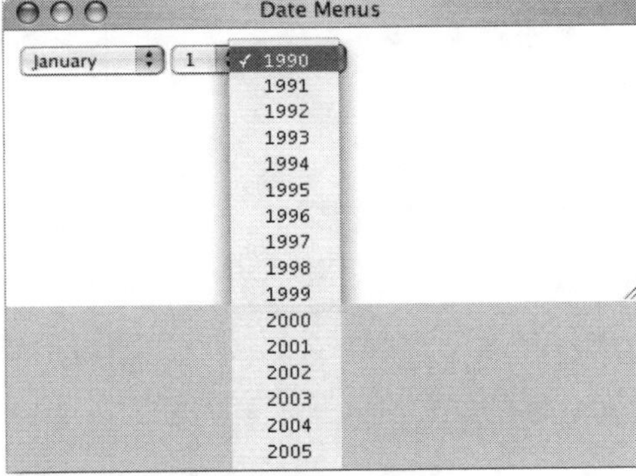

Figure 10.3 Minor changes to one line of code generate different results (compare with Figure 10.2).

6. Save your script as `menus2.php`, upload it to your Web server, and test it in your Web browser (**Figure 10.2**).

7. If desired, change the arguments in your function call to create a different year pull-down menu (**Figure 10.3**).

✔ Tips

- If you want, you can use the `$start_year = date ('Y');` line outside of the function to have the pull-down menu automatically begin with the current year. This is what you do:

  ```
  $start_year = date ('Y');
  make_date_menus ($start_year, 20);
  ```

- You can define as many functions as you want, not just one per script as the examples in this chapter portray.

- There are no limits on how many arguments a function can take.

- Once you've defined your own functions like this, you can place them in an external file and then require that file when you need access to the functions.

Setting Default Argument Values

When you're writing a function, PHP allows you to preset values for your arguments. Such a function uses the default values unless it receives an argument that then overwrites the default. In other words, by setting a default value for an argument, you render that particular argument optional when calling the function.

You'd set an argument's default value if you wanted to assume a certain value but still allow for other possibilities. However, keep in mind that the default arguments should always be written after the other standard arguments (those without defaults). This is because PHP directly assigns values to arguments in the order they're received from the call line. Thus, it isn't possible to omit a value for the first argument but include one for the second (this would mean you sent one value, and it would automatically be equated to the first argument, not the second).

For example, suppose a function is written like this:

```
function calculate_total ($qty, $price =
→ 20.00, $tax = 0.06) {...
```

If you call the function with this line

```
calculate_total (3, 0.07);
```

with the intention of setting `$qty` to 3, leaving `$price` at 20.00, and changing the `$tax` to 0.07, there will be problems. The end result will be that `$qty` is set to 3, `$price` is set to 0.07, and `$tax` remains at 0.06, which isn't the desired outcome. The proper way to achieve that affect would be to code

```
calculate_total (3, 20.00, 0.07);
```

Let's rework the `make_date_menus()` function to incorporate the notion of setting default argument values.

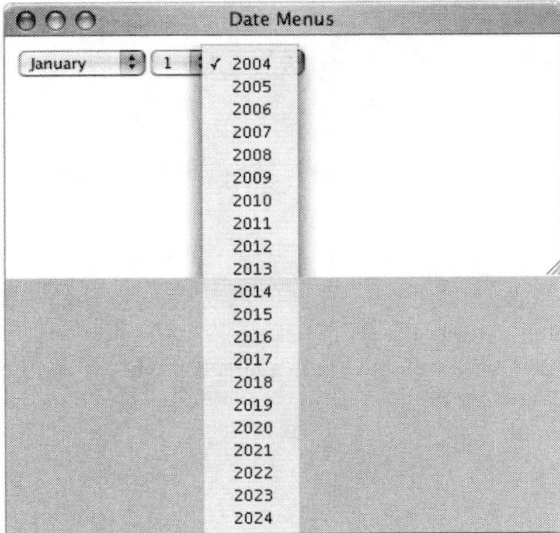

Figure 10.4 Now the script uses a default value for one function argument. This doesn't affect the end result but does make the script easier to use.

To write a function that uses default values:

1. Open `menus2.php` (Script 10.2) in your text editor, if it isn't open already.

2. Add a default value to the `$num_years` variable in the `make_date_menus()` function (**Script 10.3**):

   ```
   function make_date_menus
   → ($start_year, $num_years = 10) {
   ```

   You've now set the value of `$num_years` to be 10 as a default. If two arguments are sent to the function, then `$num_years` will be set to the second value instead of the default, working as it did previously.

3. Save your script as `menus3.php`, upload it to your Web server, and test it in your Web browser (**Figure 10.4**).

continues on next page

Script 10.3 The function still takes two arguments, but only one of them is required. If no `$num_years` value is passed to the function, its value will be 10.

```
<!DOCTYPE html PUBLIC "-//W3C//DTD XHTML 1.0 Transitional//EN"
        "http://www.w3.org/TR/xhtml1/DTD/xhtml1-transitional.dtd">
<html xmlns="http://www.w3.org/1999/xhtml">
<head>
    <meta http-equiv="content-type" content="text/html; charset=iso-8859-1" />
    <title>Date Menus</title>
</head>
<body>
<?php // Script 10.3 - menus3.php
// This script defines and calls a function that takes arguments.

// Address error handling.
ini_set ('display_errors', 1);
error_reporting (E_ALL & ~E_NOTICE);

// This function makes three pull-down menus for the months, days, and years.
// This function requires two arguments be passed to it:
    // A start year argument (the year the pull-down menu should begin)
    // The number of years to create
function make_date_menus ($start_year, $num_years = 10) {

```

(script continues on next page)

4. If you want, change your function call (line 50) to read

   `make_date_menus (2004);`

   Calling the function with this code works without a problem, only this time 10 more years are displayed in the pull-down menu instead of 20.

5. Save the script and run it again (**Figure 10.5**).

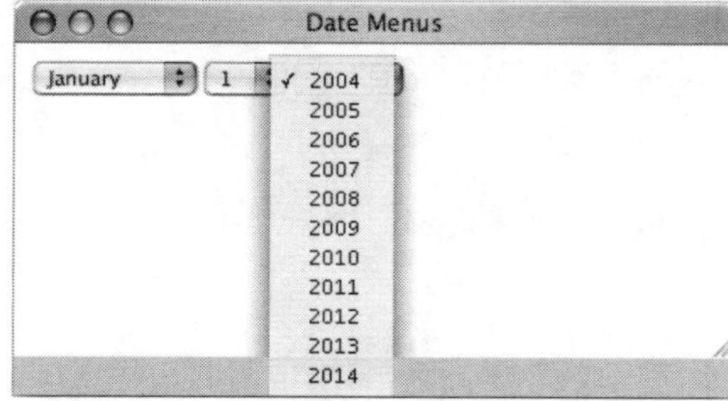

Figure 10.5 Passing only one parameter to the function causes it to use the default number of years to print (the start year plus 10 more).

Script 10.3 *continued*

```
22      // Array to store the months.
23      $months = array (1 => 'January', 'February', 'March', 'April', 'May', 'June', 'July',
        'August', 'September', 'October', 'November', 'December');
24
25      // Make the month pull-down menu.
26      print '<select name="month">';
27      foreach ($months as $key => $value) {
28          print "\n<option value=\"$key\">$value</option>";
29      }
30      print '</select>';
31
32      // Make the day pull-down menu.
33      print '<select name="day">';
34      for ($day = 1; $day <= 31; $day++) {
35          print "\n<option value=\"$day\">$day</option>";
36      }
37      print '</select>';
38
39      // Make the year pull-down menu.
40      print '<select name="year">';
41      for ($y = $start_year; $y <= ($start_year + $num_years); $y++) {
42          print "\n<option value=\"$y\">$y</option>";
43          $year++;
44      }
45      print '</select>';
46  } // End of function.
47
48  // Make the form.
49  print '<form action="" method="post">';
50  make_date_menus(2004, 20);
51  print '</form>';
52
53  ?>
54  </body>
55  </html>
```

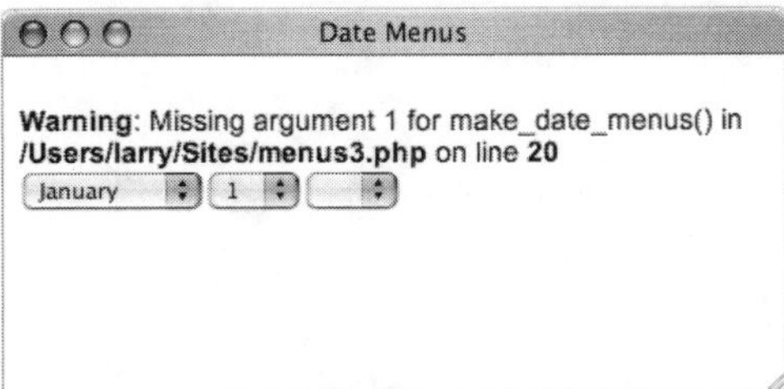

Figure 10.6 As with any function (user-defined or built into PHP), passing an incorrect number of arguments when calling it yields an error message.

✔ Tips

- If you fail to pass the proper number of arguments to a function, you'll see an error message (**Figure 10.6**).
- To pass no value to a function for a particular argument, use an empty string ('') or the word `NULL` (without quotes). Either of these values will override the default value, if one is established.
- As mentioned way back in Chapter 1, "Getting Started with PHP," the PHP manual marks optional function arguments using square brackets. For example, when you use the `number_format()` function, the number of decimals to round to is optional:

  ```
  string number_format ( float number
  → [, int decimals])
  ```

Creating and Using Functions that Return a Value

Once you've begun writing functions that take an argument, the next step is to have a function return a value. To do so requires just two more steps. First, you use the `return` statement within the function. Second, you must assign the output somehow when you call the function. Commonly, you'll assign the returned value to a variable; but you can also, for example, directly print the output. Here is the basic format for a function that takes an argument and returns a value:

```
function function_name ($argument) {
    statement(s);
    return $value;
}
```

Normally this function will be used with a line of code such as this:

```
$variable = function_name ($parameter);
```

Note that you assign the returned value of the function to a variable. Here's another (rather trivial) example:

```
function print_hello ($name) {
   return "Hello, $name!";
}
print print_hello ('Peyton');
```

To best demonstrate this concept, let's create a function that performs a simple calculation and formats the result. This script will display an HTML form where a user enters a quantity and price. When the form is submitted (back to this same page), a total value will be determined and printed.

Returning Multiple Values

User-defined functions frequently return just a single value but can return multiple values using the notion of arrays. Here's how you go about this:

```
function some_function ($arg1, $arg2)
{
   // Do whatever.
   return array ( $value1, $value2);
}
```

Then, to call this function, you code as follows:

```
list ($var1, $var2) = some_function
→ ($p1, $p2);
```

The end result is that `$value1` from the function is assigned to `$var1` in the PHP script, and `$value2` from the function is assigned to `$var2`.

To create and use a function that returns a value:

1. Create a new PHP document in your text editor, beginning with the standard HTML head (**Script 10.4**):

```
<!DOCTYPE html PUBLIC "-//W3C//
→ DTD XHTML 1.0 Transitional//EN"
"http://www.w3.org/TR/xhtml1/DTD/
→ xhtml1-transitional.dtd">
<html xmlns="http://www.w3.org/1999/
→ xhtml">
<head>
    <meta http-equiv="content-type"
    → content="text/html; charset=
    → iso-8859-1" />
    <title>Cost Calculator</title>
</head>
<body>
```

2. Begin the PHP code:

```
<?php // Script 10.4 - calculator.php
ini_set ('display_errors', 1);
error_reporting (E_ALL & ~E_NOTICE);
```

3. Define the function:

```
function calculate_total ($quantity,
→ $price) {
    $total = $quantity * $price;
    $total = number_format ($total,
    2);
    return $total;
}
```

This function takes two arguments—a quantity and a price—and multiplies them to create a total. This value is then formatted before it's returned by the function.

continues on next page

Script 10.4 This script both displays and handles an HTML form in order to perform some basic calculations. The script uses a function that takes two arguments and returns a single value.

```
<!DOCTYPE html PUBLIC "-//W3C//DTD XHTML 1.0 Transitional//EN"
        "http://www.w3.org/TR/xhtml1/DTD/xhtml1-transitional.dtd">
<html xmlns="http://www.w3.org/1999/xhtml">
<head>
    <meta http-equiv="content-type" content="text/html; charset=iso-8859-1" />
    <title>Cost Calculator</title>
</head>
<body>
<?php // Script 10.4 - calculator.php
// This script displays and handles an HTML form.
// Users can select a quantity and price to be calculated.

// Address error handling.
ini_set ('display_errors', 1);
error_reporting (E_ALL & ~E_NOTICE);

// This function makes the calculations.
function calculate_total ($quantity, $price) {

    $total = $quantity * $price; // Calculation
    $total = number_format ($total, 2); // Formatting
```

(script continues on next page)

Although this may seem like a silly use of a function, the benefits of putting even a one-step calculation into a function are twofold: First, the calculation will be easier to find and modify at a later date with your function located at the beginning of your script instead of hidden in the rest of the code; and second, should you want to repeat the action again in a script, you can do so without duplicating code.

4. Begin the conditional to see if the form was submitted:

```
if (isset ($_POST['submit'])) {
```

Because this page both displays and handles the HTML form, you use a conditional that checks for the presence of a `$_POST['submit']` variable. If this variable is set, the script should handle the form. If it isn't, the script should display the form.

Script 10.4 *continued*

```
    return $total; // Return the value.

} // End of function.

if (isset ($_POST['submit'])) { // Handle form.

    // Check for values.
    if ( is_numeric ($_POST['quantity']) AND is_numeric ($_POST['price']) ) {

        // Call the function and print the results.
        $total = calculate_total ($_POST['quantity'], $_POST['price']);
        print "<p>Your total comes to $<b>$total</b></p>";

    } else { // Inappropriate values entered.
        print "<p>Please enter a valid quantity and price!</p>";
    }

} else { // Display form.

    print '<form action="calculator.php" method="post">
    <p>Quantity: <input type="text" name="quantity" size="3" /></p>
    <p>Price: <input type="text" name="price" size="5" /></p>
    <input type="submit" name="submit" value="Calculate!" />
    </form>';

}
?>
</body>
</html>
```

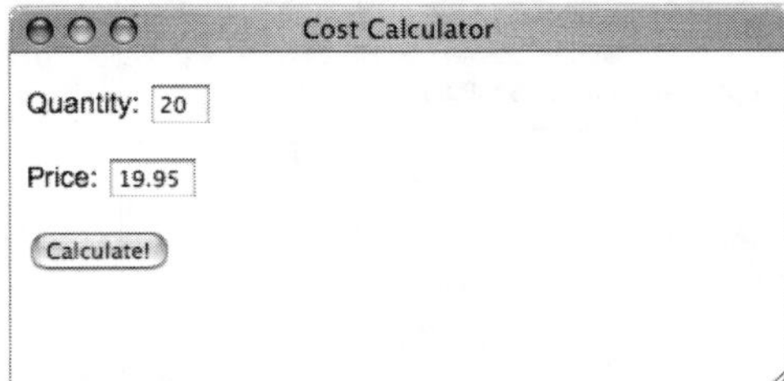

Figure 10.7 This simple form takes two values on which calculations will be made (see Figure 10.8).

5. Handle the form data:

```
if ( is_numeric ($_POST['quantity'])
→ AND is_numeric ($_POST['price']) ) {
   $total = calculate_total
   → ($_POST['quantity'],
   → $_POST['price']);
   print "<p>Your total comes to
   → $<b>$total</b></p>";
} else {
   print "<p>Please enter a valid
   → quantity and price!</p>";
}
```

   This part of the PHP code—which handles the form if it has been submitted—first checks that a numeric quantity and price were entered. If so, the total is determined by calling the `calculate_total()` function and assigning the result to the `$total` variable. This result is then printed out.

   If either of the form variables was not properly submitted, a message is printed indicating such.

6. Display the HTML form:

```
} else {
   print '<form action="calculator.php"
   → method="post">
   <p>Quantity: <input type="text"
   → name="quantity" size="3" /></p>
   <p>Price: <input type="text"
   → name="price" size="5" /></p>
   <input type="submit" name="submit"
   → value="Calculate!" />
   </form>';
}
```

   The form itself is quite simple (**Figure 10.7**), requesting two different values from the user.

continues on next page

7. Complete the PHP code and the HTML page:

```
?>
</body>
</html>
```

8. Save the page as `calculator.php`, upload it to your Web server, and test it in your Web browser (**Figure 10.8**).

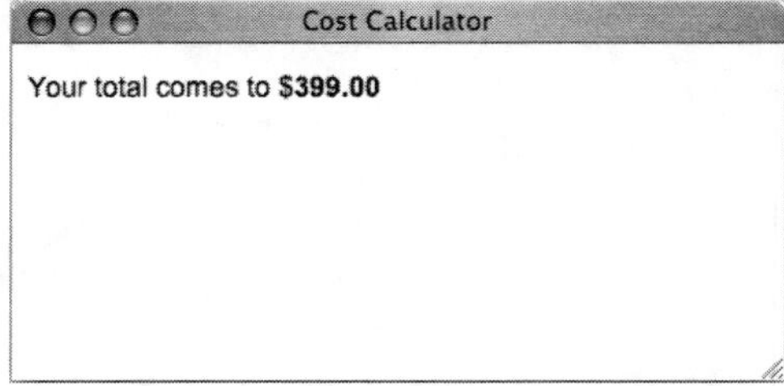

Figure 10.8 The result of the calculation, which takes place within a user-defined function.

✔ Tip

- You can have only one `return` statement executed in a function, but the same function can have multiple `return` statements. As an example, you may want to write a function that checks for a condition and returns whether the condition was satisfied. In such a case, you'd code as follows in your function:

```
if (condition) {
   return TRUE;
} else {
   return FALSE;
}
```

The result returned by the function is either TRUE or FALSE, indicating whether the stated condition was met.

Understanding Variable Scope

The concept of variable scope wasn't introduced in Chapter 2, "Variables," because without an understanding of functions, scope makes little sense. Now that you have a reasonable familiarity with functions, this section will revisit the topic of variables and discuss in some detail how exactly variables and functions work together.

As you saw in the second section of this chapter, "Creating and Calling Functions that Take Arguments," you can send variables to a function by passing them as arguments. However, you can also call a variable from within a function using the `global` statement. This is possible because of variable scope. The *scope* of a variable is essentially the realm in which it exists. By default, the variables you write in a script exist for the life of that script. Conversely, environment variables (such as `$_SERVER['PHP_SELF']`) exist throughout the server.

continues on next page

Functions, though, create a new level of scope. Function variables—the arguments of a function as well as any variables defined within the function—exist only within that function and aren't accessible outside of it (that is, they're local variables with local scope). Likewise, a variable from outside a function can only be referenced by passing it to the function as an argument or by using the `global` statement. The `global` statement roughly means, "I want this variable within the function to be the same as it is outside of the function." In other words, the `global` statement turns a local variable with local scope into a global variable with global scope. Any changes made to the variable within the function are also passed on to the variable when it's outside of the function (assuming the function is called, that is), without using the `return` command.

The syntax of the `global` statement is as follows:

```
function function_name ($argument) {
    global $variable;
   statement(s);
}
```

As long as *$variable* exists outside of the function, it will also have the same value within the function.

This leads to another issue regarding functions and variables: Because of variable scope, a variable within a function is a different entity (perhaps with a different value) than a variable outside of the function, *even if the two variables use the exact same name* (and assuming you don't use the `global` statement within the function). Let's go over this more explicitly.

Frequently, you'll use a function call line like this one:

```
function_name ($value1);
```

The function (here, `function_name ($argument1)`) then equates the value of `$argument1` to that of `$value1`, so their values are the same but their names are different. However, if the name of the argument in the function is also `$value1` (so the function-creation line reads `function_name ($value1)`), the `$value1` variable within the function assumes the same value as the original `$value1` outside of the function—but they're still two separate variables. The one has a scope within the function, and the other has a scope outside of it.

So, you don't have to come up with different names. You can use the exact same name in the function and the call line for the sake of convenience (it becomes easy to remember what arguments are passed that way), but remember that they aren't the same variable. What happens to a variable's value within a function stays within the function (unless you use the `global` statement, which does make the two variables the same).

To demonstrate variable scope, let's rework the `calculator.php` script using the `global` statement.

To use the global statement:

1. Open `calculator.php` in your text editor (Script 10.4).
2. Before the function definition, add the following (**Script 10.5**):

   `$tax = 8.75;`

   You create a `$tax` variable with a set value to be used in the cost calculations. It's assigned a value outside of the function because it will be used later in the main body of the script.

continues on next page

Script 10.5 The function in this script can use the `$tax` variable—even though it hasn't been passed to the function—thanks to the `global` statement.

Script

```
<!DOCTYPE html PUBLIC "-//W3C//DTD XHTML 1.0 Transitional//EN"
        "http://www.w3.org/TR/xhtml1/DTD/xhtml1-transitional.dtd">
<html xmlns="http://www.w3.org/1999/xhtml">
<head>
    <meta http-equiv="content-type" content="text/html; charset=iso-8859-1" />
    <title>Cost Calculator</title>
</head>
<body>
<?php // Script 10.5 - calculator.php (second version after Script 10.4)
// This script displays and handles an HTML form.
// Users can select a quantity and price to be calculated.

// Address error handling.
ini_set ('display_errors', 1);
error_reporting (E_ALL & ~E_NOTICE);

// Define the tax rate.
$tax = 8.75;

// This function makes the calculations.
function calculate_total ($quantity, $price) {
```

(script continues on next page)

3. Within the function definition, add a `global` statement:

   `global $tax;`

   This statement tells the function to incorporate the same `$tax` variable as the one that exists outside of the function.

4. Before the `$total` in the function is formatted, recalculate the value using the tax rate:

   `$taxrate = ($tax / 100) + 1;`

   `$total = $total * $taxrate;`

   To add the tax to the total value, you start by dividing the tax by 100, to create a percentage. Then you add 1 to this value to get a multiplier. This result is then multiplied by the total to come up with the new, final total.

Script 10.5 *continued*

```

    global $tax;

    $total = $quantity * $price; // Calculation
    $taxrate = ($tax / 100) + 1;
    $total = $total * $taxrate; // Add the tax.
    $total = number_format ($total, 2); // Formatting

    return $total; // Return the value.

} // End of function.

if (isset ($_POST['submit'])) { // Handle form.

    // Check for values.
    if ( is_numeric ($_POST['quantity']) AND is_numeric ($_POST['price']) ) {

        // Call the function and print the results.
        $total = calculate_total ($_POST['quantity'], $_POST['price']);
        print "<p>Your total comes to $<b>$total</b>, including the $tax percent tax.</p>";

    } else { // Inappropriate values entered.
        print "<p>Please enter a valid quantity and price!</p>";
    }

} else { // Display form.

    print '<form action="calculator.php" method="post">
    <p>Quantity: <input type="text" name="quantity" size="3" /></p>
    <p>Price: <input type="text" name="price" size="5" /></p>
    <input type="submit" name="submit" value="Calculate!" />
    </form>';

}
?>
</body>
</html>
```

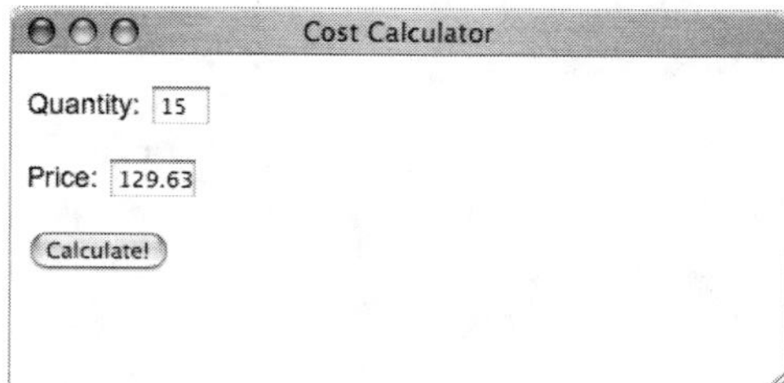

Figure 10.9 Run the form again...

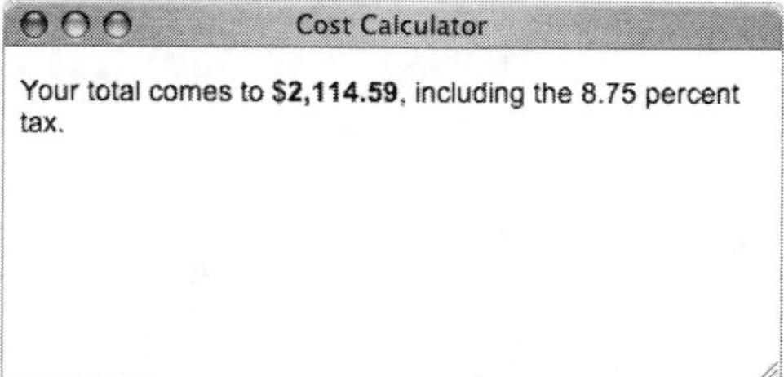

Figure 10.10 ...and the calculation now makes use of a global `$tax` variable.

Notice that you use a `$taxrate` variable (based on `$tax`) to perform these calculations. This is because you'll print out the value of `$tax` later, and any changes made to it here will be reflected (because it's a global variable).

5. Alter the main `print()` statement so that it prints the tax rate:

```
print "<p>Your total comes to
→ $<b>$total</b>, including the $tax
→ percent tax.</p>";
```

The `$tax` variable defined at the beginning of the script is printed out at the end. If you hadn't used the `$taxrate` variable within the function and made the alterations to the global `$tax` instead, those calculations would be reflected in the value printed here.

6. Save your script, upload it to your Web server, and test it in your Web browser (**Figures 10.9** and **10.10**).

✔ Tips

- Constants and the superglobal arrays (`$_GET`, `$_POST`, `$_COOKIE`, and `$_SESSION`) have the added benefit that they're always available inside functions without requiring the `global` statement (which is why they are called *superglobal*).
- When it comes to naming conventions for function arguments, there are different schools of thought. On the one hand, using the same name in the function as a variable outside of the function makes it easy to remember how values match up. On the other hand, using generic argument names in your function makes it less script-specific. You can also use a hybrid method by appending a lowercase *f* to the beginning of function names, such as `$f_quantity` and `$f_tax`. Some programmers identify global variables as `$g_variable`. Again, the key is to remain consistent with your naming policy.

Advanced Function Concepts

This chapter covers the basics of defining and using your own functions in PHP scripts, but there are a few more advanced topics you can consider.

A *static* variable is one that belongs to a function and whose value is initialized the first time that function is called. This value is then remembered by the function for each subsequent call (within the same PHP script). In other words, a static variable gives a function a little memory:

```
function print_number () {
   static $num = 1;
   print $num++;
}
print_number(); // Prints 1
print_number(); // Prints 2
```

In all the examples in this chapter, the variables have been passed to a function by value. There is an alternative: passing a variable by *reference*. When you do this, any changes made to the variable within the function affect the variable as it exists outside of the function:

```
function increment ($num) {
   $num++;
}
$n = 10;
increment ($n); // $n is still 10.
increment (&$n); // $n is 11.
```

Alternatively, this can be forced on all values sent to a function by using the following:

```
function increment (&$num) {...
```

Recursive functions call themselves. This isn't a problem as long as the function has an *out* (something that will cause the function to stop calling itself); otherwise, an infinite loop will be created. This example prints the numbers 1 through 10:

```
function print_to_ten () {
   static $n = 1;
   print $n;
   $n++;
   while ($n <= 10) {
      print_to_ten();
   }
}
print_to_ten();
```

PHP also lets you call functions using a variable's name. Using the previous function, you could do this:

```
$var = 'print_number';
$var();
```

This is a ridiculous example, but the idea is useful if you want to make truly abstract and flexible code.

Finally, using the `func_num_args()`, `func_get_arg()`, and `func_get_args()` functions, you can make a function take a variable number of arguments.

See the PHP manual for more information on any of these concepts if you're so inclined.

11 Files and Directories

To truly take your Web applications to the next level, you'll need a method of storing and retrieving data. E-commerce sites, Internet portals, and template-driven content providers all have a system for permanently writing information to the server and retrieving that information as needed.

There are two primary ways of storing data with PHP: using files (and directories) or databases. This chapter will discuss the former, and the next chapter will introduce the latter. It's worth your time to comprehend both methods (in fact, a database is just a really fancy system for writing to and reading from data stored in files on the server).

Although a database can be more powerful and secure than a file-based system, you may be surprised at how much you can do by sending and retrieving information from simple text documents on the server!

In this chapter, you'll learn about file permissions and then learn to write to, read from, and lock files. After that, you'll see how to handle file uploads with PHP, how to create directories, and an alternate method for reading data from a file. These last two examples will also demonstrate a simple file-based registration and log-in system that you can use in your Web applications.

File Permissions

Before you work through the examples of writing to and reading from a file, this section will briefly mention file permissions. The topic is large enough that you may want to pursue it further but this discussion will get you started.

Permissions identify who can do what to the file or directory. The options are *read*, *write*, and *execute* (actually, files can be designated *executable*, whereas directories are made *searchable*). On top of that, these options can be set differently for three unique types of users: the *owner* of the file (the person who put it on the server or created it); members of a particular *group*, which a server administrator sets; and, *others* (those who don't fall into the previous two categories). There is also the implied *everyone* level, which includes all of the previously mentioned users.

Normally, a file's *owner* is given read and write permissions by default, whereas *groups* and *others* are able to read a file or directory. For the examples in this chapter, PHP needs to be able to write to some files and directories, so you must be able to expand the permissions. Being able to write to a file or directory can be a security issue and should only be designated an option when absolutely necessary. Keep this in mind, and pay attention to some of the security tips mentioned throughout this chapter.

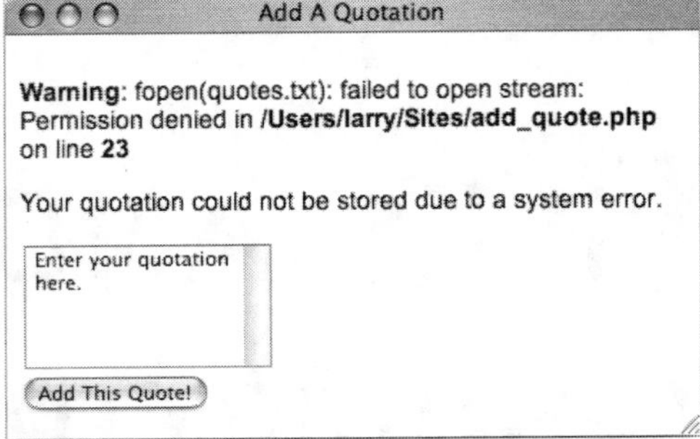

Figure 11.1 The *...failed to open stream: Permission denied...* message is the result of attempting to do something to a file that isn't allowed by the server. Here the server is denying the `fopen()` function that is attempting to open `quotes.txt` for the purpose of writing to it.

Creating the text file

In the first example, you'll work with a text file on the server named `quotes.txt`. If the file doesn't have the correct permissions to do what your PHP script is asking it to, you'll see an error message similar to that shown in **Figure 11.1**. Before proceeding through this chapter, you should create `quotes.txt` on the server and establish its permissions.

To create quotes.txt:

1. Open your text editor and create a new document.
2. Without typing anything into the file, save it as `quotes.txt`.
3. Move the file into the proper directory of your PHP-enabled computer or upload the file to your Web server (see the sidebar for tips on placing the file).

✔ Tips

- The `file_exists()` function returns TRUE if a submitted filename is found on the server. This can be used to test for the existence of a file before doing anything with it.

```
if (file_exists ('/path/to/
→ quotes.txt')) { …
```

- Assuming that PHP has write permissions on a directory, you can create a blank document within that directory using PHP. This is accomplished using the `touch()` function:

```
touch ('quotes.txt');
```

A More Secure File Structure

Having writable files and directories on the server is a bit of a security risk. If the Web server (and everyone else) can write to the file or directory, then what's to stop malicious users from trying to hack your system using this same gateway?

In general, the security issue is more important for directories than for files. This is because anyone can write anything to an open directory, including viruses, evil scripts, and Trojan horses.

The best security measure you can take in such instances is to place your writable files and directories outside of the Web directory. In other words, if your Web pages go in `C:\inetpub\wwwroot` or `/Users/your_username/Sites`, then if you place items in `C:\inetpub` or `/Users/your_username`, they are accessible to the locally running PHP but not to others over the Internet. The examples in this chapter follow this structure, and you should do so as well.

Setting a file's permissions

The previous sequence may seem like an odd series of steps, but in order to set the permissions on a file, the file must exist first. You do want the file to be blank, though, because you'll use PHP to write data to it later.

The desired end result for this example is to give either *others* or *everyone* permission to *read* and *write* (but not *execute*) `quotes.txt`. How you accomplish this depends on:

- Whether you're running PHP on your own computer or on a remote server
- The operating system of the PHP-enabled computer

Unfortunately, it would be impossible to offer steps for how every user should set the permissions under any circumstances, but here are some rough guidelines and steps to get you going.

To set a file's permissions on a remote server:

- Some ISPs offer their users a Web-based control panel where they can set file permissions (**Figure 11.2**) as well set other hosting parameters.
- If you have Telnet or ssh access to the server (which would presumably be running some form of Unix), follow these steps:

  1. Connect to the server.
  2. Type `cd /path/to/quotes/directory`, and press Enter.

     This should put you in the same directory as the `quotes.txt` file. You may or may not need to take this step, depending on what directory you're in after connecting.
  3. Type `chmod 0666 quotes.txt`, and press Enter.

     This should change the file's permissions. If it fails, you'll need to use `sudo chmod 0666 quotes.txt` and then enter your password at the prompt. If that fails, speak with the server's administrator.
- You may be able to change a file's permissions using your FTP client (**Figure 11.3**).

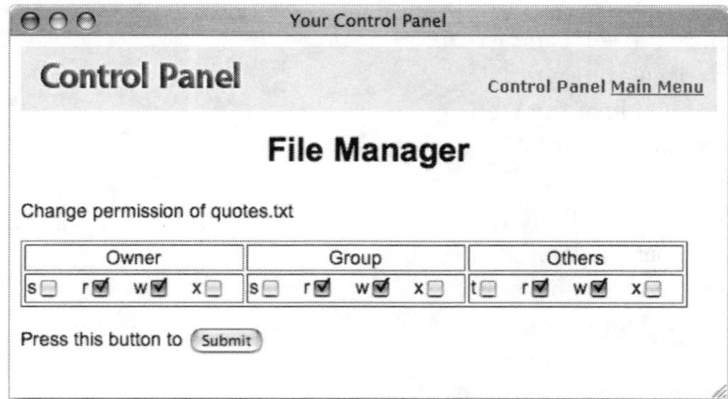

Figure 11.2 This control panel, provided by a hosting company, lets you adjust a file's permissions.

Figure 11.3 The Fetch FTP application uses this pop-up window to allow you to set a file's permissions.

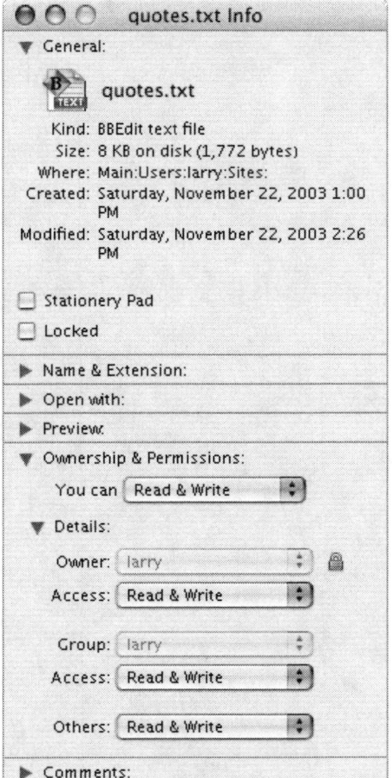

Figure 11.4 The Mac OS X Get Info panel lets you adjust a file's ownership and permissions, among other things.

To set a file's permissions on your computer:

- If you're working on your own Windows computer, you may not need to change the permissions. To test this theory, try each example first. If you see the *Permission denied* error message (Figure 11.1), use the next suggestion to rework the permissions.
- Windows users who need to change the permissions can do so by viewing the file or directory's properties. The resulting panel will differ for each version of Windows, but basically you just need to tweak who can access the file and how.
- Mac OS X users must select the file in the Finder and choose Get Info from the File menu. From there, use the Ownership & Permissions subpanel to adjust the file's permissions (**Figure 11.4**).
- On Unix (including users of Linux and Mac OS X) you can also use the `chmod 0666 quotes.txt` line in a terminal window, assuming that you have authority to do so.

✔ Tips

- Most operating systems have no *PHP* user. Instead, the *PHP* user is essentially the user the Web server application (for example, Apache, PWS, or IIS) is running as. On the Unix family, Apache often runs as *nobody*. On Windows, the Web server frequently runs as the same user who is logged in (and who probably created the file), meaning there be no need to alter a file's permissions.
- If you're already familiar with Telnet and `chmod`, you probably also understand what the `0666` number means; but here's an explanation for those of you who aren't familiar with it. The `0` is just a prefix, and each `6` corresponds to *write* (`2`) plus *read* (`4`) permission—first assigning `6` to the *owner*, then to the *group*, and then to *others*. Comparatively, `0777` allows *write* (`2`) plus *read* (`4`) plus *execute* (`1`) permission to all three types of users. This numbering is applicable for Unix variant operating systems (Linux, Solaris, and Mac OS X).
- PHP has several functions for changing a file or directory's permissions, including `chgrp()`, `chown()`, and `chmod()`. However, they will only work if PHP already has permission to modify the file or directory in question.

fopen() Modes

Mode	Meaning
r	Reading only; begin reading at the start of the file.
r+	Reading or writing; begin at the start of the file.
w	Writing only; create the file if it doesn't exist, and overwrite any existing contents.
w+	Reading or writing; create the file if it doesn't exist, and overwrite any existing contents (when writing).
a	Writing only; create the file if it doesn't exist, and append the new data to the end of the file (retain any existing data and add to it).
a+	Reading or writing; create the file if it doesn't exist, and append the new data to the end of the file (when writing).
x	Writing only; create the file if it doesn't exist, but do nothing (and issue a warning) if the file does exist.
x+	Reading or writing; create the file if it doesn't exist, but do nothing (and issue a warning) if the file already exists (when writing).

Table 11.1 Which mode to use when opening a file is rather self-evident. The most important things to keep in mind are whether you'll be reading, writing, or both, and what to do with any existing file contents (append to or overwrite).

Writing to Files

Because you need to write something to a file in order to read something from it, this chapter explores writing first. Writing to a file on the server is a three-step process: first, open the file; second, write your data to it; and third, close the file. Fortunately, PHP's built-in functions for doing these steps are quite obvious:

```
$fp = fopen ('filename', 'mode');
fwrite ($fp, 'data to be written');
fclose ($fp);
```

To write to a file, you must create a file pointer when opening it. This file pointer, assigned to the appropriately named `$fp` variable, is used by PHP to refer to the open file. (If you want to be more explicit, use `$file_pointer` as the variable name.)

The most important consideration when opening the file is what *mode* you use. Depending on what you intend to do with the file, the mode dictates how to open it. The most forgiving mode is `a+`, which allows you to read or write to a file. It creates the file if it doesn't exist, and it appends—hence *a*—new data to the end of the file automatically. Conversely, `r` only allows you to read from a file. **Table 11.1** lists all the possible modes. Each mode can also be appended with a `b` flag, which forces files to be opened in binary mode. This is a safer option for files that might be read on multiple operating systems.

The `fwrite()` function writes the new data (sent as the second argument in the function call) to the file in accordance with the selected mode. You want each piece of data to be written on its own line, so each submission should conclude with the appropriate line break for the operating system of the computer running PHP. This would be

- \n on Unix and Mac OS X
- \r\n on Windows

For the last step of the writing process, you close the file by once again referring to the file pointer while calling the `fclose()` function.

Let's create a form that stores user-submitted quotations in a plain text file. Later in this chapter, another PHP script will retrieve and randomly display these quotations.

To write to an external file:

1. Create a new PHP document in your text editor, beginning with the standard HTML head (**Script 11.1**):

```
<!DOCTYPE html PUBLIC "-//W3C//
→ DTD XHTML 1.0 Transitional//EN"
"http://www.w3.org/TR/xhtml1/DTD/
→ xhtml1-transitional.dtd">
<html xmlns="http://www.w3.org/1999/
→ xhtml">
<head>
    <meta http-equiv="content-type"
    → content="text/html; charset=
    → iso-8859-1" />
    <title>Add A Quotation</title>
</head>
<body>
```

Script 11.1 This script takes a user-submitted quotation and stores it in a text file. Before doing so, though, it checks that a quotation was entered, adjusts for the server's Magic Quotes setting, and, finally, makes certain that it can open the file for writing.

```
<!DOCTYPE html PUBLIC "-//W3C//DTD XHTML 1.0 Transitional//EN"
        "http://www.w3.org/TR/xhtml1/DTD/xhtml1-transitional.dtd">
<html xmlns="http://www.w3.org/1999/xhtml">
<head>
    <meta http-equiv="content-type" content="text/html; charset=iso-8859-1" />
    <title>Add A Quotation</title>
</head>
<body>
<?php // Script 11.1 - add_quote.php
// This script displays and handles an HTML form.
// This script takes text input and stores it in a text file.

// Address error handling.
ini_set ('display_errors', 1);
error_reporting (E_ALL & ~E_NOTICE);

if (isset ($_POST['submit'])) { // Handle form.

    if ( !empty ($_POST['quote']) ) {   // Check for the required value.

        if ($fp = fopen ('../quotes.txt', 'ab')) { // Try to open the file.
```

(script continues on next page)

2. Create a section of PHP code:

```
<?php // Script 11.1 - add_quote.php
ini_set ('display_errors', 1);
error_reporting (E_ALL & ~E_NOTICE);
```

3. See if the form has been submitted:

```
if (isset ($_POST['submit'])) {
```

This page both displays and handles the HTML form. This conditional checks to see if the form has been submitted, in which case the quotation should be written to the text file.

4. Check that a quotation was entered:

```
if ( !empty ($_POST['quote']) ) {
```

This simple conditional checks that a quotation was entered by seeing that the `$_POST['quote']` variable isn't empty.

5. Attempt to open the file for writing:

```
if ($fp = fopen ('../quotes.txt',
→ 'ab')) {
```

By placing the `fopen()` statement in a conditional, you make the PHP script attempt to write to the file only if it could be successfully opened for writing. At the same time, the file pointer is created.

The file opened is `quotes.txt`, which should be located in the directory above this script (which is presumably in the Web directory root). The mode being used is `ab`, meaning that the file should be opened for writing and the data being written should be appended to any existing data. The `b` flag is added so that the file is opened in a binary safe mode. That may not be necessary, but it can't hurt.

6. Remove any slashes if Magic Quotes is enabled:

```
if (ini_get ('magic_quotes_gpc')) {
   $data = stripslashes
   → ($_POST['quote']);
} else {
   $data = $_POST['quote'];
}
```

This clever little conditional checks to see if Magic Quotes GPC is turned on, using the `ini_get()` function. This function returns TRUE or FALSE, indicating whether the submitted setting is enabled. If Magic Quotes GPC is enabled, then extra slashes will be added to the string that should be removed. If Magic Quotes GPC isn't enabled, then the existing variable's value will be fine.

continues on next page

Script 11.1 *continued*

```

            // Adjust for magic quotes.
            if (ini_get ('magic_quotes_gpc')) {
                $data = stripslashes ($_POST['quote']);
            } else {
                $data = $_POST['quote'];
            }

            fwrite ($fp, "$data\n"); // Write the data. Use \r\n on Windows.
            fclose ($fp); // Close the file.

            // Print a message.
            print "<p>Your quotation has been stored.</p>";

```

(script continues on next page)

7. Write the data to the file, close the file, and then print a message:

```
fwrite ($fp, "$data\n");
fclose ($fp);
print "<p>Your quotation has been stored.</p>";
```

The first line writes the data (which is either the original string or one with any slashes removed) to the file. In this example, you use the `\n` newline character to mark the end of the line. If you're using Windows, replace `\n` with `\r\n`.

After that, the file is closed by referring to the same file pointer, and a simple message is displayed to the user.

8. Complete the conditionals:

```
        } else {
            print "<p>Your quotation could not be stored due to a system error.</p>";
        }
    } else {
        print "<p>Please enter a quotation!</p>";
    }
}
```

The first `else` completes the conditional that checks whether PHP couldn't open the file for writing. The second `else` completes the conditional that checks whether no quotation was entered. The final closing curly brace marks the end of the main `$_POST['submit']` conditional.

Because this page handles the form and then displays it again (so that the user may keep entering quotations), the form isn't displayed as part of an `else` statement as it has been in other examples in this book.

Script 11.1 *continued*

```
            } else { // Could not open the file.
                print "<p>Your quotation could
                not be stored due to a system
                error.</p>";
            }

        } else { // Failed to enter a quotation.
            print "<p>Please enter a
            quotation!</p>";
        }

    } // End of SUBMIT IF.

    // Leave PHP and display the form.
    ?>

    <form action="add_quote.php"
    method="post">
    <p>
    <textarea name="quote" rows="5" cols=
    "30">Enter your quotation here.</textarea>
    <br />
    <input type="submit" name="submit"
    value="Add This Quote!" />
    </p>
    </form>
    </body>
    </html>
```

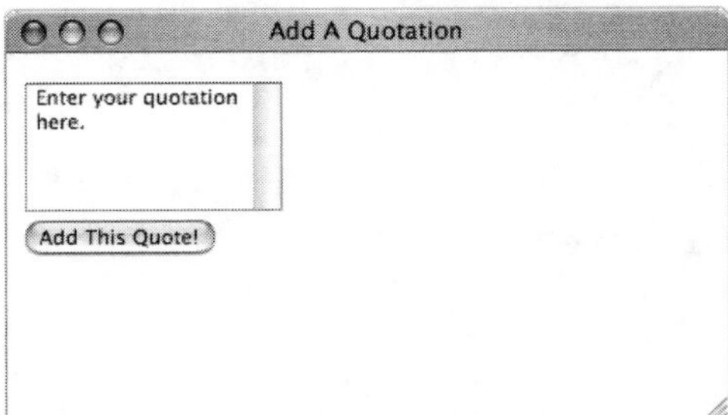

Figure 11.5 This very simple form lets a user submit a quotation that will be written to a text file.

9. Complete the PHP section:

```
?>
```

Because the rest of this script is standard HTML, you exit out of the PHP code by closing the PHP tag.

10. Create the HTML form:

```
<form action="add_quote.php"
→ method="post">
<p>
<textarea name="quote" rows="5"
→ cols="30">Enter your quotation
→ here.</textarea>
<br />
<input type="submit" name="submit"
→ value="Add This Quote!" />
</p>
</form>
```

This HTML form (**Figure 11.5**) presents a text box where the user can enter a quotation. The text box has a preset value of *Enter your quotation here.*, created by putting that text between the `<textarea>` tags.

As you must with any script that both handles and displays a form, be certain that the name of your submit button matches the `$_POST` array index being used in the `if (isset ($_POST['submit']))` conditional.

11. Complete the HTML page:

```
</body>
</html>
```

continues on next page

12. Save the file as `add_quote.php`, upload it to your Web server in the directory below `quotes.txt` (or place both in the appropriate directories on your PHP-enabled computer), and test it in your Web browser (**Figures 11.6** and **11.7**).
13. Test the script a few more times to add several quotations to the text file.
14. If you want, open the `quotes.txt` file in a text editor to confirm that the data has been written to it.

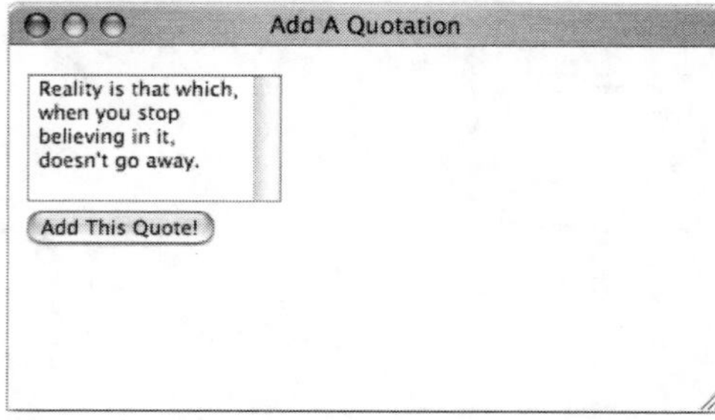

Figure 11.6 Filling out the form (using a quotation by Phillip K. Dick)...

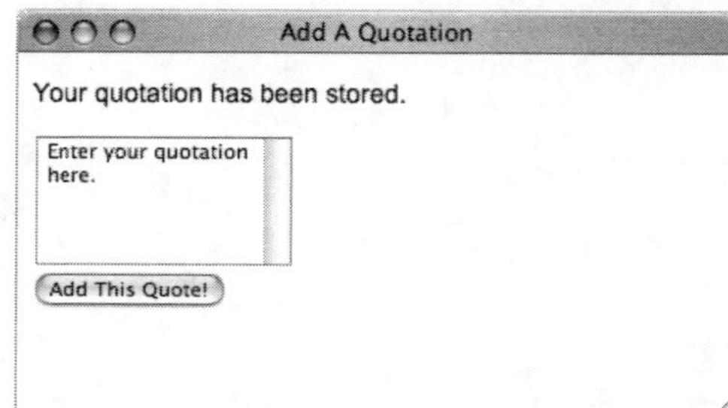

Figure 11.7 ...and the result if all went well.

✔ Tips

- If you receive a permissions error when you run this script (see Figure 11.1), either the permissions aren't set properly or the PHP script couldn't access the data file. This can happen if you misspell the filename or incorrectly reference the file's path on the server.
- Having a writable file on your server can be a bit of a security risk. See the sidebar "A More Secure File Structure" earlier in this chapter for ways to improve on the security of a script like `add_quote.php`.
- PHP 5 added a `file_put_contents()` function to the language. It replaces the `fopen()`, `fwrite()`, `fclose()` process. It was still being developed when this book was written, so see the manual for more information if you're running version 5 of PHP.
- If your version of PHP is running in safe mode or has the `open_basedir` directive set, you may be limited in using PHP to access files and directories. Check your `phpinfo()` script to see these settings for your server.

- You can also use PHP to write to and read from files on remote computers.
- If a script or Web application will be accessing the same file multiple times, it may make sense to assign the filename and path (where it is on the server) to a variable, for the sake of convenience. Then you can feed this variable to the `fopen()` function.
- As an extra step of safe-checking, you can use the `is_writable()` function to determine whether the server will allow you to write data to the file before you attempt to open it. Here is how you'd begin to incorporate it (this is only a part of the script):

```
if (is_writable ('../quotes.txt')) {
   // Attempt to open...
} else {
   print 'The file is not writable!';
}
```

- If you want, you can add an *author* text input to the form so that both the quotation and the person who said it can be recorded. Later examples in this chapter show how to record and retrieve multiple elements.

Locking Files

Although the last example worked fine, it could be improved on. If only a single user was submitting the form at one time, there would be no problems. But what if two or more users submitted different quotations simultaneously? In such a case, there would be a high probability of problems.

The solution is to temporarily lock the file while PHP is writing to it. You can do so using the `flock()` function:

```
$fp = fopen ('filename.txt', 'a+b');
flock ($fp, locktype)
```

The different lock types are represented by the constants listed in **Table 11.2**.

As an example, to temporarily lock a file during a write, use this code:

```
$fp = fopen ('filename.txt', 'a+b');
flock ($fp, LOCK_EX);
fwrite ($fp, 'data to be written');
flock ($fp, LOCK_UN);
```

To demonstrate, let's rewrite `add_quote.php` to lock the file during the writing process.

flock() Lock Types

Lock	Meaning
LOCK_SH	Shared lock for reading purposes
LOCK_EX	Exclusive lock for writing purposes
LOCK_UN	Release of a lock
LOCK_NB	Non-blocking lock

Table 11.2 These locks let you protect a file while data is being written to it.

To use file locks:

1. Open add_quote.php (Script 11.1) in your text editor, if it isn't already open.
2. Before the fwrite() line, add the following (**Script 11.2**):
   `flock ($fp, LOCK_EX);`
   This command places an exclusive lock on the file so that other scripts can't write to it at the same time.
3. After the fwrite() line, add:
   `flock ($fp, LOCK_UN);`
   This command unlocks the file so that it can be accessed again.

continues on next page

Script 11.2 The modified version of the add_quote.php script locks the data file for better security and reliability.

```
<!DOCTYPE html PUBLIC "-//W3C//DTD XHTML 1.0 Transitional//EN"
        "http://www.w3.org/TR/xhtml1/DTD/xhtml1-transitional.dtd">
<html xmlns="http://www.w3.org/1999/xhtml">
<head>
    <meta http-equiv="content-type" content="text/html; charset=iso-8859-1" />
    <title>Add A Quotation</title>
</head>
<body>
<?php // Script 11.2 - add_quote.php (second version after Script 11.1)
// This script displays and handles an HTML form.
// This script takes text input and stores it in a text file.

// Address error handling.
ini_set ('display_errors', 1);
error_reporting (E_ALL & ~E_NOTICE);

if (isset ($_POST['submit'])) { // Handle form.

    if ( !empty ($_POST['quote']) ) {   // Check for the required value.

        if ($fp = fopen ('../quotes.txt', 'ab')) { // Try to open the file.

            // Adjust for magic quotes.
            if (ini_get ('magic_quotes_gpc')) {
                $data = stripslashes ($_POST['quote']);
            } else {
                $data = $_POST['quote'];
            }

            flock ($fp, LOCK_EX);
            fwrite ($fp, "$data\n"); // Write the data. Use \r\n on Windows.
            flock ($fp, LOCK_UN);
            fclose ($fp); // Close the file.

            // Print a message.
            print "<p>Your quotation has been stored.</p>";
```

(script continues on next page)

4. Save the file, upload it to your Web server, and test it again in your Web browser (**Figures 11.8** and **11.9**).

✔ Tips

- The `flock()` function won't work on some file systems, including NFS (Network File System) and FAT. This means people using PHP on older versions of Windows (like Windows 98) can't use `flock()`.
- For locking to work, every script that writes to a file needs to use locking.
- In truth, the benefit added by locking a file is only marginal (but every little bit helps). A more secure and reliable method of storing data is to use a database. You'll learn more about this in the next chapter.

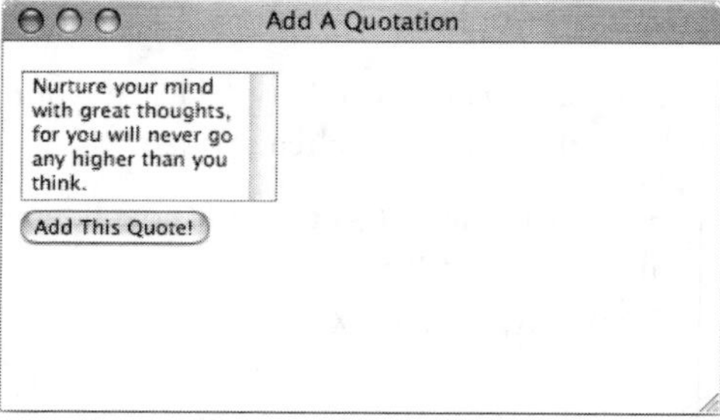

Figure 11.8 Using the form once again (using Benjamin Disraeli this time)...

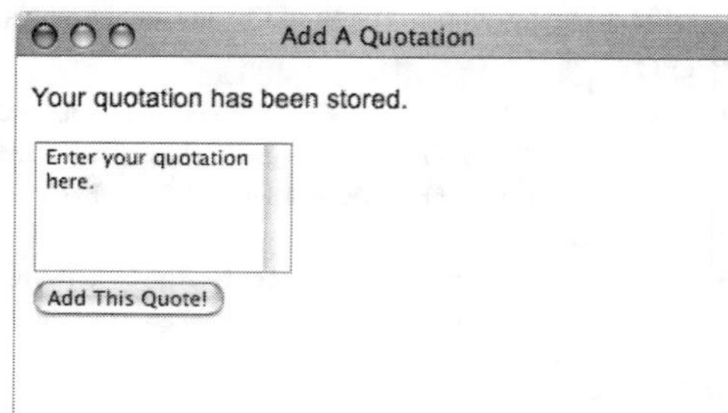

Figure 11.9 ...the quotation is still stored without a problem.

Script 11.2 *continued*

```

        } else { // Could not open the file.
            print "<p>Your quotation could not be stored due to a system error.</p>";
        }

    } else { // Failed to enter a quotation.
        print "<p>Please enter a quotation!</p>";
    }

} // End of SUBMIT IF.

// Leave PHP and display the form.
?>

<form action="add_quote.php" method="post">
<p>
<textarea name="quote" rows="5" cols="30">Enter your quotation here.</textarea>
<br />
<input type="submit" name="submit" value="Add This Quote!" />
</p>
</form>
</body>
</html>
```

Reading from Files

Now that you've coded a script that writes data to a file, it's time to create one that can read the information. Reading data from a file is much easier than writing to it. Instead of creating a file pointer and using the `fopen()` function, you can read the file in one fell swoop:

```
$array = file ('filename.txt');
```

The `file()` function is a valuable built-in tool in PHP. It reads everything from a file and places that information into an array. Each array element contains one line from the file, where each line is terminated by a newline (`\n` or `\r\n`).

If `filename.txt` contains two lines of information, each of which ends with a newline, the corresponding array will contain two elements. The first element will be equal to the first line of `filename.txt`, and the second element will be equal to the second line. Once the data is stored into an array, you can easily manipulate or print it, as you learned in Chapter 7, "Using Arrays."

Now you'll use this knowledge to create a script that randomly displays one of the stored quotations.

To read from a file:

1. Create a new PHP document in your text editor, beginning with the standard HTML header (**Script 11.3**):

```
<!DOCTYPE html PUBLIC "-//W3C//
→ DTD XHTML 1.0 Transitional//EN"
"http://www.w3.org/TR/xhtml1/DTD/
→ xhtml1-transitional.dtd">
<html xmlns="http://www.w3.org/1999/
→ xhtml">
<head>
   <meta http-equiv="content-type"
   → content="text/html; charset=
   → iso-8859-1" />
   <title>View A Quotation</title>
</head>
<body>
```

2. Open a PHP code section:

```
<?php // Script 11.3 - view_quote.php
ini_set ('display_errors', 1);
error_reporting (E_ALL & ~E_NOTICE);
```

3. Read the file contents and store them in an array:

```
$data = file ('../quotes.txt');
```

The function reads the file data into an array called `$data`. Each element of `$data` is a string, which is the submitted quotation.

4. Pick a random number based on the number of elements in `$data`:

```
$n = count ($data);
$rand = rand (0, ($n - 1));
```

In the first step, you count how many elements (which is to say, how many quotations) are in the `$data` array. Then you use the `rand()` function to select a random number.

If `$data` has 10 elements, they're indexed between 0 and 9, so that's the range you want to use for `rand()`. To calculate this range for a variable number of lines in the text file, use 0 and one less than the number of elements in `$data`.

Script 11.3 The `view_quote.php` file retrieves all the quotations from the text file and displays one at random.

```
<!DOCTYPE html PUBLIC "-//W3C//DTD XHTML 1.0 Transitional//EN"
        "http://www.w3.org/TR/xhtml1/DTD/xhtml1-transitional.dtd">
<html xmlns="http://www.w3.org/1999/xhtml">
<head>
    <meta http-equiv="content-type" content="text/html; charset=iso-8859-1" />
    <title>View A Quotation</title>
</head>
<body>
<?php // Script 11.3 - view_quote.php
// This script displays and handles an HTML form.
// This script takes text input and stores it in a text file.

// Address error handling.
ini_set ('display_errors', 1);
error_reporting (E_ALL & ~E_NOTICE);

// Read the file's contents into an array.
$data = file ('../quotes.txt');

// Count the number of items in the array.
$n = count ($data);

// Pick a random item.
$rand = rand (0, ($n - 1));

// Print the quotation.
print '<p>' . trim ($data[$rand]) . '</p>';

?>

</body>
</html>
```

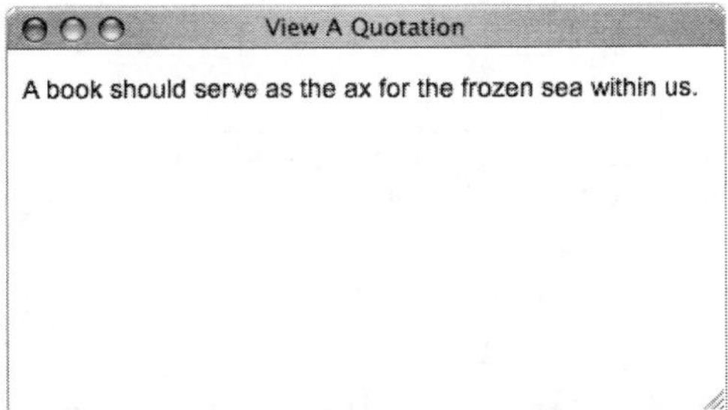

Figure 11.10 A random quotation is displayed each time the page is viewed. This one is by Franz Kafka, in case you were curious.

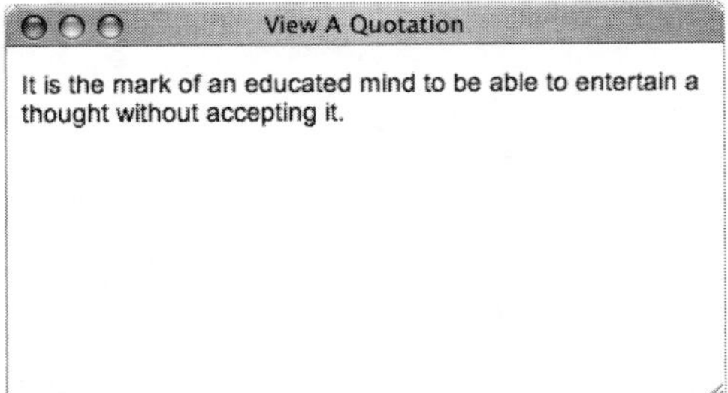

Figure 11.11 Subsequent viewings of the `view_quote.php` script display different quotations from the text file. Here is one from Aristotle.

5. Print out the quotation:

```
print '<p>' . trim ($data[$rand]) .
→ '</p>';
```

A simple `print()` statement involving concatenation is used to print the random quotation. To retrieve the quotation, you refer to the `$data` array and use the generated `$rand` number as the index. The retrieved quotation is then trimmed to cut off the newline characters from the end of the quotation.

6. Complete the PHP code and the HTML page:

```
?>
</body>
</html>
```

7. Save the file as `view_quote.php`, upload it to your Web server (in the same directory as `add_quote.php`), and test it in your Web browser (**Figure 11.10**).

8. Reload the page in your Web browser to view another random quote (**Figure 11.11**).

✔ Tips

- If you want to be extra careful, you can use the `is_readable()` function to test that PHP can read a file before you call the `file()` function.
- The `file_get_contents()` function works exactly like `file()` but returns the entire file as one long string, rather than as an array.
- The `readfile()` function reads through a file and sends the contents to the Web browser window.
- Later in the chapter, you'll learn a more complex method of reading a file using `fgets()` and `fgetcsv()`.
- If you are using a version of PHP prior to 4.2, you'll need to "seed" the `rand()` function before using it. See Chapter 4, "Using Numbers," or the PHP manual for specifics.

Handling File Uploads

As this book has demonstrated, handling HTML forms using PHP is a remarkably easy achievement. Regardless of the data being submitted, PHP can handle it easily and directly. The same is true when the user uploads a file via an HTML form.

In order to give the user the option of uploading a file, you must make three changes to the standard HTML form. First, the initial `form` line must include the code `enctype="multipart/form-data"`, which lets the browser know to expect different types of form data.

Second, a special hidden input type should be added:

```
<input type="hidden"
name="MAX_FILE_SIZE" value="30000">
```

This is a recommendation to the browser of how large a file, in bytes, can be uploaded.

Third, the `<input type="file" name="my_file">` element is used to create the necessary form field (**Figures 11.12** and **11.13**).

The `file` type of form input allows the user to select a file on their computer, which, upon submission, will be uploaded to the server. Once this has occurred, you can then use PHP to handle the file.

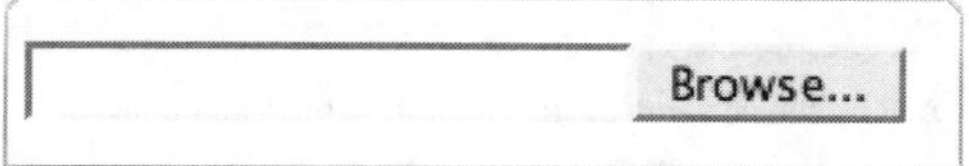

Figure 11.12 This is how Netscape Navigator interprets the `file` input type.

Figure 11.13 This is how the Safari Web browser interprets the `file` input type (prior to selecting a file).

$_FILES Error Codes

Code	Meaning
0	No error has occurred.
1	The file exceeds the `upload_max_filesize` setting in `php.ini`.
2	The file exceeds the `MAX_FILE_SIZE` setting in the HTML form.
3	The file was only partially uploaded.
4	No file was uploaded.

Table 11.3 If PHP can't move an uploaded file, it will use one of these error codes to describe the problem.

Configuring PHP for File Uploads

In order for file uploading to work, a number of settings in your `php.ini` configuration file must be set. These may or may not be enabled in your configuration, so you should check them by viewing the `php.ini` file or running a `phpinfo()` script.

For starters, `file_uploads` must be on. Second, the `upload_tmp_dir` value must be set to a directory on the server where PHP can place files (in other words, it must exist and be modifiable by the Web server).

The `upload_max_filesize` and `post_max_size` settings dictate how large a file can be sent. Whereas the `MAX_FILE_SIZE` hidden form input is a recommendation to the Web browser, these two settings control whether the file is uploaded.

Finally, if really large files will be uploaded (many megabytes or larger), you may need to increase the `memory_limit` and `max_execution_time` settings to give PHP the time and the resources to do what it needs to do.

In the PHP script, you refer to the `$_FILES` variable (think of it as the file equivalent of `$_POST`) to address the uploaded file. The `$_FILES` array contains five elements:

- `name`, the name of the file as it was on the user's computer
- `type`, the mime type of the file (for example, *image/jpg*)
- `size`, the size of the file in bytes
- `tmp_name`, the temporary name of the file as it's stored on the server
- `error`, an error code if something goes wrong (**Table 11.3**)

When a file is uploaded, the server places it in a temporary directory. You can then use the `move_uploaded_file()` function to store the file in its final destination:

```
move_uploaded_file ($_FILES['file_input_
→ name']['tmp_name'], '/path/to/
→ destination/filename');
```

For PHP to be able to take these steps, you must set several configurations in the `php.ini` file (see the sidebar), and the Web server needs write access to both the temporary and final destination directories.

You'll write a basic script that uploads a file and stores it on the server. Like the add_quote.php script, this example also both creates the HTML form and processes it, all in one page. First, though, you'll create a writable directory as the destination point.

To create a writable directory:

1. Create a new folder called uploads, located outside of the Web directory root (**Figure 11.14**).
2. Using the steps outlined in the first section of this chapter, set the permissions so that everyone can write to, read from, and search (0777 in Unix terms) the directory.

To use PHP for file uploads:

1. Create a new PHP document, beginning with the HTML header (**Script 11.4**):
```
<!DOCTYPE html PUBLIC "-//W3C//
→ DTD XHTML 1.0 Transitional//EN"
"http://www.w3.org/TR/xhtml1/DTD/
→ xhtml1-transitional.dtd">
<html xmlns="http://www.w3.org/1999/
→ xhtml">
<head>
   <meta http-equiv="content-type"
   → content="text/html; charset=
   → iso-8859-1" />
   <title>Upload a File</title>
</head>
<body>
```
2. Create a section of PHP code:
```
<?php // Script 11.4 - upload_file.php
ini_set ('display_errors', 1);
error_reporting (E_ALL & ~E_NOTICE);
```

continues on page 320

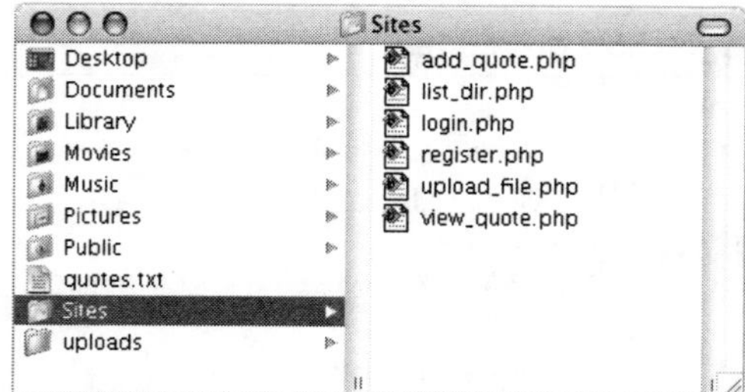

Figure 11.14 For this example, a writable uploads directory must exist. Here, it's placed in the same directory as the Web root folder called Sites. Thus uploads is in the directory above the one in which the upload_file.php script resides and is not accessible via the Internet.

Script 11.4 The simplicity of this script should indicate how naturally PHP handles file uploads. There are two steps to uploading files: change the HTML form accordingly, and use `move_uploaded_file()` to move the file to the desired location.

Script

```
<!DOCTYPE html PUBLIC "-//W3C//DTD XHTML 1.0 Transitional//EN"
        "http://www.w3.org/TR/xhtml1/DTD/xhtml1-transitional.dtd">
<html xmlns="http://www.w3.org/1999/xhtml">
<head>
    <meta http-equiv="content-type" content="text/html; charset=iso-8859-1" />
    <title>Upload a File</title>
</head>
<body>
<?php // Script 11.4 - upload_file.php
// This script displays and handles an HTML form.
// This script takes a file upload and stores it on the server.

// Address error handling.
ini_set ('display_errors', 1);
error_reporting (E_ALL & ~E_NOTICE);

if (isset ($_POST['submit'])) { // Handle form.

    // Try to move the uploaded file.
    if (move_uploaded_file ($_FILES['thefile']['tmp_name'], "../uploads/{$_FILES['thefile']
    ['name']}")) {

        print '<p>Your file has been uploaded.</p>';

    } else { // Problem!

        print '<p>Your file could not be uploaded because: <b>';

        // Print a message based upon the error.
        switch ($_FILES['thefile']['error']) {
            case 1:
                print 'The file exceeds the upload_max_filesize setting in php.ini';
                break;
            case 2:
                print 'The file exceeds the MAX_FILE_SIZE setting in the HTML form';
                break;
            case 3:
                print 'The file was only partially uploaded';
                break;
            case 4:
                print 'No file was uploaded';
                break;
        }
        print '</b>.</p>';
    }

} // End of SUBMIT IF.

```

(script continues on next page)

3. Check whether the form has been submitted:

```
if (isset ($_POST['submit'])) {
```

Once again, this script both displays and handles the HTML form. If it has been submitted, the uploaded file should be addressed.

4. Attempt to move the uploaded file to its final destination:

```
if (move_uploaded_file ($_FILES['thefile']['tmp_name'], "../uploads/{$_FILES['thefile']['name']}")) {
```

The `move_uploaded_file()` function attempts to move the uploaded file (identified by `$_FILES['thefile']['tmp_name']`) to its new location (`../uploads/{$_FILES['thefile']['name']}`). The location is the `uploads` directory, which is located in the folder above the one this script is in. The file's name will be the same as it was on the user's computer.

Placing this function as a condition in an `if` statement makes it easy to respond based on whether the move worked.

5. Print messages indicating the success of the operation:

```
   print '<p>Your file has been uploaded.</p>';
} else {
   print '<p>Your file could not be uploaded because: <b>';
```

The first `print()` statement is executed if the move worked. The `else` applies if it didn't work, in which case an error message is begun. This message will be made more explicit in Step 6.

Script 11.4 *continued*

```
// Leave PHP and display the form.
?>

<form action="upload_file.php" enctype="multipart/form-data" method="post">
<p>Upload a file using this form: <br /><br />
<input type="hidden" name="MAX_FILE_SIZE" value="30000" />
<input type="file" name="thefile" /><br /><br />
<input type="submit" name="submit" value="Upload This File" />
</p>
</form>
</body>
</html>
```

6. Print out the error message if the move didn't work:

```
switch ($_FILES['thefile']['error']) {
   case 1:
      print 'The file exceeds the
      → upload_max_filesize setting
      → in php.ini';
      break;
   case 2:
      print 'The file exceeds the
      → MAX_FILE_SIZE setting in the
      → HTML form';
      break;
   case 3:
      print 'The file was only
      → partially uploaded';
      break;
   case 4:
      print 'No file was uploaded';
      break;
}
```

If a move doesn't work, the `$_FILES['thefile']['error']` variable contains a number indicating the appropriate error message. By using this in a `switch` conditional, the PHP script can print out the appropriate error message.

You wouldn't normally place something like this on a public site (it's a little too much information), but it's exceptionally good for helping you to debug a problem.

7. Complete the error message, and close both conditionals:

```
      print '</b>.</p>';
   }
}
```

continues on next page

8. Exit out of PHP can create the HTML form:

```
?>
<form action="upload_file.php"
→ enctype="multipart/form-data"
→ method="post">
<p>Upload a file using this form:
→ <br /><br />
<input type="hidden" name=
→ "MAX_FILE_SIZE" value="30000" />
<input type="file" name="thefile" />
→ <br /><br />
<input type="submit" name="submit"
→ value="Upload This File" />
</p>
</form>
```

The HTML form is simple (**Figure 11.15**), containing only a `file` input type and a submit button. It differs from other HTML forms in this book in that it uses the `encytpe` attribute and a `MAX_FILE_SIZE` hidden input type.

Be careful when giving your `file` input a name, because this value must exactly match the index used in the `$_FILES` variable. Here, you use a generic *thefile*.

9. Complete the HTML page:

```
</body>
</html>
```

10. Save the page as `upload_file.php`, upload it to your Web server (in the directory below `uploads`), and test it in your Web browser (**Figures 11.16, 11.17**, and **11.18**).

11. Check the `uploads` directory to ensure that the file was placed there.

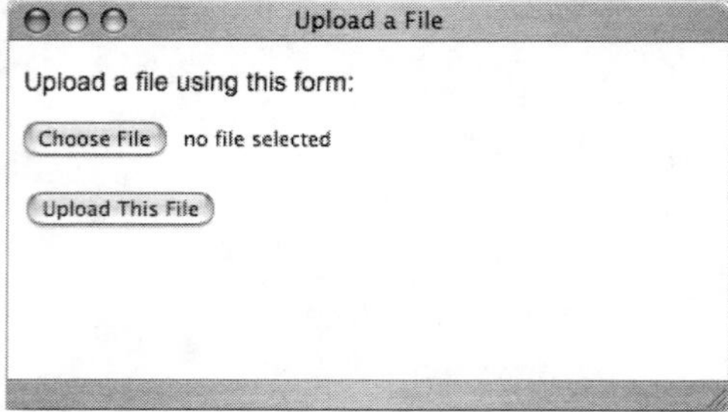

Figure 11.15 This HTML form lets the user select a file on their computer to upload to the server.

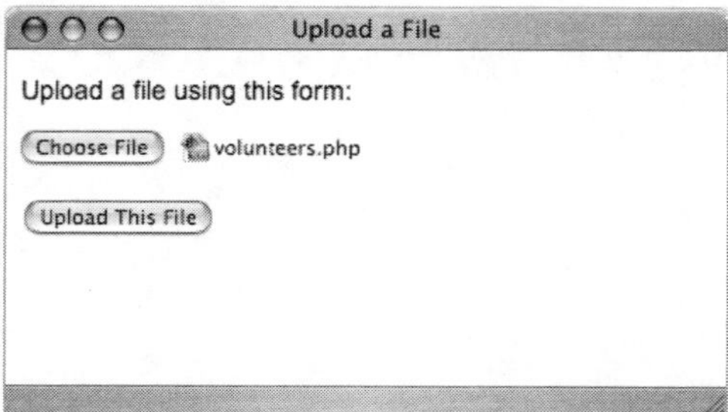

Figure 11.16 Select a file on your computer to upload. If your Web browser displays a text box next to the file button, the selected filename (and possibly path) appears in that text box.

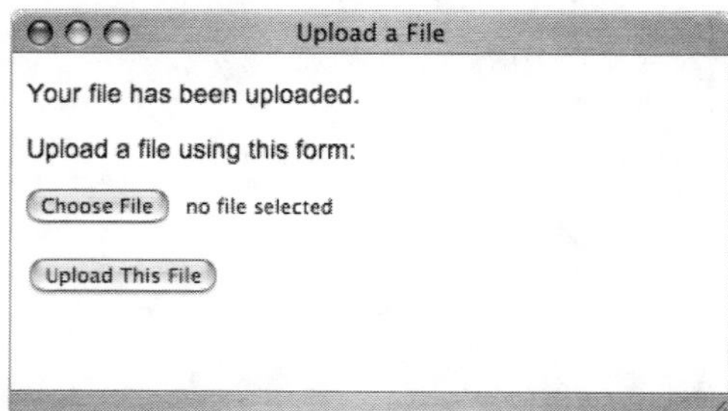

Figure 11.17 If the file was uploaded and moved successfully, a message is printed and the form is displayed again.

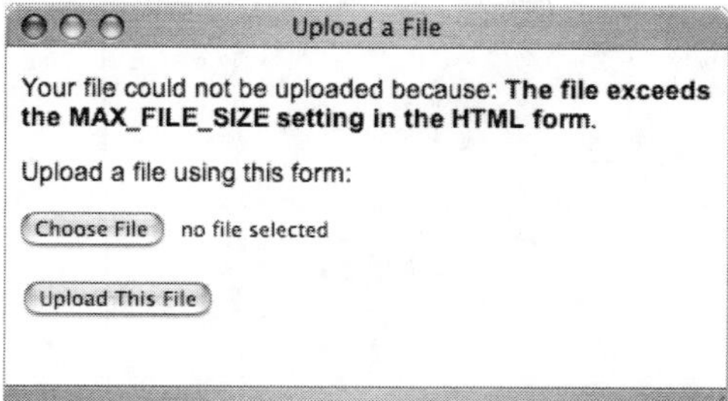
Upload a File

Your file could not be uploaded because: **The file exceeds the MAX_FILE_SIZE setting in the HTML form.**

Upload a file using this form:

Choose File no file selected

Upload This File

Figure 11.18 If a problem occurred, the script indicates the reason why.

✔ Tips

- If the file couldn't be moved and a permissions denied error is shown, check the permissions on the `uploads` directory. Then check that the path to the directory used in the script is correct and that there are no spelling errors.
- As you might discover, files uploaded through the Web browser are owned (in terms of permissions) by the Web server application.
- From a security standpoint, it's better to rename an uploaded file. To do so, you'll need to devise a system that generates a new, unique filename and stores both the original and the new filename in a text file or a database.
- A script can handle multiple file uploads as long as they have different names. In such a case, you need only one `MAX_FILE_SIZE` hidden input. In the PHP script, you'd apply the `move_uploaded_file()` function to `$_FILES['filename1']`, `$_FILES['filename2']`, and so on.
- To create a progress bar indicating how the upload process is going, check out `http://sourceforge.net/projects/megaupload/`.
- You can limit a file upload to a specific size or type by referencing the appropriate index (for example, `$_FILES['thefile']['size']`) in your PHP script (after the file has been uploaded).
- Use `unlink()` to delete a file without moving or copying it.
- You can use the `copy()` function to make a copy of a file on the server. Prior to version 4.0.3 of PHP (when the `move_uploaded_file()` function was added), PHP handled uploaded files by using `copy()` to move the files and `unlink()` to delete the temporary files.

Navigating Directories

The previous PHP scripts worked with files, but you can also do many things with directories using PHP. In this example, you'll write a script that lists a directory's contents, but first you'll need to understand the usage and syntax of many of the functions you'll use.

To navigate through a directory, you begin by opening the directory with `opendir()`:

```
$dp = opendir ('dirname');
```

This creates a pointer, which can be used as a reference to this open directory. From there, you can use the `readdir()` function in a `while` loop:

```
while ($item = readdir ($dp)) {
   // Do something with $item.
}
```

Finally, you close the directory using `closedir()`:

```
closedir ($dp);
```

This structure should look very similar to the way you write data to a file.

While you're working with files, you'll use the `filesize()` function in this example; it determines how large a file is in bytes. This value can be assigned to a variable or be printed:

```
$number = filesize ('filename');
```

Similarly, the `filemtime()` retrieves the modification time of a file. It returns a timestamp, which can be formatted using the `date()` function.

A PHP 5 Alternative

New to PHP version 5 is the `scandir()` function, which simplifies the `opendir()`, `readdir()`, `closedir()` sequence. In fact, `scandir()` works a lot like the `file()` function, but on directories, not files. In one step, this function places the names of the contents of a directory into an array.

If you're using PHP 5, you can write this script by dropping the `opendir()`, `closedir()`, and `rewinddir()` functions. Instead, use

```
$files = scandir ($search_dir);
```

at the top of the script.

Then replace each `while` loop with the following:

```
foreach ($files as $item) {
}
```

The contents of the `while` loops—the two different `if` conditionals—can go within these new `foreach` loops.

Script 11.5 This script displays the contents of a directory. First the subdirectories are listed, followed by the files (with their sizes and modification dates) in a table.

```
<!DOCTYPE html PUBLIC "-//W3C//DTD XHTML 1.0 Transitional//EN"
        "http://www.w3.org/TR/xhtml1/DTD/xhtml1-transitional.dtd">
<html xmlns="http://www.w3.org/1999/xhtml">
<head>
    <meta http-equiv="content-type" content="text/html; charset=iso-8859-1" />
    <title>Directory Contents</title>
</head>
<body>
<?php // Script 11.5 - list_dir.php
// This script lists the directories and files in a directory.

// Address error handling.
ini_set ('display_errors', 1);
error_reporting (E_ALL & ~E_NOTICE);

// Set the directory name and open it.
$search_dir = '.';
$dp = opendir ($search_dir);

// List the directories first.
while ($item = readdir ($dp) ) {
    if ( (is_dir ($item)) AND (substr ($item, 0, 1) != '.') ) {
        print "$item<br />\n";
    }
}

rewinddir ($dp); // Reset the pointer.

// Create a table header.
print '<hr /><br />
<table cellpadding="2" cellspacing="2" align="left">
<tr>
<td><b>File Name</b></td>
<td><b>File Size</b></td>
<td><b>Last Modified</b></td>
</tr>';

```

(script continues on next page)

Finally, PHP includes several functions that identify attributes. This chapter has already mentioned `is_writable()` and `is_readable()`, but there are also `is_dir()` and `is_file()`. They return TRUE if the item in question is a directory or a file, respectively.

You'll put all of these capabilities together into one page, which will constitute a Web-based control panel for viewing a directory's contents.

To create the directory control panel:

1. Create a new PHP document in your text editor, beginning with the standard HTML header (**Script 11.5**):

```
<!DOCTYPE html PUBLIC "-//W3C//DTD XHTML 1.0 Transitional//EN"
"http://www.w3.org/TR/xhtml1/DTD/xhtml1-transitional.dtd">
<html xmlns="http://www.w3.org/1999/xhtml">
<head>
    <meta http-equiv="content-type" content="text/html; charset=iso-8859-1" />
    <title>Directory Contents</title>
</head>
<body>
```

2. Begin the PHP code:

```
<?php // Script 11.5 - list_dir.php
ini_set ('display_errors', 1);
error_reporting (E_ALL & ~E_NOTICE);
```

continues on next page

3. Identify the directory to be opened, and open it:

```
$search_dir = '.';
$dp = opendir ($search_dir);
```

By establishing this value as a variable at the top of the PHP script, it will be easy to find and change as needed. Here you use the period to refer to the current directory. You could also use an absolute path to another directory (`/Users/larry/Documents` or `c:\\myfiles\\directory`) or a relative path (`../myfiles`), as long as PHP has permission to read the named directory.

The second line associates the open directory with a directory pointer, which will be used several times throughout the script.

4. List the subdirectories of this directory:

```
while ($item = readdir ($dp) ) {
   if ( (is_dir ($item)) AND (substr
   → ($item, 0, 1) != '.') ) {
      print "$item<br />\n";
   }
}
```

This `while` loop accesses every item in the directory, assigning each one to the `$item` variable. You first want to list every directory, so you use the `is_dir()` function to confirm the item's type. Then you check that it isn't the current directory (marked by a single period on Unix systems) or the parent directory (marked by a double period on Unix systems). If this conditional is TRUE, then the item's name is printed out, followed by an HTML break and a newline (to make neater HTML source).

Script 11.5 *continued*

```
// List the files.
while ($item = readdir ($dp) ) {
    if ( (is_file ($item)) AND (substr
    ($item, 0, 1) != '.') ) {

        // Get the file size.
        $fs = filesize ($item);

        // Get the file's modification
        date.
        $lm = date ('F j, Y', filemtime
        ($item));

        // Print the information.
        print "<tr>
        <td>$item</td>
        <td>$fs bytes</td>
        <td>$lm</td>
    </tr>\n";

    } // Close the IF.

} // Close the WHILE.

print '</table>'; // Close the HTML table.

closedir ($dp); // Close the directory.

?>
</body>
</html>
```

5. Reset the directory pointer:

```
rewinddir ($dp);
```

Next the script goes through the directory listing again, checking for files. Before this can happen, the pointer (an imaginary thing marking where in the directory the listing is) needs to be reset back to the beginning. This is accomplished with the `rewinddir()` function.

6. Create a break, and start a table for the files:

```
print '<hr /><br />
<table cellpadding="2"
→ cellspacing="2" align="left">
<tr>
<td><b>File Name</b></td>
<td><b>File Size</b></td>
<td><b>Last Modified</b></td>
</tr>';
```

The script also displays the files' size and modification date. To make this look nicer, the results are placed in an HTML table.

7. Begin looping through the files in this directory:

```
while ($item = readdir ($dp) ) {
   if ( (is_file ($item)) AND (substr
   → ($item, 0, 1) != '.') ) {
```

Like the directory listings, this loop checks that the item is a file and that it isn't a hidden file (on Unix systems, hidden files have names that begin with a single period).

continues on next page

8. Calculate the file's size and modification date, and then print out the information:

```
$fs = filesize ($item);
$lm = date ('F j, Y', filemtime
→ ($item));
print "<tr>
<td>$item</td>
<td>$fs bytes</td>
<td>$lm</td>
</tr>\n";
```

The first line calls the `filesize()` function to retrieve the file's size in bytes. The second line calls the `filemtime()` function, which returns a timestamp of the file's modification time. This is then fed into the `date()` function, along with the proper formatting, to return a string like *November 24, 2003*. Finally, these two items and the file's name are printed in the appropriate columns of the table.

9. Complete the conditional and the loop:

```
    }
}
```

10. Close the table and the directory:

```
print "</table>";
closedir ($dp);
```

11. Complete the PHP code and the HTML page:

```
?>
</body>
</html>
```

12. Save the file as `list_dir.php`, upload it to your Web server, and test it in your Web browser (**Figure 11.19**).

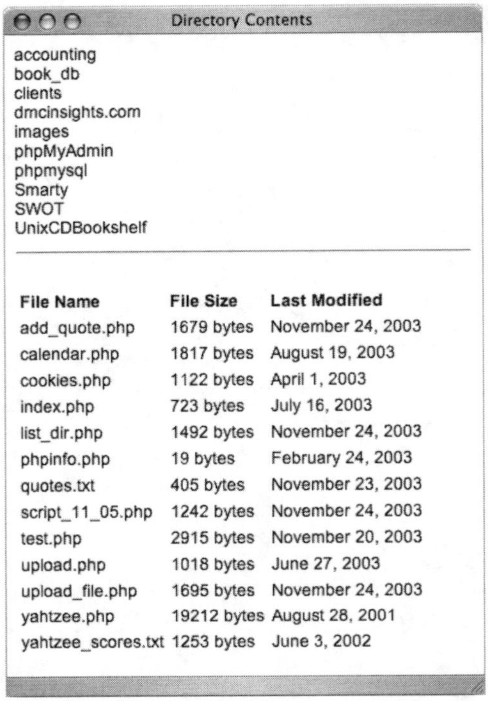

Directory Contents

accounting
book_db
clients
dmcinsights.com
images
phpMyAdmin
phpmysql
Smarty
SWOT
UnixCDBookshelf

File Name	File Size	Last Modified
add_quote.php	1679 bytes	November 24, 2003
calendar.php	1817 bytes	August 19, 2003
cookies.php	1122 bytes	April 1, 2003
index.php	723 bytes	July 16, 2003
list_dir.php	1492 bytes	November 24, 2003
phpinfo.php	19 bytes	February 24, 2003
quotes.txt	405 bytes	November 23, 2003
script_11_05.php	1242 bytes	November 24, 2003
test.php	2915 bytes	November 20, 2003
upload.php	1018 bytes	June 27, 2003
upload_file.php	1695 bytes	November 24, 2003
yahtzee.php	19212 bytes	August 28, 2001
yahtzee_scores.txt	1253 bytes	June 3, 2002

Figure 11.19 The `list_dir.php` script shows the contents of a directory. The top part lists the subfolders, and the bottom table lists the files.

✔ Tips

- Notice that you need to use double backslashes to create absolute path names on a Windows server. This is necessary because the single backslash, used in Windows path names, is the escape character. So, it must be escaped to be taken literally.
- The `glob()` function lets you search a directory for files whose name matches a pattern (like **.jpg* or *filename*.doc*).
- Other file functions you might appreciate include `fileperms()`, which returns the file's permissions; `fileatime()`, which returns the last time a file was accessed; and `fileowner()`, which returns the user who owns the file.
- To find out about other file and directory functions, look in the PHP manual under *Directories* and *Filesystem*.

Creating Directories

Understanding how to read from and write to files on the server is only part of the data storage process. It's likely you'll also want to use directories for this purpose as well.

The command for creating a directory in PHP is

```
mkdir ('directory_name', permissions);
```

The directory name is the name of the directory to be created. This can also be a path:

```
mkdir ('C:\\inetpub\\users\\eleanor');
```

On Windows servers, the permissions are ignored and therefore not required (as in the previous example). On other servers, the permissions are `0777` by default (see the "File Permissions" section of this chapter to learn what those numbers mean).

With this in mind, let's create a script that makes a new directory for a user when the user registers. This script also records the username and password to a text file, so that the user can be validated when logging in. You'll begin by creating the parent directory (which must be writable so that PHP can create subdirectories in it) and the `users.txt` data file.

Script 11.6 The `register.php` script serves two purposes: it records the user's information in a text file and creates a new directory for that user's stuff.

```
<!DOCTYPE html PUBLIC "-//W3C//DTD XHTML 1.0 Transitional//EN"
        "http://www.w3.org/TR/xhtml1/DTD/xhtml1-transitional.dtd">
<html xmlns="http://www.w3.org/1999/xhtml">
<head>
    <meta http-equiv="content-type" content="text/html; charset=iso-8859-1" />
    <title>Register</title>
</head>
<body>
<?php // Script 11.6 - register.php
// This script displays and handles an HTML form.
// This script registers a user by storing their information in a text file and creating a directory for them.

// Address error handling.
ini_set ('display_errors', 1);
error_reporting (E_ALL & ~E_NOTICE);

if (isset ($_POST['submit'])) { // Handle form.

    $problem = FALSE; // No problems so far.

    // Check for each value.
    if (empty ($_POST['username'])) {
        $problem = TRUE;
        print '<p>Please enter a username!</p>';
    }

    if (empty ($_POST['password1'])) {
        $problem = TRUE;
        print '<p>Please enter a password!</p>';
    }

    if ($_POST['password1'] != $_POST['password2']) {
        $problem = TRUE;
        print '<p>Your password did not match your confirmed password!</p>';
    }

```

(script continues on next page)

To create the directory and the data file:

1. Create a new folder called `users`, located outside of the Web directory root.
2. Using the steps outlined in the first section of this chapter, set the permissions so that everyone can write to, read from, and search (`0777` in Unix terms) the directory.

   If you're running Windows, this step will most likely not be necessary.
3. In your text editor, create a new, blank document.
4. Save this file in the `users` directory with the name `users.txt`.
5. Again using the steps outlined earlier in the chapter, set the permissions on `users.txt` so that everyone can write to and read from the file (`0666` in Unix terms).

   Again, this will probably not be necessary if you're running Windows on your PHP server.

To create the registration script:

1. Create a new PHP document in your text editor, beginning with the standard HTML header (**Script 11.6**):

```
<!DOCTYPE html PUBLIC "-//W3C//
→ DTD XHTML 1.0 Transitional//EN"
"http://www.w3.org/TR/xhtml1/DTD/
→ xhtml1-transitional.dtd">
<html xmlns="http://www.w3.org/1999/
→ xhtml">
<head>
   <meta http-equiv="content-type"
   → content="text/html; charset=
   → iso-8859-1" />
   <title>Register</title>
</head>
<body>
```

continues on next page

2. Begin the PHP code:

   ```
   <?php // Script 11.6 - register.php
   ini_set ('display_errors', 1);
   error_reporting (E_ALL & ~E_NOTICE);
   ```

3. Check whether the form has been submitted:

   ```
   if (isset ($_POST['submit'])) {
   ```

   Once again, this page both displays and handles the HTML form. This is accomplished using a conditional that checks for the value of the `$_POST['submit']` variable.

Script 11.6 *continued*

```
    if (!$problem) { // If there weren't any problems...

        if ($fp = fopen ('../users/users.txt', 'ab')) { // Open the file.

            // Create the data to be written.
            $dir = time() . rand (0, 4596);
            $data = $_POST['username'] . "\t" . crypt($_POST['password1']) . "\t" . $dir . "\n"; // \r\n on Windows

            // Write the data and close the file.
            fwrite ($fp, $data);
            fclose ($fp);

            // Create the directory.
            mkdir ("../users/$dir");

            // Print a message.
            print '<p>You are now registered!</p>';

        } else { // Couldn't write to the file.
            print '<p>You could not be registered due to a system error.</p>';
        }

    } else { // Forgot a field.
        print '<p>Please try again!</p>';
    }

} else { // Display the form.

// Leave PHP and display the form.
?>
```

(script continues on next page)

Script 11.6 *continued*

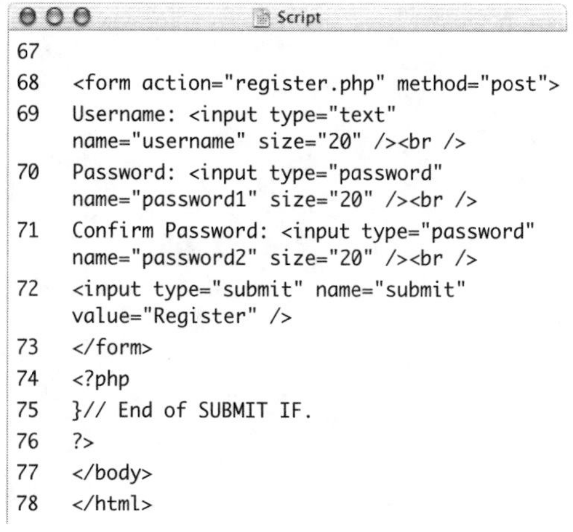

```
<form action="register.php" method="post">
Username: <input type="text" name="username" size="20" /><br />
Password: <input type="password" name="password1" size="20" /><br />
Confirm Password: <input type="password" name="password2" size="20" /><br />
<input type="submit" name="submit" value="Register" />
</form>
<?php
}// End of SUBMIT IF.
?>
</body>
</html>
```

4. Validate the registration information:

```
$problem = FALSE;
if (empty ($_POST['username'])) {
    $problem = TRUE;
    print '<p>Please enter a username! </p>';
}
if (empty ($_POST['password1'])) {
    $problem = TRUE;
    print '<p>Please enter a password! </p>';
}
if ($_POST['password1'] != $_POST['password2']) {
    $problem = TRUE;
    print '<p>Your password did not match your confirmed password! </p>';
}
```

The registration form is a simpler version of earlier registration forms developed in this book. The same validation process you previously developed is used to check the submitted username and passwords. The `$problem` variable is used as a flag to indicate whether a problem occurred.

5. Check for problems:

```
if (!$problem) {
```

Again, the `$problem` variable lets you know if it's OK to register the user. If no problems occurred, it's safe to continue.

continues on next page

6. Attempt to open the `users.txt` file:

```
if ($fp = fopen ('../users/users.txt',
→ 'ab')) {
```

Like before, the data file is opened as part of a conditional, so that the script can respond to its success. The file being opened is in the `users` directory, which is in the directory above this script. The file is opened using the `ab` mode, appending data to the file.

7. Create the data to be written to the file, and then write it:

```
$dir = time() . rand (0, 4596);
$data = $_POST['username'] . "\t" .
→ crypt($_POST['password1']) . "\t" .
→ $dir . "\n";
fwrite ($fp, $data);
fclose ($fp);
```

The name of the directory being created is a number based on the time the user registered and a random value. This system helps to guarantee that the directory created is both unique and has a valid name.

Instead of storing a single string as you previously have, this script stores three separate pieces of information: the user's name; an encrypted version of the password (using the `crypt()` function); and the directory name, created in the previous line.

To distinguish between the pieces of information, you insert a tab (created using the `\t` code). A newline is used to mark the end of the line (Windows users should use `\r\n` instead).

8. Create the user's directory, and print a message:

```
mkdir ("../users/$dir");
print '<p>You are now registered!
→ </p>';
```

The `mkdir()` function creates the directory in the `users` directory. The directory is named whatever random number was generated earlier and has open permissions.

9. Complete the conditionals:

```
    } else {
        print '<p>You could not be
        → registered due to a system
        → error.</p>';
    }
} else {
    print '<p>Please try again!</p>';
}
```

The first `else` completes the conditional if the script couldn't open the `users.txt` file for writing. The second `else` completes the conditional if the user failed to complete the form properly.

10. Add an `else` clause to the main conditional, and exit out of PHP:

```
} else {
?>
```

Unlike the previous examples in this chapter, this PHP script first displays the form and then handles it. Whereas the other scripts would then display the form again, this one does not, as the form creation is part of an `else` statement. Because the rest of the page is just HTML, you exit out of PHP to create the form.

11. Display the HTML form:

```
<form action="register.php"
→ method="post">
Username: <input type="text"
→ name="username" size="20" /><br />
Password: <input type="password"
→ name="password1" size="20" /><br />
Confirm Password: <input type=
→ "password" name="password2"
→ size="20" /><br />
<input type="submit" name="submit"
→ value="Register" />
</form>
```

You can add many things to this form, like the user's name or email address.

continues on next page

CREATING DIRECTORIES

12. Complete the main conditional:

```
<?php
}
?>
```

This final closing curly brace closes the main submit conditional. For it to work, a new PHP section must be created first.

13. Complete the HTML page:

```
</body>
</html>
```

14. Save the file as `register.php`, upload it to your Web server, and test it in your Web browser (**Figures 11.20** and **11.21**).

15. If you want, open the `users.txt` file in your text editor to see its contents (**Figure 11.22**).

✔ Tips

- You can also ensure that the page worked as it should by looking in the `users` directory for the new subdirectories.
- The `rmdir()` function deletes an existing directory, assuming PHP has permission to do so.
- At some point, you may want to create a system to guarantee unique usernames. The process for doing so is simple enough: Before you attempt to create the directory, use PHP to check your list of existing usernames for a match to the just-registered name. If no match is found, the new name is acceptable. If the username is already in use, the PHP can create an error message requesting a new username.

Figure 11.20 The registration form is quite basic but serves its purpose.

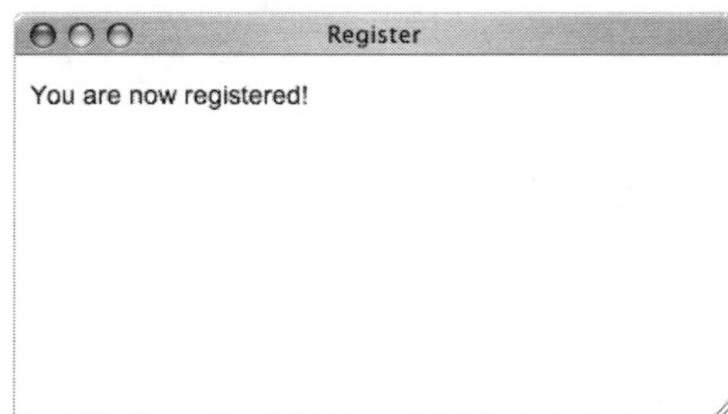

Figure 11.21 This is what the user sees if the registration process worked.

Figure 11.22 The `users.txt` file lists three tab-delineated fields of information: the username, an encrypted version of the user's password, and their associated directory name.

Reading Files Incrementally

In the view_quote.php script (Script 11.3), an entire file was read into an array using the file() function. But what if you want to read in only a little of the file at a time? Then you need to use the fgets() function.

The fgets() function returns a string of a certain length. It's most often placed in a while loop that uses the feof() function to make sure the end of the file hasn't been reached. For example:

```
$fp = fopen ('filename', 'rb');
while (!feof ($fp)) {
   $string = fgets ($fp, 1024);
}
fclose ($fp);
```

In this example, the fgets() function returns 1023 bytes of data at a time (the 1024 indicated length minus 1). The length requested should be a number larger than a single line of text in the file.

In an example where the data is stored in a delineated format (commonly using a comma, hence a CSV—comma-separated values), you can use the fgetcsv() function instead. It breaks the string into parts, using the marked separator, and returns an array:

```
$array = fgetcsv ($fp, length,
→ delimiter);
$array = fgetcsv ($fp, 1024, "\t");
```

Again, this function returns 1023 bytes of data, but it breaks the string into an array using the tab (\t) as an indicator of where to make elements. This function is the equivalent of using the fgets() and explode() functions together.

As an example, let's create a log-in script that uses the `users.txt` file created in the previous example. It will continue to read a file until a matching username/password combination has been found.

To read a file incrementally:

1. Create a new PHP document in your text editor, beginning with the standard HTML header (**Script 11.7**):

```
<!DOCTYPE html PUBLIC "-//W3C//
→ DTD XHTML 1.0 Transitional//EN"
"http://www.w3.org/TR/xhtml1/DTD/
→ xhtml1-transitional.dtd">
<html xmlns="http://www.w3.org/1999/
→ xhtml">
<head>
   <meta http-equiv="content-type"
   → content="text/html; charset=
   → iso-8859-1" />
   <title>Login</title>
</head>
<body>
```

2. Create the PHP section:

```
<?php // Script 11.7 - login.php
ini_set ('display_errors', 1);
error_reporting (E_ALL & ~E_NOTICE);
```

3. Check whether the form has been submitted:

```
if (isset ($_POST['submit'])) {
```

4. Create a dummy variable to use as a flag:

```
$loggedin = FALSE;
```

The `$loggedin` variable is used to indicate whether the user entered the correct username/password combination. When the script first starts, it's assumed that they have not.

Script 11.7 The `login.php` script uses the information stored in `users.txt` (created by Script 11.6) to validate a user.

Script

```
<!DOCTYPE html PUBLIC "-//W3C//DTD XHTML 1.0 Transitional//EN"
        "http://www.w3.org/TR/xhtml1/DTD/xhtml1-transitional.dtd">
<html xmlns="http://www.w3.org/1999/xhtml">
<head>
    <meta http-equiv="content-type" content="text/html; charset=iso-8859-1" />
    <title>Login</title>
</head>
<body>
<?php // Script 11.7 - login.php
// This script displays and handles an HTML form.
// This script logs a user in by checking the stored values in text file.

// Address error handling.
ini_set ('display_errors', 1);
error_reporting (E_ALL & ~E_NOTICE);

if (isset ($_POST['submit'])) { // Handle the form.

    $loggedin = FALSE; // Not currently logged in.

    // Open the file.
    $fp = fopen ('../users/users.txt', 'rb');

    // Loop through the file.
    while ( $line = fgetcsv ($fp, 100, "\t")) {

        // Check the file data against the submitted data.
        if ( ($line[0] == $_POST['username']) AND ($line[1] == crypt ($_POST['password'], $line[1]) ) ) {

            $loggedin = TRUE; // Correct username/password combination.

            // Stop looping through the file.
            break;

        } // End of IF.

    } // End of WHILE.
```

(script continues on next page)

Script 11.7 *continued*

```
        fclose ($fp); // Close the file.

        // Print a message.
        if ($loggedin) {
            print '<p>You are now logged in.
            </p>';
        } else {
            print '<p>The username and
            password you entered do not match
            those on file.</p>';
        }

    } else { // Display the form.

    // Leave PHP and display the form.
    ?>

    <form action="login.php" method="post">
    Username: <input type="text"
    name="username" size="20" /><br />
    Password: <input type="password"
    name="password" size="20" /><br />
    <input type="submit" name="submit"
    value="Login" />
    </form>
    <?php
    }// End of SUBMIT IF.
    ?>
    </body>
    </html>
```

5. Open the file for reading:

   ```
   $fp = fopen ('../users/users.txt',
   → 'rb');
   ```

   Unlike the `file()` function, the `fgetcsv()` function requires a file pointer. Therefore, the `users.txt` file must be opened with the `fopen()` function, using the appropriate mode. Here, that mode is `rb`, meaning the file should be opened for reading in a binary safe mode.

6. Loop through each line of the file:

   ```
   while ( $line = fgetcsv ($fp, 100,
   → "\t")) {
   ```

   This `while` loop reads another 100 bytes or one line of the file—whichever comes first—with each iteration. The data being read is broken into an array, using the tab to indicate the separate elements.

   Because the `users.txt` file stores its data in the format *username tab password tab directory newline*, the `$line` array contains three elements indexed at 0 (username), 1 (password), and 2 (directory).

7. Check the submitted values against the retrieved values:

   ```
   if ( ($line[0] == $_POST['username'])
   → AND ($line[1] == crypt ($_POST
   → ['password'], $line[1]) ) ) {
   ```

   This two-part conditional checks the submitted username against the stored username (`$line[0]`) and checks the submitted password against the stored password (`$line[1]`). However, because the stored password was encrypted, it needs to be checked against an encrypted version of the submitted password.

   To check the submitted password against the encrypted version, you call the `crypt()` function again, passing the submitted password and the stored, encrypted version as arguments.

continues on next page

8. If a match was found, set `$loggedin` to TRUE and exit the `while` loop:

```
$loggedin = TRUE;
break;
```

If the conditional is TRUE, the submitted username and password match those on file. In this case, the `$loggedin` flag is set to TRUE, and the `break` statement is used to exit the `while` loop. The benefit of this system is that only as much of the file is read as is required to find a match.

9. Close the conditional, the `while` loop, and the file:

```
    }
}
fclose ($fp);
```

10. Print a message to the user:

```
if ($loggedin) {
    print '<p>You are now logged in.
    → </p>';
} else {
    print '<p>The username and pass
    → word you entered do not match
    → those on file.</p>';
}
```

Using the `$loggedin` flag, the script can now say whether the user is "logged in." You could add some functionality to this process by storing the user's directory in a session and then sending them to a file-upload page.

11. Continue the main submit conditional, and exit PHP:

```
} else {
?>
```

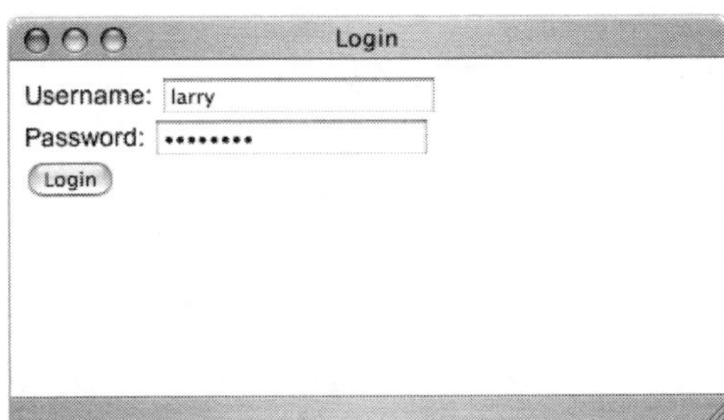

Figure 11.23 The log-in form takes a username and password.

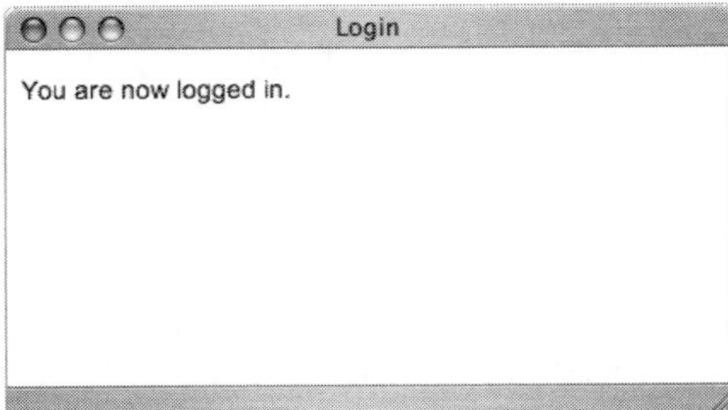

Figure 11.24 If the submitted username and password match those previously recorded, the user sees this message.

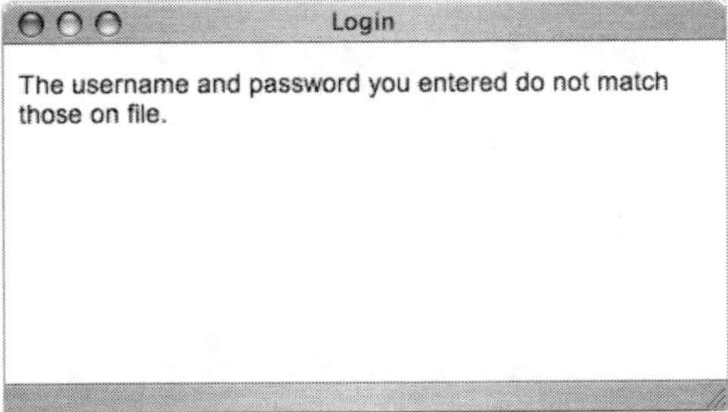

Figure 11.25 The result if the user submits a username and password combination that doesn't match the values previously recorded.

12. Create the HTML form:

```
<form action="login.php"
→ method="post">
Username: <input type="text"
→ name="username" size="20" /><br />
Password: <input type="password"
→ name="password" size="20" /><br />
<input type="submit" name="submit"
→ value="Login" />
</form>
```

13. Return to PHP to complete the main conditional:

```
<?php
}
?>
```

14. Finish the HTML page:

```
</body>
</html>
```

15. Save the file as `login.php`, upload it to your Web server, and test it in your Web browser (**Figures 11.23**, **11.24**, and **11.25**).

✔ Tips

- As of PHP 4.2, the `length` argument in `fgets()` is optional and defaults to 1 Kbyte (1024 bytes). As of PHP 4.3, the `length` argument defaults so that it automatically returns all the data until the end of the line.
- As of PHP 4.3, the `fgetcsv()` function takes another optional argument: the string being used to enclose the elements.
- If a line is blank, `fgetcsv()` returns an array containing a single null value.

12 Intro to Databases

Strange as it may sound, the Internet wouldn't be where it is today if not for the existence of databases. In fact, PHP probably wouldn't be as popular or as useful if not for its built-in support for numerous types of databases.

There are currently many existing database servers or Database Management Systems (DBMS), which function on different platforms. On any operating system, Oracle is generally considered one of the best DBMS, but its price puts it out of the running for all but the largest and best-financed applications. For Windows and Windows NT, you'll often encounter Access or SQL Server, both of which are fine but not cross-platform compliant.

This chapter will use MySQL as the example DBMS. Although MySQL—which is available for most platforms—isn't as powerful as other database servers, it has enough speed and functionality for most purposes. And its price—free for most uses—makes it the most common choice for Web development.

This chapter shows you how to develop a simple database that creates a *blog* (a Web-based journal). Although you'll learn enough here to get started, you may want to visit Appendix B, "Resources," once you've finished this chapter to find some references where you can learn more about the topic.

Introduction to SQL

A *database* is a collection of tables (tables being made up of columns and rows) that stores information. Databases are created, updated, and read using SQL (Structured Query Language). There are surprisingly few commands in SQL (**Table 12.1**), which is both a blessing and a curse.

SQL was designed to be written a lot like the English language, which makes it very user friendly; but it does take some thought to create more elaborate SQL statements with only the handful of available terms.

Using PHP to work with MySQL comes down to sending SQL commands to MySQL using the `mysql_query()` function. The best way to debug problems that occur is to print out the query being executed and run the query on the database using a separate application. This way, you can see if it's an SQL/MySQL problem or a PHP one. Your two best tools in this cause are

- The MySQL monitor (**Figure 12.1**), a command-line tool for interacting with MySQL
- phpMyAdmin (**Figure 12.2**), a PHP-based MySQL interface

For a demonstration of using the MySQL monitor, see Appendix A. For information on phpMyAdmin, see www.phpmyadmin.net.

Common SQL Commands

Command	Purpose
CREATE	Creates a database or table
DELETE	Deletes records from a table
DROP	Deletes a database or table
INSERT	Adds records to a table
SELECT	Retrieves records from a table
UPDATE	Updates records in a table

Table 12.1 These are the most essential SQL commands.

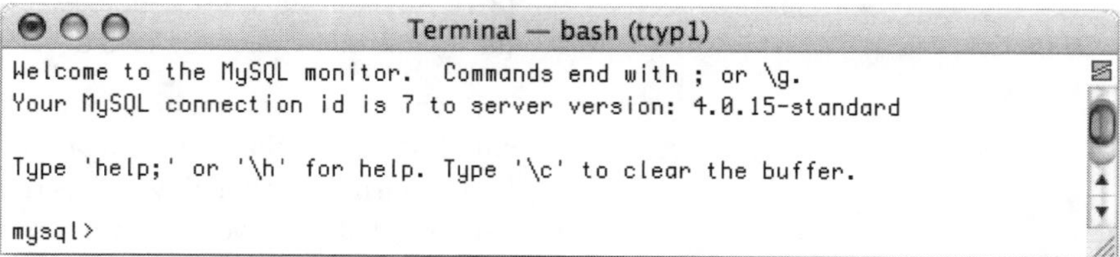

Figure 12.1 The MySQL monitor comes with the MySQL database software and can be used to execute queries without the need for a PHP script.

✔ Tips

- Technically, a DBMS is the software that interfaces with the database proper. However, more and more people are using the terms *database* and *DBMS* synonymously.
- Several other applications are available for interacting with MySQL. Some are free, and others cost. A quick search using Google for *MySQL*, *admin*, and your operating system should turn up some results.
- A popular alternative to MySQL is PostgreSQL. Unlike MySQL, it's free for all uses, and it contains some advanced features that MySQL is just beginning to incorporate.
- Be aware that adding a database into your Web applications creates more potential for errors, so check and double-check your work as you go.

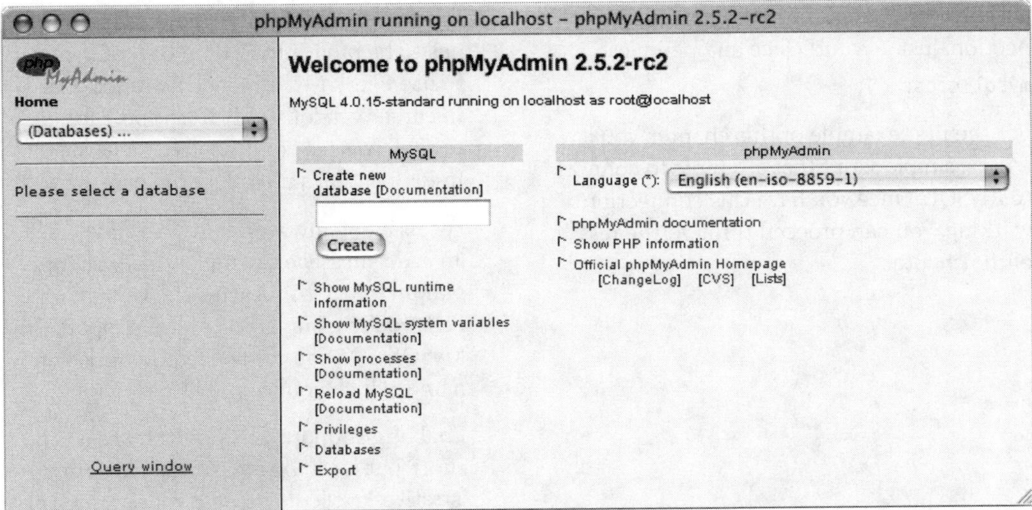

Figure 12.2 phpMyAdmin is perhaps the most popular software written in PHP. It provides a Web-based interface for a MySQL database.

Connecting to MySQL

When you worked with text files in Chapter 11, "Files and Directories," you saw that you first had to create a file pointer while opening the file. This pointer then acted as a reference point to that open file. You use a similar process when working with databases. First, you have to establish a connection to the database server (in this case, MySQL). This connection is then used as the access point for any future commands. The syntax for connecting to a database is

```
$dbc = mysql_connect ('localhost',
→ 'username', 'password');
```

The database connection (`$dbc`) is established using three arguments: the host, which is almost always *localhost*; the username; and the password for that username.

If you're using a database through a hosting company, the company will most likely provide you with the username and password to use. If you're running MySQL on your own computer, see Appendix A to learn how you create a user.

Once you're done working with a database, it's considered good form to close the connection, just as you'd close an open file:

```
mysql_close ();
```

For the first example of this chapter, you'll write a simple script that attempts to connect to MySQL. Once you have this connection working, you can proceed through the rest of the chapter.

MySQL Support in PHP

Support for the MySQL database server has to be built into PHP in order for you to use PHP's MySQL-specific functions. In earlier versions of PHP, support for MySQL was part of the software by default. In PHP 5, that's no longer the case.

For users of any version of PHP, if you see an error message saying *...undefined function mysql_...*, this means the version of PHP you're using doesn't have support for MySQL. (Or, you misspelled the function name, which you should also check.)

Enabling support for MySQL takes a little effort, but it can be done if you have administrative-level control over your server. For more information, see the PHP manual.

Script 12.1 Being able to connect to the MySQL server is the most important step. This script tests that process.

```
Script
<!DOCTYPE html PUBLIC "-//W3C//DTD XHTML 1.0 Transitional//EN"
        "http://www.w3.org/TR/xhtml1/DTD/xhtml1-transitional.dtd">
<html xmlns="http://www.w3.org/1999/xhtml">
<head>
    <meta http-equiv="content-type" content="text/html; charset=iso-8859-1" />
    <title>Connect to MySQL</title>
</head>
<body>
<?php // Script 12.1 - mysql_connect.php
// This script connects to the MySQL server.

// Address error handling.
ini_set ('display_errors', 1);
error_reporting (E_ALL & ~E_NOTICE);

// Attempt to connect to MySQL and print out messages.
if ($dbc = mysql_connect ('localhost', 'username', 'password')) {

    print '<p>Successfully connected to MySQL.</p>';

    mysql_close(); // Close the connection.

} else {

    print '<p>Could not connect to MySQL.</p>';

}

?>
</body>
</html>
```

To connect to MySQL:

1. Create a new PHP document in your text editor, beginning with the standard HTML header (**Script 12.1**).

```
<!DOCTYPE html PUBLIC "-//W3C//DTD XHTML 1.0 Transitional//EN"
"http://www.w3.org/TR/xhtml1/DTD/xhtml1-transitional.dtd">
<html xmlns="http://www.w3.org/1999/xhtml">
<head>
    <meta http-equiv="content-type" content="text/html; charset=iso-8859-1" />
    <title>Connect to MySQL</title>
</head>
<body>
```

2. Create the section of PHP code:

```
<?php // Script 12.1 - mysql_connect.php
ini_set ('display_errors', 1);
error_reporting (E_ALL & ~E_NOTICE);
```

3. Connect to MySQL, and report on the results:

```
if ($dbc = mysql_connect ('localhost', 'username', 'password')) {
    print '<p>Successfully connected to MySQL.</p>';
    mysql_close();
} else {
    print '<p>Could not connect to MySQL.</p>';
}
```

   By placing the connection attempt as the condition in an `if-else` statement, you make it easy to report on whether the connection worked.

continues on next page

This chapter will continue to use *username* and *password* as values. For your scripts, you'll need to replace these with the values provided by your Web host or set when you add a user using the steps outlined in Appendix A.

If a connection was established, a positive message is printed and then the connection is closed. Otherwise, an opposite message is printed, and there is no need to close the database connection (because it wasn't opened).

4. Complete the PHP code and the HTML page:

```
?>
</body>
</html>
```

5. Save the file as `mysql_connect.php`, upload it to your Web server (or place in the proper directory of your PHP-enabled computer), and test it in your Web browser (**Figure 12.3**).

   If you see results like those in **Figure 12.4**, double-check the username and password values. They should match up with those provided to you by your Web host or those you used to create the user. You can always test your connection username and password by using them in the MySQL monitor (again, see Appendix A).

   If you see *call to undefined function mysql_connect...*, your version of PHP doesn't support MySQL (see the sidebar).

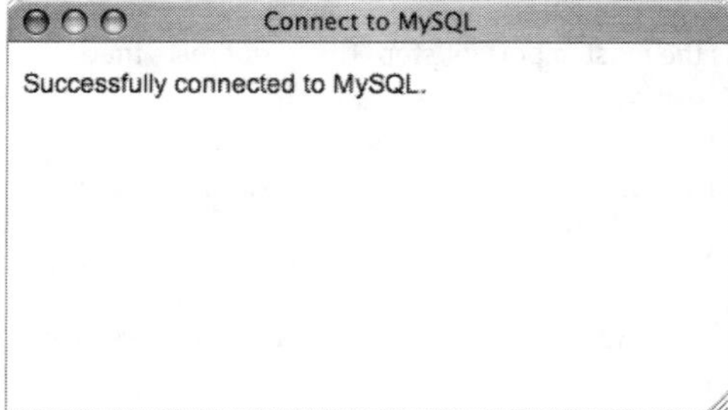

Figure 12.3 If PHP has support for MySQL and the username/password/host combination you used was correct, you should see this simple message.

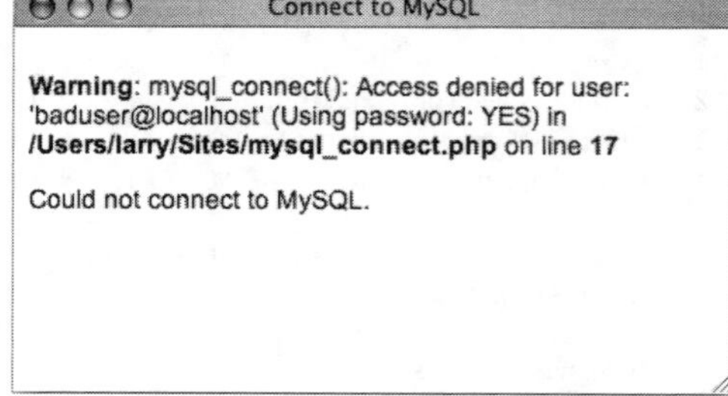

Figure 12.4 If PHP couldn't connect to MySQL, you'll probably see something like this.

✔ Tips

- Most of the MySQL-related PHP functions take an optional argument that is the database connection (`$dbc` in this case). All the examples in this chapter omit this argument, but you'll frequently see the functions used with or without it.

- The *localhost* value is used as the host name when both the PHP script and the MySQL database reside on the same computer. You can use PHP to connect to a MySQL database running on a remote server by changing the host name in the PHP script and creating the proper permissions in MySQL.
- PHP has built-in support for most databases, including dBase, FilePro, mSQL, MySQL, Oracle, PostgreSQL, and Sybase. If you're using a type of database that doesn't have direct support—for example, Access or SQL Server—you'll need to use PHP's ODBC (Open Database Connectivity) functions along with that database's ODBC drivers to interface with the database.
- The combination of using PHP and MySQL is so common now that you may run across two terms that identify servers configured with both PHP and MySQL: *LAMP* (*Linux* operating system, *Apache* Web server, *MySQL* DBMS, *PHP*) and *WAMP* (*Windows* operating system, *Apache* Web server, *MySQL* DBMS, *PHP*).
- You'll be working with MySQL, so all the functions you use in this chapter are MySQL specific. For example, to connect to a database in MySQL, the proper function is `mysql_connect()` but if you're using PostgreSQL, you'd instead write `pg_connect()`. If you aren't using a MySQL DBMS, use the PHP manual (available through `www.PHP.net`) to find the appropriate function names.
- At the time of this writing, PHP is in the process of adding a series of MySQLi (Improved MySQL Extension) functions. These are intended to be used with MySQL 4.1, once it's released. If you're using MySQL 4.1 or greater and want to take advantage of its advanced capabilities, see the PHP manual for more information.

MySQL Error Handling

Before this chapter gets too deep into working with MySQL, it would be best to discuss some error-handling techniques up front. Common errors you'll encounter are

- Failure to connect to MySQL
- Failure in selecting a database
- Inability to run a query
- No results being returned by a query
- Data not being inserted into a table

Experience will teach you why these errors normally occur, but immediately seeing what the problem is when running your scripts can save you much debugging time. To have your scripts give informative reports about errors that occur, use the `mysql_error()` function. This function returns a textual version of the error that the MySQL server returned.

Along with this function, you may want to use two PHP tools for handling errors. The `@` symbol, when used preceding a function name, suppresses any error messages or warnings the function might invoke. More potent is `die()`, which terminates the execution of a script and sends any message within the parentheses to the Web browser. For example:

```
die ('Could not connect to MySQL.');
```

As a rule of thumb, use `die()` with any function whose successful execution is mandated by the remainder of the script (such as connecting to MySQL and selecting the database). Use `@` with functions that might be problematic but wouldn't necessitate stopping the script.

Script 12.2 By adding error control to the script (the @ symbol and the die() function), you can more purposefully address problems that occur.

```
<!DOCTYPE html PUBLIC "-//W3C//DTD XHTML 1.0 Transitional//EN"
    "http://www.w3.org/TR/xhtml1/DTD/xhtml1-transitional.dtd">
<html xmlns="http://www.w3.org/1999/xhtml">
<head>
    <meta http-equiv="content-type" content="text/html; charset=iso-8859-1" />
    <title>Connect to MySQL</title>
</head>
<body>
<?php // Script 12.2 - mysql_connect.php (second version after Script 12.1)
// This script connects to the MySQL server.

// Address error handling.
ini_set ('display_errors', 1);
error_reporting (E_ALL & ~E_NOTICE);

// Attempt to connect to MySQL and print out messages.
if ($dbc = @mysql_connect ('localhost', 'username', 'password')) {

    print '<p>Successfully connected to MySQL.</p>';

    mysql_close(); // Close the connection.

} else {

    die ('<p>Could not connect to MySQL because: <b>' . mysql_error() . '</b></p>');

}

?>
</body>
</html>
```

To use error handling:

1. Open `mysql_connect.php` (Script 12.1) in your text editor.

2. Suppress any PHP errors created by the `mysql_connect()` function by changing the `if` conditional as follows (**Script 12.2**):

   ```
   if ($dbc = @mysql_connect ('localhost',
   → 'username', 'password')) {
   ```

   Rather than have PHP print out its error messages when the `mysql_connect()` function backfires (Figure 12.4), they're suppressed here using the @ symbol. The errors still occur, but they're handled by the change made in the next step.

3. Replace the `print()` statement after the `else` with this line:

   ```
   die ('<p>Could not connect to MySQL
   → because: <b>' . mysql_error() .
   → '</b></p>');
   ```

   Instead of printing a message or relying on whatever error PHP kicks out (see Figure 12.4), the script now prints the MySQL error in bold. You accomplish this by sending some HTML concatenated with the `mysql_error()` function as the argument to `die()`.

continues on next page

4. Save the file, upload it to your Web server, and test it again in your Web browser (**Figure 12.5**).

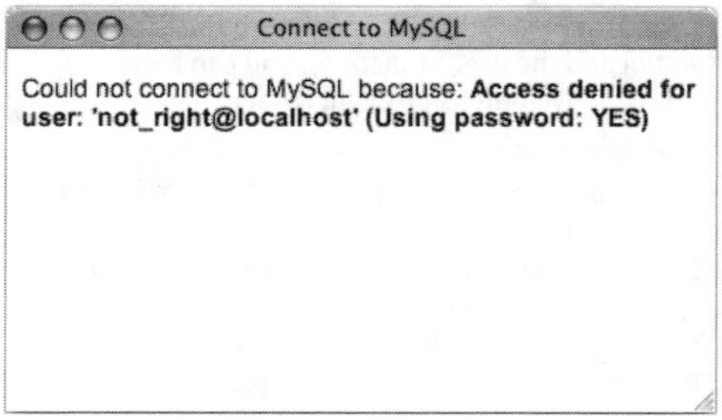

✔ Tips

- In this chapter, error messages are revealed to assist in the debugging process. Live Web sites should not have this level of explicit error messages being shown to the user.
- You can use the @ symbol to suppress errors, notices, or warnings stemming from any function, not just a MySQL-related one. For example:

  ```
  @include ('./filename.php');
  ```
- Similarly, `die()` isn't MySQL specific. It can be used in many situations and without the `mysql_error()` function.
- The `die()` function is an alias for `exit()`, and technically, they are both language constructs, not functions. Regardless, both `exit()` and `die()` can be called with or without parentheses but requires the parentheses if you also want it to print a message.

Connect to MySQL

Could not connect to MySQL because: **Access denied for user: 'not_right@localhost' (Using password: YES)**

Figure 12.5 Using PHP's error-control functions, you can adjust how errors are handled. If there was a problem, this result looks better than Figure 12.4. If the script connected, the result is like that in Figure 12.3, because neither of the error-management tools is used.

Creating and Selecting a Database

Before you do anything with a database, you need to create and select it. Whether you can do this depends on the database permissions of the user connecting to MySQL.

Database permissions are a bit more complicated than file permissions, but you need to understand this fact: Different types of users can be assigned different database capabilities. For example, a DBMS administrator can create new databases and delete existing ones (you may have dozens of databases in your DBMS), but a lower-level administrator may only be able to create and modify tables within a single database. The most basic user may just be able to read from, but not modify, tables.

If you're using a Web hosting company, it will most likely give you the second type of access—control over a single database but not the DBMS itself—and establish the initial database for you. If you're working on your own server or have administrative access, you have the capability to create new users and databases.

To create a database with PHP, you use the `mysql_query()` function with the `CREATE DATABASE` *`databasename`* SQL command:

```
mysql_query ('CREATE DATABASE
→ mydatabase');
```

Once you've done this, you can select the database using `mysql_select_db()`:

```
mysql_select_db ('mydatabase');
```

Note that you only ever need to create a database once, but it must always be selected before any other queries are run on it. In other words, some developers need to perform this first step, but everyone must take the second step with every PHP script.

In this example, you'll create a new database and then select it. To repeat, creating a database requires that you have administrator access. If your Web host restricts your access, it should create the initial database for you upon request; you can just write the second part of this script, which selects the database.

To create and select a database:

1. Open `mysql_connect.php` (Script 12.2) in your text editor.

2. After the first `print()` statement, create the new database, if necessary (**Script 12.3**):

   ```
   if (@mysql_query ('CREATE DATABASE myblog')) {
      print '<p>The database has been created.</p>';
   } else {
      die ('<p>Could not create the database because: <b>' . mysql_error() . '</b></p>');
   }
   ```

   If you need to create the database, use this construct to handle the task cleanly and effectively. The query—`CREATE DATABASE myblog`—is run using the `mysql_query()` function. The `@` symbol is used to suppress any error messages, which are instead handled by the `die()` function in conjunction with the `mysql_error()` function. If the database could not be created, a simple message is printed.

Script 12.3 Creating a new database consists of three steps: connecting to the database, running a `CREATE DATABASE` query using the `mysql_query()` function, and then closing the connection.

```
<!DOCTYPE html PUBLIC "-//W3C//DTD XHTML 1.0 Transitional//EN"
        "http://www.w3.org/TR/xhtml1/DTD/xhtml1-transitional.dtd">
<html xmlns="http://www.w3.org/1999/xhtml">
<head>
    <meta http-equiv="content-type" content="text/html; charset=iso-8859-1" />
    <title>Create the Database</title>
</head>
<body>
<?php // Script 12.3 - create_db.php
// This script connects to the MySQL server.
// This script also creates and selects the database.

// Address error handling.
ini_set ('display_errors', 1);
error_reporting (E_ALL & ~E_NOTICE);

// Attempt to connect to MySQL and print out messages.
if ($dbc = @mysql_connect ('localhost', 'username', 'password')) {

    print '<p>Successfully connected to MySQL.</p>';

    if (@mysql_query ('CREATE DATABASE myblog')) {
        print '<p>The database has been created.</p>';
    } else {
        die ('<p>Could not create the database because: <b>' . mysql_error() . '</b></p>');
    }

    if (@mysql_select_db ('myblog')) {
        print '<p>The database has been selected.</p>';
    } else {
        die ('<p>Could not select the database because: <b>' . mysql_error() . '</b></p>');
    }

```

(script continues on next page)

Script 12.3 *continued*

```
    mysql_close(); // Close the connection.

} else {

    die ('<p>Could not connect to MySQL because: <b>' . mysql_error() . '</b></p>');

}

?>
</body>
</html>
```

Create the Database

Successfully connected to MySQL.

The database has been created.

The database has been selected.

Figure 12.6 If the database could be created and selected, you'll see this result in the Web browser.

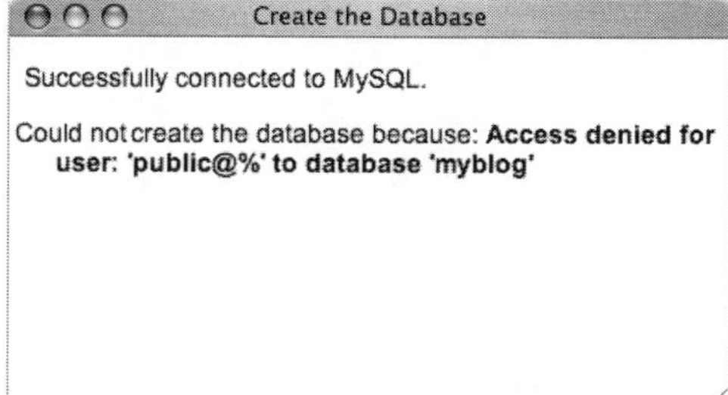

Figure 12.7 If the user doesn't have the authority to create a database, you'll see a message like this. A similar result will occur if the user doesn't have permission to select the database.

3. Select the database:

```
if (@mysql_select_db ('myblog')) {
    print '<p>The database has been
    → selected.</p>';
} else {
    die ('<p>Could not select the
    → database because: <b>' .
    → mysql_error() . '</b></p>');
}
```

   This structure parallels the `mysql_connect()` and `mysql_query()` conditionals, suppressing any error messages, reporting on the results, and using the `die()` function to terminate the script if the database couldn't be selected.

   Every PHP script that runs queries on a database must connect to MySQL and select the database in order to work.

4. If you want, change the page title to reflect this script's new purpose:

```
<title>Create the Database</title>
```

5. Save your script as `create_db.php`, upload it to your Web server, and test in your Web browser (**Figures 12.6** and **12.7**).

✔ Tips

- You probably won't create databases with any frequency and may not normally do so using a PHP script. Still, this example demonstrates both how you execute simple queries using PHP as well as the SQL command needed to create a database.
- You haven't done so in these examples, but in general it's a good idea to set your database information—host name, username, password, and database name—as variables or constants. Then you can plug them into the appropriate functions. By doing so, you can separate the database specifics from the functionality of the script, allowing you to easily port that code to other applications.

Creating a Table

Once the initial database has been created and selected, you can begin to create individual tables in it. A database can consist of multiple tables, but in this simple example you'll create one table in which data will be stored.

To create a table in the database, you'll use SQL—the language that databases understand. Because SQL is a lot like spoken English, the proper query to create a new table reads like so:

```
CREATE TABLE the_tablename (column1,
→ column2, etc.)
```

For each column, separated by commas, you first indicate the column name and then the column type. Common types are TEXT, VARCHAR (a variable number of characters), DATETIME, and INT (integer). Because it's highly recommended that you create a first column that acts as the *primary key* (a column used to refer to each row), a simple CREATE statement could be

```
CREATE TABLE my_table (id INT PRIMARY
→ KEY, information TEXT)
```

A table's primary key is a special column of unique values that is used to refer to the table's rows. The database makes an index of this column in order to more quickly navigate through the table. A table can have only one primary key, which you normally set up as an automatically incremented column of integers. The first row has a key of 1, the second has a key of 2, and so forth. Referring back to the key always retrieves the values for that row.

You can visit the MySQL Web site for more information on SQL. By following the directions in this section, though, you should be able to accomplish some basic database tasks. The table that you'll create in this example looks like **Table 12.2**.

blob_entries Table

Column Name	Column Type
blog_id	Positive, non-null, automatically incrementing integer
title	Text up to 100 characters in length
entry	Text of any length
date_entered	A timestamp including both the date and the time the row was added

Table 12.2 This table will be used for all of the examples in this chapter.

Script 12.4 You handle creating a table (and most other database requests) by writing the appropriate query and then using the mysql_query() function.

```
<!DOCTYPE html PUBLIC "-//W3C//DTD XHTML 1.0 Transitional//EN"
        "http://www.w3.org/TR/xhtml1/DTD/xhtml1-transitional.dtd">
<html xmlns="http://www.w3.org/1999/xhtml">
<head>
    <meta http-equiv="content-type" content="text/html; charset=iso-8859-1" />
    <title>Create a Table</title>
</head>
<body>
<?php // Script 12.4 - create_table.php
// This script connects to the MySQL server, selects the database, and creates a table.

// Address error handling.
ini_set ('display_errors', 1);
error_reporting (E_ALL & ~E_NOTICE);

// Connect and select.
if ($dbc = @mysql_connect ('localhost', 'username', 'password')) {

    if (!@mysql_select_db ('myblog')) {
        die ('<p>Could not select the database because: <b>' . mysql_error() . '</b></p>');
    }

} else {
    die ('<p>Could not connect to MySQL because: <b>' . mysql_error() . '</b></p>');
}


// Define the query.
$query = 'CREATE TABLE blog_entries (
    blog_id INT UNSIGNED NOT NULL AUTO_INCREMENT PRIMARY KEY,
    title VARCHAR(100) NOT NULL,
    entry TEXT NOT NULL,
    date_entered DATETIME NOT NULL
    )';

```

(script continues on next page)

In this example, you'll create a table that stores information submitted via an HTML form. In the next section of the chapter, you'll write the script that inserts the submitted data into the table created here.

To create a new table:

1. Begin a new PHP document in your text editor, starting with the standard HTML header (**Script 12.4**):

```
<!DOCTYPE html PUBLIC "-//W3C//DTD XHTML 1.0 Transitional//EN"
"http://www.w3.org/TR/xhtml1/DTD/xhtml1-transitional.dtd">
<html xmlns="http://www.w3.org/1999/xhtml">
<head>
    <meta http-equiv="content-type" content="text/html; charset=iso-8859-1" />
    <title>Create a Table</title>
</head>
<body>
```

2. Begin a section of PHP code:

```
<?php // Script 12.4 - create_table.php
ini_set ('display_errors', 1);
error_reporting (E_ALL & ~E_NOTICE);
```

continues on next page

3. Connect to the MySQL server, and select the database:

```
if ($dbc = @mysql_connect ('localhost', 'username', 'password')) {
   if (!@mysql_select_db ('myblog'))
   {
      die ('<p>Could not select the database because: <b>' . mysql_error() . '</b></p>');
   }
} else {
   die ('<p>Could not connect to MySQL because: <b>' . mysql_error() . '</b></p>');
}
```

This is a simplified version of the code used in the previous script. The main difference is that no messages are printed if each step was successful (we'll assume everything's working by this point).

4. Create the query for making the table:

```
$query = 'CREATE TABLE blog_entries (
   blog_id INT UNSIGNED NOT NULL AUTO_INCREMENT PRIMARY KEY,
   title VARCHAR(100) NOT NULL,
   entry TEXT NOT NULL,
   date_entered DATETIME NOT NULL
   )';
```

Script 12.4 *continued*

```
// Run the query.
if (@mysql_query ($query)) {
    print '<p>The table has been created.</p>';
} else {
    die ('<p>Could not create the table because: <b>' . mysql_error() . '</b>.</p><p>The query being run was: ' . $query . '</p>');
}

mysql_close(); // Close the connection.

?>
</body>
</html>
```

Let's break the query into more recognizable parts. First, to create a new table, you write CREATE TABLE *tablename* (where *tablename* is replaced by the actual, desired table name). Then, within parentheses, you list every column you want with each column separated by a comma. Your table and column names should be alphanumeric, with no spaces.

The first column in the table is called blog_id; it's an unsigned integer (INT UNSIGNED—which means that it can only be a positive whole number). By including the words NOT NULL, you indicate that this column must have a value for each row. The values automatically increase by one for each row added (AUTO INCREMENT) and stand as the primary key.

The next two columns consist of text. One, called title, is limited to 100 characters. The second, entry, can be nearly limitless in size. Each of these fields is also marked as NOT NULL, making them required fields.

Finally, the date_entered column is a timestamp that marks when each record was added to the table.

5. Execute the query:

```
if (@mysql_query ($query)) {
   print '<p>The table has been
   → created.</p>';
} else {
   die ('<p>Could not create the table
   → because: <b>' . mysql_error() .
   → '</b>.</p><p>The query being run
   → was: ' . $query . '</p>');
}
```

continues on next page

To create the table, you call the `mysql_query()` function using the `$query` variable as the argument. If a problem occurred, the MySQL error is printed, along with the value of the `$query` variable. This last step is a particularly useful debugging technique.

6. Close the database connection:

```
mysql_close();
```

7. Complete the PHP code and the HTML page:

```
?>
</body>
</html>
```

8. Save the script as `create_table.php`, upload it to your Web server, and test it in your Web browser (**Figures 12.8** and **12.9**).

✔ Tips

- It's not necessary to write your SQL queries partially in all capital letters as you have here, but doing so helps to distinguish your SQL keywords from the table and column names.
- On larger Web applications, it's highly recommended that you place the database connection and selection code (lines 17 through 25 here) in a separate file, located outside of the Web directory. Then, each page that requires the database can include this external file.
- The `mysql_query()` function returns TRUE if a query was successfully run on a database. That result doesn't necessarily mean the desired result occurred.
- This chapter presents the basics of MySQL and SQL-related knowledge (including column types). You'll want to check out other resources—listed in Appendix B—once you're comfortable with the fundamentals.

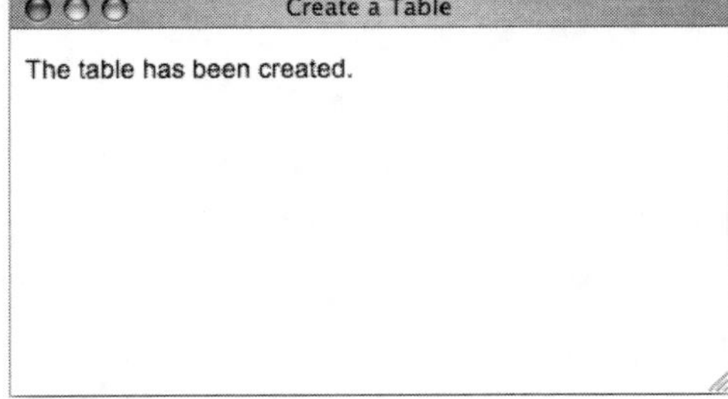

Figure 12.8 If all went well, all you'll see is this message.

Create a Table

Could not create the table because: **You have an error in your SQL syntax. Check the manual that corresponds to your MySQL server version for the right syntax to use near 'blog_id INT UNSIGNED NOT NULL AUTO_INCREMENT PRIMARY KEY, titl.**

The query being run was: CREATE TABLE blog_entries blog_id INT UNSIGNED NOT NULL AUTO_INCREMENT PRIMARY KEY, title VARCHAR(100) NOT NULL, entry TEXT NOT NULL, date_entered DATETIME NOT NULL)

Figure 12.9 Between the MySQL error message and printing out the query being executed, you should be able to figure out what the problem is if the script does not work properly.

Inserting Data into a Database

As mentioned, this database will be used as a blog, an online journal. Blog entries—consisting of a title and text—will be added to the database using one page and then displayed on another page. It's a simple but relevant use of a database.

In the last section, you created the table, which consists of four columns: `blog_id`, `title`, `entry`, and `date_entered`. The process of adding information to a table is similar to creating the table itself in terms of which functions you use, but the SQL query is different. To insert records, you use the `INSERT` SQL command using either of the following models:

```
INSERT INTO tablename values ('value1',
→ 'value2', 'value3', etc.)
INSERT INTO tablename (column1_name,
→ column2_name) values ('value1',
→ 'value2')
```

The query begins with `INSERT INTO` *`tablename`*. Then you can either specify which columns you're inserting values for or not. The latter is more specific and is therefore preferred, but it can be tedious if you're populating a slew of columns. In either case, you must be certain to list the right number and type of values for each column in the table.

The values are placed within parentheses, with the value for each column within single quotation marks and each value separated by a comma. If the value being inserted is a number, it doesn't need to be placed within single quotation marks but it still requires the comma.

You run this query on the database using the `mysql_query()` function. Because these queries are often elaborate, it helps to assign each query to a variable and send that variable to the `mysql_query()` function.

To demonstrate, let's create a page that adds blog entries to the database. Like many of the examples in the previous chapter, this one will both display and handle the HTML form.

To enter data into a database from an HTML form:

1. Begin a new document in your text editor, starting with the HTML header (**Script 12.5**):

```
<!DOCTYPE html PUBLIC "-//W3C//DTD XHTML 1.0 Transitional//EN"
"http://www.w3.org/TR/xhtml1/DTD/xhtml1-transitional.dtd">
<html xmlns="http://www.w3.org/1999/xhtml">
<head>
   <meta http-equiv="content-type" content="text/html; charset=iso-8859-1" />
   <title>Add a Blog Entry</title>
</head>
<body>
```

2. Create the initial PHP section:

```
<?php // Script 12.5 - add_entry.php
ini_set ('display_errors', 1);
error_reporting (E_ALL & ~E_NOTICE);
```

3. Check whether the form has been submitted:

```
if (isset ($_POST['submit'])) {
```

Script 12.5 The query statement for adding information to a database is straightforward enough, but be sure to match the number of values in parentheses to the number of columns in the database table.

```
<!DOCTYPE html PUBLIC "-//W3C//DTD XHTML 1.0 Transitional//EN"
        "http://www.w3.org/TR/xhtml1/DTD/xhtml1-transitional.dtd">
<html xmlns="http://www.w3.org/1999/xhtml">
<head>
    <meta http-equiv="content-type" content="text/html; charset=iso-8859-1" />
    <title>Add a Blog Entry</title>
</head>
<body>
<?php // Script 12.5 - add_entry.php
// This script adds a blog entry to the database.

// Address error handling.
ini_set ('display_errors', 1);
error_reporting (E_ALL & ~E_NOTICE);

if (isset ($_POST['submit'])) { // Handle the form.

    // Connect and select.
    if ($dbc = @mysql_connect ('localhost', 'username', 'password')) {

        if (!@mysql_select_db ('myblog')) {
            die ('<p>Could not select the database because: <b>' . mysql_error() . '</b></p>');
        }

    } else {
        die ('<p>Could not connect to MySQL because: <b>' . mysql_error() . '</b></p>');
    }

    // Define the query.
    $query = "INSERT INTO blog_entries (blog_id, title, entry, date_entered) VALUES (0, '{$_POST['title']}', '{$_POST['entry']}', NOW())";

```

(script continues on next page)

Script 12.5 *continued*

```
    // Execute the query.
    if (@mysql_query ($query)) {
        print '<p>The blog entry has been added.</p>';
    } else {
        print "<p>Could not add the entry because: <b>" . mysql_error() . "</b>. The query was $query.</p>";
    }

    mysql_close();

}

// Display the form.
?>
<form action="add_entry.php" method="post">
<p>Entry Title: <input type="text" name="title" size="40" maxsize="100" /></p>
<p>Entry Text: <textarea name="entry" cols="40" rows="5"></textarea></p>
<input type="submit" name="submit" value="Add to the Blog!" />
</form>
</body>
</html>
```

4. Connect to and select the database:

```
if ($dbc = @mysql_connect ('localhost',
→ 'username', 'password')) {
   if (!@mysql_select_db ('myblog')) {
      die ('<p>Could not select the
      → database because: <b>' .
      → mysql_error() . '</b></p>');
   }
} else {
   die ('<p>Could not connect to
   → MySQL because: <b>' .
   → mysql_error() . '</b></p>');
}
```

As an alternative, you can place this section of code in a separate file, store it outside of the Web directory, and then include it using the following:

```
require_once ('../mysql_connect.php');
```

5. Define the `INSERT` query:

```
$query = "INSERT INTO blog_entries
→ (blog_id, title, entry, date_
→ entered) VALUES (0, '{$_POST
→ ['title']}', '{$_POST['entry']}',
→ NOW())";
```

The query begins with the necessary `INSERT INTO` *`tablename`* code. Then it lists the columns for which values will be submitted. After that is the word `VALUES`, followed by four values (one for each column, in order) within single quotation marks and separated by commas. When you assign this query to the `$query` variable, you use double quotation marks both to access the `$_POST['title']` and `$_POST['entry']` variable values and to avoid conflicts with the single quotation marks used to demarcate the values.

continues on next page

Because the `blog_id` column has been set to `AUTO_INCREMENT`, you can use 0 as the value and MySQL will automatically use the next logical value for that column. To set the value of the `date_entered` column, you use the MySQL `NOW()` function. It inserts the current time as that value.

6. Run the query on the database:

```
if (@mysql_query ($query)) {
   print '<p>The blog entry has been
   → added.</p>';
} else {
   print "<p>Could not add the entry
   → because: <b>" . mysql_error() .
   → "</b>. The query was $query.</p>";
}
```

The query, once defined, is run using the `mysql_query()` function. By calling this function as the condition of an `if-else` statement, you can print simple messages indicating the result of the query execution.

As an essential debugging tool, if the query didn't run properly, the MySQL error and the query being run are both printed to the Web browser (**Figure 12.10**).

7. Close the database connection, and complete the main conditional and the PHP section:

```
   mysql_close();
}
?>
```

This curly brace closes the submit conditional. From here on out, the form will be displayed.

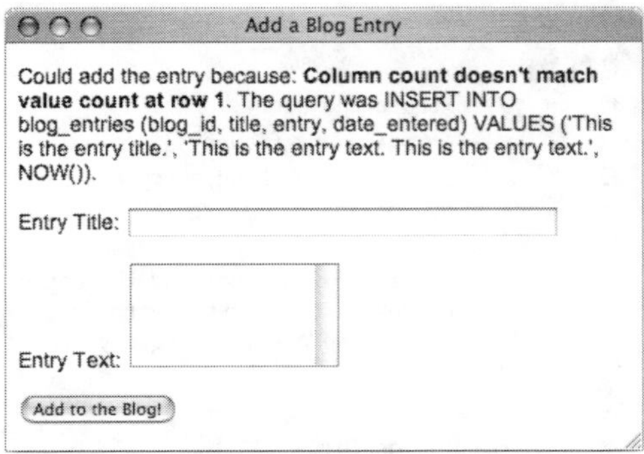

Figure 12.10 If the `INSERT` query didn't work, the MySQL error is printed along with the query that was run.

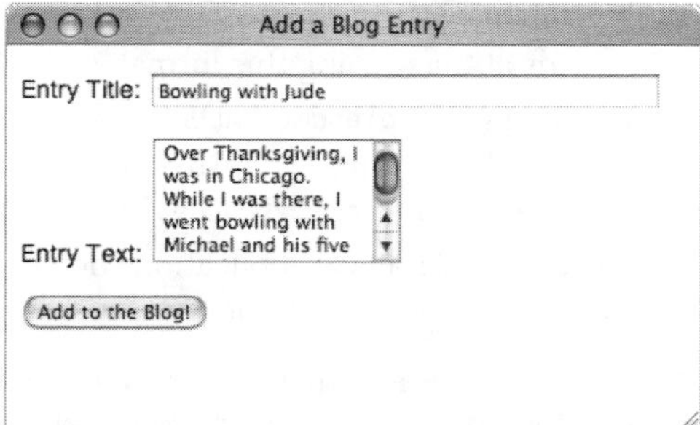

Figure 12.11 This is the form for adding an entry to the database.

Figure 12.12 If the `INSERT` query ran properly, a message is printed and the form is displayed again.

8. Create the form:

```
<form action="add_entry.php"
→ method="post">
<p>Entry Title: <input type="text"
→ name="title" size="40" maxsize=
→ "100" /></p>
<p>Entry Text: <textarea
name="entry" → cols="40"
rows="5"></textarea></p>
<input type="submit" name="submit"
→ value="Add to the Blog!" />
</form>
```

The HTML form is very simple, requiring only a title for the blog entry and the entry itself. As a good rule of thumb, use the same name for your form inputs as the corresponding column names in the database. Doing so makes errors less likely.

9. Finish the HTML page:

```
</body>
</html>
```

10. Save the script as `add_entry.php`, upload it to your Web server, and test it in your Web browser (**Figures 12.11** and **12.12**).

✔ Tips

- If Magic Quotes GPC is enabled in your PHP configuration, you'll need to use the `stripslashes()` function to remove extraneous slashes from the submitted values.
- You haven't done so here, but it's normally a good idea to apply the `trim()` function to remove extraneous white space from values being inserted into a database.
- If you want to be able to check your SQL statements without making them obviously viewable to the user, add this line of code to your script:

  ```
  print "<!--The query is $query -->";
  ```

  Now the PHP script will write the query as an HTML comment, making it viewable by looking at the page source (**Figure 12.13**).
- MySQL allows you to insert several records at once, using this format:

  ```
  INSERT INTO tablename VALUES
  ('value1', 'value2', 'value3'),
  ('value1', 'value2', 'value3');
  ```

  Most other database applications don't support this construct, though.
- To retrieve the automatically incremented number created for an `AUTO_INCREMENT` column, use the `mysql_insert_id()` function.

Source of http://localhost/add_entry.php

```
<!DOCTYPE html PUBLIC "-//W3C//DTD XHTML 1.0 Transitional//EN"
        "http://www.w3.org/TR/xhtml1/DTD/xhtml1-transitional.dtd">
<html xmlns="http://www.w3.org/1999/xhtml">
<head>
    <meta http-equiv="content-type" content="text/html; charset=iso-8859-1" />
    <title>Add a Blog Entry</title>
</head>
<body>
<p>The blog entry has been added.</p><!-- INSERT INTO blog_entries (blog_id, title,
entry, date_entered) VALUES (0, 'Bowling with Jude', 'Over Thanksgiving, I was in
Chicago. While I was there, I went bowling with Michael and his five year old son,
Jude.', NOW()) --><form action="add_entry.php" method="post">
<p>Entry Title: <input type="text" name="title" size="40" maxsize="100" /></p>
<p>Entry Text: <textarea name="entry" columns="40" rows="5"></textarea></p>
<input type="submit" name="submit" value="Add to the Blog!" />
</form>
</body>
</html>
```

Figure 12.13 During development of a Web site, you can print your SQL queries as an HTML comment in order to double-check exactly what the code is doing.

Retrieving Data from a Database

The next process this chapter demonstrates for working with databases is retrieving data from a populated table. You still use the mysql_query() function, but retrieving data is slightly different than inserting data—you have to assign the retrieved information to a variable in order to use it. This section goes through this process one step at a time.

The basic syntax for retrieving data is the SELECT query:

```
SELECT what_columns FROM what_tables
```

The easiest query for reading data from a table is

```
SELECT * FROM tablename
```

The asterisk is the equivalent of saying *every column*. If you only require certain columns to be returned, you can limit your query, like so:

```
SELECT title, entry FROM blogs_entries
```

This query requests that only the information from two columns (title and entry) be gathered. Keep in mind that this structure doesn't limit what rows (or records) are returned, just what columns for those rows.

Another way to restrict your query is to add a conditional restricting which rows are returned, accomplished using a WHERE clause:

```
SELECT * FROM tablename WHERE
→ (first_name='Larry')
```

Here you want the information from every column in the table, but only from the rows where the first_name column is equal to *Larry*. This is a good example of how SQL uses only a few terms effectively and flexibly.

The main difference in retrieving data from a database as opposed to inserting data into a database is that you need to handle the query differently. You may want to assign the results of the query to a variable:

```
$result = mysql_query ($query);
```

In layman's terms, this variable now knows what the result of the query is (technically, it points to the returned rows in the MySQL server). To access multiple rows of information retrieved, you should run the `$result` variable through a loop:

```
while ($row = mysql_fetch_array
→ ($result)) {
   // Do something with $row.
}
```

With each iteration of the loop, the next row of information from the query (referenced by `$result`) is turned into an array called `$row`. This process continues until no more rows of information are found.

As with any array, when you retrieve records from the database, you must refer to the columns exactly as they're defined in the database (the keys are case-sensitive). So, in this example, you must use `$row['entry']` instead of `$row['Entry']`. For this reason, it's recommended that you use entirely lower-case column names when you create a table.

The best way to comprehend this system is to try it. You'll write a script that reads the information stored in the `blog_entries` table (you may want to run through `add_entry.php` a couple more times to build up the table).

To retrieve data from a table:

1. Begin a new PHP script, starting with the standard HTML header (**Script 12.6**):

```
<!DOCTYPE html PUBLIC "-//W3C//
→ DTD XHTML 1.0 Transitional//EN"
"http://www.w3.org/TR/xhtml1/DTD/
→ xhtml1-transitional.dtd">
<html xmlns="http://www.w3.org/1999/
→ xhtml">
<head>
   <meta http-equiv="content-type"
   → content="text/html; charset=
   → iso-8859-1" />
   <title>View My Blog</title>
</head>
<body>
```

continues on next page

Script 12.6 The SQL query for retrieving all data from a table is quite simple; but in order for PHP to access every returned record, you must loop through the results one row at a time.

```
<!DOCTYPE html PUBLIC "-//W3C//DTD XHTML 1.0 Transitional//EN"
        "http://www.w3.org/TR/xhtml1/DTD/xhtml1-transitional.dtd">
<html xmlns="http://www.w3.org/1999/xhtml">
<head>
    <meta http-equiv="content-type" content="text/html; charset=iso-8859-1" />
    <title>View My Blog</title>
</head>
<body>
<?php // Script 12.6 - view_blog.php
// This script retrieves blog entries from the database.

// Address error handling.
ini_set ('display_errors', 1);
error_reporting (E_ALL & ~E_NOTICE);

// Connect and select.
if ($dbc = @mysql_connect ('localhost', 'username', 'password')) {

    if (!@mysql_select_db ('myblog')) {
        die ('<p>Could not select the database because: <b>' . mysql_error() . '</b></p>');
    }

} else {
    die ('<p>Could not connect to MySQL because: <b>' . mysql_error() . '</b></p>');
}
```

(script continues on next page)

2. Define your PHP section:

```
<?php // Script 12.6 - view_blog.php
ini_set ('display_errors', 1);
error_reporting (E_ALL & ~E_NOTICE);
```

3. Connect to and select the database:

```
if ($dbc = @mysql_connect ('localhost', 'username', 'password')) {
   if (!@mysql_select_db ('myblog')) {
      die ('<p>Could not select the database because: <b>' . mysql_error() . '</b></p>');
   }
} else {
   die ('<p>Could not connect to MySQL because: <b>' . mysql_error() . '</b></p>');
}
```

4. Define the SELECT query:

```
$query = 'SELECT * FROM blog_entries ORDER BY date_entered DESC';
```

This basic query tells the database that you'd like to see every column of every row in the `blog_entries` table. The returned records should be sorted, as indicated by the `ORDER BY` clause, by the order in which they were entered (recorded in the `date_entered` column), starting with the most recent first. This last option is indicated by `DESC`, which is short for *descending*. If the query was `ORDER BY date_entered ASC`, the most recent addition would be retrieved last.

5. Run the query:

```
if ($r = mysql_query ($query)) {
```

The `SELECT` query is run like any other. However, the result of the query is assigned to a `$result` (or, more tersely, `$r`) variable, which will be referenced later.

Script 12.6 *continued*

```

// Define the query.
$query = 'SELECT * FROM blog_entries ORDER BY date_entered DESC';

if ($r = mysql_query ($query)) { // Run the query.

    // Retrieve and print every record.
    while ($row = mysql_fetch_array ($r)) {
        print "<p><h3>{$row['title']}</h3>
        {$row['entry']}<br />
        <a href=\"edit_entry.php?id={$row['blog_id']}\">Edit</a>
        <a href=\"delete_entry.php?id={$row['blog_id']}\">Delete</a>
        </p><hr />\n";
    }

} else { // Query didn't run.
    die ('<p>Could not retrieve the data because: <b>' . mysql_error() . "</b>. The query was $query.</p>");
} // End of query IF.

mysql_close(); // Close the database connection.

?>
</body>
</html>
```

6. Print out the returned results:

```
while ($row = mysql_fetch_array ($r)) {
   print "<p><h3>{$row['title']}</h3>
   {$row['entry']}<br />
   <a href=\"edit_entry.php?id=
   → {$row['blog_id']}\">Edit</a>
   <a href=\"delete_entry.php?id=
   → {$row['blog_id']}\">Delete</a>
   </p><hr />\n";
}
```

This loop sets the variable `$row` to an array containing the first record returned in `$r`. The loop then executes the following commands (the `print()` statement). Once the loop gets back to the beginning, it assigns the next row, if it exists. It continues to do this until there are no more rows of information to be obtained.

Because the `mysql_fetch_array()` function was used, you can refer to each individual column in the row as you would any other array. The array's keys are the names of the columns from the table—hence, `blog_id`, `title`, and `entry` (there's no need to print out the `date_entered`).

7. Handle the errors if the query didn't run:

```
} else {
   die ('<p>Could not retrieve the
   → data because: <b>' . mysql_
   → error() . "</b>. The query was
   → $query.</p>");
}
```

If the query couldn't run on the database, it should be printed out, along with the MySQL error.

8. Close the database connection:

```
mysql_close();
```

continues on next page

9. Complete the PHP section and the HTML page:

```
?>
</body>
</html>
```

10. Save the script as `view_blog.php`, upload it to your Web browser, and test it in your Web browser (**Figure 12.14**).

11. If you want, add another record to the blog using the `add_entry.php` page (Script 12.5), and run this page again (**Figure 12.15**).

✔ Tips

- The `mysql_fetch_array()` function takes another argument, which is a constant indicating what kind of array should be returned. `MYSQL_ASSOC` returns an associative array, whereas `MYSQL_NUM` returns a numerically indexed array.
- The `mysql_num_rows()` function returns the number of records returned by a `SELECT` query.
- It's possible to paginate returned records so that 10 or 20 appear on each page (like the way Google works). Doing so requires more advanced coding than can be taught in this book, though. See one of the author's other, more advanced books, or look online for code examples and tutorials.
- You might want to apply the `nl2br()` function to the blog entry (`$row['entry']`) to turn new lines in the entry into HTML `<br />` tags.

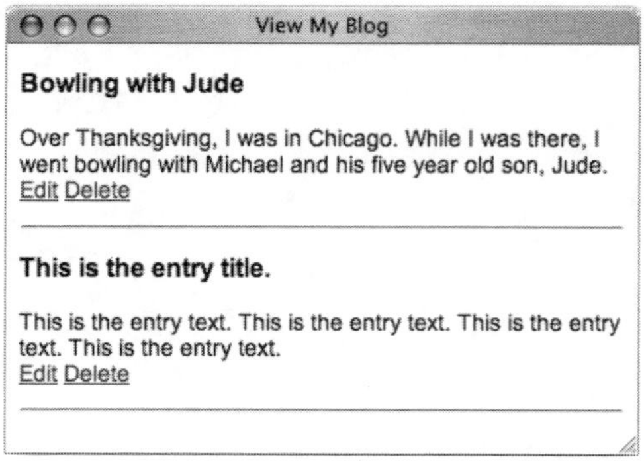

View My Blog

Bowling with Jude

Over Thanksgiving, I was in Chicago. While I was there, I went bowling with Michael and his five year old son, Jude.
Edit Delete

This is the entry title.

This is the entry text. This is the entry text. This is the entry text. This is the entry text.
Edit Delete

Figure 12.14 Being able to pull out data from a database and create a dynamic Web page is a great use of PHP and something you'll never be able to accomplish with HTML alone.

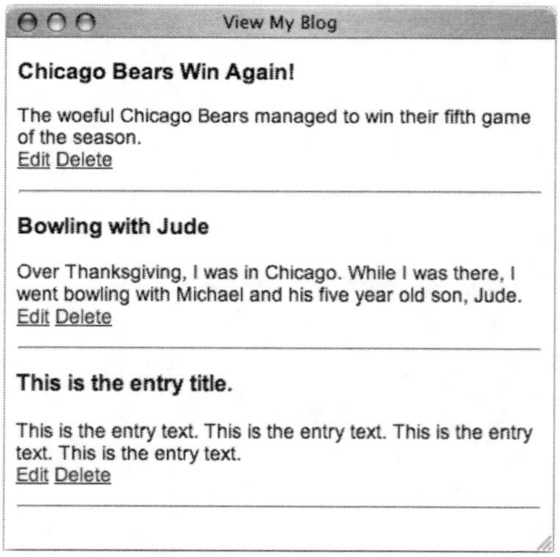

View My Blog

Chicago Bears Win Again!

The woeful Chicago Bears managed to win their fifth game of the season.
Edit Delete

Bowling with Jude

Over Thanksgiving, I was in Chicago. While I was there, I went bowling with Michael and his five year old son, Jude.
Edit Delete

This is the entry title.

This is the entry text. This is the entry text. This is the entry text. This is the entry text.
Edit Delete

Figure 12.15 Thanks to the SELECT query, which orders the returned records by the date they were entered, the most recently added entry is always listed first.

Deleting Data in a Database

Sometimes you might also want to run a DELETE query on a database. Such a query removes records from the database. The syntax for a delete query is

```
DELETE FROM tablename WHERE column=value
```

The WHERE clause isn't required, but if it's omitted, you'll remove every record from the table. You should also understand that once you delete a record, there's no way to recover it (unless you have a backup of the database).

As a safeguard, if you want to delete only a single record from a table, add the LIMIT clause to the query:

```
DELETE FROM tablename WHERE column=value
→ LIMIT 1
```

This query ensures that only one record is deleted at most. Once you've defined your query, it's again executed using the mysql_query() function, like any other "simple" query.

To see if the query worked, you can use the mysql_affected_rows() function. This function returns the number of rows affected by an INSERT, DELETE, or UPDATE query.

As an example, let's write the delete_entry.php script, which is linked from the view_blog.php page. It will receive the entry identification number, confirm that the user wants to delete this record, and then remove it.

To delete data from a database:

1. Start a new PHP document in your text editor, beginning with the standard HTML header (**Script 12.7**):

```
<!DOCTYPE html PUBLIC "-//W3C//DTD XHTML 1.0 Transitional//EN"
"http://www.w3.org/TR/xhtml1/DTD/xhtml1-transitional.dtd">
<html xmlns="http://www.w3.org/1999/xhtml">
<head>
    <meta http-equiv="content-type" content="text/html; charset=iso-8859-1" />
    <title>Delete a Blog Entry</title>
</head>
<body>
```

2. Start your PHP code:

```
<?php // Script 12.7 - delete_entry.php
ini_set ('display_errors', 1);
error_reporting (E_ALL & ~E_NOTICE);
```

3. Connect to and select the database:

```
if ($dbc = @mysql_connect ('localhost', 'username', 'password')) {
    if (!@mysql_select_db ('myblog')) {
        die ('<p>Could not select the database because: <b>' . mysql_error() . '</b></p>');
    }
} else {
    die ('<p>Could not connect to MySQL because: <b>' . mysql_error() . '</b></p>');
}
```

Script 12.7 The DELETE SQL command permanently removes a record (or records) from a table.

```
<!DOCTYPE html PUBLIC "-//W3C//DTD XHTML 1.0 Transitional//EN"
        "http://www.w3.org/TR/xhtml1/DTD/xhtml1-transitional.dtd">
<html xmlns="http://www.w3.org/1999/xhtml">
<head>
    <meta http-equiv="content-type" content="text/html; charset=iso-8859-1" />
    <title>Delete a Blog Entry</title>
</head>
<body>
<?php // Script 12.7 - delete_entry.php
// This script deletes a blog entry.

// Address error handling.
ini_set ('display_errors', 1);
error_reporting (E_ALL & ~E_NOTICE);

// Connect and select.
if ($dbc = @mysql_connect ('localhost', 'username', 'password')) {

    if (!@mysql_select_db ('myblog')) {
        die ('<p>Could not select the database because: <b>' . mysql_error() . '</b></p>');
    }

```

(script continues on next page)

4. Check whether the form has been submitted:

```
if (isset ($_POST['submit'])) {
```

5. Define and execute the query:

```
$query = "DELETE FROM blog_entries
→ WHERE blog_id={$_POST['id']} LIMIT
→ 1";
$r = mysql_query ($query);
```

This query deletes the record whose `blog_id` has a value of `$_POST['id']`. The ID value comes from the form, where it's stored as a hidden input. By adding the `LIMIT 1` clause to the query, you can guarantee that only one record, at most, is removed.

6. Check the result of the query:

```
if (mysql_affected_rows() == 1) {
    print '<p>The blog entry has been
    → deleted.</p>';
} else {
    print "<p>Could not delete the
    → entry because: <b>" .
    → mysql_error() . "</b>. The query
    → was $query.</p>";
}
```

The `mysql_affected_rows()` function returns the number of rows altered by the most recent query. If the query ran properly, one row was deleted, so this function should return 1. If so, a message is printed. Otherwise, the MySQL error and query are printed.

continues on next page

Script 12.7 *continued*

```
} else {
    die ('<p>Could not connect to MySQL because: <b>' . mysql_error() . '</b></p>');
}

if (isset ($_POST['submit'])) { // Handle the form.

    // Define the query.
    $query = "DELETE FROM blog_entries WHERE blog_id={$_POST['id']} LIMIT 1";
    $r = mysql_query ($query); // Execute the query.

    // Report on the result.
    if (mysql_affected_rows() == 1) {
        print '<p>The blog entry has been deleted.</p>';
    } else {
        print "<p>Could not delete the entry because: <b>" . mysql_error() . "</b>. The query was
        $query.</p>";
    }

} else { // Display the entry in a form.

    // Check for a valid entry ID in the URL.
    if (is_numeric ($_GET['id']) ) {
```

(script continues on next page)

7. Display the form if it hasn't been submitted:

```
} else {
```

The next section of the script displays the blog entry, because this `else` takes effect if the form hasn't yet been submitted.

8. Check for a valid entry ID, and execute the query:

```
if (is_numeric ($_GET['id']) ) {
    $query = "SELECT * FROM
    → blog_entries WHERE
    → blog_id={$_GET['id']}";
    if ($r = mysql_query ($query)) {
```

To display the blog entry, the page must confirm that a numeric ID is received by the page. Because it should come in the URL (when the user clicks the link in `view_blog.php`), you reference `$_GET['id']`.

The query is like the `SELECT` query used in the previous example, except that the `WHERE` clause has been added to retrieve a specific record. This query is then run on the database using the `mysql_query()` function.

Script 12.7 *continued*

```

        // Define the query.
        $query = "SELECT * FROM blog_entries WHERE blog_id={$_GET['id']}";
        if ($r = mysql_query ($query)) { // Run the query.

            $row = mysql_fetch_array ($r); // Retrieve the information.

            // Make the form.
            print '<form action="delete_entry.php" method="post">
            <p>Are you sure you want to delete this entry?</p>
            <p><h3>' . $row['title'] . '</h3>' .
            $row['entry'] . '<br />
            <input type="hidden" name="id" value="' . $_GET['id'] . '" />
            <input type="submit" name="submit" value="Delete this Entry!" /></p>
            </form>';

        } else { // Couldn't get the information.
            print "<p>Could not retrieve the entry because: <b>" . mysql_error() . "</b>. The query was $query.</p>";
        }

    } else { // No ID set.
        print '<p><b>You must have made a mistake in using this page.</b></p>';
    }

} // End of main IF.

mysql_close(); // Close the database connection.

?>
</body>
</html>
```

9. Retrieve the record, and display the entry in a form:

```
$row = mysql_fetch_array ($r);
print '<form action=
→ "delete_entry.php" method="post">
<p>Are you sure you want to delete
→ this entry?</p>
<p><h3>' . $row['title'] . '</h3>' .
$row['entry'] . '<br />
<input type="hidden" name="id"
→ value="' . $_GET['id'] . '" />
<input type="submit" name="submit"
→ value="Delete this Entry!" /></p>
</form>';
```

Instead of retrieving all the records using a `while` loop, as you did in the previous example, you use one call to the `mysql_fetch_array()` function to assign the returned record to the `$row` variable. Using this array, the record to be deleted can be displayed.

The form first shows the blog entry, much as it did in the `view_blog.php` script. The most important consideration is that the blog identification number, which is passed to the script as `$_GET['id']`, is stored in a hidden input. The `DELETE` query uses that value to remove the proper record.

10. Complete the conditionals:

```
        } else {
            print "<p>Could not retrieve
            → the entry because: <b>" .
            → mysql_error() . "</b>. The
            → query was $query.</p>";
        }
    } else {
        print '<p><b>You must have made
        → a mistake in using this
        → page.</b></p>';
    }
}
```

continues on next page

The first `else` is the result if the query didn't run on the database. Again, the MySQL error is printed as well as the query. The second `else` comes into play if the page doesn't receive a numeric ID, in which case a valid record couldn't be retrieved.

11. Close the database connection, and complete the page:

```
mysql_close();
?>
</body>
</html>
```

12. Save the script as `delete_entry.php`, upload it to your Web server, and test it in your Web browser (**Figures 12.16** and **12.17**).

    To test this script, you must first run `view_blog.php`. Then, click one of the Delete links to access `delete_entry.php` (Figure 12.16).

✔ Tips

- You can empty a table completely by running the query `TRUNCATE TABLE tablename`. This approach is preferred over using `DELETE FROM tablename`. `TRUNCATE` will completely drop and rebuild the table, which is better for the database.
- It's a fairly common error to try to run the query `DELETE * FROM tablename`, like a `SELECT` query. Remember that `DELETE` doesn't use the same syntax as `SELECT`, because you aren't deleting specific columns.
- Admittedly, you probably don't want to create an application that displays records and lets any user delete them at will. Instead, you'd probably have one version of the `view_blog.php` script without the Edit and Delete links (for the public) and this version for your administration of the blog.

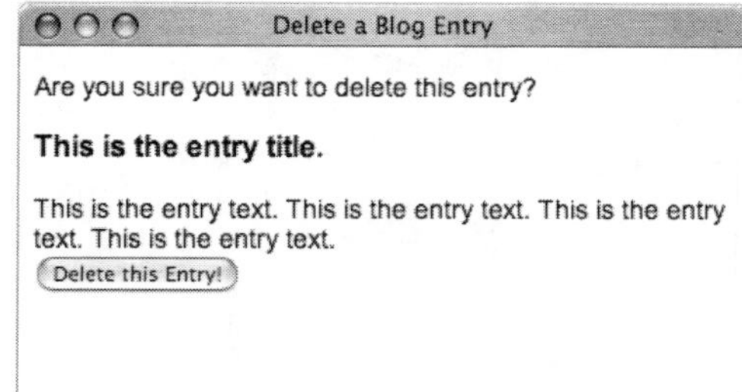

Figure 12.16 When the user arrives at this page, the blog entry is revealed and the user must confirm that they want to delete it.

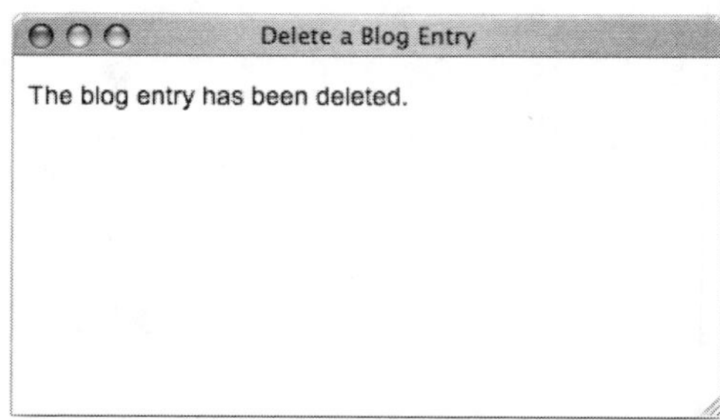

Figure 12.17 If the delete query worked properly, the user sees this result.

Updating Data in a Database

The final type of query this chapter will cover is the `UPDATE` query. It's used to alter the values of a record's columns. The syntax is as follows:

```
UPDATE tablename SET column1_name=value,
→ column2_name=value2 WHERE column=value
```

As with an `INSERT` query, if the values are strings, they should be placed within single quotation marks:

```
UPDATE users SET first_name='Eleanor',
→ age=1 WHERE user_id=142
```

As with a `DELETE` query, you should use a `WHERE` clause to limit the rows that are affected. If you don't do this, every record in the database will be updated.

To test that an update worked, you can again use the `mysql_affected_rows()` function to return the number of records altered.

To demonstrate, let's write a page for editing a blog entry. It will let the user alter an entry's title and text, but not the date entered or the blog ID number.

To update data in a database:

1. Start a new PHP document in your text editor, beginning with the standard HTML header (**Script 12.8**).

```
<!DOCTYPE html PUBLIC "-//W3C//
→ DTD XHTML 1.0 Transitional//EN"
"http://www.w3.org/TR/xhtml1/DTD/
→ xhtml1-transitional.dtd">
<html xmlns="http://www.w3.org/1999/
→ xhtml">
<head>
   <meta http-equiv="content-type"
   → content="text/html; charset=
   → iso-8859-1" />
   <title>Edit a Blog Entry</title>
</head>
<body>
```

2. Start your PHP code:

```
<?php // Script 12.8 - edit_entry.php
ini_set ('display_errors', 1);
error_reporting (E_ALL & ~E_NOTICE);
```

3. Connect to and select the database:

```
if ($dbc = @mysql_connect
('localhost', → 'username',
'password')) {
   if (!@mysql_select_db ('myblog')) {
      die ('<p>Could not select the
      → database because: <b>' .
      → mysql_error() . '</b></p>');
   }
} else {
   die ('<p>Could not connect to
   → MySQL because: <b>' .
   → mysql_error() . '</b></p>');
}
```

Script 12.8 You can edit records in a database table by using an UPDATE SQL command.

```
<!DOCTYPE html PUBLIC "-//W3C//DTD XHTML 1.0 Transitional//EN"
        "http://www.w3.org/TR/xhtml1/DTD/xhtml1-transitional.dtd">
<html xmlns="http://www.w3.org/1999/xhtml">
<head>
    <meta http-equiv="content-type" content="text/html; charset=iso-8859-1" />
    <title>Edit a Blog Entry</title>
</head>
<body>
<?php // Script 12.8 - edit_entry.php
// This script edits a blog entry using an UPDATE query.

// Address error handling.
ini_set ('display_errors', 1);
error_reporting (E_ALL & ~E_NOTICE);

// Connect and select.
if ($dbc = @mysql_connect ('localhost', 'username', 'password')) {

    if (!@mysql_select_db ('myblog')) {
        die ('<p>Could not select the database because: <b>' . mysql_error() . '</b></p>');
    }

```

(script continues on next page)

4. Check whether the form has been submitted:

```
if (isset ($_POST['submit'])) {
```

5. Define and execute the query:

```
$query = "UPDATE blog_entries SET
→ title='{$_POST['title']}',
→ entry='{$_POST['entry']}' WHERE
→ blog_id={$_POST['id']}";
$r = mysql_query ($query);
```

The `UPDATE` query sets the `title` column equal to the value entered in the form's title input and the `entry` column equal to the value entered in the form's entry textarea. Only the record whose `blog_id` is equal to `$_POST['id']`, which comes from a hidden form input, is updated.

6. Report on the success of the query:

```
if (mysql_affected_rows() == 1) {
    print '<p>The blog entry has been
    → updated.</p>';
} else {
    print "<p>Could not update the
    → entry because: <b>" .
    → mysql_error() . "</b>. The query
    → was $query.</p>";
}
```

If one row was affected, then a success message is returned. Otherwise, the MySQL error and the query are sent to the Web browser.

continues on next page

Script 12.8 *continued*

```
} else {
    die ('<p>Could not connect to MySQL because: <b>' . mysql_error() . '</b></p>');
}

if (isset ($_POST['submit'])) { // Handle the form.

    // Define the query.
    $query = "UPDATE blog_entries SET title='{$_POST['title']}', entry='{$_POST['entry']}' WHERE
    blog_id={$_POST['id']}";
    $r = mysql_query ($query); // Execute the query.

    // Report on the result.
    if (mysql_affected_rows() == 1) {
        print '<p>The blog entry has been updated.</p>';
    } else {
        print "<p>Could not update the entry because: <b>" . mysql_error() . "</b>. The query was
        $query.</p>";
    }

} else { // Display the entry in a form.

    // Check for a valid entry ID in the URL.
    if (is_numeric ($_GET['id']) ) {
```

(script continues on next page)

7. Begin the conditional for displaying the form:

```
} else {
```

Because the page both displays and handles the form, this `else` part of the conditional displays the form if it hasn't been submitted.

8. Check for a valid entry ID, and run the query on the database:

```
if (is_numeric ($_GET['id']) ) {
    $query = "SELECT * FROM
    → blog_entries WHERE
    → blog_id={$_GET['id']}";
    if ($r = mysql_query ($query)) {
```

To edit the blog, you need to retrieve the current values from the database. You use a `SELECT` query, like the one used in `delete_entry.php`, along with the blog ID value that's sent to this page in the URL (when the user clicks the link in `view_blog.php`).

9. Retrieve the data, and display it in a form:

```
$row = mysql_fetch_array ($r);
print '<form action="edit_entry.php"
→ method="post">
<p>Entry Title: <input type="text"
→ name="title" size="40"
→ maxsize="100" value="' .
→ $row['title'] . '" /></p>
<p>Entry Text: <textarea name="entry"
→ columns="40" rows="5">' .
→ $row['entry'] . '</textarea></p>
<input type="hidden" name="id"
→ value="' . $_GET['id'] . '" />
<input type="submit" name="submit"
→ value="Update this Entry!" />
</form>';
```


Script 12.8 *continued*

```

        // Define the query.
        $query = "SELECT * FROM blog_entries WHERE blog_id={$_GET['id']}";
        if ($r = mysql_query ($query)) { // Run the query.

            $row = mysql_fetch_array ($r); // Retrieve the information.

            // Make the form.
            print '<form action="edit_entry.php" method="post">
        <p>Entry Title: <input type="text" name="title" size="40" maxsize="100" value="' .
        $row['title'] . '" /></p>
        <p>Entry Text: <textarea name="entry" columns="40" rows="5">' . $row['entry'] .
        '</textarea></p>
        <input type="hidden" name="id" value="' . $_GET['id'] . '" />
        <input type="submit" name="submit" value="Update this Entry!" />
        </form>';

        } else { // Couldn't get the information.
            print "<p>Could not retrieve the entry because: <b>" . mysql_error() . "</b>. The
            query was $query.</p>";
        }
```

(script continues on next page)

Script 12.8 *continued*

```
    } else { // No ID set.
        print '<p><b>You must have made a
        mistake in using this page.</b>
        </p>';
    }

} // End of main IF.

mysql_close(); // Close the database
connection.

?>
</body>
</html>
```

Again, a single call to `mysql_fetch_array()` assigns the values for the record in question to the `$row` variable. The form is then created; it's much like the form for adding a blog entry. There are two significant changes: First, the inputs obtain preset values by referring to the `$row` variable; second, the record's ID is stored as a hidden input so that the update query knows which record to alter.

10. Complete the conditionals:

```
        } else {
            print "<p>Could not retrieve
            → the entry because: <b>" .
            → mysql_error() . "</b>. The
            → query was $query.</p>";
        }
    } else {
        print '<p><b>You must have made
        → a mistake in using this
        → page.</b></p>';
    }
}
```

As in the previous example, the first `else` takes affect if the entry couldn't be retrieved from the database. The second `else` is relevant if the page doesn't receive a numeric ID.

11. Close the database connection, and complete the page:

```
mysql_close();
?>
</body>
</html>
```

continues on next page

12. Save the file as `edit_entry.php`, upload it to your Web server, and test it in your Web browser (**Figures 12.18** and **12.19**).

    As in the previous example, to edit an entry, you must click its Edit link in the `view_blog.php` page.

13. Revisit `view_blog.php` to confirm that the changes were made (**Figure 12.20**).

✔ Tips

- The `blog_id` is a primary key, meaning that its value should never change. By using a primary key in your table, you can change every other value in the record but still refer to the row using that column.
- If you run an update on a table but don't change a record's values, `mysql_affected_rows()` will return 0.
- It can't hurt to add a `LIMIT 1` clause to an `UPDATE` query, to ensure that only one row, at most, is affected.

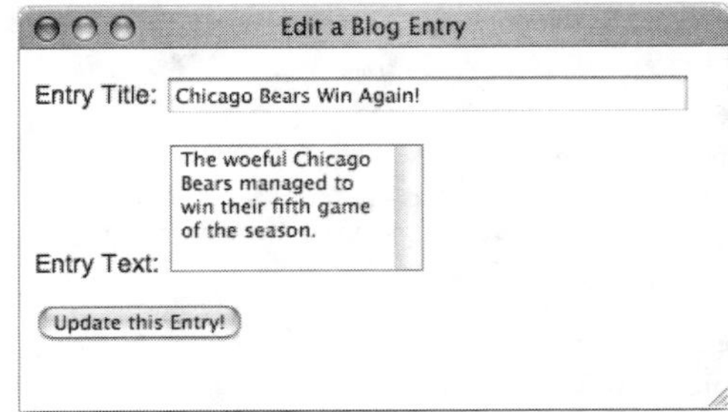

Figure 12.18 When the user arrives at the edit page, the form is shown with the existing values.

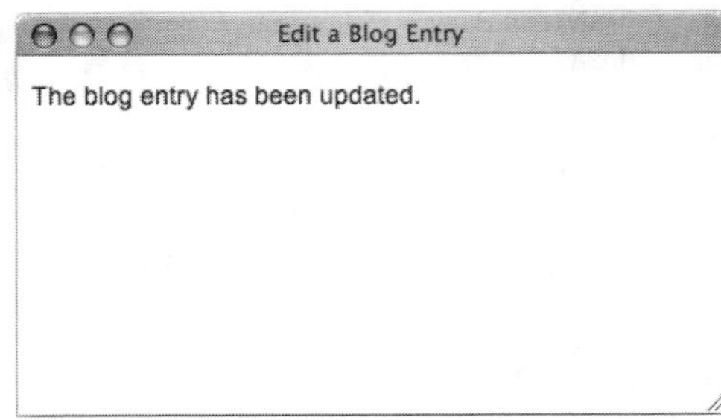

Figure 12.19 Upon submitting the form, the user sees a message like this.

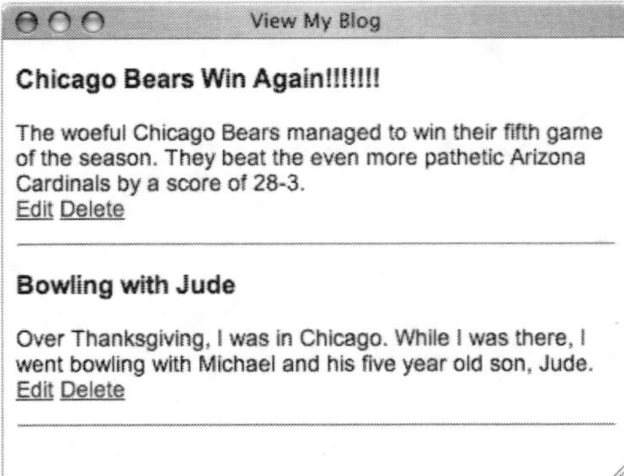

Figure 12.20 Reloading the `view_blog.php` script reflects the changes made to the entry.

13

Regular Expressions

If there were just two things you should understand about regular expressions, they would be that regular expressions are supremely useful in advanced programming and that they're easy to use but taxing to write. However, once you understand the rules for writing regular expressions, that extra knowledge will pay off in spades because regular expressions can vastly improve the quality of your programming.

This chapter will identify what regular expressions are, discuss the rules for constructing them (in great detail), and provide some useful examples demonstrating their capabilities.

What Are Regular Expressions?

Think of regular expressions as an elaborate system of matching patterns. For example, a United State zip code is in the format #####-####, where # stands for an integer between 0 and 9 and the last four digits (plus the hyphen) are optional. Therefore, any valid zip code can be identified if it matches this pattern:

```
^([0-9]{5})(-{1}[0-9]{4})?$
```

Writing the pattern is the hardest part of using regular expressions. After you've created it, you then use one of PHP's built-in functions to check a value against the pattern.

PHP supports two types of regular expressions: POSIX Extended and PCRE (Perl compatible). The latter are more powerful and slightly faster, but this chapter covers the former, which are easier to learn. PHP has six POSIX functions for working with regular expressions. These are listed in **Table 13.1**.

In order to explain how patterns are created, this section starts by introducing literals and then discusses metacharacters (special symbols) and how to group characters together. Next you'll learn about quantifiers and conclude with classes. The combination of literals, metacharacters, groupings, quantifiers, and classes defines your pattern.

As a formatting rule, this section defines patterns within quotes ("`pattern`") and indicates what the pattern matches in *italics*.

POSIX Extended Functions

Function	Purpose	Case Sensitive?
`ereg()`	Match a pattern	Yes
`eregi()`	Match a pattern	No
`ereg_replace()`	Match and replace a pattern	Yes
`eregi_replace()`	Match and replace a pattern	No
`split()`	Split a string using a pattern	Yes
`spliti()`	Split a string using a pattern	No

Table 13.1 PHP uses these six functions to work with POSIX regular expressions. Each function that concludes with an "i" is case-insensitive.

✔ Tips

- Some text editors, such as BBEdit for Macintosh, TextPad for Windows, and emacs for Unix, allow you to use regular expressions to match and replace patterns within and throughout several documents (**Figure 13.1**). This may be another good reason to learn regular expressions and is something to consider when choosing your text editor.
- If you learned regular expressions in Unix, Perl, or another technology, you might be able to begin using PHP's PCRE functions with just a little explanation. See the PHP manual for the proper functions to use and their syntax.

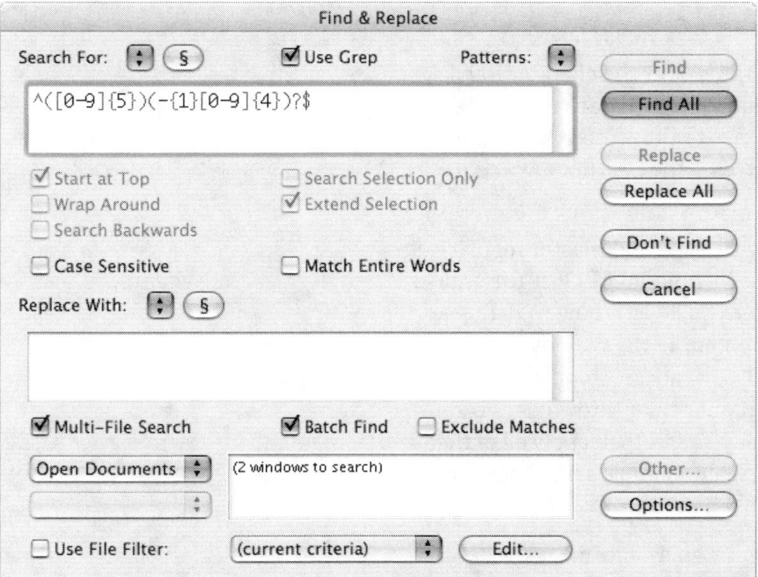

Figure 13.1 Within BBEdit's standard Find & Replace dialog box, you have the option of using regular expressions (even across several files or folders) by checking the Use Grep box. BBEdit can also store regular expression patterns for you and has some built in.

Matching Patterns

Two functions are built into PHP expressly for the purpose of matching a pattern within a string: `ereg()` and `eregi()`. The only difference between the two is that `ereg()` treats patterns as case-sensitive, whereas `eregi()` is case-insensitive, making it less particular. The latter is generally recommended for common use, unless you need to be more explicit (perhaps for security purposes, as with passwords). Both functions are evaluated to TRUE if the pattern is matched or FALSE if it isn't.

Here are two different ways to use these functions:

```
eregi ('pattern', 'string');
```

or

```
$pattern = 'pattern';
$string = 'string';
eregi ($pattern, $string);
```

Throughout the rest of the chapter, you'll assign the pattern to a variable, as in the second example, to draw more attention to the pattern itself—the heart of any regular expression.

The best way to learn and master regular expressions is by practicing. Over the course of this chapter you'll learn how to define a pattern by combining the various building blocks: literals, metacharacters, groupings, and classes. Rather than throw pages of information at you and then apply all of that at once, let's create a simple script that tests a string against a pattern.

This script will display a form that takes two te[illegible] puts: the regular expression pattern [illegible] string (or, potentially, number) being [illegible] The script will then submit these [illegible] elf and report on whether that [illegible] s that pattern. You'll use this [illegible] e with patterns through [illegible] er.

To match a pattern:

1. Create a new PHP document in your text editor, beginning with the standard HTML header (**Script 13.1**):

```
<!DOCTYPE html PUBLIC "-//W3C//DTD
→ XHTML 1.0 Transitional//EN"
"http://www.w3.org/TR/xhtml1/DTD/
→ xhtml1-transitional.dtd">
<html xmlns="http://www.w3.org/1999/
→ xhtml">
<head>
   <meta http-equiv="content-type"
   → content="text/html; charset=
   → iso-8859-1" />
   <title>Testing Regular Expression
   → Patterns</title>
</head>
<body>
```

2. Create a PHP section:

```
<?php // Script 13.1 -
test_pattern.php
ini_set ('display_errors', 1);
error_reporting (E_ALL & ~E_NOTICE);
```

3. Check to see whether the form has been submitted:

```
if ( isset ($_POST['submit'])) {
```

Because this page both displays and handles the HTML form, a conditional is used to check for the value of a submit variable.

continues on next page

Script 13.1 This simple script lets you enter a pattern and a string or number to test regular expressions. It even factors in your Magic Quotes settings.

Script

```
<!DOCTYPE html PUBLIC "-//W3C//DTD XHTML 1.0 Transitional//EN"
        "http://www.w3.org/TR/xhtml1/DTD/xhtml1-transitional.dtd">
<html xmlns="http://www.w3.org/1999/xhtml">
<head>
    <meta http-equiv="content-type" content="text/html; charset=iso-8859-1" />
    <title>Testing Regular Expression Patterns</title>
</head>
<body>
<?php // Script 13.1 - test_pattern.php
// This script takes a submitted string and checks it against a submitted pattern.

// Address error handling.
ini_set ('display_errors', 1);
error_reporting (E_ALL & ~E_NOTICE);

if ( isset ($_POST['submit'])) { // Has the form been submitted?

    if (ini_get('magic_quotes_gpc')) { // Adjust if Magic Quotes is turned on.

        $pattern = stripslashes ($_POST['pattern']);
        $string = stripslashes ($_POST['string']);

    } else { // Use the posted values as is.

```

(script continues on next page)

4. Adjust for Magic Quotes, if they're enabled:

```
if (ini_get('magic_quotes_gpc')) {
   $pattern = stripslashes
   → ($_POST['pattern']);
   $string = stripslashes
   → ($_POST['string']);
} else {
   $pattern = $_POST['pattern'];
   $string = $_POST['string'];
}
```

The `ini_get()` function returns TRUE if a setting is turned on. If Magic Quotes is enabled, the pattern and string values coming from the form might contain extra slashes that will ruin the accuracy of the regular expressions. To adjust for this, you remove the slashes using `stripslashes()`.

If Magic Quotes isn't enabled, the `ini_get()` function returns FALSE, and the `$pattern` and `$string` variables are assigned their values using the `$_POST` superglobals.

Script 13.1 *continued*

```
        $pattern = $_POST['pattern'];
        $string = $_POST['string'];

    }

    // Trim off extraneous spaces, just in case.
    $pattern = trim ($pattern);
    $string = trim ($string);

    // Print the results.
    print "<p>The result of checking<br /><i>$string</i><br />against<br /><b>$pattern</b><br />is ";
    if (eregi ($pattern, $string) ) {
        print 'TRUE!</p>';
    } else {
        print 'FALSE!</p>';
    }

} else { // Form has not been submitted.

    // Set the variables to blank values.
    $string = '';
    $pattern = '';

}
// Display the HTML form.
?>
<form action="test_pattern.php" method="post">
<p>Regular Expression Pattern: <input type="text" name="pattern" value="<?php print $pattern; ?>"
size="50" /></p>
<p>Test String: <input type="text" name="string" value="<?php print $string; ?>" size="50" /></p>
<input type="submit" name="submit" value="Test!" />
</form>
</body>
</html>
```

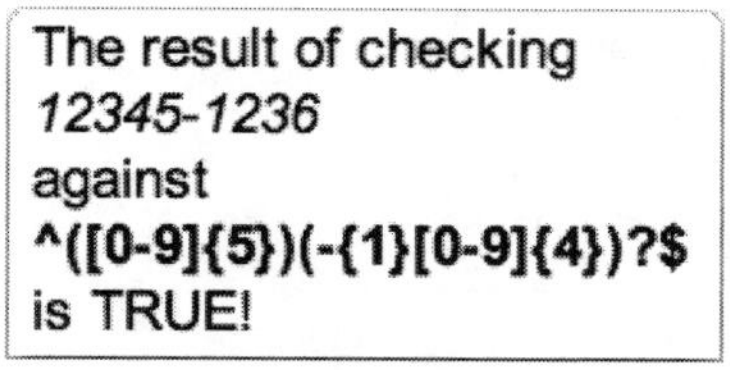

The result of checking
12345-1236
against
^([0-9]{5})(-{1}[0-9]{4})?$
is TRUE!

Figure 13.2 The script reprints the values that were entered in the form.

5. Remove any extra spaces from the submitted values:

```
$pattern = trim ($pattern);
$string = trim ($string);
```

In order to also improve the accuracy of the regular expressions, any extra spaces are removed from the beginning and end of the variables using `trim()`. This step will be more important once your patterns define the characters a string must begin and end with (in which case a space could make a valid string invalid).

6. Begin printing out the results:

```
print "<p>The result of checking
→ <br /><i>$string</i><br />against
→ <br /><b>$pattern</b><br />is ";
```

The main purpose of this script is to run a regular expression using a submitted pattern and a string. While you're reporting on the results, it will be beneficial to see the submitted pattern and string again. These values are printed out here, along with some formatting (and many break tags to make the result flow over several lines; **Figure 13.2**).

7. Check for a match, and report on its success:

```
if (eregi ($pattern, $string) ) {
   print 'TRUE!</p>';
} else {
   print 'FALSE!</p>';
}
```

continues on next page

The `eregi()` function—which is case-insensitive—is the condition for an `if-else` statement. If the string matches the pattern, `eregi()` returns TRUE and that result is printed. Otherwise, the string didn't match the pattern. (Each `print()` statement also closes the paragraph begun in Step 6, in case you were wondering what those closing </p> tags were doing.)

8. Create blank variables if the form hasn't been submitted:

```
} else {
   $string = '';
   $pattern = '';
}
```

The HTML form displays the submitted string and pattern as the default values for those inputs (**Figure 13.3**). Because these variables won't have a default value when the page is first loaded (at which point the form hasn't been submitted), they're initially set to an empty value.

9. Close the PHP section, and create the HTML form:

```
?>
<form action="test_pattern.php"
→ method="post">
<p>Regular Expression Pattern:
→ <input type="text" name="pattern"
→ value="<?php print $pattern; ?>"
→ size="50" /></p>
<p>Test String: <input type="text"
→ name="string" value="<?php print
→ $string; ?>" size="50" /></p>
<input type="submit" name="submit"
→ value="Test!" />
</form>
```

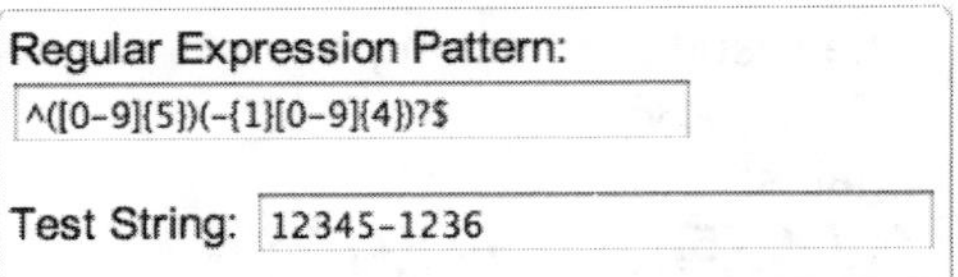

Figure 13.3 The form is *sticky*—it remembers the values that were entered in its previous use.

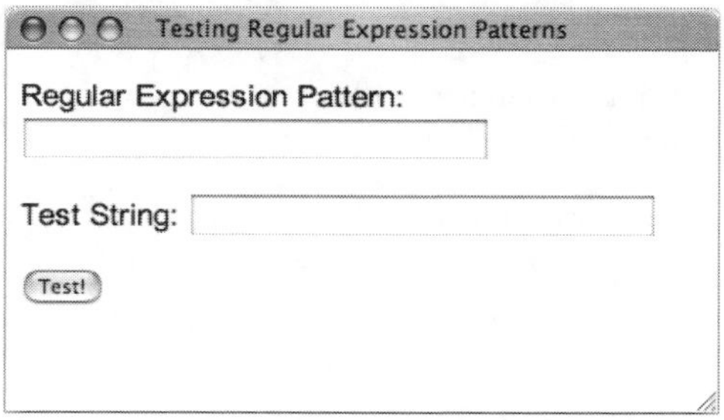

Testing Regular Expression Patterns

Regular Expression Pattern:

Test String:

Test!

Figure 13.4 This form takes the user input for a regular expression pattern and a string.

This is a very simple HTML form containing just two text inputs and a submit button. The text inputs have preset values; they use `print()` statements to print the values of `$pattern` and `$string`. For this script to work, remember that the `name` attribute of the submit button (literally, *submit*) must match the index used in the main conditional (`isset ($_POST ['submit'])`).

10. Complete the HTML page:

```
</body>
</html>
```

11. Save the script as `test_pattern.php`, upload it to your Web server (or save it in the proper directory of your PHP-enabled computer), and load it in your Web browser (**Figure 13.4**).

✔ Tips

- When it comes time for you to create a script that validates a certain string format—like an email address, a name, or a URL—use this script to test your pattern.
- Remember that regular expressions in PHP are case-sensitive by default. The `eregi()` function used in this example overrules this standard behavior.

Using Literals

The first type of character you'll use for defining patterns is a literal. A *literal* is a value that is written exactly as it is interpreted. For example, the pattern `"a"` matches the letter *a*, `"ab"` matches *ab*, and so forth.

One trick to understanding literals is that they make a match assuming the literal is found anywhere in a string. So, assuming you're using a case-insensitive regular expression function (like `eregi()`), the literal `"cat"` will match any of the following strings:

- *catalog*
- *That darn cat*
- *My name is Catherine.*

This flexibility with respect to where in a string a pattern is matched applies for all patterns—not just literals—unless you use special characters, as you'll see next. But first, let's use the test script to see literals and `eregi()` in action.

To use literals:

1. Load `test_pattern.php` in your Web browser.
2. Enter `"ann"` as your pattern and *annette* as your string (**Figure 13.5**).
3. Submit the form to see the results (**Figure 13.6**).

   As you'd expect, a match is made because the string *annette* begins with *ann*.

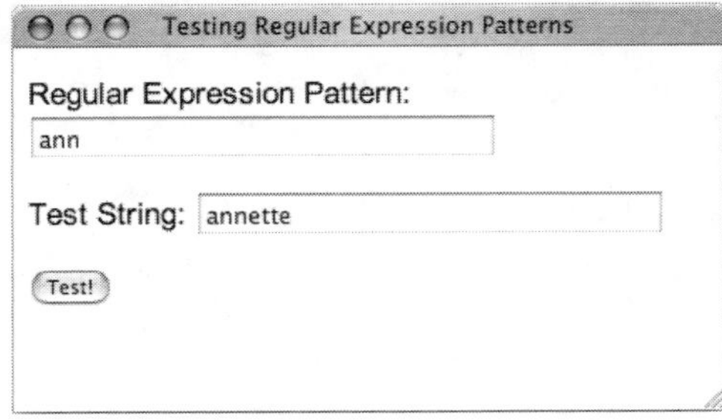

Figure 13.5 The first regular expression test checks a literal ("ann") against a string.

Testing Regular Expression Patterns

The result of checking
annette
against
ann
is TRUE!

Regular Expression Pattern:
ann

Test String: annette

Test!

Figure 13.6 A match is made.

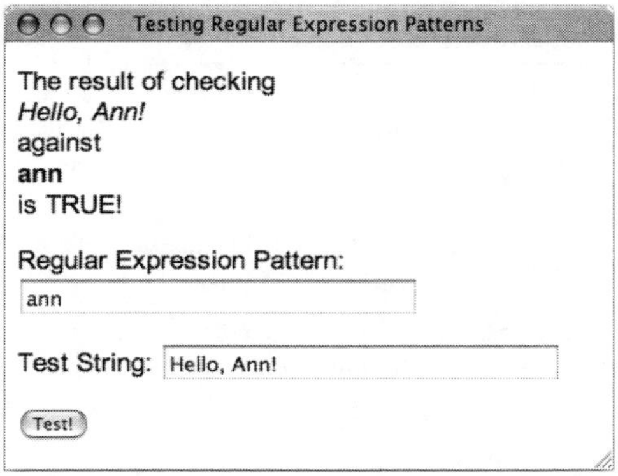

Figure 13.7 Another match is made even though "ann" is in the middle of the string and capitalized.

4. Retest using the same pattern but *Hello, Ann!* as your string (**Figure 13.7**).

   Again, a match is made because the letters *ann* are found within the string.

5. Continue testing until you're comfortable with the concept of matching literals.

   Any string you submit will make a match as long as it includes *ann* somewhere, regardless of case.

✔ Tip

- The examples in this section are purely for demonstration purposes. You should never use a pattern containing just literals in a regular expression. If you need to match specific text, the `strstr()` function is more efficient.

Using Metacharacters

Just one step beyond literals in terms of complexity are *metacharacters* (**Table 13.2**). These are special symbols that have a meaning beyond their literal value. Whereas "a" simply means *a*, the first metacharacter, the period (.), matches any single character ("." matches *a*, *b*, *c*, *1*, *&*, and so on). This is pretty straightforward, although you should note that if you want to refer to a metacharacter literally, you must escape it, much like you escape a quotation mark to print it. Hence "\." matches the period.

Two metacharacters specify where certain characters must be found. The caret (^)—pronounced like the vegetable and sometimes referred to as the *hat*—marks the beginning of a pattern. So, whereas "abc" matches *someabcstring*, "^abc" doesn't (it matches *abcsomestring*).

There is also the dollar sign ($). It works like the caret but marks the end of a pattern. Therefore, "a$" matches any string ending with an *a*, like *somestringa*.

You can combine metacharacters and literals to make more demanding patterns. For example, "^a$" only matches *a*; "^a.$" matches any two-character string beginning with *a*, followed by whatever; and "^.a$" corresponds to any two-character string ending with *a*.

Regular expressions also use the pipe (|), which is the equivalent of *or*. Therefore, "^a|b$" matches any string that either begins with *a* or ends with *b*. More practically, "gre|ay" matches both potential spellings of the color.

Metacharacters

Character	Name	Meaning
.	Period	Any single character
^	Caret	Beginning of a string
$	Dollar sign	End of a string
|	Pipe	Alternatives (*or*)
()	Parentheses	Group

Table 13.2 Each of these characters has a special meaning when used with regular expressions.

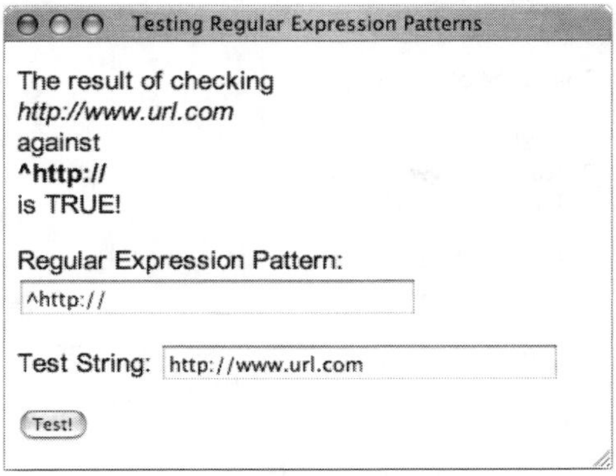

Testing Regular Expression Patterns

The result of checking
http://www.url.com
against
^http://
is TRUE!

Regular Expression Pattern:
^http://

Test String: http://www.url.com

Test!

Figure 13.8 This is the beginning of a pattern for matching valid URLs.

Using the basic symbols established so far, you can begin to incorporate parentheses to group characters into more involved patterns. Think of parentheses as being used to establish a new literal. Whereas "`yes|no`" matches many things, including *yeso* or *yeno* (*ye* plus either *s* or *n* plus *o*), "`(yes)|(no)`", accepts either of those two words in their entirety, which is certainly what you'd rather look for.

To use metacharacters:

1. Load `test_pattern.php` in your Web browser, if it isn't loaded already.
2. Enter "`^http://`" as your pattern and *http://www.url.com* as your string.

   One way to check for a valid URL is to look for the *http://* start. This pattern insists that the submitted code begin with those characters.
3. Submit the form to see the results (**Figure 13.8**).

   As long as the submitted string begins with *http://*, it will pass the regular expression. This isn't an absolute way to check for a valid URL, but it's a start.

continues on next page

4. Retest using `"^(http://)|(www.)"` as your pattern and *www.url.com* as your string (**Figure 13.9**).

   If you want, you can broaden the pattern so that the submitted URL begins with either *http://* or *www.*

5. Continue testing until you're comfortable with the concepts of metacharacters and groupings (**Figure 13.10**).

✔ Tips

- To include special characters (`^.[]$()|*?{}\`) in a pattern, you need to *escape* them (put a backslash before them). This is true for the metacharacters and the grouping symbols (parentheses and brackets). You can also use the backslash to match new lines (`"\n"`) and tabs (`"\t"`), as you would in a `print()` statement.
- Another benefit of grouping is the ability to use back referencing. This technique is covered in the "Matching and Replacing Patterns" section of this chapter.
- Using the pipe within patterns is referred to as *alternation*.

Testing Regular Expression Patterns

The result of checking
www.url.com
against
^(http://)|(www.)
is TRUE!

Regular Expression Pattern: ^(http://)|(www.)

Test String: www.url.com

Test!

Figure 13.9 A more flexible pattern uses grouping and the pipe.

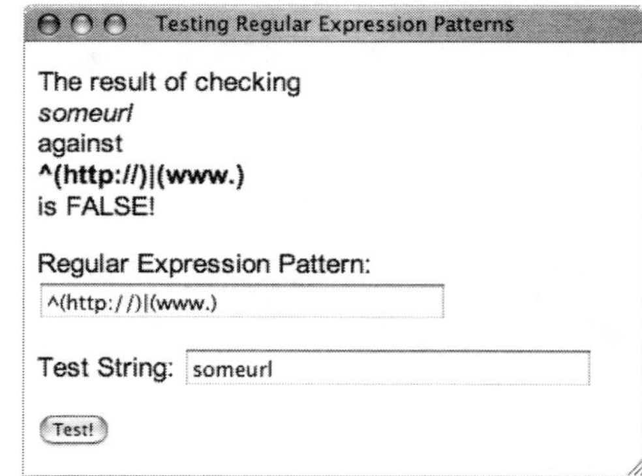

Figure 13.10 Strings that don't begin with either *http://* or *www.* don't pass the regular expression.

Quantifiers

Character	Meaning
?	Zero or one occurrences
*	Zero or more occurrences
+	One or more occurrences
{x}	Exactly *x* occurrences
{x, y}	Between *x* and *y* occurrences (inclusive)
{x,}	At least *x* occurrences

Table 13.3 Quantifiers specify how many times a character or grouping should appear in a value.

Using Quantifiers

Three special metacharacters called *quantifiers* allow for multiple occurrences in a pattern (**Table 13.3**). The question mark (?) matches zero or one of a thing, the asterisk (*) is used to match zero or more of a thing, and the plus matches one or more of a thing. This explanation uses the imprecise *thing* because quantifiers can be applied to single characters, groupings (parentheticals), or classes.

So "a?" matches up to one *a* (*a* or no *a*'s match), "a*" matches zero or more a's (*a*, *aa*, *aaa*, and so on), and "a+" matches one or more a's (*a*, *aa*, *aaa*, and so on, but there must be at least one).

To match a certain quantity of a thing, put the quantity between curly braces ({}), stating either a specific number, a minimum, or a minimum and a maximum. Thus, "a{3}" matches *aaa*; "a{3,}" matches *aaa*, *aaaa*, and so on (three or more a's); and "a{3,5}" matches just *aaa*, *aaaa*, and *aaaaa* (between three and five).

Using parentheses, you can apply quantifiers to groupings. Hence, "a{3}" matches *aaa*, but "(abc){3}" matches *abcabcabc*. As a better example, "bon+" matches a string beginning with *bon* followed by one or more *n*'s (say, *bonnet*), but "(bon)+" matches a string beginning with *bon*, followed by zero or more *bon*'s (*bonbon*).

To use quantifiers:

1. Load `test_pattern.php` in your Web browser, if it isn't loaded already.
2. Enter `"^(0|1|2|3|4|5|6|7|8|9){5}$"` as your pattern and a five-digit zip code as your string, and submit the form to see the results (**Figure 13.11**).

   A valid United States zip code is a number five digits long. To check for this, you use the caret to indicate that the submitted string must begin with what follows. In parentheses, you list all the numerals, with the pipe in between them. This grouping says that the characters can be a zero or a one or a two or a three, and so forth. Then the `{5}` quantifier specifies exactly how many characters must be used out of the grouping. Finally, the dollar sign indicates that this (the five numbers) must be the end of the string.
3. Retest using the same pattern but using a valid or invalid zip code as your string (**Figure 13.12**).
4. Continue testing until you're comfortable using quantifiers.

✔ Tips

- The regular expression used in this example is a complicated way to validate a zip code. When you learn about classes in the next section of this chapter, you'll see a shorthand notation for representing numerals.
- When you use curly braces to specify a number of characters, you must always include the minimum number, but the maximum is optional. Thus `"a{3}"` and `"a{3,}"` are acceptable, but `"a{,3}"` isn't.

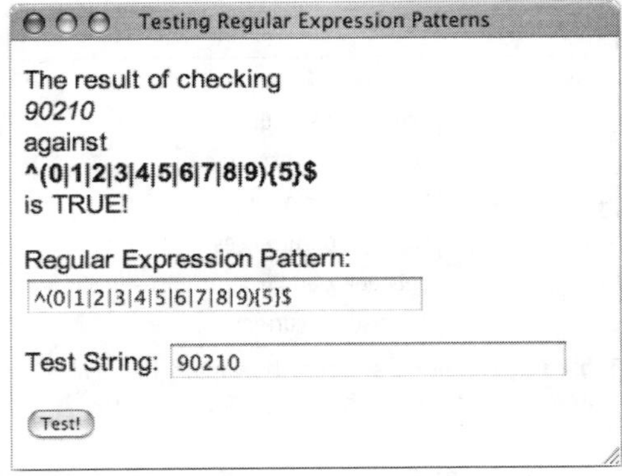

Figure 13.11 This unseemly pattern checks for a valid five-digit zip code.

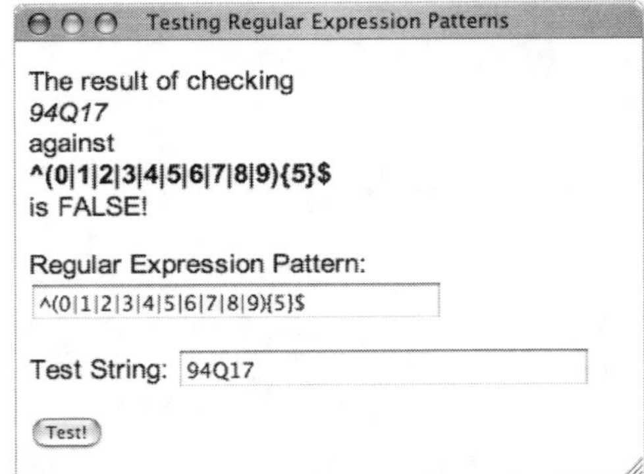

Figure 13.12 A single letter placed within the zip code causes it to no longer match the pattern.

Character Classes

CLASS	MEANING
[a-z]	Any lowercase letter
[a-zA-Z]	Any letter
[0-9]	Any numeral
[\f\r\t\n\v]	Any white space
[aeiou]	Any vowel
[[:alnum:]]	Any letter or number
[[:alpha:]]	Any letter (same as [a-zA-Z])
[[:blank:]]	Any tabs or spaces
[[:digit:]]	Any numeral(same as [0-9])
[[:lower:]]	Any lowercase letter
[[:upper:]]	Any uppercase letter
[[:punct:]]	Any punctuation character (. , ; : -)
[[:space:]]	Any white space

Table 13.4 PHP's built-in classes are shorthand for commonly searched characters.

Using Classes

As the previous example demonstrates, trying to factor in a range of possible characters (like every numeral) can make for tedious patterns. This would be even worse if you wanted to check for any 10-letter word (in which case there would be 26 allowable characters). As a shorthand notation for commonly searched characters, you can define and utilize *classes* (more formally referred to as *character classes*).

You create classes by placing characters within square brackets (`[]`). For example, you can match any vowel with `"[aeoiu]"`. Or, you can use the hyphen to indicate a range of characters: `"[a-z]"` matches any lowercase letter, `"[A-Z]"` matches any uppercase letter, and `"[0-9]"` matches any digit.

Classes can also use quantifiers: `"^[a-z]{3}$"` matches any lowercase word that's three letters long. Or, you can combine multiple ranges within a class: `"[A-Za-z]"` is any letter, and `"[A-Za-z0-9]"` is any alphanumeric character.

One odd thing you should remember is that, within the square brackets, the caret symbol—which is normally used to indicate an accepted beginning of a string—is used to exclude a character. So, `"[^a]"` matches any character that isn't *a*.

PHP defines some classes that will be most useful to you in your programming (**Table 13.4**). These classes have slightly different notations but are used the same way.

By defining your own classes and using those built into PHP, you can make better patterns for regular expressions.

To use classes:

1. Load `test_pattern.php` in your Web browser, if it isn't loaded already.

2. Enter `"^([0-9]{5})(-{1}[0-9]{4})?$"` as your pattern and a 5- or 10-digit zip code as your string, and submit the form to see the results (**Figure 13.13**).

   This is the zip code pattern mentioned in the first section of this chapter—now you can understand what it means. The caret indicates that the submitted string must begin with what follows. In the first parentheses, it's indicated that five digits are required, using the `[0-9]` class.

   The second parenthetical starts with the hyphen, of which there must be exactly one. Then four digits are required. This whole grouping can either exist or not (the question mark indicates that zero or one of this grouping is valid). The dollar sign marks the conclusion of the pattern.

   Using this pattern, zip codes like *12345* and *12345-6789* will match, whereas *123456789* and *12345-* won't.

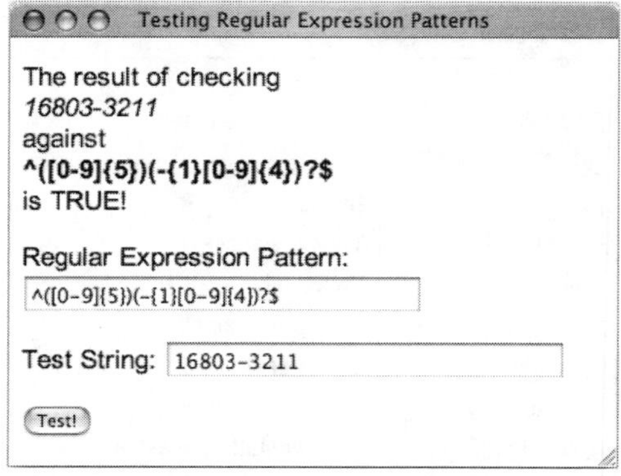

Figure 13.13 This pattern allows for any valid U.S. zip code.

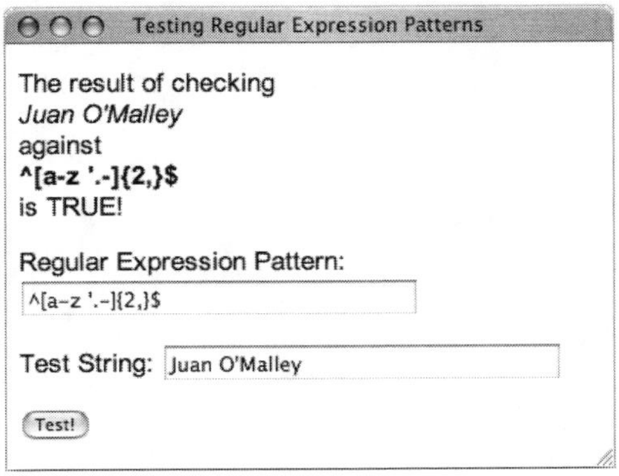

The result of checking
Juan O'Malley
against
^[a-z '.-]{2,}$
is TRUE!

Regular Expression Pattern: ^[a-z '.-]{2,}$

Test String: Juan O'Malley

Test!

Figure 13.14 The pattern being used here—`"^[a-z '-]{2,}$"`—checks for a valid name value.

3. Test the pattern `"^[a-z '.-]{2,}$"` against common names (**Figure 13.14**).

   To check that someone entered a valid name, use this loose pattern. It has a class that allows for letters, spaces, an apostrophe, a period, and a hyphen. This pattern successfully matches names like *Homer J. Simpson*, *Juan O'Malley*, and *Joe Baga-donuts*.

4. Continue testing until you're comfortable working with character classes.

✔ Tips

- The biggest problem with using regular expressions is coming up with a pattern that is neither too strict nor too loose. For example, while the pattern for testing a valid name is fairly good, it still wouldn't allow some names (like Danish ones). As a programmer, your goal is to find the pattern that is appropriately strict enough for the task at hand.
- The dollar sign and the period have no special meaning inside of a class.
- Some operating systems throw errors if you use the hyphen in a class without marking a range. In other words, `"[a-z]"` is OK, but `"['.-]"` isn't. To work around this, you can escape the hyphen with the backslash: `"^[a-z '.\-]{2,}$"`.

Matching and Replacing Patterns

The ereg() and eregi() functions are great for validating strings, but you can take your programming one step further by matching a pattern and then replacing it with a slightly different pattern or with specific text. The syntax for using the two functions is as follows:

```
eregi_replace ('pattern', 'replace',
→ 'string');
```

or

```
$pattern = 'pattern';
$replace = 'replace';
$string = 'string';
$new_string = eregi_replace ($pattern,
→ $replace, $string);
```

You might want to use this approach to turn a user-entered Web site address (a URL) into a clickable HTML link, by encapsulating it in `<a href="url"></a>` tags. Let's write a new script to do just that.

Back Referencing

There is one more concept to discuss with regard to establishing patterns and making replacements: *back referencing.*

In the zip code matching pattern, `"^([0-9]{5})(-{1}[0-9]{4})?$"`, notice that there are two groupings within parentheses—`([0-9]{5})` and `(-{1}[0-9]{4})`. Within a regular expression pattern, PHP automatically numbers parenthetical groupings beginning at 1. Back referencing allows you to refer to each individual section by using a double backslash (`\\`) in front of the corresponding number. For example, if you match the zip code *94710-0001* with this pattern, referring back to `\\1` will give you *94710.*

This may make more sense once you see the example. It refers to `\\0`, which represents the entire, matched URL.

To match and replace a pattern:

1. Begin a new PHP document in your text editor, starting with the standard HTML header (**Script 13.2**):

```
<!DOCTYPE html PUBLIC "-//W3C//DTD
→ XHTML 1.0 Transitional//EN"
"http://www.w3.org/TR/xhtml1/DTD/
→ xhtml1-transitional.dtd">
<html xmlns="http://www.w3.org/1999/
→ xhtml">
<head>
    <meta http-equiv="content-type"
    → content="text/html; charset=
    → iso-8859-1" />
    <title>Make URL Click-able</title>
</head>
<body>
```

2. Start the PHP section:

```
<?php // Script 13.2 - convert_url.php
ini_set ('display_errors', 1);
error_reporting (E_ALL & ~E_NOTICE);
```

3. Check that the form has been submitted, and trim spaces from the submitted URL:

```
if ( isset ($_POST['submit'])) {
   $url = trim ($_POST['url']);
```

Unlike the previous script, this one won't adjust for the presence of Magic Quotes. If the submitted URL contains quotation marks, it won't be a valid URL anyway, so it should fail the regular expression.

Script 13.2 The `eregi_replace()` function turns the user-submitted URL into a hot-clickable link automatically. This is possible due largely to back referencing.

```
<!DOCTYPE html PUBLIC "-//W3C//DTD XHTML 1.0 Transitional//EN"
        "http://www.w3.org/TR/xhtml1/DTD/xhtml1-transitional.dtd">
<html xmlns="http://www.w3.org/1999/xhtml">
<head>
    <meta http-equiv="content-type" content="text/html; charset=iso-8859-1" />
    <title>Make URL Click-able</title>
</head>
<body>
<?php // Script 13.2 - convert_url.php
// This script turns a valid URL into an HTML link.

// Address error handling.
ini_set ('display_errors', 1);
error_reporting (E_ALL & ~E_NOTICE);

if ( isset ($_POST['submit'])) { // Has the form been submitted?

    // Trim off extraneous spaces, just in case.
    $url = trim ($_POST['url']);

```

(script continues on next page)

4. Establish the patterns being used:

```
$pattern1 = '^((http|https|ftp)://)
→ {1}([[:alnum:]-])+(\.)
→ ([[:alnum:]-]){2,4}([[:alnum:]/
→ +=%&_.~?-]*)$';
$pattern2 = '^([[:alnum:]-])+(\.)
→ ([[:alnum:]-]){2,4}([[:alnum:]/
→ +=%&_.~?-]*)$';
```

These two patterns are essentially the same except that the first tests for the presence of *http://*, *https://*, and *ftp://* whereas the second one doesn't. You'll see why in Steps 6 and 7.

Both patterns are fairly generic. They test for the presence of letters, digits, and the hyphen. Then it checks for a single period, followed by a two- to four-letter section (*.com*, *.edu*, and so on). After that can come pretty much anything. This pattern allows for extra domains (*.uk*), pathnames (*/directory*), and so forth.

5. Test the submitted URL against the first pattern:

```
if (eregi ($pattern1, $url)) {
```

The heart of the script is this `if-elseif-else` conditional. It begins by checking for a URL that matches the first pattern (in other words, a URL that begins with *http://*, *https://*, or *ftp://*).

Script 13.2 *continued*

```
    // Establish the patterns.
    $pattern1 = '^((http|https|ftp)://){1}([[:alnum:]-])+(\.)([[:alnum:]-]){2,4}([[:alnum:]/+=
    %&_.~?-]*)$';
    $pattern2 = '^([[:alnum:]-])+(\.)([[:alnum:]-]){2,4}([[:alnum:]/+=%&_.~?-]*)$';

    // Test the submitted value against the patterns.
    if (eregi ($pattern1, $url)) { // Check for an existing http/https/ftp.

        $url = eregi_replace ($pattern1, '<a href="\\0">\\0</a>', $url);
        print "<p>Here is the URL: $url<br />The code is now: " . htmlentities ($url) . '</p>';

    } elseif (eregi ($pattern2, $url)) { // No http/https/ftp, add http://.

        $url = eregi_replace ($pattern2, '<a href="http://\\0">\\0</a>', $url);
        print "<p>Here is the URL: $url<br />The code is now: " . htmlentities ($url) . '</p>';

    } else { // Invalid URL.
        print'<p>Please enter a valid URL.</p>';
    }

} // End of main conditional.
// Display the HTML form.
?>
<form action="convert_url.php" method="post">
<p>URL: <input type="text" name="url" size="30" /></p>
<input type="submit" name="submit" value="Convert" />
</form>
</body>
</html>
```

6. Make the code replacement, and print the results:

```
$url = eregi_replace ($pattern1,
→ '<a href="\\0">\\0</a>', $url);
print "<p>Here is the URL: $url<br />
→ The code is now: " . htmlentities
→ ($url) . '</p>';
```

If the first pattern is matched, then the URL is turned into the URL enclosed within `<a href=""></a>` tags. This converted URL is printed so that it appears as a clickable link. It's also printed after being run through the `htmlentities()` function so that you can see the generated code without looking at the source.

7. Repeat Step 6 using the second pattern:

```
} elseif (eregi ($pattern2, $url)) {
   $url = eregi_replace ($pattern2,
   → '<a href="http://\\0">\\0</a>',
   → $url);
   print "<p>Here is the URL: $url
   → <br />The code is now: " .
   → htmlentities ($url) . '</p>';
```

If the submitted URL matches the second pattern, then it doesn't begin with *http://*, *https://*, or *ftp://*. In this case, most of the code is the same as in Step 7, except that the URL is preceded with *http://* to make it a valid link.

8. Print a message if the URL is invalid:

```
} else {
   print'<p>Please enter a valid URL.
   → </p>';
}
```

If the submitted URL doesn't match either of the patterns, an error message is printed.

continues on next page

9. Complete the main conditional, and close the PHP code:

```
}
?>
```

10. Create the HTML form:

```
<form action="convert_url.php"
→ method="post">
<p>URL: <input type="text"
name="url" size="30" /></p>
<input type="submit" name="submit"
→ value="Convert" />
</form>
```

This form just has a URL text input.

11. Complete the HTML page:

```
</body>
</html>
```

12. Save the script as `convert_url.php`, upload it to your Web server, and run the page in your Web browser.

13. Test the script using a valid URL (**Figure 13.15**).

✔ Tips

- If `eregi_replace()` doesn't find a match, the original string is returned.
- The `ereg()` and `eregi()` functions can also return matched patterns in an optional third argument, meaning that the code in this example could be replicated using those two functions.
- The `split()` and `spliti()` functions work like `explode()` in that they turn a string into an array. The difference is that these functions let you use regular expressions to define the separator.
- The Perl-compatible version of the `ereg_replace()` function is `preg_replace()`.

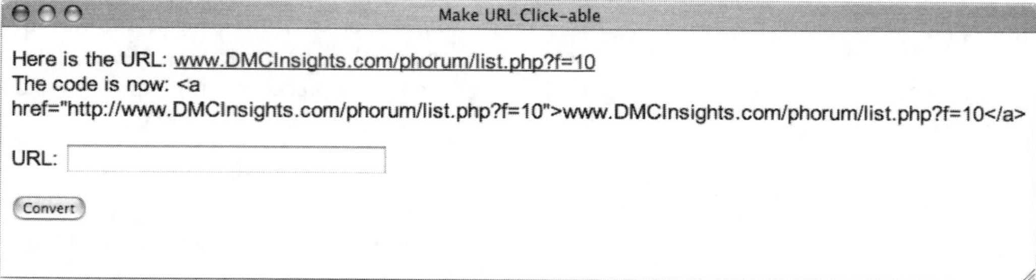

Figure 13.15 With the `eregi_replace()` function, you're able to turn a submitted URL, with or without the *http://* prefix, into a clickable link

Installation and Configuration

A

Many PHP users, especially those just learning the language, may never need to install and configure PHP or MySQL. However, should you decide to take this route, rest assured that it isn't necessarily that complicated and the price of all the required software—free—makes it an even more appealing option. When you use your own PHP installation, you ensure that the preferred version of PHP, supporting exactly those features you desire, is available for your programming use.

You need to answer two questions before beginning installation: what operating system will the server run, and what Web server application will you use? This section demonstrates how to install PHP and MySQL on Windows and on Mac OS X (if you're already using Linux, this section assumes you know what you're doing in this area). With respect to the Web server, Apache comes with Mac OS X and; for Windows, you'll install Internet Information Server (IIS), Microsoft's high-end alternative.

After the installation section, this appendix demonstrates some basics for working with MySQL and configuring PHP. The PHP and MySQL manuals cover installation and configuration in a reasonable amount of detail. You may want to also peruse them, particularly if you encounter problems.

Installing on Windows 2000

Getting PHP and a Web server to work on a Windows machine (it doesn't have to be Windows 2000) is just a matter of using the appropriate installers and following their instructions. You can install PHP and MySQL on any version of Windows and use Apache, Xitami, IIS (Internet Information Server), or PWS (Personal Web Sharing) as your Web server.

If you want to take the easiest route, all-in-one installers are available that will install and configure Apache, PHP, and MySQL. Some will even install phpMyAdmin or other software at the same time. Some options along these lines include:

- AppServ (`www.appservnetwork.com`)
- PHP Triad (`http://sourceforge.net/projects/phptriad`)
- Merlin Server (`www.abriasoft.com`)
- WinLAMP (`www.datacaptech.com/winlamp.php`)

To reiterate, you might have the best luck using one of these installers. In case you'd rather go through the steps yourself, this section demonstrates how to install IIS, PHP, and MySQL. Once you've completed these steps—or used an all-in-one installer—continue through this appendix for information on creating MySQL users and configuring PHP.

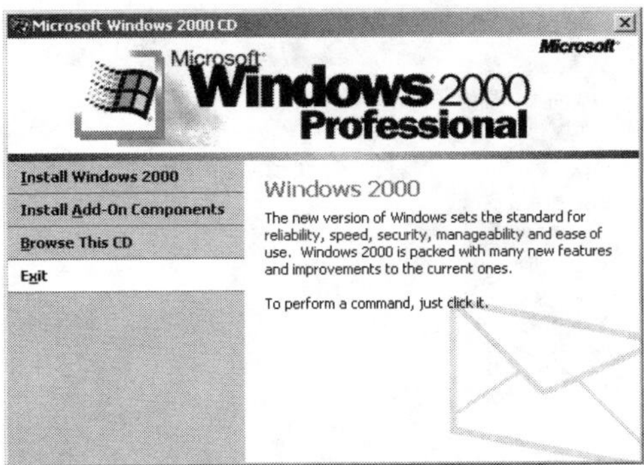

Figure A.1 The main menu for the Windows 2000 CD-ROM.

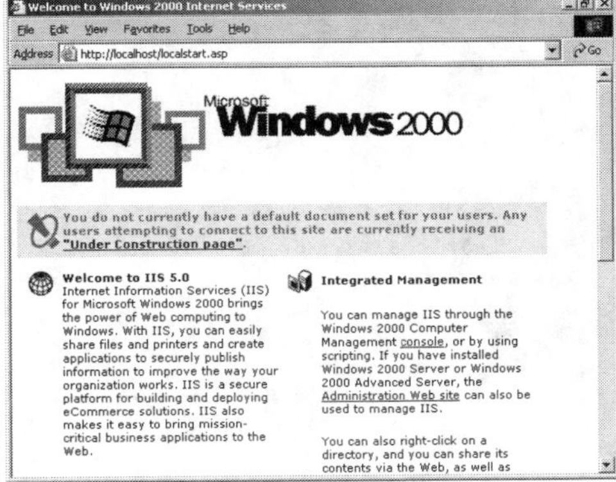

Figure A.2 Your browser should display this page if IIS is running.

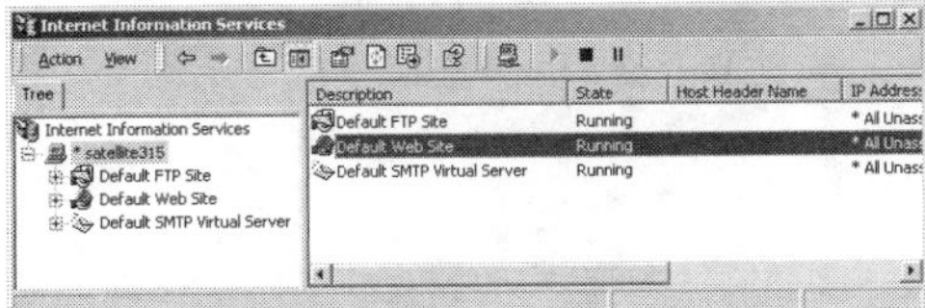

Figure A.3 Use the Internet Information Services control panel to stop IIS.

To install PHP and IIS:

1. Insert your operating system CD into your CD-ROM drive and click Install Add-On Components (**Figure A.1**).

   You can install IIS using the CD-ROM that came with the operating system. If you don't have this option, you'll need to use another Web server or one of the all-in-one installers.

2. Select Internet Information Services (IIS) for installation and click Next.

3. After the installation process finishes, test that IIS is working by going to `http://localhost` in your Web browser (**Figure A.2**).

   You should see a default message like the one in this figure. It confirms that the Web server is running.

4. Stop IIS (**Figure A.3**).

   Before installing PHP, you need to stop the Web server. To do so, go to Start > Settings > Control Panel > Administrative Tools > Internet Services Manager. In the window that appears (see the figure), click the name of your computer in the "Tree" pane, and then right-click Default Web Site in the "Description" column. Select Stop from the menu that appears.

5. Download the latest version of PHP from `www.php.net/downloads`.

   For the Windows operating systems, PHP is available in two versions. Download the installer, not the package.

6. Unzip the PHP file and run the installer.

   The PHP installation process has several steps, including reading the license agreement, selecting an installation type (Standard is recommended), and selecting the installation folder (use `C:\php`).

continues on next page

7. Enter the SMTP information (**Figure A.4**).

   If you have access to an SMTP (Standard Mail Transfer Protocol) server, enter that information here. Otherwise, enter dummy values (in which case the `mail()` function won't work until you manually configure it).

8. Choose which server is being used (**Figure A.5**).

   The installer lets you choose which Web server PHP should be configured. Because you're installing it with IIS, you should select Microsoft IIS 4 or higher.

9. Complete the process.

   In the final steps, PHP copies over all the necessary files. Then it asks you to confirm the IIS Script mapping (you can use the default setup). Once everything is complete, a message is displayed (**Figure A.6**).

10. Restart IIS.

    To start the Web server, follow the guidelines in Step 4; select Start in the menu that that appears after you right-click Default Web Site.

✔ Tips

- If you'd like to use a different Web server, this process will still work (install the server, stop the server, run the PHP installer, restart the server). The PHP installer recognizes many Web servers (see Figure A.5), although you may have to do some configuration.
- If you have problems with the installation, refer to the PHP manual and specifically check out the user-submitted comments.

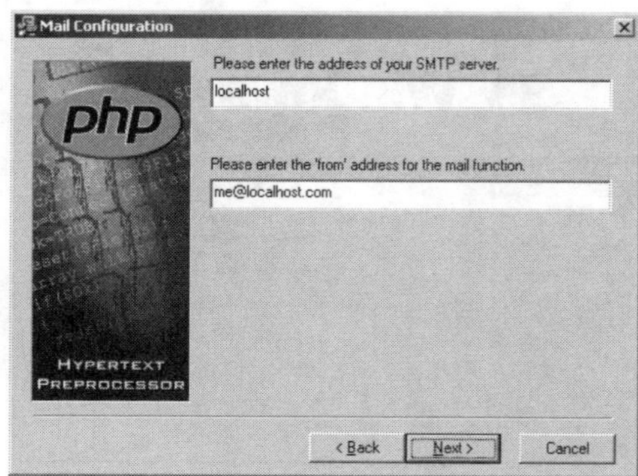

Figure A.4 Values entered here can always be changed later in the `php.ini` file (see "PHP Configuration").

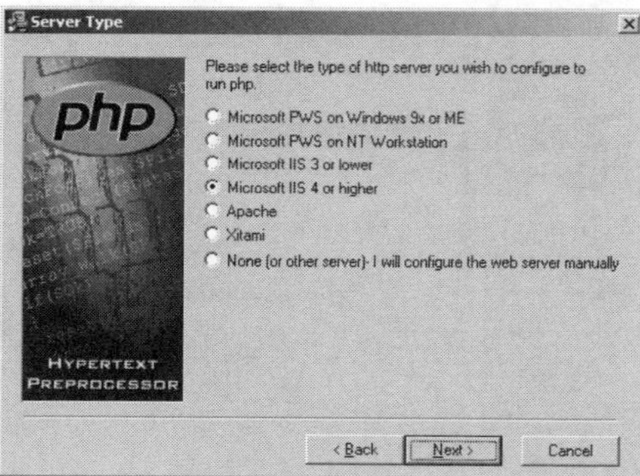

Figure A.5 The PHP installer recognizes and configures most of the popular Web server applications.

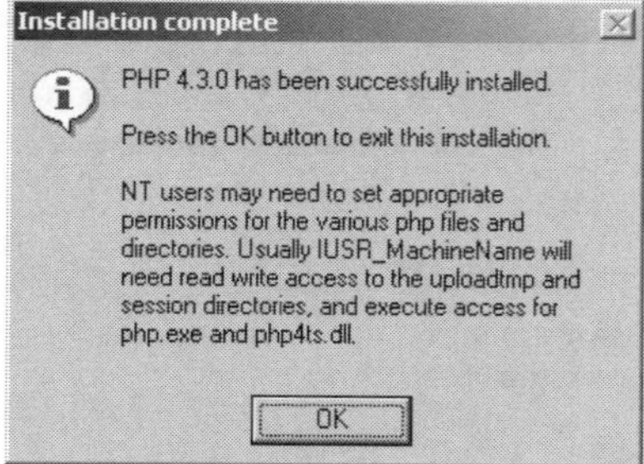

Figure A.6 The PHP installation is complete.

Installing on Windows 2000

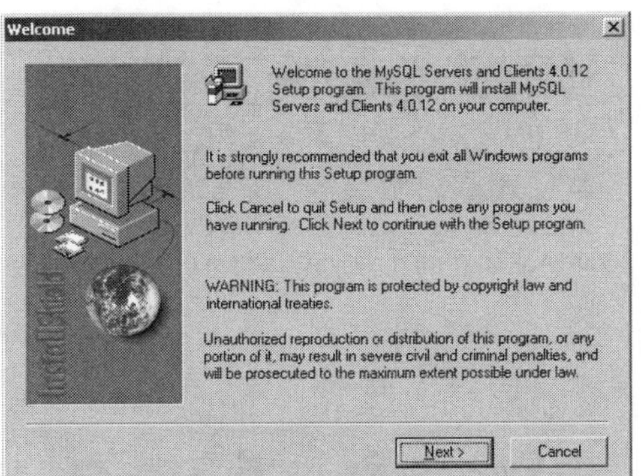

Figure A.7 Run the `setup.exe` file (the Setup Launcher) to begin the process.

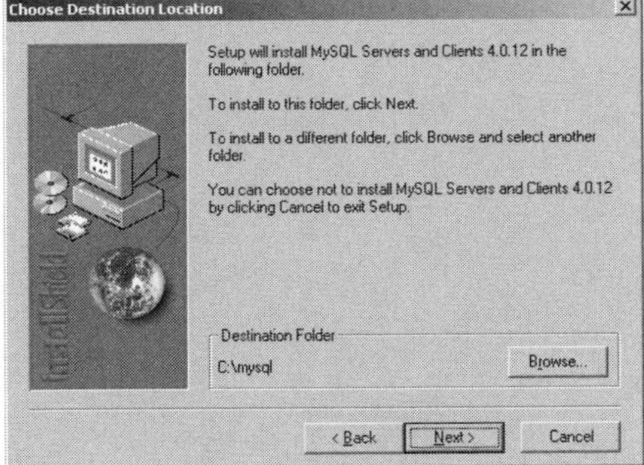

Figure A.8 Pay attention as to where MySQL is being installed. This location will be relevant as you work with the software.

To install MySQL on Windows:

1. Download the Zip file from the MySQL Web site.

   Download the *production* version of the software, not the *alpha* or *recent* version.

2. Unzip the downloaded file.

   Using an application such as WinZip, decompress the downloaded file. When you're prompted, it doesn't really matter where you choose to unzip the files. However, when you're installing MySQL (Step 3), it's best to do so into the `C:\mysql` directory—plan accordingly.

3. Run the `setup.exe` application by double-clicking the file (**Figure A.7**).

   Follow the various steps, selecting a destination (**Figure A.8**) and installation type (Typical, Compact, or Custom) when prompted. In this case, choose the Typical installation into the `C:\mysql` directory.

   If you're using a version of Windows NT, you must be logged in as an administrator-level user with permission to install software.

To start MySQL on Windows:

1. Open a DOS prompt.

   To work with MySQL, you'll need to familiarize yourself with the command prompt. You can normally access it by clicking the Start menu, select Run, and typing `cmd` in the Run prompt. Press Enter to see a DOS prompt (also known as a *console*).

continues on next page

2. Move to the mysql\bin directory:

   `cd C:\mysql\bin`

   To start, stop, and work with MySQL, you must be in the proper directory. The installer places all the utilities in the `bin` directory. If you used the default installation, the `cd C:\mysql\bin` command will get you there.

3. Start the MySQL server (**Figure A.9**):

   `mysqld --console`

   You should see a number of messages, concluding with *ready for connections*. The `--console` parameter tells MySQL to report messages to the console window (as opposed to the error log). On some versions of Windows, you won't get another command prompt until MySQL is stopped, so you'll need to create another console window to enter more commands.

4. You can stop the MySQL server using this command (**Figure A.10**):

   `mysqladmin -u root shutdown`

   Until you've established a root user password, this command stops a running MySQL server. Once you've set that password, you use `mysqladmin -u root -p shutdown` instead.

✔ Tips

- The bin directory contains a few versions of `mysqld`, including `mysqld-nt` for NT versions of Windows, `mysqld-max`, and `mysqld-opt`. Using `mysqld` is perfect for most users.

- You aren't required to install MySQL into a `C:\mysql` directory, but doing so is a good idea. If, for some reason, you prefer to install the software elsewhere, specify the correct directory when `setup.exe` prompts you.

Figure A.9 Starting the MySQL server on Windows.

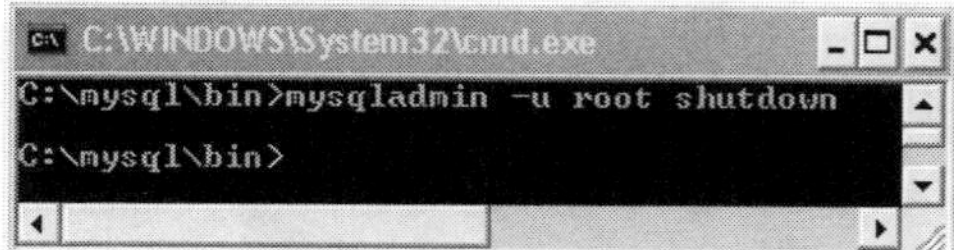

Figure A.10 Stopping MySQL using the `mysqladmin` utility.

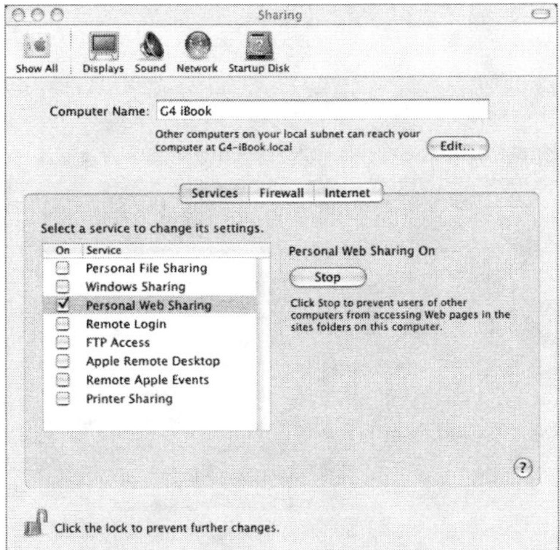

Figure A.11 Use the Sharing System Preferences panel to turn off Personal Web Sharing before installing PHP.

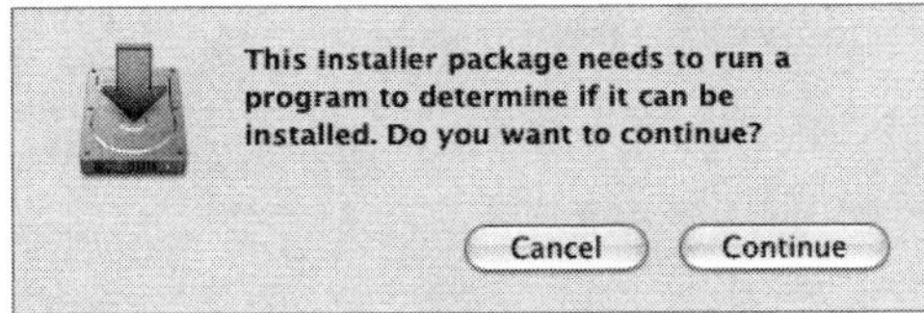

Figure A.12 This warning lets you approve what the installer is doing.

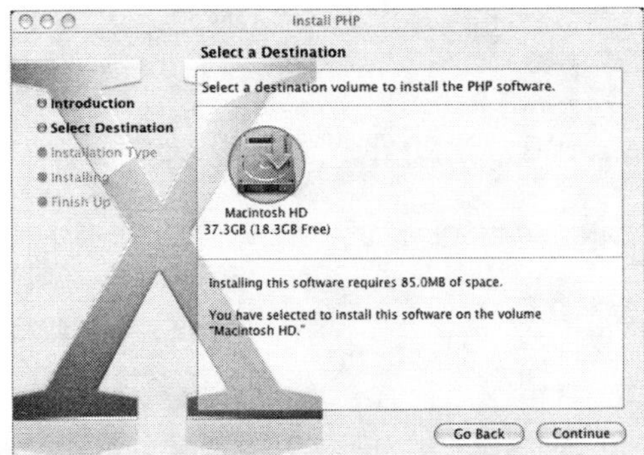

Figure A.13 Install PHP on the same volume as Mac OS X.

Installing on Mac OS X

Thanks to some ready-made packages, installing MySQL and PHP on Mac OS X is surprisingly easy. Mac OS X already uses Apache as its Web server and comes with a version of PHP installed but not enabled. Using the instructions in this section, you'll install a more current, better version of PHP, thanks to Marc Liyanage, who does a ton of work supporting the Mac operating system.

Before you follow these steps, make sure you're running at least version 10.2 of Mac OS X. Also turn off Personal Web Sharing (**Figure A.11**) and stop any running versions of MySQL.

To install PHP:

1. Download the package from `www.entropy.ch/software/macosx/php`.
2. Mount the downloaded disk image by double-clicking the file.

   The downloaded file will have a name like `Entropy-PHP-`*`version`*`.dmg`. For example, at the time of this writing, the package is `Entropy-PHP-4.3.4-1.dmg`.
3. After the disk image mounts, start the installer by double-clicking the PHP package.

   The package will be named `php-`*`version`*`.pkg`. In this example, it's `php-4.3.4.pkg`.
4. Click Continue if the installer says that it needs to run a program to determine if it can be installed (**Figure A.12**).
5. Click Continue.
6. Select the destination volume, and click Continue (**Figure A.13**).

   If you have multiple volumes on your computer, select the one that also has the operating system.

continues on next page

7. Click Install.
8. Enter your administrator's password at the prompt.

   The installation takes a couple of minutes.
9. Click Close when the installation is complete.
10. Open the System Preferences.
11. Click on Sharing underneath the Internet & Network heading.
12. Make sure Personal Web Sharing is on (Figure A.11).

To install MySQL on Mac OS X:

1. Download the latest production version of MySQL from `www.mysql.com`.
2. Mount the disk image (**Figure A.14**).

   The downloaded file will be named something like `mysql-standard-`*`version`*`.dmg`.
3. Open the disk image, and run the package installer.
4. Click Continue on the opening page.
5. Read the Important Information, and click Continue (**Figure A.15**).
6. Read the Software License Agreement, and click Continue.
7. Click Agree at the prompt.
8. Select the destination volume, and click Continue.
9. Click Install.
10. Enter the administrator's name and password at the prompt.
11. Click Close after the installer has finished (**Figure A.16**).

Figure A.14 The disk image file (left) must be mounted (right) to access the installer.

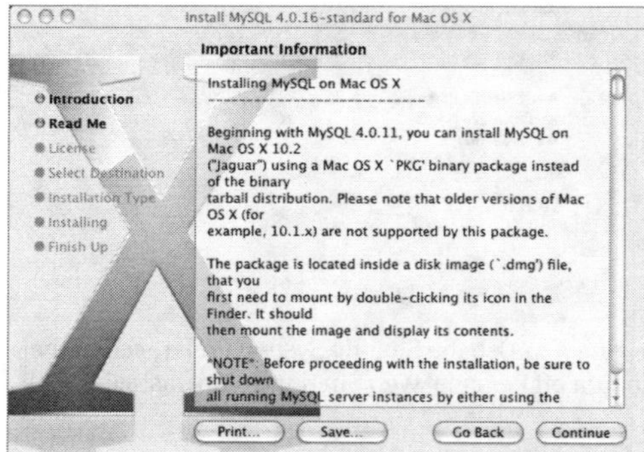

Figure A.15 This screen tells you some important information about the installation.

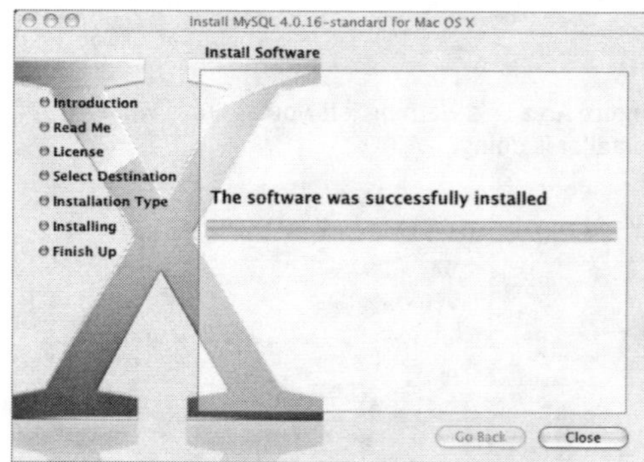

Figure A.16 MySQL has been successfully installed.

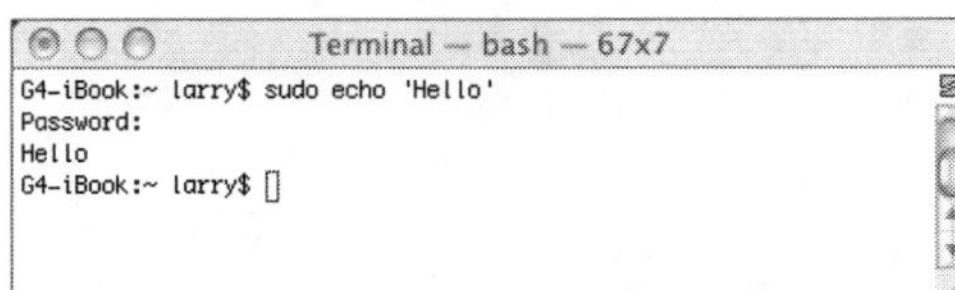

Figure A.17 Get sudo working before you start MySQL.

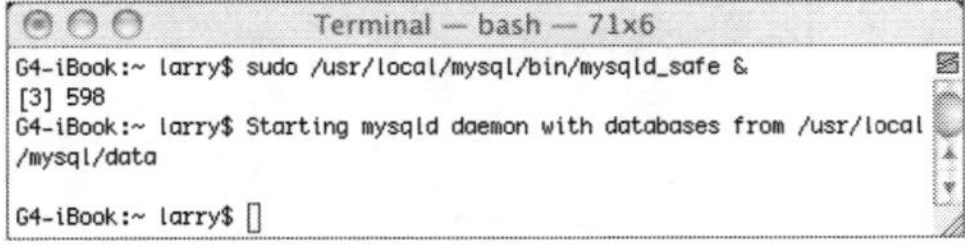

Figure A.18 Starting the MySQL server.

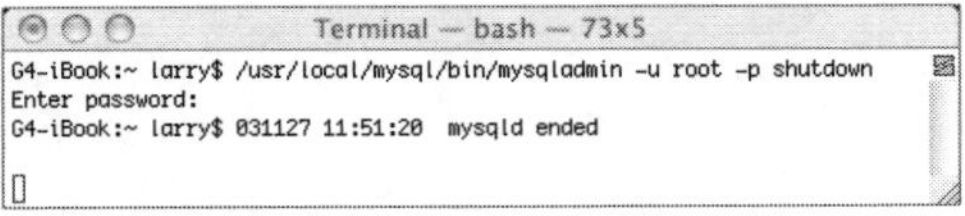

Figure A.19 Stopping the MySQL server.

To start MySQL on Mac OS X:

1. Open the Terminal application.
2. Type `sudo echo 'Hello'`, and press Return (**Figure A.17**).

   This may seem like a strange step, but what you're accomplishing here is successful use of the `sudo` command. This must be done because requiring a password in the next step will cause problems.

   You'll need to enter the administrator's password (for your operating system). After that works, `sudo` won't require a password again unless you've been idle for more than five minutes.
3. Type `sudo /usr/local/mysql/bin/mysqld_safe &` and press Return (**Figure A.18**).

   This line starts the MySQL server. The ampersand tells Terminal to run the process in the background.
4. Press Return again to get the prompt.

   Now you can move on to the next section to see how to create users.
5. To stop MySQL, type `/usr/local/mysql/bin/mysqladmin -u root -p shutdown` and press Return (**Figure A.19**).

   Use `-p` if you've already set the password for the root user, and then enter the password at the prompt. If you haven't yet set a root user password, type:

   ```
   /usr/local/mysql/bin/mysqladmin
   → -u root shutdown
   ```

   Notice that you don't need to use `sudo` to stop MySQL.
6. Press Return again to get the prompt.

✔ Tips

- If you're running a version of Mac OS X earlier than 10.2, you'll need to compile PHP and MySQL from the source. See the respective manuals for more information.
- Apple's software updates will frequently alter your PHP installation because they may replace the existing `httpd.conf` file. The easiest fix is to reinstall PHP.
- Server Logistics (`www.serverlogistics.com`) also has PHP, Apache, and MySQL packages available. The MySQL package creates a System Preferences panel that allows you to start and stop the MySQL server without using the Terminal.
- If you want MySQL to automatically start when you turn on your computer, install the MySQL Startup Item that comes with the MySQL Installer.
- If you installed the MySQL Startup Item, you can start MySQL using this command:

  ```
  sudo /Library/StartupItems/MySQL/
  → MySQL start
  ```
- Mac OS X Server comes with both PHP and MySQL installed.
- You start version 3.x of MySQL with the `safe_mysqld` command, whereas version 4.x uses `mysqld_safe`.

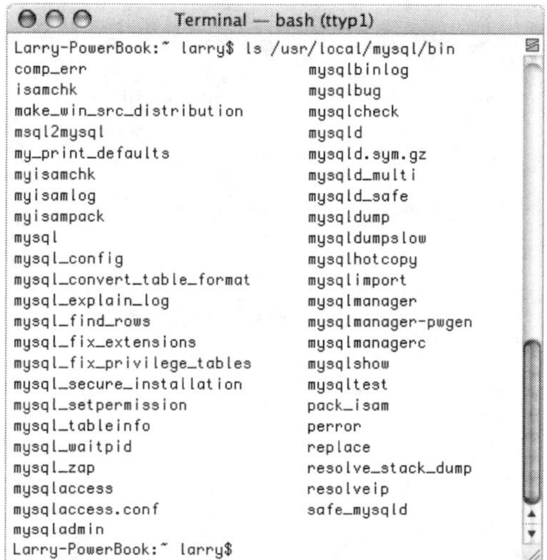

Figure A.20 Mac users can see the contents of a directory using the `ls` command. Windows users should use `dir`.

Using the MySQL Monitor

The MySQL software comes with an important tool called the MySQL monitor or the MySQL client. This application provides an interface for communicating with the MySQL server. It's a command-line tool that must be accessed using the Terminal application on Linux and Mac OS X or through the command (DOS) prompt on Windows.

To use the MySQL monitor:

1. Make sure the MySQL server is running.
2. Access a command prompt.

   On Mac OS X and Unix, you can accomplish this by running the Terminal application.

   On Windows, click the Start Menu, select Run, and then type `cmd` and press Enter at the prompt.
3. Determine the path to the MySQL monitor.

   To connect to the monitor, you need to type in the full path name to the utility. This path depends on where you installed the software, but it's most likely

   `C:\mysql\bin\mysql` (Windows)

   or

   `/usr/local/mysql/bin/mysql`
   (Mac OS X and Unix)

   You can confirm the proper path by running the appropriate command and seeing the result, by listing the contents of that directory and finding `mysql` there (**Figure A.20**), or by searching for "mysql" on your computer.

continues on next page

4. Attempt to connect to the MySQL monitor.

   To connect, enter the pathname plus `-u` *`username`* `-p`. So, the command might be

   `c:\mysql\bin\mysql -u username -p` (Windows)

   or

   `/usr/local/mysql/bin/mysql -u`
   `→ username -p` (Unix and Mac OS X)

   Replace *`username`* with the user name you want to use. If you haven't yet created any other users, this will be `root`. If you haven't yet established a root password, you can omit the `-p` flag.

5. Enter the password at the prompt (**Figure A.21**).

   The password requested is the MySQL password for the user named during the connection. You'll see this prompt only if you used the `-p` option in Step 4.

6. List and select a database (**Figure A.22**):

   `SHOW DATABASES;`

   `USE myblog;`

   The `SHOW DATABASES` command is an SQL query that lists every database hosted on that MySQL installation. To select a specific database, use the SQL command `USE` *`databasename`*. Notice that each command must be terminated with a semicolon.

7. Exit the MySQL monitor.

   To do so, type `exit` or `quit`.

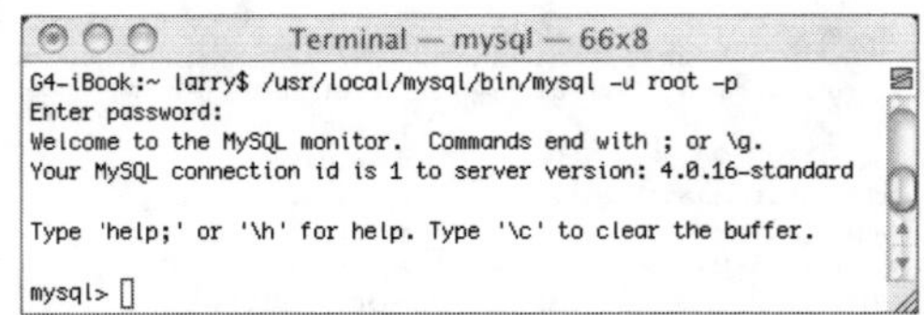

Figure A.21 Successfully accessing the MySQL monitor.

Figure A.22 List every database, and select which one you want to work with.

✔ Tips

- If you see a *Can't connect to local MySQL server through socket...* error message, it normally means MySQL isn't running.
- Remember that the MySQL monitor is your best tool for debugging PHP scripts that work with MySQL. You can use the MySQL monitor to check user permissions and to run queries outside of the PHP script.
- Any queries you run in the MySQL monitor must conclude with a semicolon. Conversely, when you run a query from a PHP script, you shouldn't use a closing semicolon (on the query itself).

Creating MySQL Users

Once you've successfully installed MySQL, you need to begin creating users. The initial MySQL installation comes with one user (named *root*) with no password set. At the very least, you should create a password for this user.

After that, you can create other users with more limited permissions. As a rule, you shouldn't use the root user for normal day-to-day operations.

Setting the root user password

One of the first uses of the MySQL monitor is to assign a password to the root user. When you install MySQL, no such value is established. This is certainly a security risk that should be remedied before you begin to use the server. Just to clarify, your databases can have several users, just as your operating system might. MySQL users are different from operating system users, even if they share a common name. Therefore, the MySQL root user is a different entity than the operating system's root user—it has different powers and even different passwords (preferably but not necessarily).

Most importantly, understand that the MySQL server must be running in order for you to use the MySQL monitor. If MySQL isn't currently running, start it now using the steps outlined earlier in the appendix.

To assign a password to the root user:

1. Access your system from a command-line interface.

   This will be Terminal on Mac OS X and Unix or the command prompt on Windows.

2. Connect to the MySQL monitor:

   `C:\mysql\bin\mysql -u root` (Windows)

   or

   `/usr/local/mysql/bin/mysql -u root` (Mac OS X and Unix)

   If you're on Windows, you can `cd` to the directory and then type `mysql -u root`, or do it all in one step. If you're using a Unix system, you'll have better luck typing in the whole command at once.

3. Enter the following command, replacing *thepassword* with the password you want to use (**Figure A.23**):

   ```
   SET PASSWORD FOR 'root'@'localhost'=
   → PASSWORD('thepassword');
   ```

   Keep in mind that passwords in MySQL are case-sensitive, so *Kazan* and *kazan* aren't interchangeable. The term `PASSWORD` that precedes the actual quoted password tells MySQL to encrypt that string.

4. Exit MySQL:

   ```
   exit
   ```

5. Test the new password by logging in to the MySQL monitor (**Figure A.24**):

   `C:\mysql\bin\mysql -u root -p` (Windows)

   or

   `/usr/local/mysql/bin/mysql -u root -p` (Mac OS X and Unix)

   Now that a password has been established, you need to add the `-p` flag to the connection command. You'll see an *Enter password:* prompt, where you enter the just-created password.

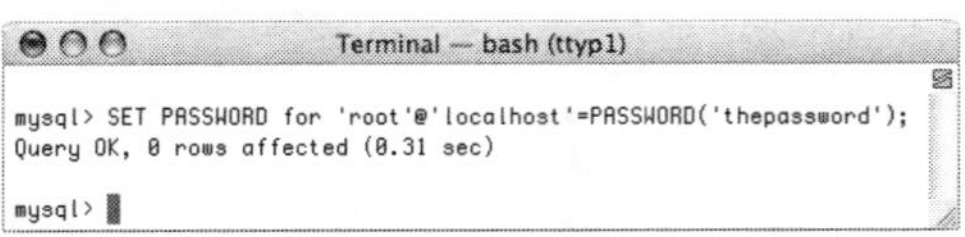

Figure A.23 You should establish a root user's password immediately after you install the software.

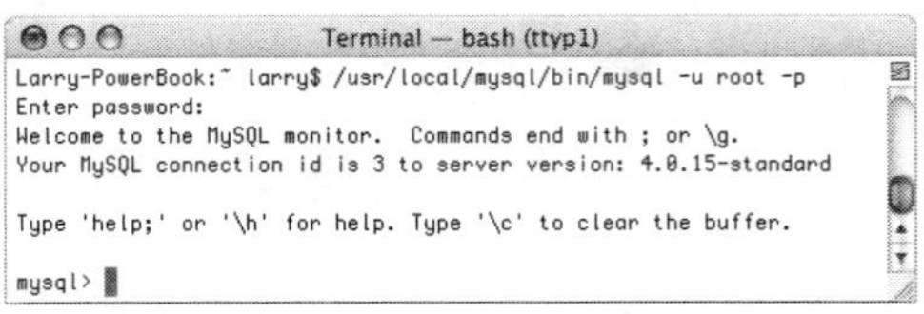

Figure A.24 Testing the root user password by attempting to log in with it.

MySQL Privileges

PRIVILEGE	ALLOWS
SELECT	Read rows from tables.
INSERT	Add new rows of data to tables.
UPDATE	Alter existing data in tables.
DELETE	Remove existing data from tables.
INDEX	Create and drop indexes in tables.
ALTER	Modify the structure of a table.
CREATE	Create new tables or databases.
DROP	Delete existing tables or databases.
RELOAD	Reload the grant tables (and therefore enact user changes).
SHUTDOWN	Stop the MySQL server.
PROCESS	View and stop existing MySQL processes.
FILE	Import data into tables from text files.
GRANT	Create new users.
REVOKE	Remove users' permissions.

Table A.1 These privileges can be granted to or revoked from MySQL users. The privileges are listed in order from the benign (SELECT) to the most dangerous (REVOKE).

Creating users and privileges

After you have MySQL successfully up and running, and after you've established a password for the root user, it's time to begin adding other users. To improve the security of your databases, you should always create new users to access your databases rather than using the root user at all times.

The MySQL privileges system was designed to ensure proper authority for certain commands on specific databases. This technology is how a Web host, for example, can let several users access several databases without concern. Each user in the MySQL system can have specific capabilities on specific databases from specific hosts (computers). The root user—the MySQL root user, not the system's—has the most power and is used to create sub-users, although sub-users can be given rootlike powers (inadvisably so).

When a user attempts to do something with the MySQL server, MySQL first checks to see if the user has permission to connect to the server at all (based on the user name, the user's password, and the information in the MySQL database's user table). Second, MySQL checks to see if the user has permission to run the specific SQL statement on the specific databases—for example, to select data, insert data, or create a new table. **Table A.1** lists the various privileges you can set on a user-by-user basis.

There are a handful of ways to set users and privileges in MySQL, but it's recommended that you do it manually using the MySQL monitor and the GRANT command. The syntax goes like this:

```
GRANT privileges ON database.* TO
→ username IDENTIFIED BY 'password';
```

For the *privileges* aspect of this statement, you can list specific privileges from Table A.1, or you can allow for all of them by using ALL (which isn't prudent). The *database*.* part of the statement specifies which database and tables the user can work on. You can name specific tables using *database.tablename* syntax or allow for every database with *.* (again, not prudent). Finally, you can specify the user name and a password.

The user name has a maximum length of 16 characters. When you're creating a user name, be sure to avoid spaces (use the underscore instead), and note that user names are case-sensitive.

The password has no length limit but is also case-sensitive. The passwords are encrypted in the MySQL database, meaning they can't be recovered in a plain text format. Omitting the IDENTIFIED BY '*password*' clause results in that user not being required to enter a password (which, once again, should be avoided).

Finally, you have the option of limiting users to particular hostnames. The hostname is either the name of the computer on which the MySQL server is running (localhost being the most common value here) or the name of the computer from which the user will be accessing the server. This can even be an IP address, should you choose. To specify a particular host, change your statement to

```
GRANT ALL ON database.* TO
→ username@localhost hostname
→ IDENTIFIED BY 'password';
```

To allow for any host, use the hostname wildcard character (%):

```
GRANT ALL ON database.* TO username@'%'
→ IDENTIFIED BY 'password';
```

Figure A.25 Creating an administrative-level user for a single database.

As an example of this process, you'll create two new users with specific privileges on the `myblog` database. Keep in mind that you can only grant permissions to users on existing databases. If your MySQL server doesn't yet have a `myblog` database, create one using `CREATE DATABASE myblog` (followed by a semicolon, as is required by the MySQL monitor).

To create new users:

1. Log in to the MySQL monitor:

   ```
   mysql -u root -p
   ```

   This is the shortened version of the command. Change it accordingly for your operating system. You must be logged in as a user capable of creating databases and other users.

2. Create a user with administrative-level privileges on the `myblog` database (**Figure A.25**):

   ```
   GRANT SELECT, INSERT, UPDATE, DELETE,
   → CREATE, DROP, ALTER, INDEX ON
   → myblog.* TO 'llama'@'localhost'
   → IDENTIFIED BY 'camel';
   ```

   This user, *llama*, can create tables, alter tables, insert data, update data, and so forth, on the `myblog` database. This essentially includes every administrative-level capability aside from creating new users. Be certain to use a password—perhaps one more clever than used here—and, preferably, specify a particular host.

continues on next page

3. Create a user with basic access to the databases (**Figure A.26**):

   ```
   GRANT SELECT, INSERT, UPDATE, DELETE
   → ON myblog.* TO 'webuser'@'localhost'
   → IDENTIFIED BY 'BroWs1ng';
   ```

   Now the generic *webuser* can browse through records (SELECT from tables) as well as add, edit, and delete them, but this user can't alter the structure of the database. When you're establishing users and privileges, work your way from the bottom up, allowing the bare minimum of access at all times.

4. Apply the changes (**Figure A.27**):

   ```
   FLUSH PRIVILEGES;
   ```

   The changes just made won't take effect until you've told MySQL to reset the list of acceptable users and privileges, which is what this command does. This is the same as typing

   ```
   mysqladmin -u root -p reload
   ```

   (you'll frequently see either) from the command line. Forgetting this step and then being unable to access the database using the newly created users is a common mistake.

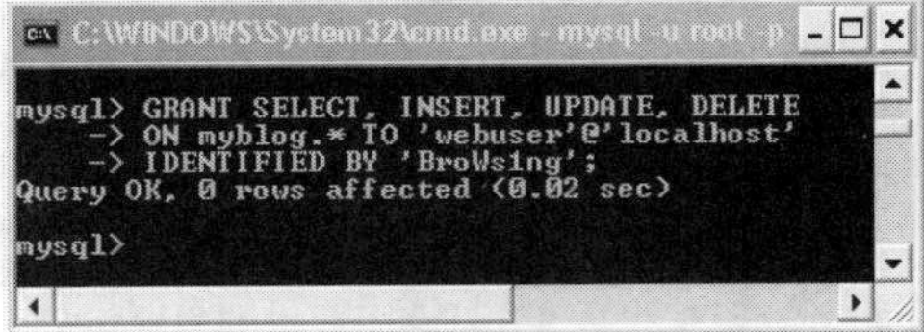

Figure A.26 This user has more restricted rights to the same database.

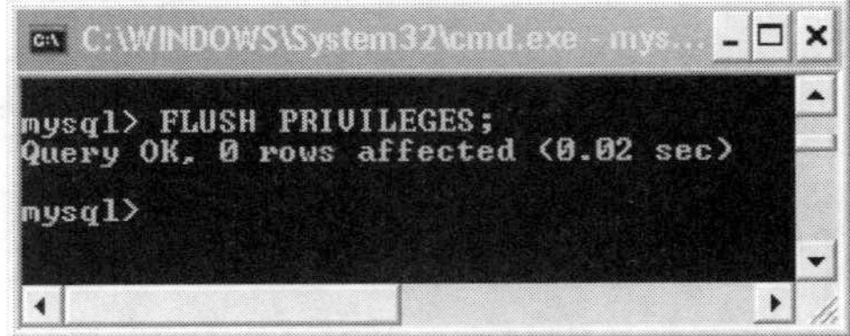

Figure A.27 Don't forget this step before you try to access MySQL using the newly created users.

✔ Tips

- Any database whose name begins with `test_` can be modified by any user who has permission to connect to MySQL. Therefore, be careful not to create a database named this way unless it truly is experimental.

- The REVOKE command removes users and permissions.

PHP Configuration

One of the benefits of installing your own version of PHP is that you can configure it as you prefer. How PHP runs is determined by the `php.ini` file, which is normally created when PHP is installed.

Here are just a few of the settings you may want to consider tweaking:

- `display_errors`

  Turn on this value while you're learning the language.

- `error_reporting`

  Turn off `E_NOTICE` so you don't get more errors than you want.

- `register_globals`

  Generally, you should leave `register_globals` off (it's more secure). But if you're having a lot of problems and don't want to use superglobals, change this setting while you learn.

Enabling Mail

The `mail()` function works only if the computer running PHP has access to sendmail or another mail server. One way to enable the `mail()` function is to set the `smtp` value in the `php.ini` file (for Windows only). This approach works, for example, if your Internet provider has an SMTP address you can use. Unfortunately, you can't use this value if your ISP's SMTP server requires authentication.

For Windows, there are also a number of free SMTP servers, like PostCast. You can install one on your computer, and then you'll have a working email server.

On Mac OS X version 10.2, you can use Sendmail Enabler (`www.roadstead.com/weblog/Tutorials/SMSource.html`) to activate sendmail. On Mac OS X version 10.3, you can use Postfix Enabler (`www.roadstead.com/weblog/Tutorials/PostfixEnabler.html`), because Panther doesn't have sendmail. If you'd rather not spend the money on either of these products, search Google for instructions on manually enabling your mail server.

Alternatively, you can search some of the PHP code libraries to learn how to use an SMTP server that requires authentication.

To alter PHP's configuration:

1. Open the `php.ini` file in any text editor.

   The file's location on your computer depends on many things. The best way to find it is to run a `phpinfo()` script in your Web browser (**Figure A.28**).

2. Change the settings as you wish.

   Depending on your operating system, you may need authority to make changes to this file.

   Many instructions are included in the file. Lines are commented-out (made inactive) by preceding them with a semicolon.

3. Save the `php.ini` file.

4. Restart your Web server.

   You don't need to restart the entire computer, just the Web server (Apache, IIS, Xitami, and so on).

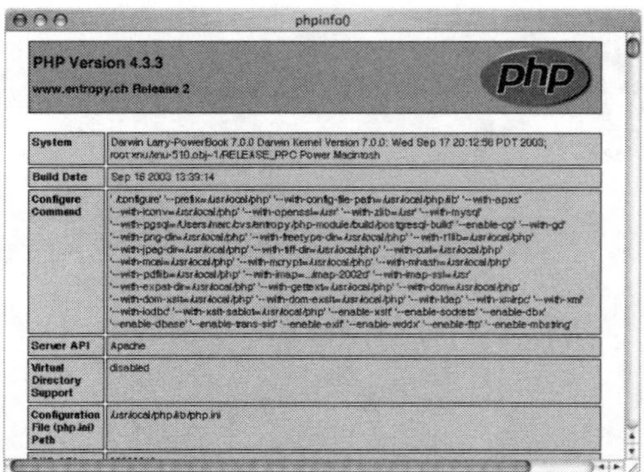

Figure A.28 The `phpinfo()` function prints the location of the active `php.ini` file as well as all the configuration information.

✔ Tips

- It's possible that your computer doesn't have a `php.ini` file. In that case, create one from scratch or take one from the downloaded PHP source code.
- You can also use the `phpinfo()` script to check that your configuration changes have taken effect.
- If you edit the `php.ini` file and restart the Web server but your changes don't take effect, make sure you're editing the proper `php.ini` file (you may have more than one on your computer).

B

Resources

This book was written to give beginning PHP programmers a good foundation on which to base their learning. A few topics have been either omitted or glossed over due to this book's focus. This appendix lists a number of useful PHP-related Internet resources; briefly discusses where to obtain more information for databases and other advanced topics; and includes a few tables, both old and new.

Along with those sites included here, you should familiarize yourself with the book's companion Web site, found at `www.DMCInsights.com/phpvqs2`. There you'll find:

- More Web links (nearly 300)
- All the scripts used in the book
- A support forum for your questions
- An errata page, listing printing errors in this book (which does happen, sadly)

When the first edition of this book was written, few good sites were available. Now there are literally dozens. The best, most obvious ones are included here, but a quick Google search will always be a great resource for you.

Online PHP Resources

If you have questions specifically about PHP, you should be able to find the answer with ease. This section of the appendix highlights the best Internet-specific tools for you to use.

The PHP manual

All PHP programmers should familiarize themselves with and possibly acquire some version of the PHP manual before beginning to work with the language. The manual is available from the official PHP site—`www.php.net/docs.php` (**Figure B.1**)—as well as from a number of other locations.

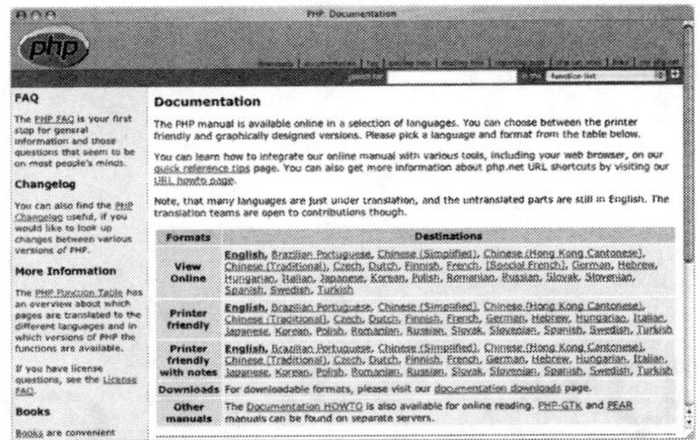

Figure B.1 The PHP home page has many different versions of the PHP manual available for download. You may want to save one version on your computer for quick reference and then check the online annotated version if you're having problems with a specific function.

You can download the manual in nearly two dozen languages in many formats. The official Web site also has an annotated version of the manual available at `www.php.net/manual/en/` (in English), where users have added helpful notes and comments. If you're having problems with a particular function, reading the manual's page for it may provide an answer.

You can quickly access the documentation page for any specific function by going to `www.php.net/functionname`. For example, the page for the `number_format()` function is `www.php.net/number_format`.

General PHP Web sites

This section mentions a few of the many useful Web sites you can turn to when you're programming, and leaves it up to you to discover the ones you like best. Most of these also contain links to other PHP-related sites.

The first, and most obvious, site to bookmark is PHP.net (`www.php.net`), the official site for PHP.

Figure B.2 Spoono is an all-around Web development site with an extra focus given to PHP.

Secondarily, you should familiarize yourself with Zend (`www.zend.com`), the home page for the creators of PHP's core. The site contains numerous downloads plus a wealth of other resources—straight from the masters, so to speak.

For information on specific topics, PHPBuilder (`www.phpbuilder.com`) is a great place to turn. The site has dozens of articles explaining how to do particular tasks using PHP. On top of that, PHPBuilder provides support forums and a code library where programmers have uploaded sample scripts.

Spoono (`www.spoono.com`, **Figure B.2**) is a good general Web development site, but it also focuses a good portion of its energies on PHP. For a cohesive look at developing dynamic Web sites using PHP, HTML, CSS, and JavaScript, this is an excellent place to turn.

One final Web reference is the PHP Coding Standard, available at `http://alltasks.net/code/php_coding_standard.html`. The standard is a document that makes recommendations for programming in PHP in terms of proper format and syntax for variable names, control structures, and so forth. You shouldn't feel obligated to abide by these rules, but they provide some solid and well-thought-out recommendations that can help minimize errors as you program.

Code repositories

There's no shortage of code libraries online these days. Due to the generous (and often showy) nature of PHP programmers, many sites have scores of PHP scripts, organized and available for download. The best online code repositories are as follows:

- WeberDev (`www.weberdev.com/maincat.php3?categoryID=106&category=PHP`)
- HotScripts (`www.hotscripts.com/PHP/`).
- PX: the PHP Code Exchange (`http://px.sklar.com`, **Figure B.3**)
- PHP Resource Index (`http://php.resourceindex.com`)
- PHP Classes Repository (`www.phpclasses.org`)

You can also find code examples at Zend and PHPBuilder or by searching the Web using Google or another search engine.

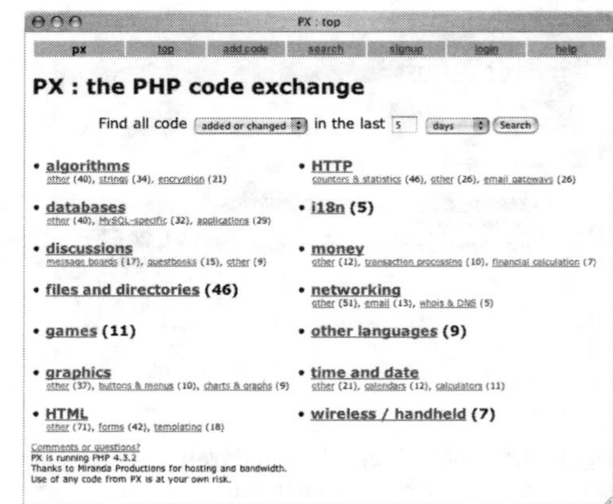

Figure B.3 PX: the PHP Code Exchange is a no-nonsense resource for downloading other users' PHP scripts.

Newsgroups and mailing lists

If you have access to newsgroups, you can use them as a great sounding board for ideas as well as a place to get your most difficult questions answered. Of course, you can always give back to the group by offering your own expertise to those in need.

The largest English-language PHP newsgroup is `comp.lang.php`. You may be able to access it through your ISP or via a pay-for-use Usenet organization. Newsgroups are also available in languages other than English.

The PHP Web site lists the available mailing lists you can sign up for at `www.php.net/mailing-lists.php` (**Figure B.4**).

Before you post to any newsgroup or mailing list, it will behoove you to read Eric Steven Raymond's "How to Ask Questions the Smart Way" at `www.catb.org/~esr/faqs/smart-questions.html`.

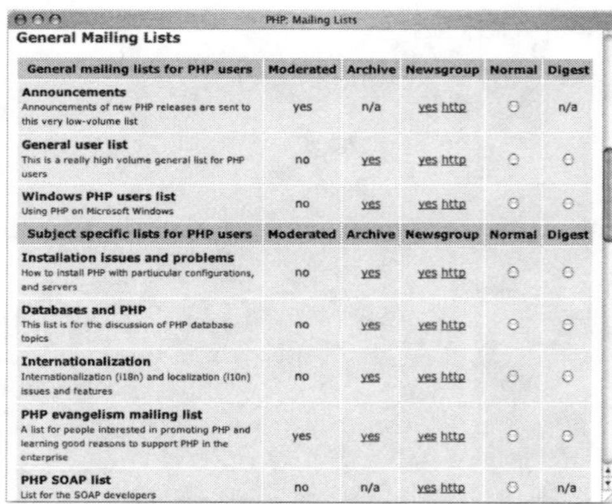

Figure B.4 The PHP mailing lists are active places where your questions can be answered quickly.

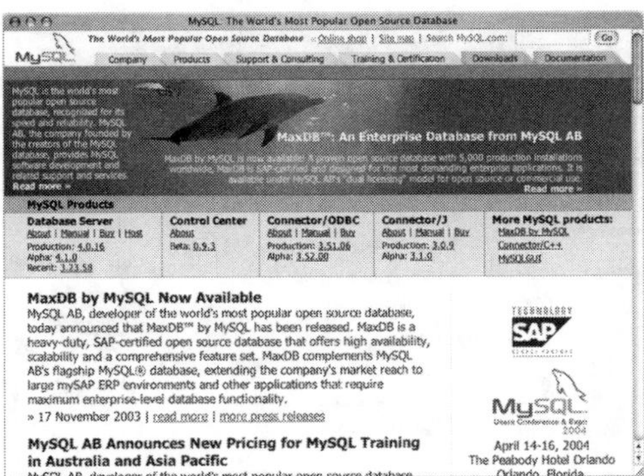

Figure B.5 The MySQL Web site has most of the documentation you'll need as well as the downloadable files for MySQL itself.

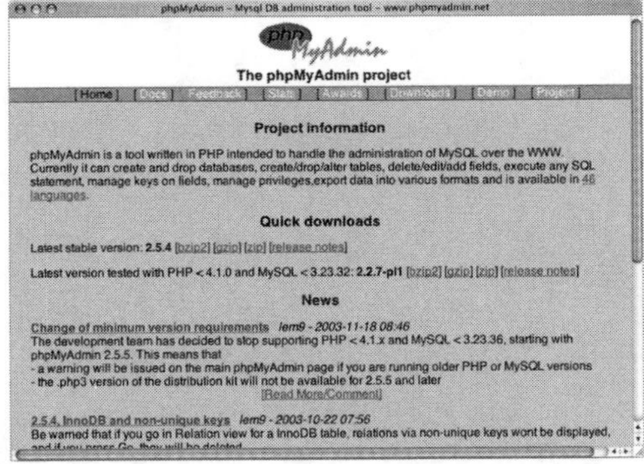

Figure B.6 The free phpMyAdmin tool is an absolute must for developers learning to work with PHP and MySQL.

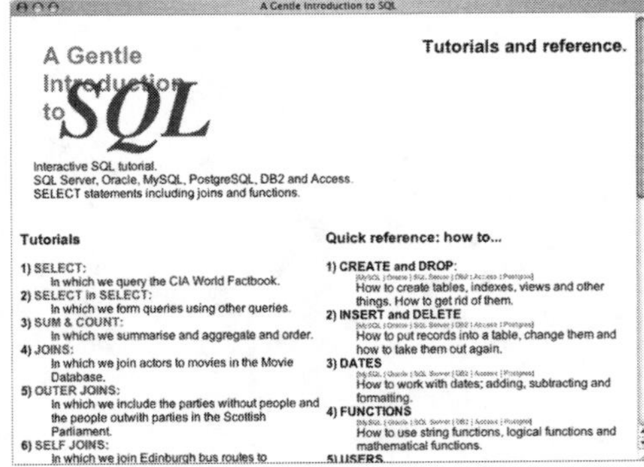

Figure B.7 This site provides tutorials and references covering the entire range of SQL usage.

Database Resources

Which database resources will be most useful to you depends, obviously, on which database management system (DBMS) you're using. The most common database used with PHP is probably MySQL, although PostgreSQL may be a close second. PHP supports most of the standard databases.

To learn more about using MySQL, begin with the official MySQL Web site (`www.mysql.com`, **Figure B.5**). You can download the MySQL manual to use as a reference while you work. A handful of books are also available specifically on MySQL, including my own *MySQL: Visual QuickStart Guide* (Peachpit Press, 2002).

You can gather information on using PostgreSQL databases by first visiting the PostgreSQL Web site (`www.postgresql.org`).

If you're using MySQL, don't forget to download and install phpMyAdmin (`www.phpmyadmin.net`, **Figure B.6**). Written in PHP, this is an invaluable tool for working with a database. If you're using PostgreSQL or even Oracle, you can find similar tools available for interfacing with them. Every database application also has its own mailing lists and newsgroups.

Another area of database resources you should delve into is SQL. Web sites discussing SQL, the language used by every database application, include the following:

- SQL Course (`www.sqlcourse.com`)
- A Gentle Introduction to SQL (`www.sqlzoo.net`, **Figure B.7**)
- W3Schools' SQL Tutorial (`www.w3schools.com/sql`)
- SQL.org (`www.sql.org`)

Advanced Topics

This book should adequately get you started using PHP, but there are a few topics that you may want to investigate further.

OOP and PEAR

The subject of objects and object-oriented programming (OOP) is not covered in this book because it's beyond the scope of a beginner's guide and you won't be restricted by not knowing about objects. When you decide you want to learn the subject, you can search the PHP sites for tutorials or start using PEAR. The PEAR library is an immense repository of PHP code, written using objects (classes, technically). Even if you don't use objects yourself or you barely understand the concept, you can still get a lot of value out of the free code on the PEAR Web site (`http://pear.php.net`, **Figure B.8**).

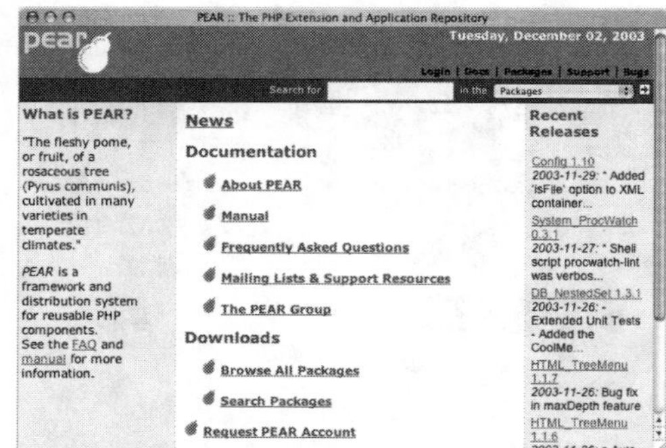

Figure B.8 Begin investigating PEAR once you become somewhat comfortable with PHP.

Security

Web servers, operating systems, databases, and PHP security are all topics that could merit their own books. Although this book tries to demonstrate writing secure Web applications, there's always room for you to learn more in this area. Start by checking out these sites:

- A Study in Scarlet (`www.securereality.com.au/studyinscarlet.txt`)
- W3C Security Resources (`www.w3.org/Security`)

The first is an article about writing secure PHP code. The second is the World Wide Web Consortium's resources page for Web-related security issues.

You should also read the relevant sections of the PHP manual and the manual for the database you're using. Searching the Internet for *PHP* and *security* will turn up many interesting articles as well.

Top Ten Frequently Asked Questions (or Problems)

A new addition to this book is a list of the most common problems you'll encounter and the most likely cause of each problem. Although it isn't exhaustive, this list should help you get through some of the hurdles you face when learning PHP:

1. Blank Web pages

   If you see a blank screen in your Web browser after submitting a form or loading a PHP script, it's most likely because an error occurred that terminated the execution of the page. First, check the HTML source code to see if it's an HTML problem. Then turn on `display_errors` in your `php.ini` configuration file to see what PHP problem could be occurring.

2. *Undefined variable* or *undefined index* error

   These errors occur when error reporting is set on its highest level; they may or may not indicate a problem. Check the spelling of each variable or array index to make sure it's correct. Then, either change the error reporting settings or initialize variables prior to referring to them.

3. Variables don't have a value

   This problem has two possible causes: You referred to a variable by the wrong name; or `register_globals` is turned off and you aren't using `$_GET`, `$_POST` and the other superglobals. Double-check your capitalization and spelling of variable names, and then be certain to use `$_GET`, `$_POST`, `$_COOKIE`, and `$_SESSION` as appropriate. If need be, use the `print_r()` function to see the name and value of every variable.

4. *Call to undefined function...* error

   Such an error message means you're attempting to use a function that PHP doesn't have. This problem can be caused by a misspelling of a function name, failure to define your own function before calling it, or using a function that's not available in your version of PHP. Check your spelling and the PHP manual for a non-user-defined function to find the problem.

5. *Headers already sent* error

   This error message indicates that you've used an HTTP header-related function (`header()`, `setcookie()`, or `session_start()`) after the Web browser has already received HTML or even a blank space. Double-check what occurs in a script before you call any of these functions, or use output buffering to avoid the hassle.

6. *Access denied* error

   If you see this message while attempting to work with a database, then the user name, password, and host combination you're using doesn't have permission to access the database. This isn't normally a PHP issue. Confirm the values that are being used, and attempt to connect to the database using a different system (such as MySQL's `MySQL` monitor).

7. *Supplied argument is not a valid MySQL result resource* error

   This is another database-related error message. The message means that a query result is being used inappropriately. Most frequently, this is because you're trying to fetch rows from a query that didn't return any records. To solve this problem, print out the query being run and test it using another tool (such as the `MySQL` monitor or phpMyAdmin). Also check that you've been consistent with your variable names.

8. Pre-set HTML form values are cut off

   You must put the `value` attribute of an HTML form input within double quotation marks. If you fail to do so, only the part of the value up to the first space will be set as that input's value.

9. Conditionals or loops behave unpredictably

   These logical errors are quite common. Check that you haven't used the wrong operator (such as = instead of ==) and that you refer to the proper variables. Then use `print()` statements to let you know what the script is doing.

10. Parse errors

    Parse errors are the most ubiquitous problems you'll deal with. Even the most seasoned PHP programmer sees them occasionally. Check that every statement concludes with a semicolon and that all quotation marks, parentheses, square braces, and curly brackets are evenly paired. If you still can't find the parse error, comment out large sections of the script using the /* and */ characters. Uncomment a section at a time until you see the parse error again. Then you'll know where in the script the problem is (or most likely is).

Tables

Through the course of this book, it has included a handful of tables of useful information. This section of the appendix combines many of these tables in one location as a convenient reference; it also includes a new table that lists operator precedence (**Tables B.1** through **B.5**).

Operator Precedence
! ++ --
* / %
+ - .
< <= > >=
== != ===
&&
||
= += -= *= /= .= %=
and
xor
or

Table B.1 This is a partial list of operator precedence from highest to lowest (for example, multiplication takes precedence over addition).

PHP's Operators

Operator	Usage	Type
+	Addition	Arithmetic
-	Subtraction	Arithmetic
*	Multiplication	Arithmetic
/	Division	Arithmetic
%	Modulus (remainder of a division)	Arithmetic
++	Incrementation	Arithmetic
--	Decrementation	Arithmetic
=	Assigns a value to a variable	Assignment
==	Equality	Comparison
!=	Inequality	Comparison
<	Less than	Comparison
>	Greater than	Comparison
<=	Less than or equal to	Comparison
>=	Greater than or equal to	Comparison
!	Negation	Logical
AND	And	Logical
&&	And	Logical
OR	Or	Logical
||	Or	Logical
.	Concatenation	String
XOR	Or not	Logical
.=	Concatenates to the value of a variable	Combined concatenation and assignment
+=	Adds to the value	Combined arithmetic and assignment
-=	Subtracts from the value of a variable	Combined arithmetic and assignment

Table B.2 This is the list of PHP's main operators and their types. It's most important to remember that a single equals sign (=) assigns a value to a variable, whereas two equals signs (==) are used together to check for equality.

fopen() Modes

Mode	Meaning
r	Read only; begin reading at the start of the file.
r+	Read or write; begin at the start of the file.
w	Write only; create the file if it doesn't exist, and overwrite any existing contents.
w+	Read or write; create the file if it doesn't exist, and overwrite any existing contents (when writing).
a	Write only; create the file if it doesn't exist, and append the new data to the end of the file (retain any existing data and add to it).
a+	Read or write; create the file if it doesn't exist, and append the new data to the end of the file (when writing).
x	Write only; create the file if it doesn't exist, but do nothing (and issue a warning) if the file does exist.
x+	Read or write; create the file if it doesn't exist, but do nothing (and issue a warning) if the file already exists (when writing).

Table B.3 The parameter you use when opening a file determines what PHP can do with that file—write to it, read from it, and so forth.

date() Function Formatting

Character	Meaning	Example
Y	Year as 4 digits	2004
y	Year as 2 digits	04
n	Month as 1 or 2 digits	2
m	Month as 2 digits	02
F	Month	February
M	Month as 3 letters	Feb
j	Day of the month as 1 or 2 digits	8
d	Day of the month as 2 digits	08
l (lowercase L)	Day of the week	Monday
D	Day of the week as 3 letters	Mon
w	Day of the week as a single digit	0 (Sunday)
z	Day of the year: 0 to 365	189
t	Number of days in the given month	31
S	English ordinal suffix for a day, as 2 characters	rd
g	Hour in 12-hour format as 1 or 2 digits	6
G	Hour in 24-hour format as 1 or 2 digits	18
h	Hour in 12-hour format as 2 digits	06
H	Hour in 24-hour format as 2 digits	18
i	Minutes	45
s	Seconds	18
a	am or pm	am
A	AM or PM	PM
U	Seconds since the epoch	1048623008

Table B.4 The various date formats may be the most common thing that you won't be able to remember. Keep this table nearby when you're using the `date()` function.

Error Reporting Levels

Number	Constant	Meaning
1	E_ERROR	Fatal run-time errors
2	E_WARNING	Non-fatal run-time warnings
4	E_PARSE	Compile-time parse errors
8	E_NOTICE	Run-time notices
16	E_CORE_ERROR	Fatal errors that occur during PHP's initial startup (PHP 4 only)
32	E_CORE_WARNING	Warnings (non-fatal errors) that occur during PHP's initial startup (PHP 4 only)
64	E_COMPILE_ERROR	Fatal compile-time errors (PHP 4 only)
128	E_COMPILE_WARNING	Compile-time warnings (non-fatal errors; PHP 4 only)
256	E_USER_ERROR	User-generated error messages (PHP 4 only)
512	E_USER_WARNING	User-generated warning messages (PHP 4 only)
1024	E_USER_NOTICE	User-generated notice messages (PHP 4 only)
	E_ALL	All of the above, as supported

Table B.5 These error-reporting options come in handy both when you're initially developing a site and once it has gone live.

INDEX

B

C

D

E

F

G

H

I

J

K

L

M

N

O

P

INDEX

Q

R

T

U

V

W

X

Z